Gakuen
CE™

Volume 3

Tachibana Higuchi

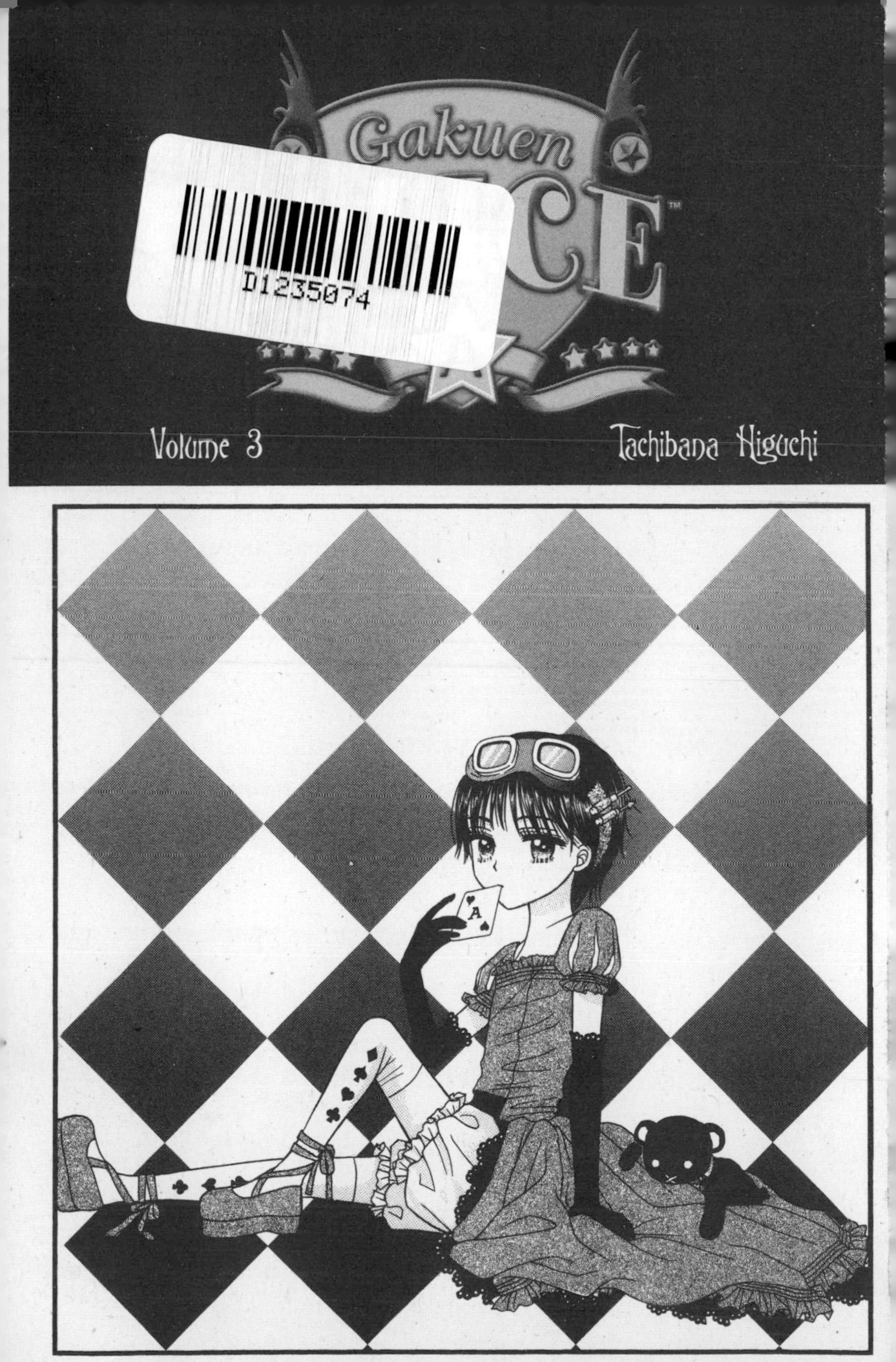
A

Gakuen Alice

Contents

Volume 3

Created by Tachibana Higuchi

HAMBURG // LONDON // LOS ANGELES // TOKYO

Gakuen Alice Volume 3
Created by Tachibana Higuchi

Translation - Haruko Furukawa
English Adaptation - Jennifer Keating
Copy Editor - Shannon Watters
Retouch and Lettering - Star Print Brokers
Production Artist - Courtney Geter
Graphic Designer - James Lee

Editor - Lillian Diaz-Przybyl
Digital Imaging Manager - Chris Buford
Pre-Production Supervisor - Lucas Rivera
Production Manager - Elisabeth Brizzi
Managing Editor - Vy Nguyen
Creative Director - Anne Marie Horne
Editor-in-Chief - Rob Tokar
Publisher - Mike Kiley
President and C.O.O. - John Parker
C.E.O. and Chief Creative Officer - Stu Levy

A  Manga

TOKYOPOP and  are trademarks or registered trademarks of TOKYOPOP Inc.

TOKYOPOP Inc.
5900 Wilshire Blvd. Suite 2000
Los Angeles, CA 90036

E-mail: info@TOKYOPOP.com
Come visit us online at www.TOKYOPOP.com

ISBN: 978-1-4278-0321-4

First TOKYOPOP printing: June 2008
10 9 8 7 6 5 4 3 2 1
Printed in the USA

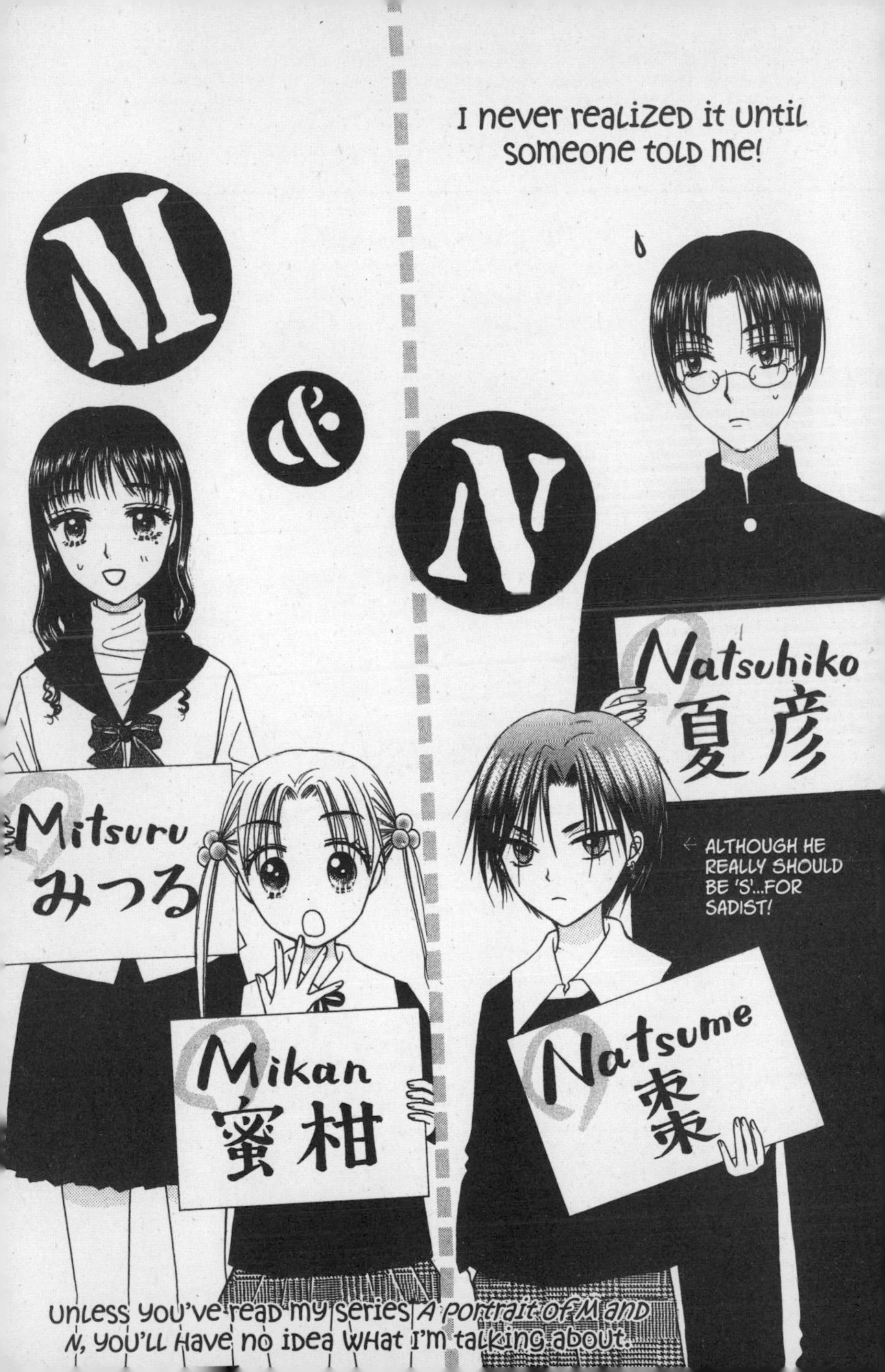
I never realized it until someone told me!
M
&
N
Natsuhiko
夏彦
← ALTHOUGH HE REALLY SHOULD BE 'S'...FOR SADIST!
Mitsuru
みつる
Natsume
棗
Mikan
蜜柑
Unless you've read my series *A Portrait of M and N*, you'll have no idea what I'm talking about.

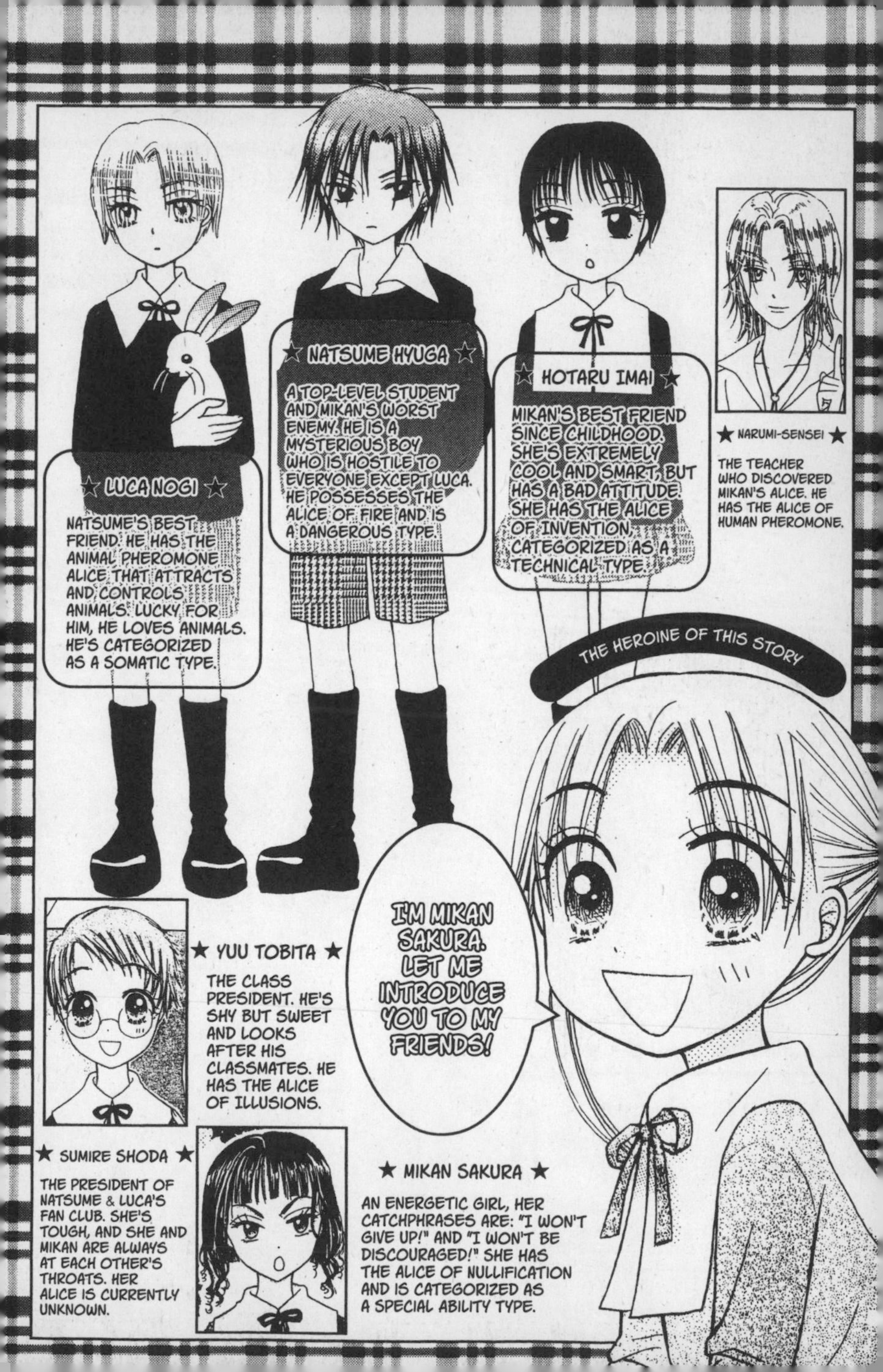
★ NARUMI-SENSEI ★
THE TEACHER WHO DISCOVERED MIKAN'S ALICE. HE HAS THE ALICE OF HUMAN PHEROMONE.
★ HOTARU IMAI ★
MIKAN'S BEST FRIEND SINCE CHILDHOOD. SHE'S EXTREMELY COOL AND SMART, BUT HAS A BAD ATTITUDE. SHE HAS THE ALICE OF INVENTION, CATEGORIZED AS A TECHNICAL TYPE.
★ NATSUME HYUGA ★
A TOP-LEVEL STUDENT AND MIKAN'S WORST ENEMY. HE IS A MYSTERIOUS BOY WHO IS HOSTILE TO EVERYONE EXCEPT LUCA. HE POSSESSES THE ALICE OF FIRE AND IS A DANGEROUS TYPE.
★ LUCA NOGI ★
NATSUME'S BEST FRIEND. HE HAS THE ANIMAL PHEROMONE ALICE THAT ATTRACTS AND CONTROLS ANIMALS. LUCKY FOR HIM, HE LOVES ANIMALS. HE'S CATEGORIZED AS A SOMATIC TYPE.
THE HEROINE OF THIS STORY
I'M MIKAN SAKURA. LET ME INTRODUCE YOU TO MY FRIENDS!
★ YUU TOBITA ★
THE CLASS PRESIDENT. HE'S SHY BUT SWEET AND LOOKS AFTER HIS CLASSMATES. HE HAS THE ALICE OF ILLUSIONS.
★ MIKAN SAKURA ★
AN ENERGETIC GIRL, HER CATCHPHRASES ARE: "I WON'T GIVE UP!" AND "I WON'T BE DISCOURAGED!" SHE HAS THE ALICE OF NULLIFICATION AND IS CATEGORIZED AS A SPECIAL ABILITY TYPE.
★ SUMIRE SHODA ★
THE PRESIDENT OF NATSUME & LUCA'S FAN CLUB. SHE'S TOUGH, AND SHE AND MIKAN ARE ALWAYS AT EACH OTHER'S THROATS. HER ALICE IS CURRENTLY UNKNOWN.

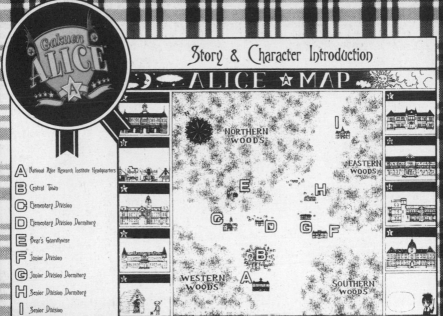

Gakuen ALICE

Story & Character Introduction

ALICE MAP

NORTHERN WOODS
EASTERN WOODS
WESTERN WOODS
SOUTHERN WOODS

- **A** National Alice Research Institute Headquarters
- **B** Central Town
- **C** Elementary Division
- **D** Elementary Division Dormitory
- **E** Bear's Guardhouse
- **F** Junior Division
- **G** Junior Division Dormitory
- **H** Senior Division Dormitory
- **I** Senior Division

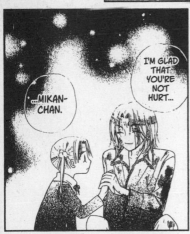

I'M GLAD THAT YOU'RE NOT HURT...
...MIKAN-CHAN.

STORY THUS FAR:

★ TWO SMALL TOWN GIRLS, MIKAN AND HOTARU, ARE BEST FRIENDS. WHEN HOTARU TRANSFERRED TO ALICE ACADEMY, A SCHOOL FOR PEOPLE WITH MYSTERIOUS POWERS (AKA 'ALICE'), MIKAN FOLLOWED HER!

★ ALTHOUGH MIKAN WAS OFFICIALLY ADMITTED INTO THE ACADEMY, SHE WAS BULLIED BY BOTH A MEAN TEACHER AND NATSUME, THE BOSS OF THE CLASS. BUT WITH HER OPEN PERSONALITY AND POSITIVE ENERGY, HER CLASS'S MOOD BEGAN TO IMPROVE!

★ ONE DAY, MIKAN DISCOVERED HER TRUSTED TEACHER, NARUMI-SENSEI, WAS SECRETLY BURNING HER LETTERS TO HER GRANDPA. IN ANGER, SHE SNUCK OUT OF THE ACADEMY, AND WAS IMMEDIATELY ATTACKED BY A GANG THAT TARGETS ALICE CHILDREN! LUCKILY, SHE WAS RESCUED BY NARUMI-SENSEI. WHY HE WAS BURNING HER LETTERS REMAINED A MYSTERY, BUT MIKAN DECIDED TO TRUST HIM AND RETURNED WITH HIM TO THE ACADEMY...

WHAT IS ALICE ACADEMY?

THE ULTIMATE TALENT SCHOOL WHERE ONLY SPECIAL PRODIGIES POSSESSED OF MYSTERIOUS POWERS CALLED "ALICES" ARE ALLOWED ADMITTANCE. AN EXTREMELY STRICT INSTITUTION, THE ACADEMY RESTRICTS OUTSIDE COMMUNICATION--EVEN BETWEEN STUDENTS AND THEIR PARENTS.

YOU PASSED THE ENTRANCE TEST.
CONGRATULATIONS. ♡

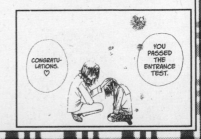

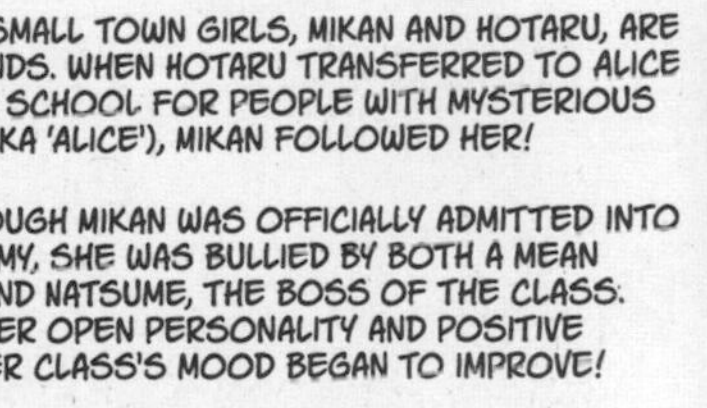

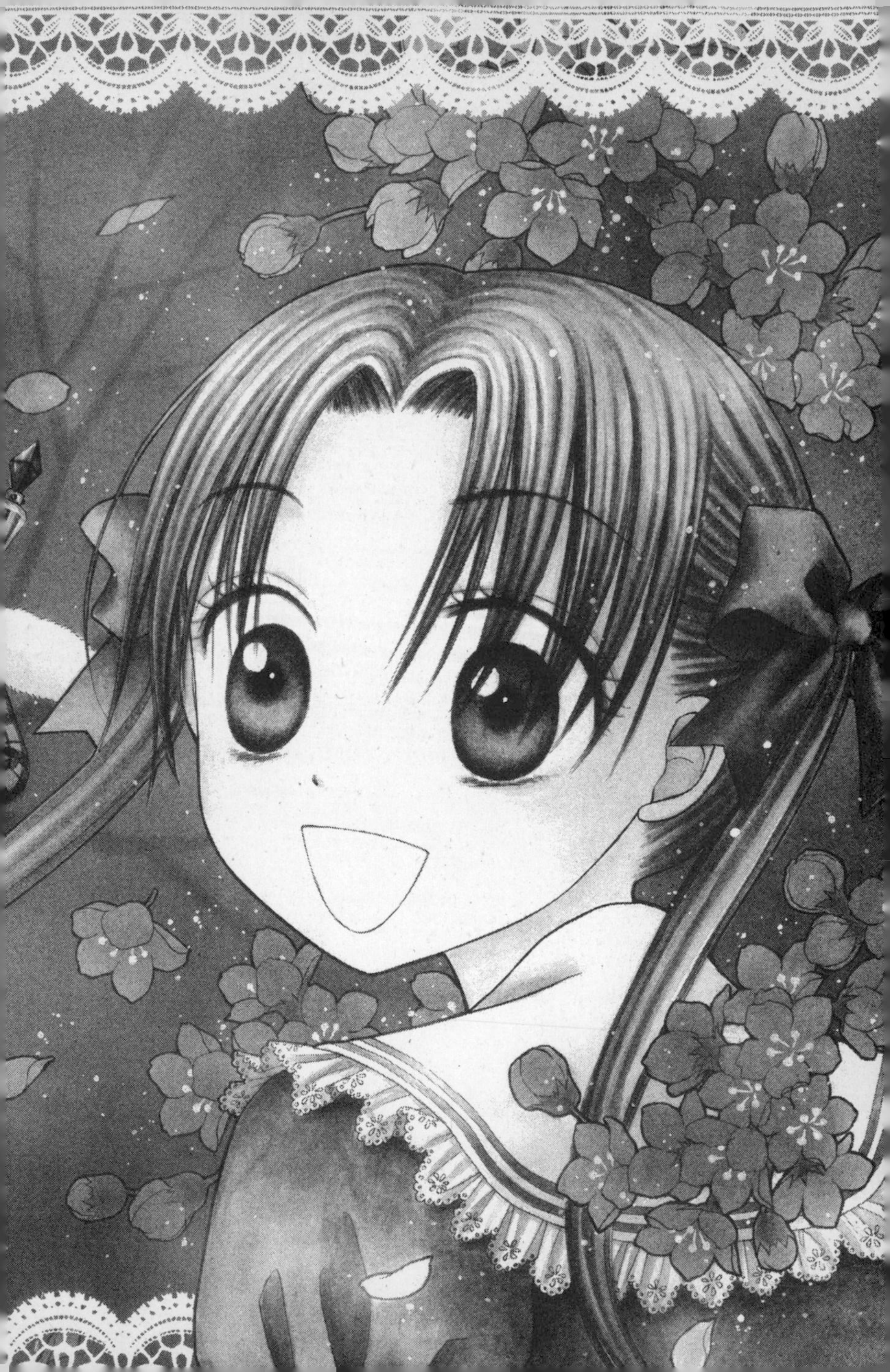

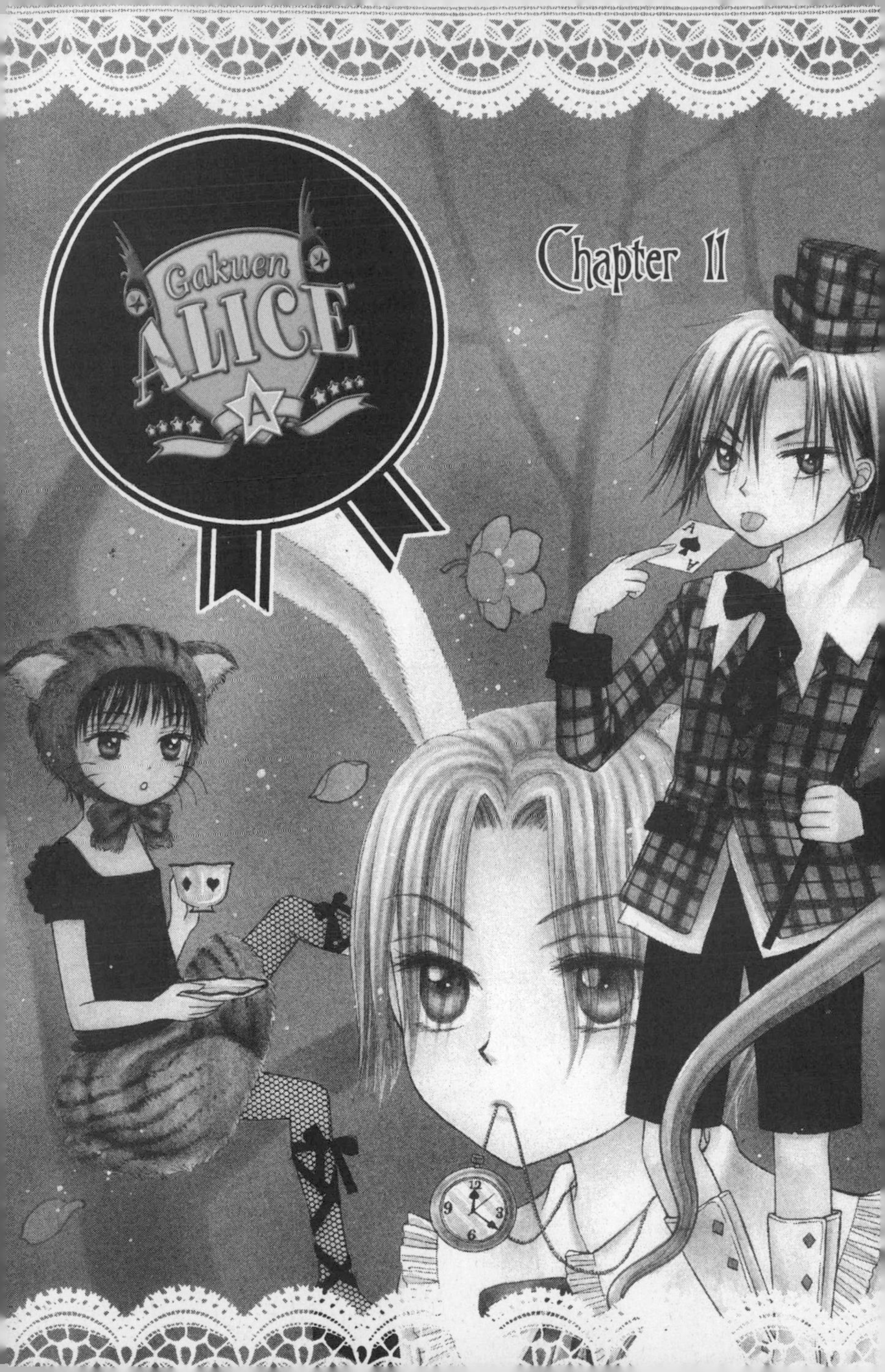
Gakuen ALICE
Chapter 11

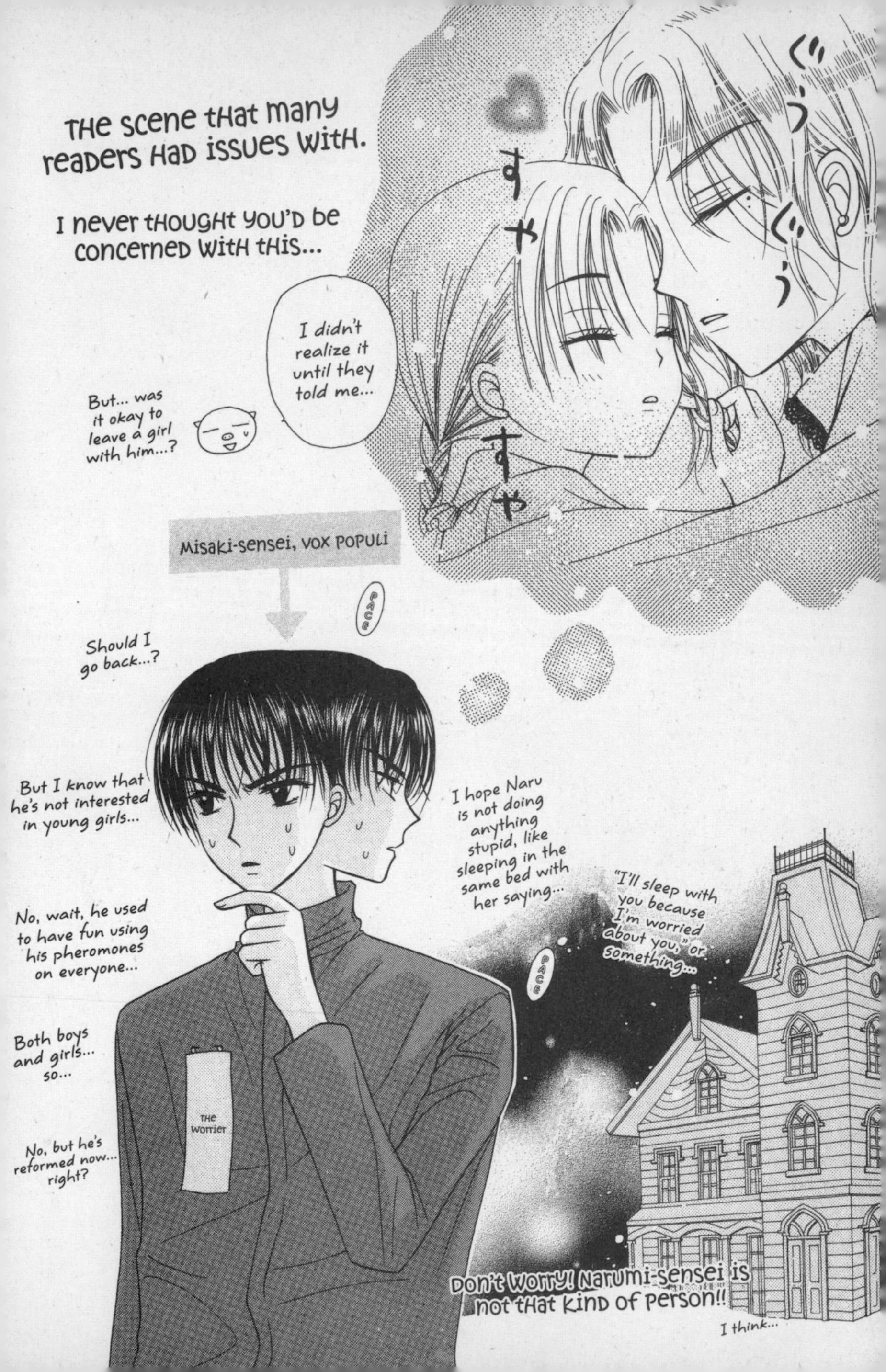
The scene that many readers had issues with.
I never thought you'd be concerned with this...
ぐうぐう
すやすや
I didn't realize it until they told me...
But... was it okay to leave a girl with him...?
Misaki-sensei, VOX POPULI
PACE
Should I go back...?
I hope Naru is not doing anything stupid, like sleeping in the same bed with her saying...
"I'll sleep with you because I'm worried about you," or something...
PACE
But I know that he's not interested in young girls...
No, wait, he used to have fun using his pheromones on everyone...
Both boys and girls... so...
No, but he's reformed now... right?
THE Worrier
Don't worry! Narumi-sensei is not that kind of person!!
I think...

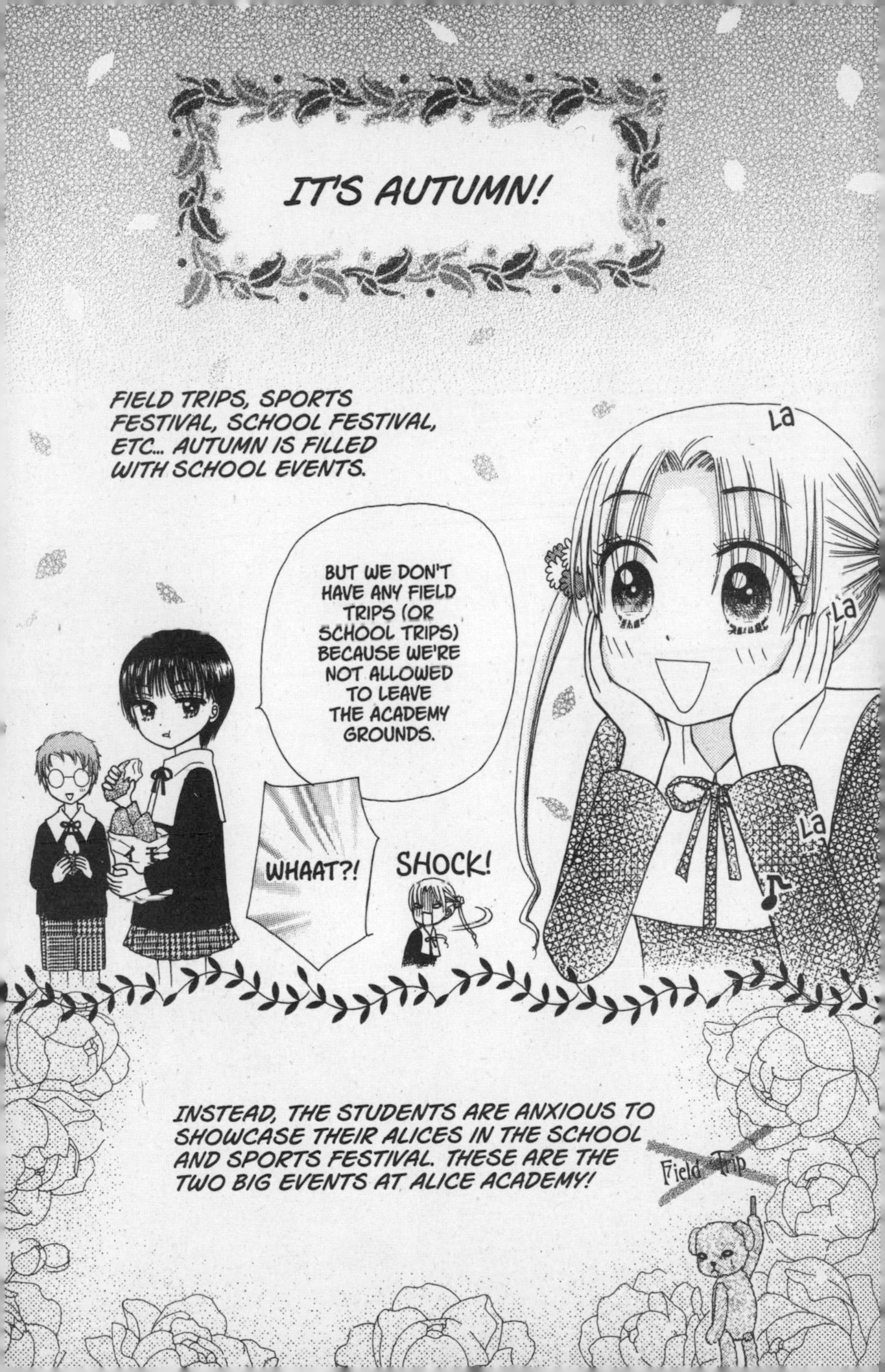
IT'S AUTUMN!
FIELD TRIPS, SPORTS FESTIVAL, SCHOOL FESTIVAL, ETC... AUTUMN IS FILLED WITH SCHOOL EVENTS.
La
La
La
BUT WE DON'T HAVE ANY FIELD TRIPS (OR SCHOOL TRIPS) BECAUSE WE'RE NOT ALLOWED TO LEAVE THE ACADEMY GROUNDS.
SHOCK!
WHAAT?!
INSTEAD, THE STUDENTS ARE ANXIOUS TO SHOWCASE THEIR ALICES IN THE SCHOOL AND SPORTS FESTIVAL. THESE ARE THE TWO BIG EVENTS AT ALICE ACADEMY!
Field Trip

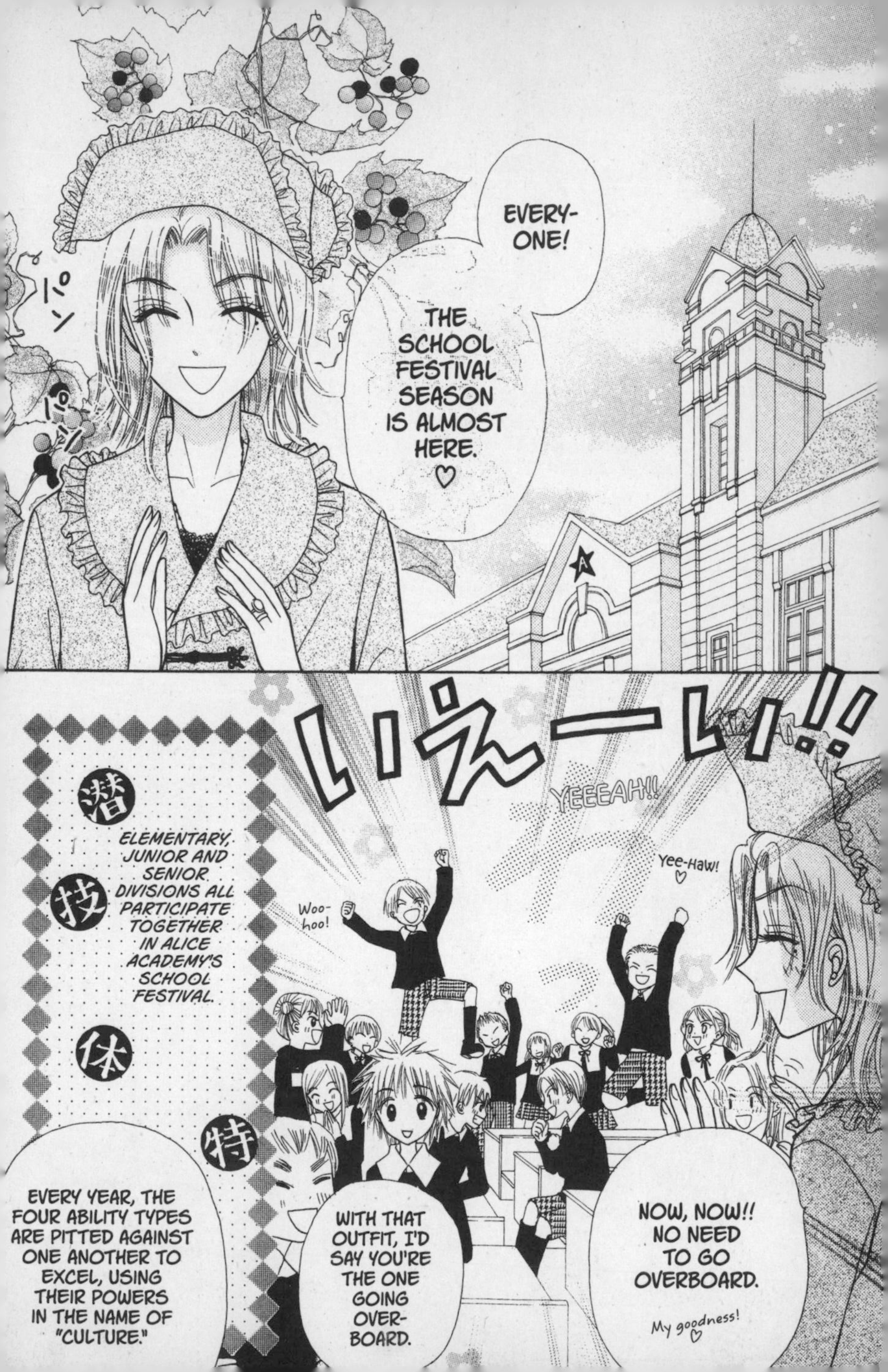
EVERY-ONE!
THE SCHOOL FESTIVAL SEASON IS ALMOST HERE. ♡
パン
パン
いえーい!!
YEEEAH!!
Yee-Haw! ♡
Woo-hoo!
潜
技
体
特
ELEMENTARY, JUNIOR AND SENIOR DIVISIONS ALL PARTICIPATE TOGETHER IN ALICE ACADEMY'S SCHOOL FESTIVAL.
NOW, NOW!! NO NEED TO GO OVERBOARD.
My goodness! ♡
WITH THAT OUTFIT, I'D SAY YOU'RE THE ONE GOING OVER-BOARD.
EVERY YEAR, THE FOUR ABILITY TYPES ARE PITTED AGAINST ONE ANOTHER TO EXCEL, USING THEIR POWERS IN THE NAME OF "CULTURE."

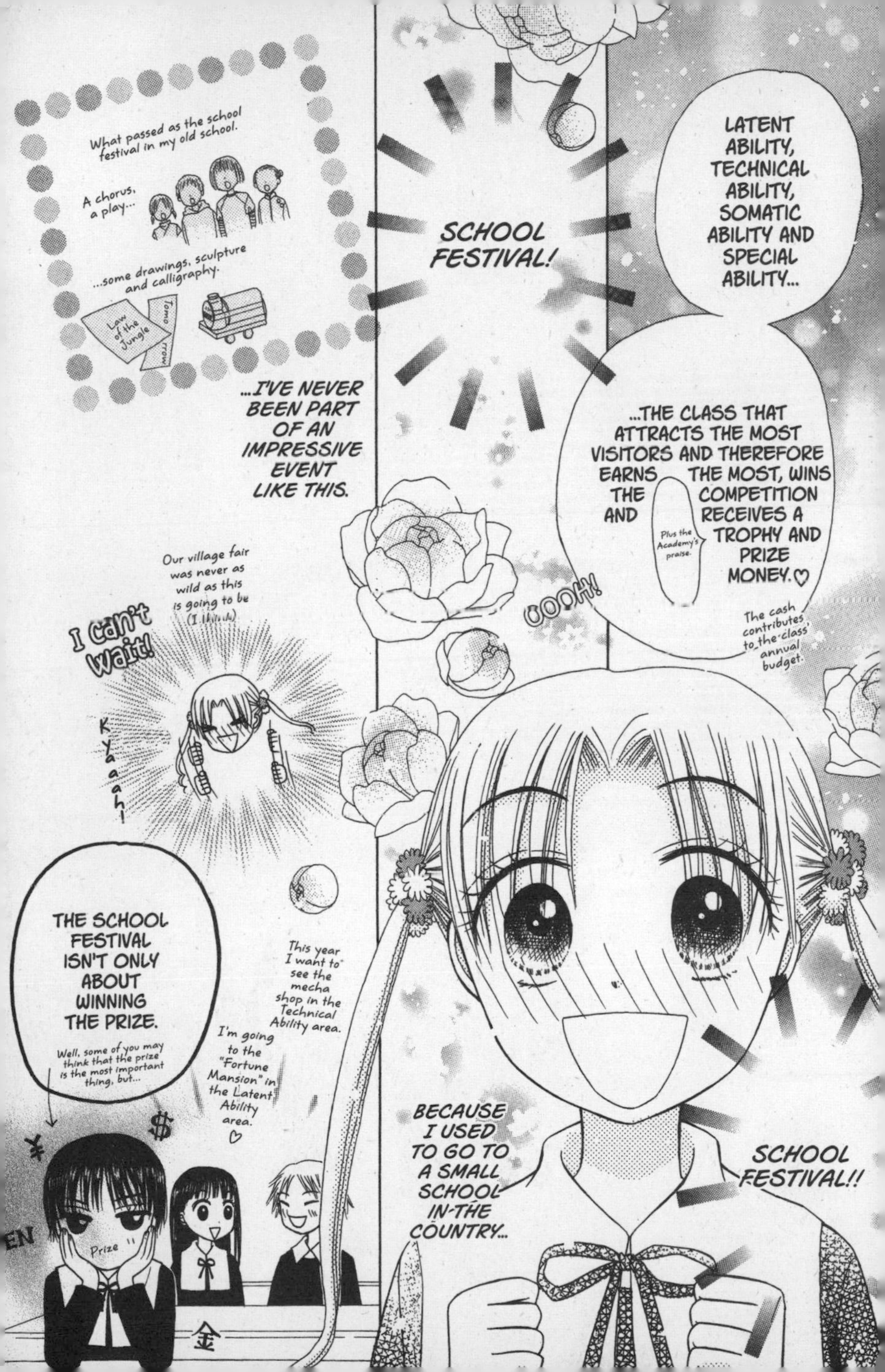
LATENT ABILITY, TECHNICAL ABILITY, SOMATIC ABILITY AND SPECIAL ABILITY...
...THE CLASS THAT ATTRACTS THE MOST VISITORS AND THEREFORE EARNS THE MOST, WINS THE COMPETITION AND RECEIVES A TROPHY AND PRIZE MONEY.♡
Plus the Academy's praise.
The cash contributes to the class' annual budget.
SCHOOL FESTIVAL!
OOOH!
SCHOOL FESTIVAL!!
BECAUSE I USED TO GO TO A SMALL SCHOOL IN THE COUNTRY...
What passed as the school festival in my old school.
A chorus, a play...
...some drawings, sculpture and calligraphy.
Law of the Jungle
Tomo rrow
...I'VE NEVER BEEN PART OF AN IMPRESSIVE EVENT LIKE THIS.
Our village fair was never as wild as this is going to be
I can't wait!
Kyaaaah!
This year I want to see the mecha shop in the Technical Ability area.
I'm going to the "Fortune Mansion" in the Latent Ability area. ♡
THE SCHOOL FESTIVAL ISN'T ONLY ABOUT WINNING THE PRIZE.
Well, some of you may think that the prize is the most important thing, but...
Prize
金

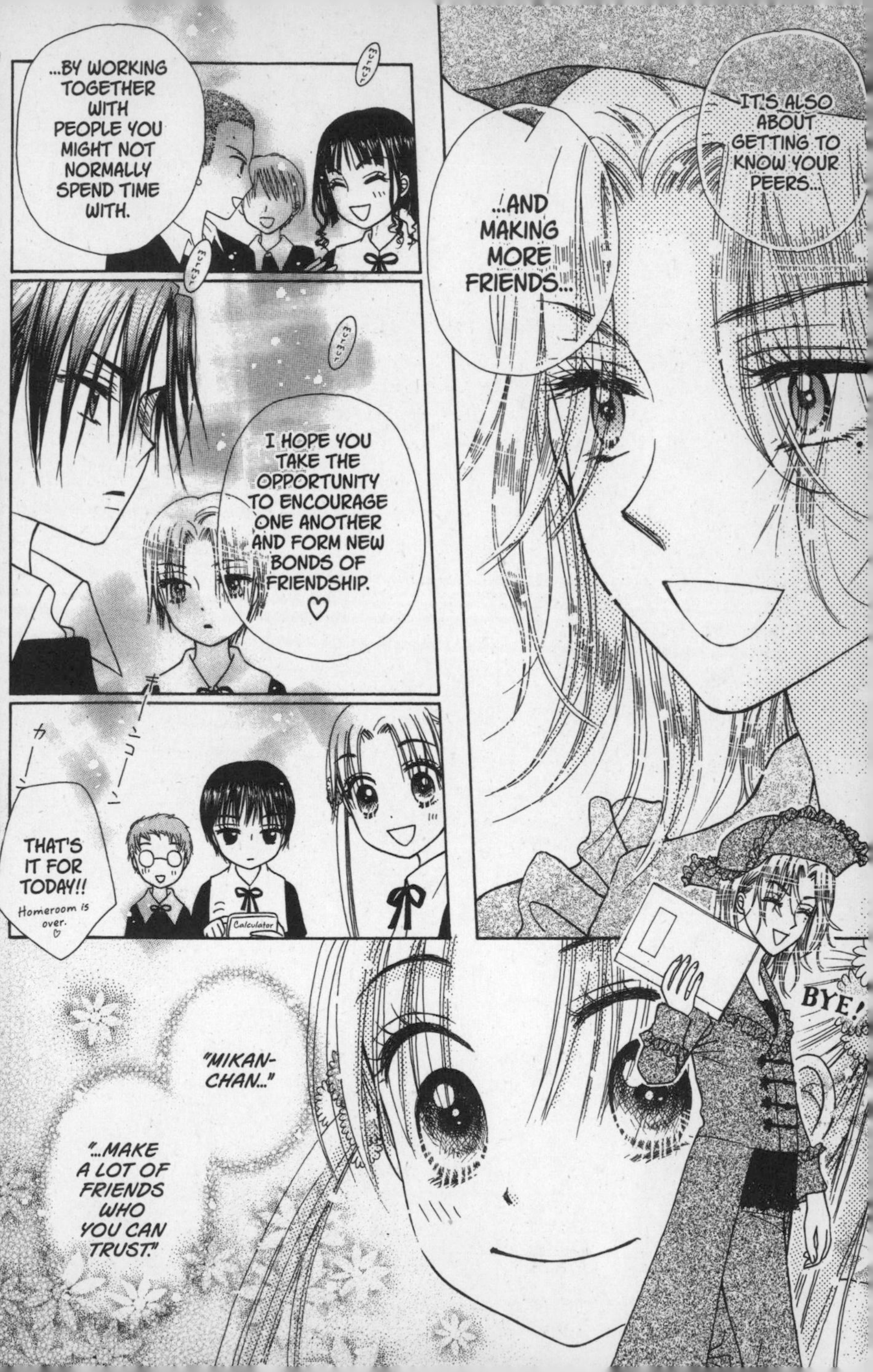
IT'S ALSO ABOUT GETTING TO KNOW YOUR PEERS...
...AND MAKING MORE FRIENDS...
...BY WORKING TOGETHER WITH PEOPLE YOU MIGHT NOT NORMALLY SPEND TIME WITH.
I HOPE YOU TAKE THE OPPORTUNITY TO ENCOURAGE ONE ANOTHER AND FORM NEW BONDS OF FRIENDSHIP. ♡
THAT'S IT FOR TODAY!!
Homeroom is over. ♡
Calculator
BYE!
"MIKAN-CHAN..."
"...MAKE A LOT OF FRIENDS WHO YOU CAN TRUST."

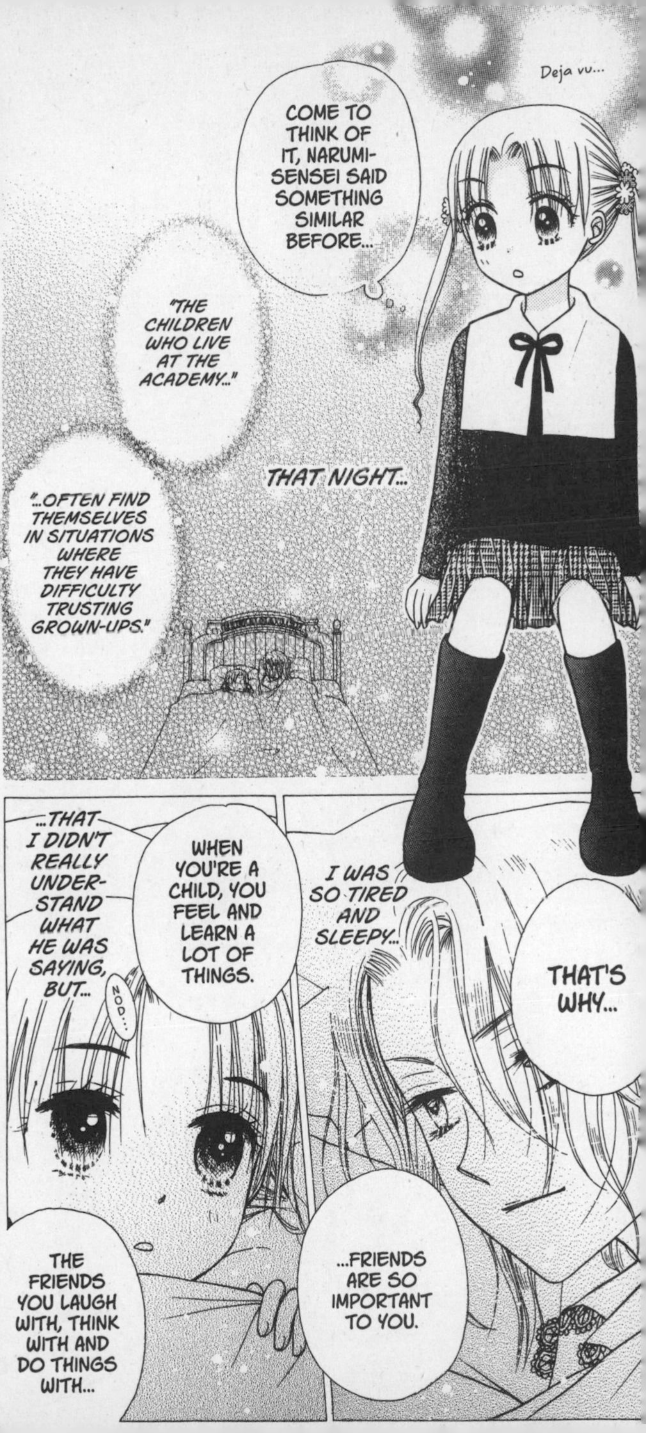
Deja vu...
COME TO THINK OF IT, NARUMI-SENSEI SAID SOMETHING SIMILAR BEFORE...
"THE CHILDREN WHO LIVE AT THE ACADEMY..."
"...OFTEN FIND THEMSELVES IN SITUATIONS WHERE THEY HAVE DIFFICULTY TRUSTING GROWN-UPS."
THAT NIGHT...
I WAS SO TIRED AND SLEEPY...
THAT'S WHY...
...FRIENDS ARE SO IMPORTANT TO YOU.
...THAT I DIDN'T REALLY UNDERSTAND WHAT HE WAS SAYING, BUT...
WHEN YOU'RE A CHILD, YOU FEEL AND LEARN A LOT OF THINGS.
NOD...
THE FRIENDS YOU LAUGH WITH, THINK WITH AND DO THINGS WITH...

Read at your own discretion.

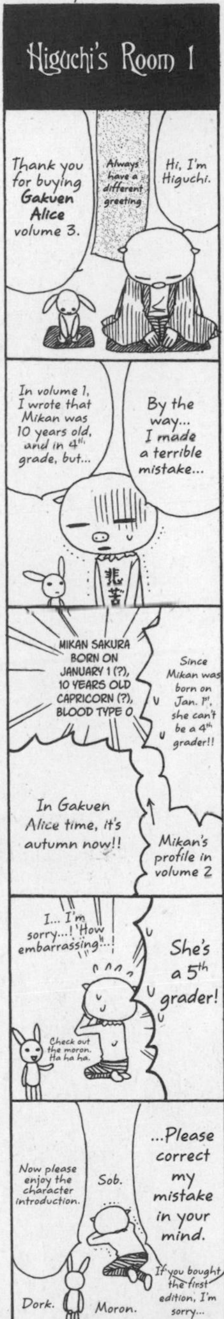
Higuchi's Room 1
Hi, I'm Higuchi.
Always have a different greeting
Thank you for buying Gakuen Alice volume 3.
By the way... I made a terrible mistake...
In volume 1, I wrote that Mikan was 10 years old, and in 4th grade, but...
悲苦
MIKAN SAKURA BORN ON JANUARY 1 (?), 10 YEARS OLD CAPRICORN (?), BLOOD TYPE O
Since Mikan was born on Jan. 1st, she can't be a 4th grader!!
In Gakuen Alice time, it's autumn now!!
Mikan's profile in volume 2
She's a 5th grader!
I... I'm sorry...! How embarrassing!...!
Check out the moron. Ha ha ha.
...Please correct my mistake in your mind.
Sob.
Now please enjoy the character introduction.
If you bought the first edition, I'm sorry...
Moron.
Dork.

Go to 2.

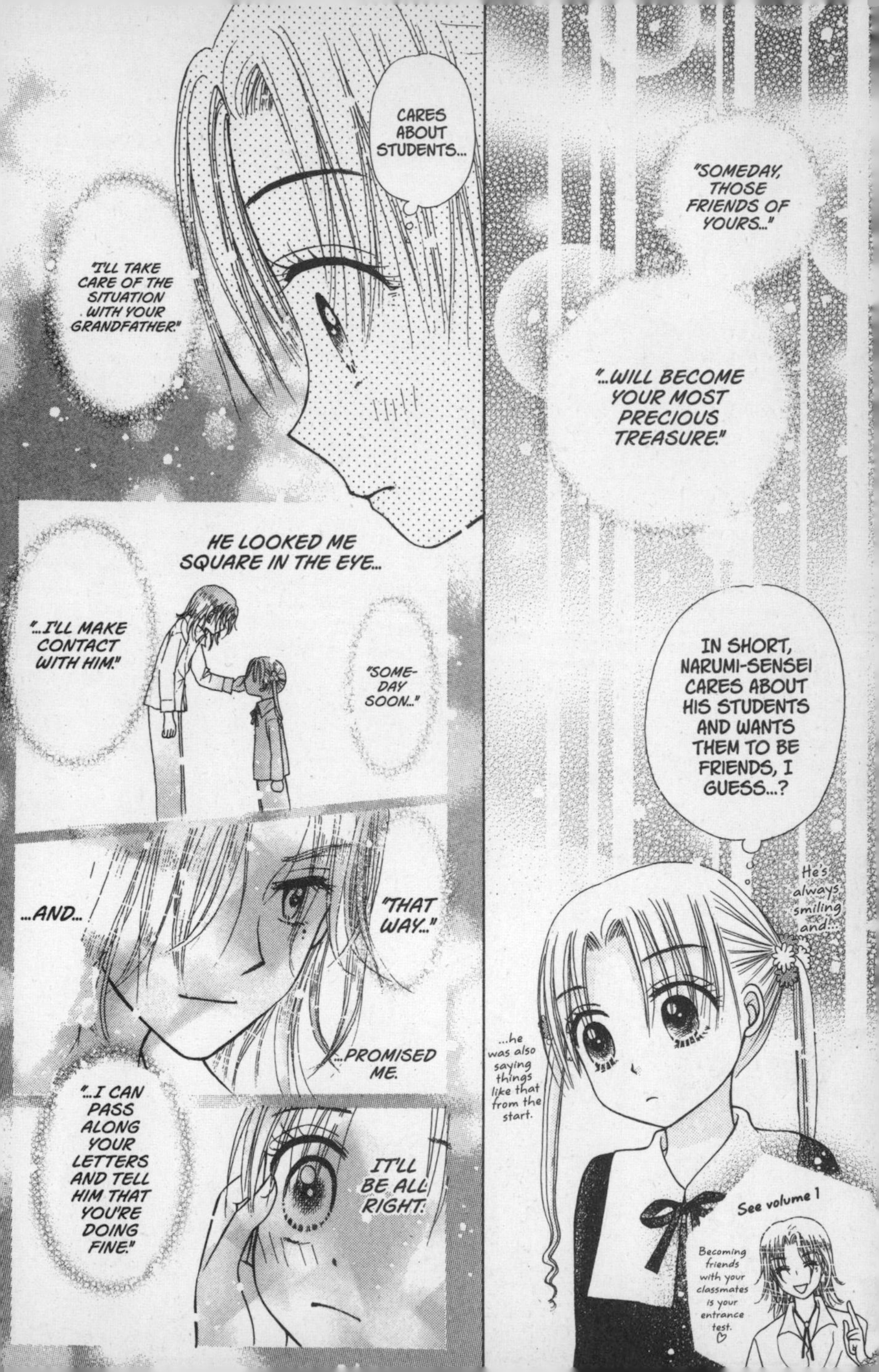
"SOMEDAY, THOSE FRIENDS OF YOURS..."
"...WILL BECOME YOUR MOST PRECIOUS TREASURE."
IN SHORT, NARUMI-SENSEI CARES ABOUT HIS STUDENTS AND WANTS THEM TO BE FRIENDS, I GUESS...?
He's always smiling and...
...he was also saying things like that from the start.
See volume 1
Becoming friends with your classmates is your entrance test. ♡
CARES ABOUT STUDENTS...
"I'LL TAKE CARE OF THE SITUATION WITH YOUR GRANDFATHER."
HE LOOKED ME SQUARE IN THE EYE...
"SOME-DAY SOON..."
"...I'LL MAKE CONTACT WITH HIM."
"THAT WAY..."
...AND...
...PROMISED ME.
IT'LL BE ALL RIGHT!
"...I CAN PASS ALONG YOUR LETTERS AND TELL HIM THAT YOU'RE DOING FINE."

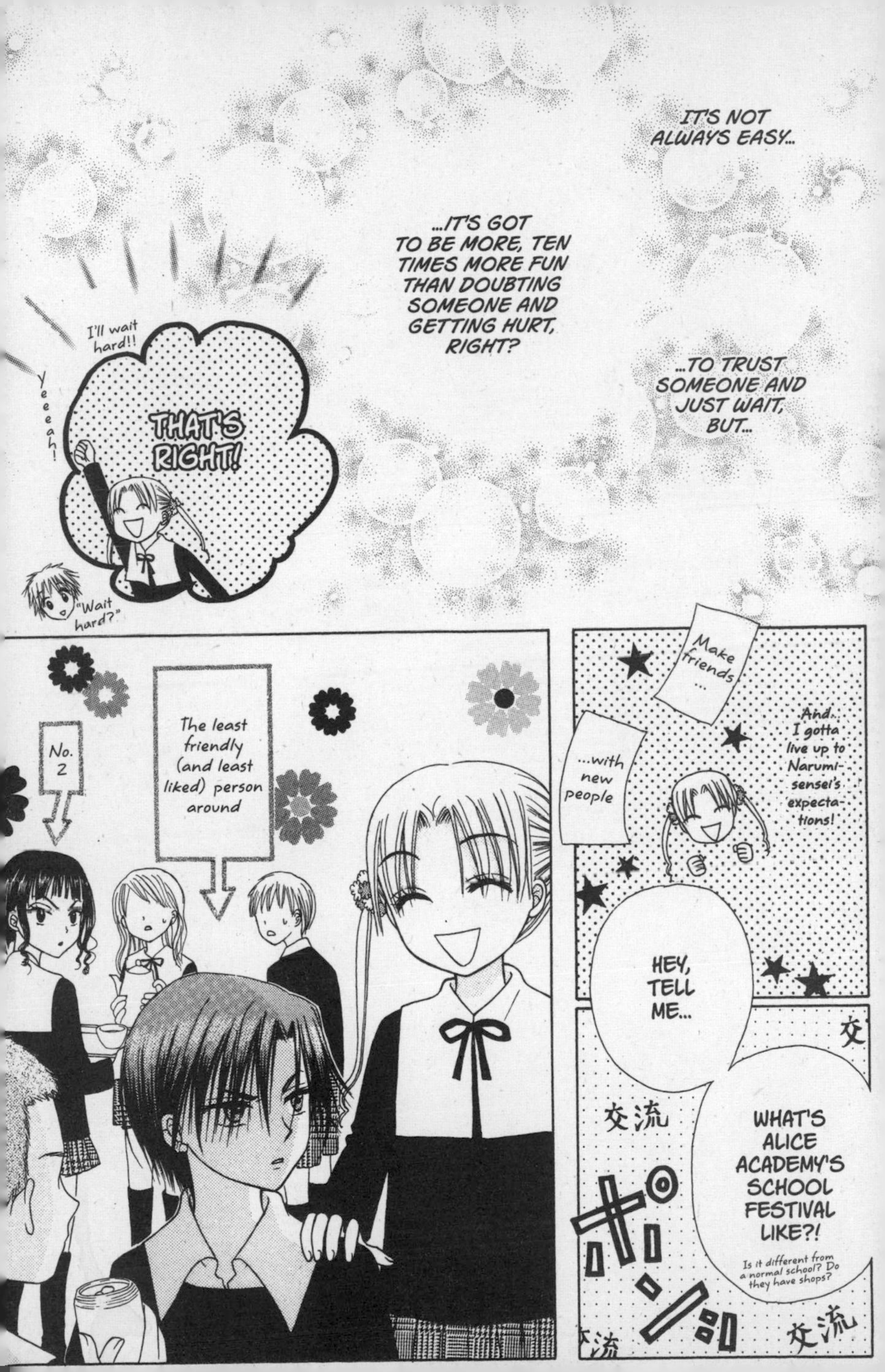
IT'S NOT ALWAYS EASY...
...TO TRUST SOMEONE AND JUST WAIT, BUT...
...IT'S GOT TO BE MORE, TEN TIMES MORE FUN THAN DOUBTING SOMEONE AND GETTING HURT, RIGHT?
THAT'S RIGHT!
I'll wait hard!!
Yeeeah!
"Wait hard?"
Make friends...
...with new people
And... I gotta live up to Narumi-sensei's expectations!
HEY, TELL ME...
WHAT'S ALICE ACADEMY'S SCHOOL FESTIVAL LIKE?!
Is it different from a normal school? Do they have shops?
交流
The least friendly (and least liked) person around
No. 2

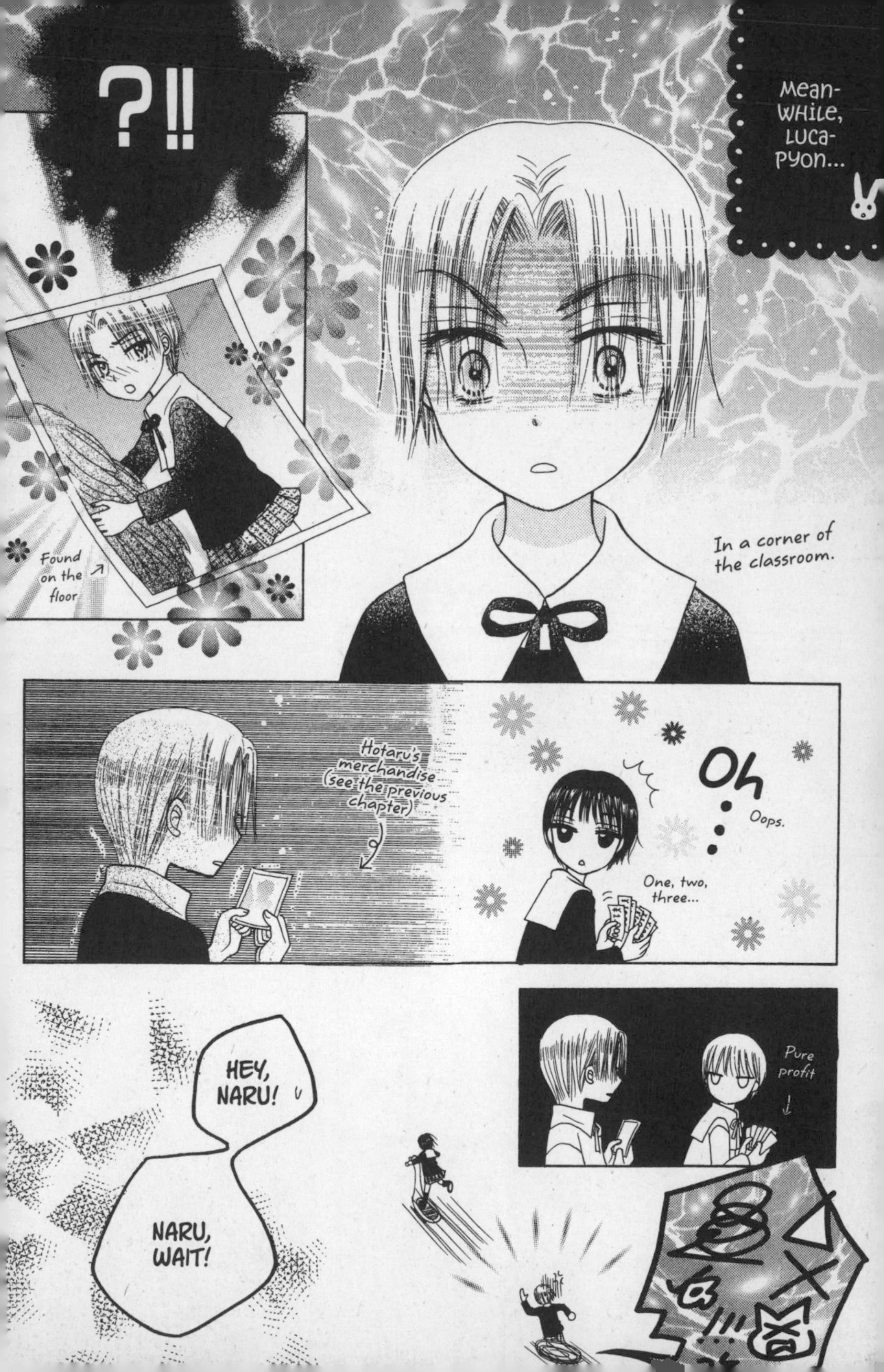
Mean-
while,
Luca-
pyon...
In a corner of the classroom.
?!!
Found on the floor
Oh...
Oops.
One, two, three...
Hotaru's merchandise (see the previous chapter)
Pure profit
HEY, NARU!
NARU, WAIT!

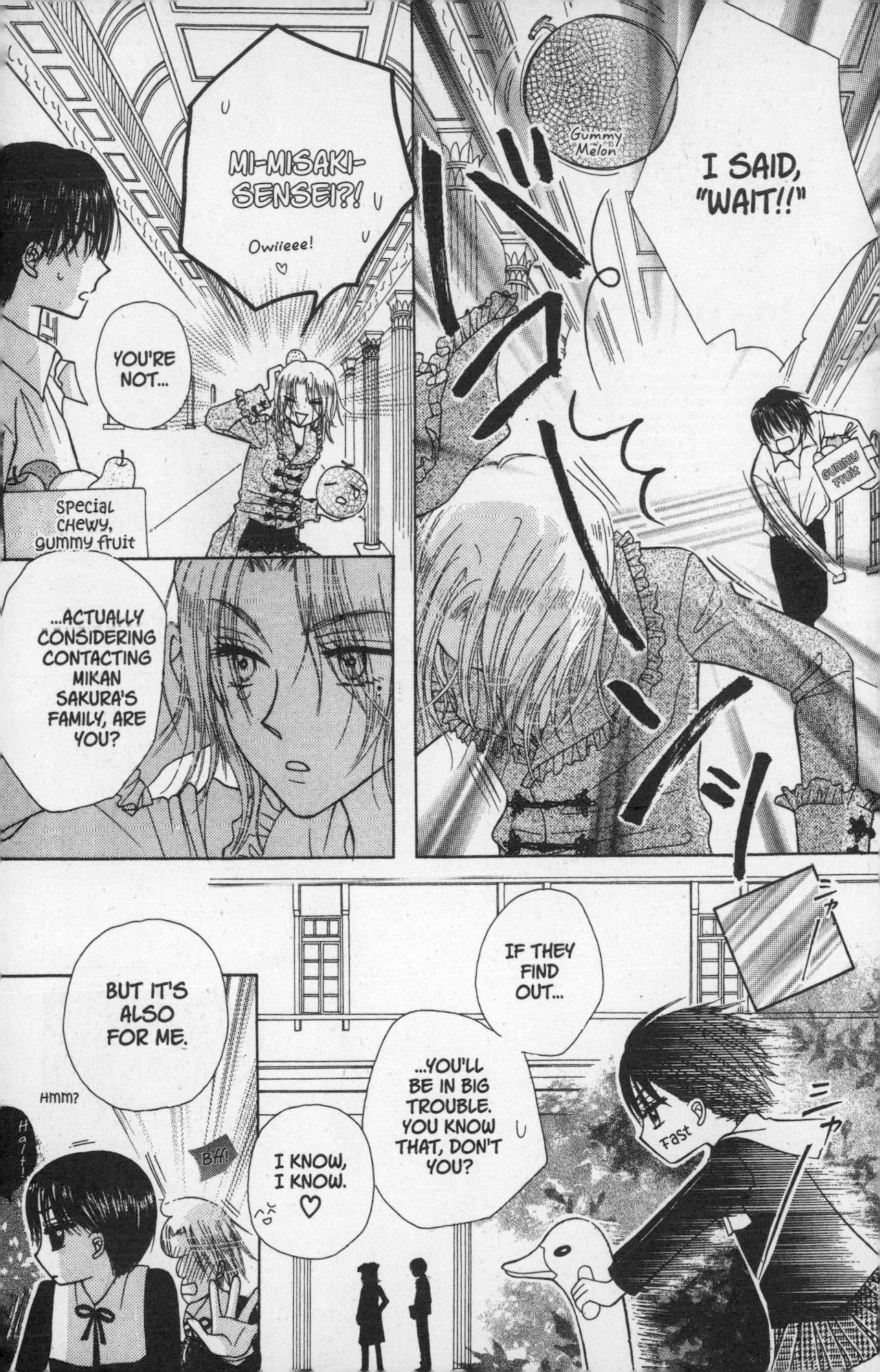
Gummy Melon
I SAID, "WAIT!!"
Gummy Fruit
MI-MISAKI-SENSEI?!
Owiieee!
YOU'RE NOT...
Special chewy, gummy fruit
...ACTUALLY CONSIDERING CONTACTING MIKAN SAKURA'S FAMILY, ARE YOU?
Fast
IF THEY FIND OUT...
...YOU'LL BE IN BIG TROUBLE. YOU KNOW THAT, DON'T YOU?
I KNOW, I KNOW. ♥
BUT IT'S ALSO FOR ME.
Bff!
Hmm?
Halt

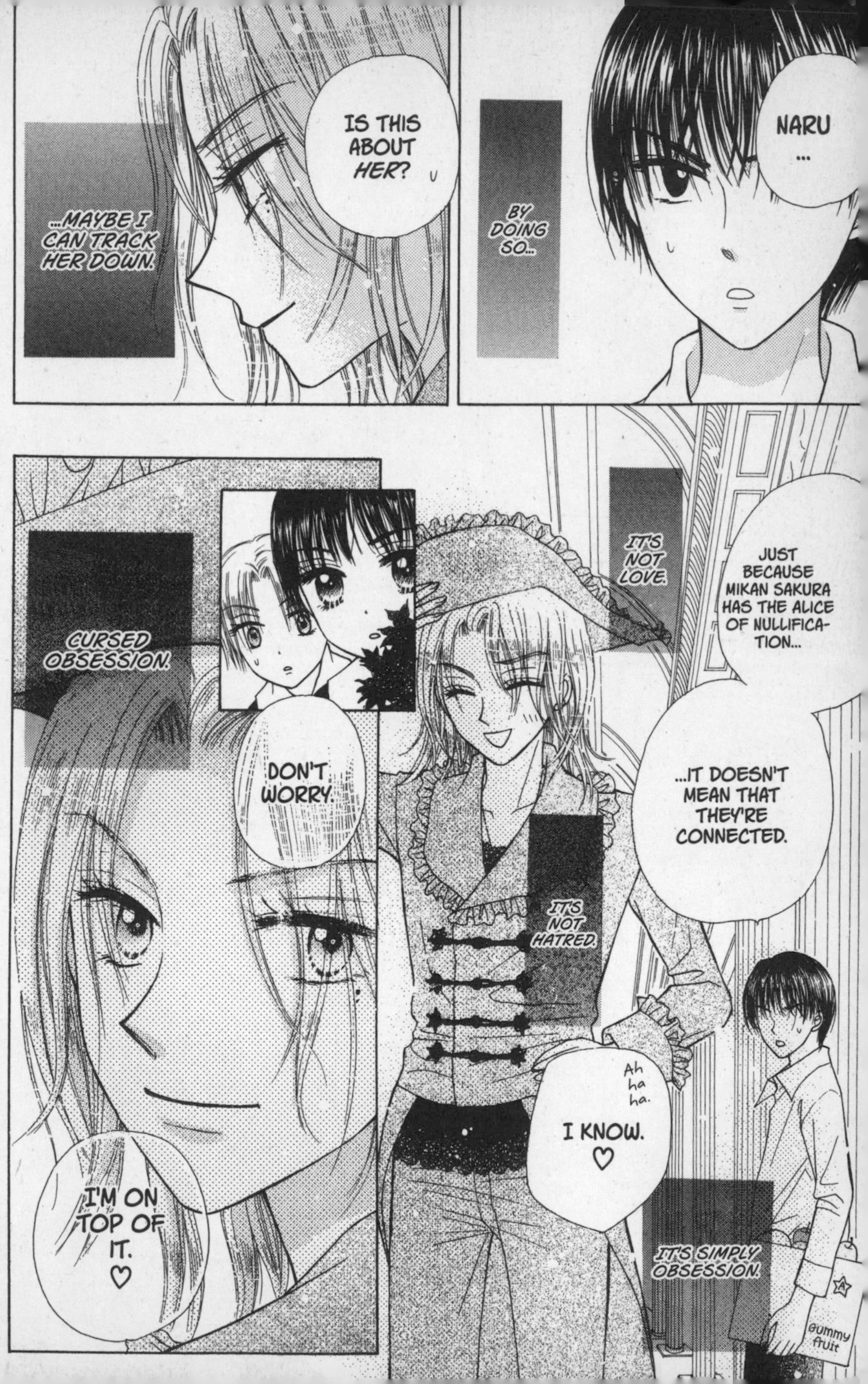
NARU ...
BY DOING SO...
IS THIS ABOUT HER?
...MAYBE I CAN TRACK HER DOWN.
JUST BECAUSE MIKAN SAKURA HAS THE ALICE OF NULLIFICATION...
IT'S NOT LOVE.
...IT DOESN'T MEAN THAT THEY'RE CONNECTED.
IT'S NOT HATRED.
CURSED OBSESSION.
DON'T WORRY.
Ah ha ha.
I KNOW. ♡
IT'S SIMPLY OBSESSION.
Gummy fruit
I'M ON TOP OF IT. ♡

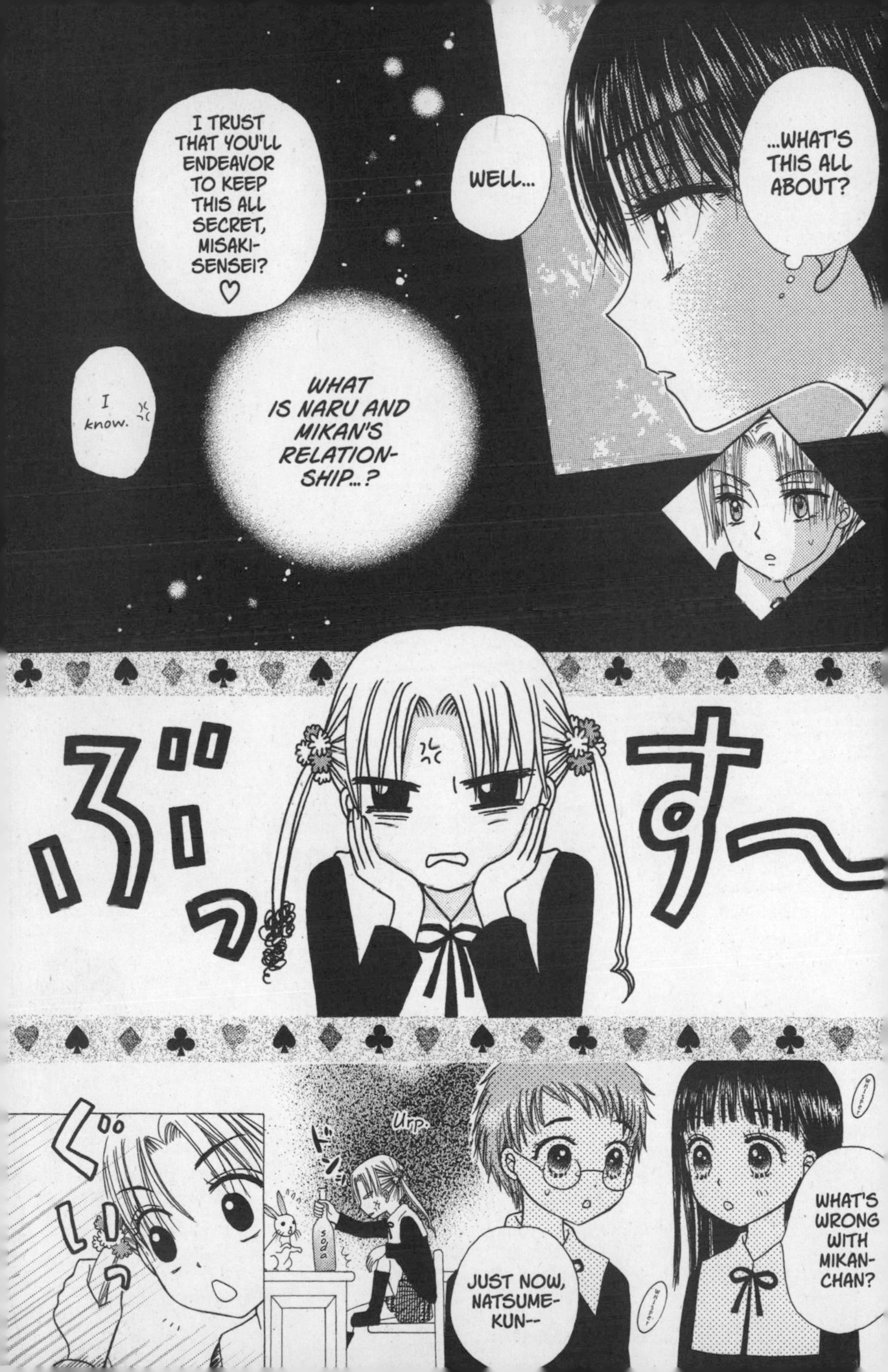
...WHAT'S THIS ALL ABOUT?
WELL...
I TRUST THAT YOU'LL ENDEAVOR TO KEEP THIS ALL SECRET, MISAKI-SENSEI? ♡
I know.
WHAT IS NARU AND MIKAN'S RELATIONSHIP...?
ぶっすー
WHAT'S WRONG WITH MIKAN-CHAN?
JUST NOW, NATSUME-KUN--
Urp.
soda
ぐっ

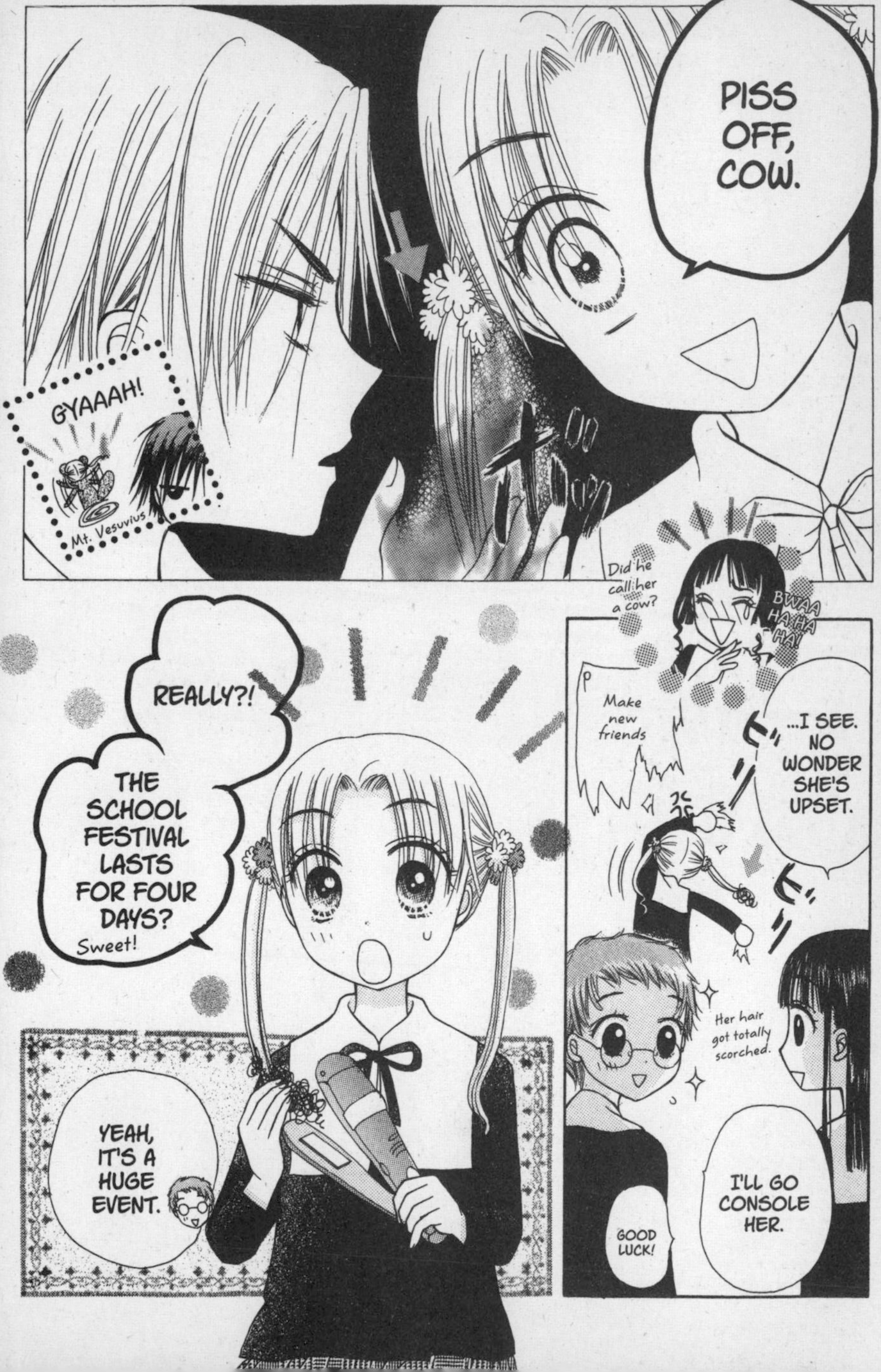
PISS OFF, COW.
GYAAAH!
Mt. Vesuvius
Did he call her a cow?
BWAAHAHAHA!
Make new friends
...I SEE. NO WONDER SHE'S UPSET.
Her hair got totally scorched.
I'LL GO CONSOLE HER.
GOOD LUCK!
REALLY?!
THE SCHOOL FESTIVAL LASTS FOR FOUR DAYS?
Sweet!
YEAH, IT'S A HUGE EVENT.

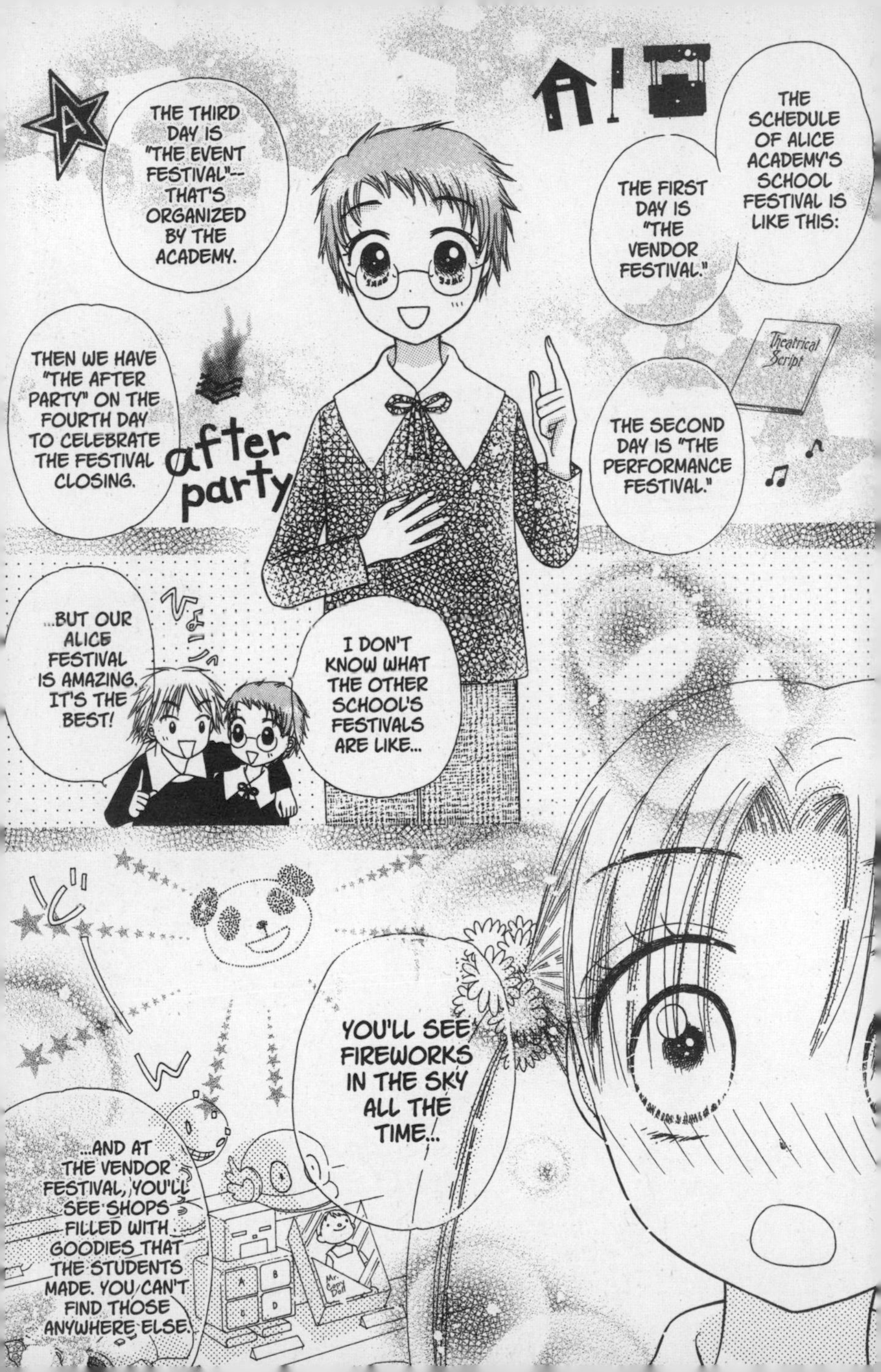
THE SCHEDULE OF ALICE ACADEMY'S SCHOOL FESTIVAL IS LIKE THIS:
THE FIRST DAY IS "THE VENDOR FESTIVAL."
Theatrical Script
THE SECOND DAY IS "THE PERFORMANCE FESTIVAL."
THE THIRD DAY IS "THE EVENT FESTIVAL"--THAT'S ORGANIZED BY THE ACADEMY.
THEN WE HAVE "THE AFTER PARTY" ON THE FOURTH DAY TO CELEBRATE THE FESTIVAL CLOSING.
after party
I DON'T KNOW WHAT THE OTHER SCHOOL'S FESTIVALS ARE LIKE...
...BUT OUR ALICE FESTIVAL IS AMAZING. IT'S THE BEST!
YOU'LL SEE FIREWORKS IN THE SKY ALL THE TIME...
...AND AT THE VENDOR FESTIVAL, YOU'LL SEE SHOPS FILLED WITH GOODIES THAT THE STUDENTS MADE. YOU CAN'T FIND THOSE ANYWHERE ELSE.
Mr. Copy Doll

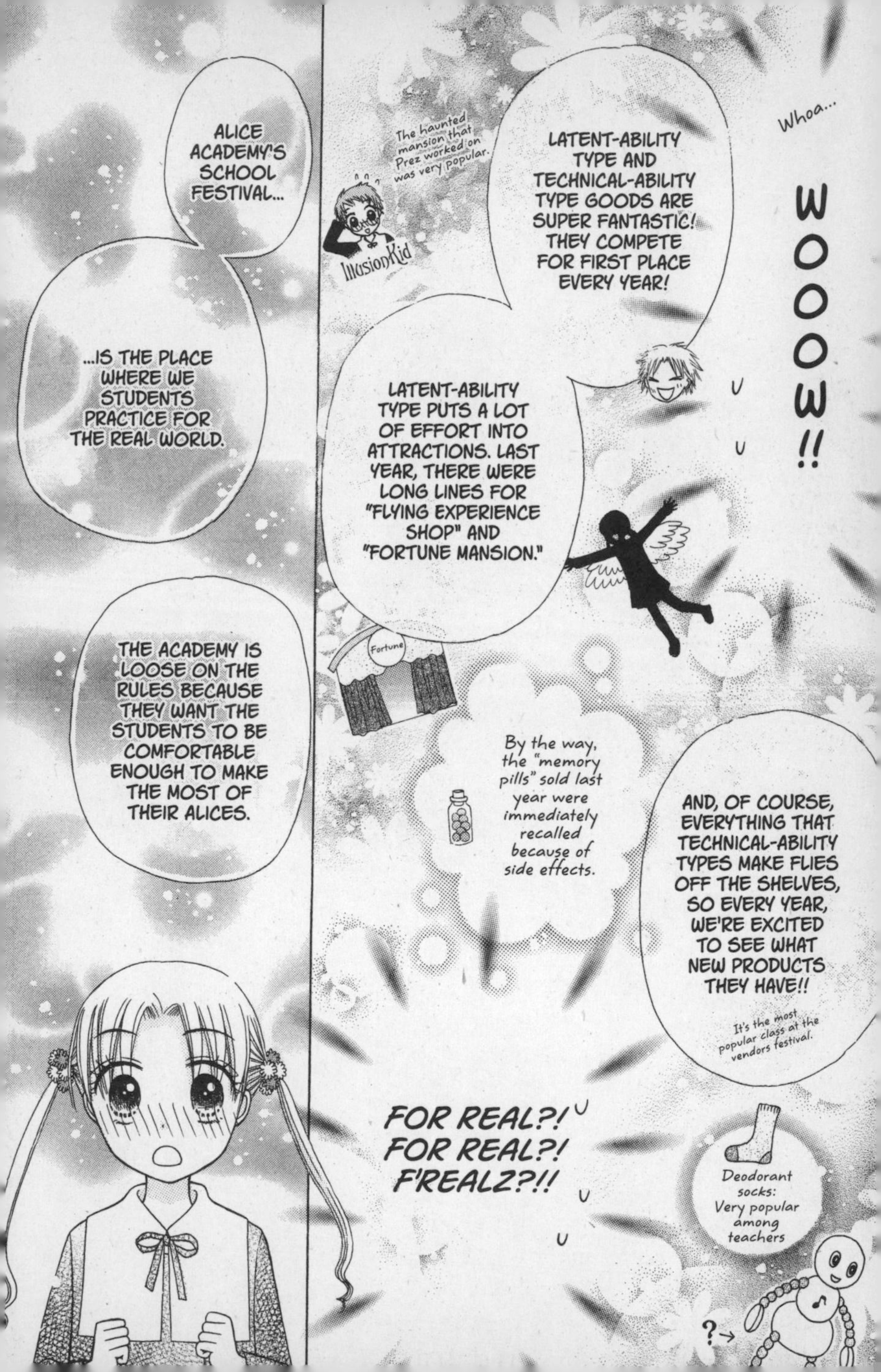
Whoa...
WOOOOW!!
LATENT-ABILITY TYPE AND TECHNICAL-ABILITY TYPE GOODS ARE SUPER FANTASTIC! THEY COMPETE FOR FIRST PLACE EVERY YEAR!
The haunted mansion that Prez worked on was very popular.
Illusion Kid
LATENT-ABILITY TYPE PUTS A LOT OF EFFORT INTO ATTRACTIONS. LAST YEAR, THERE WERE LONG LINES FOR "FLYING EXPERIENCE SHOP" AND "FORTUNE MANSION."
Fortune
AND, OF COURSE, EVERYTHING THAT TECHNICAL-ABILITY TYPES MAKE FLIES OFF THE SHELVES, SO EVERY YEAR, WE'RE EXCITED TO SEE WHAT NEW PRODUCTS THEY HAVE!!
It's the most popular class at the vendors festival.
By the way, the "memory pills" sold last year were immediately recalled because of side effects.
FOR REAL?! FOR REAL?! F'REALZ?!!
Deodorant socks: Very popular among teachers
?→
ALICE ACADEMY'S SCHOOL FESTIVAL...
...IS THE PLACE WHERE WE STUDENTS PRACTICE FOR THE REAL WORLD.
THE ACADEMY IS LOOSE ON THE RULES BECAUSE THEY WANT THE STUDENTS TO BE COMFORTABLE ENOUGH TO MAKE THE MOST OF THEIR ALICES.

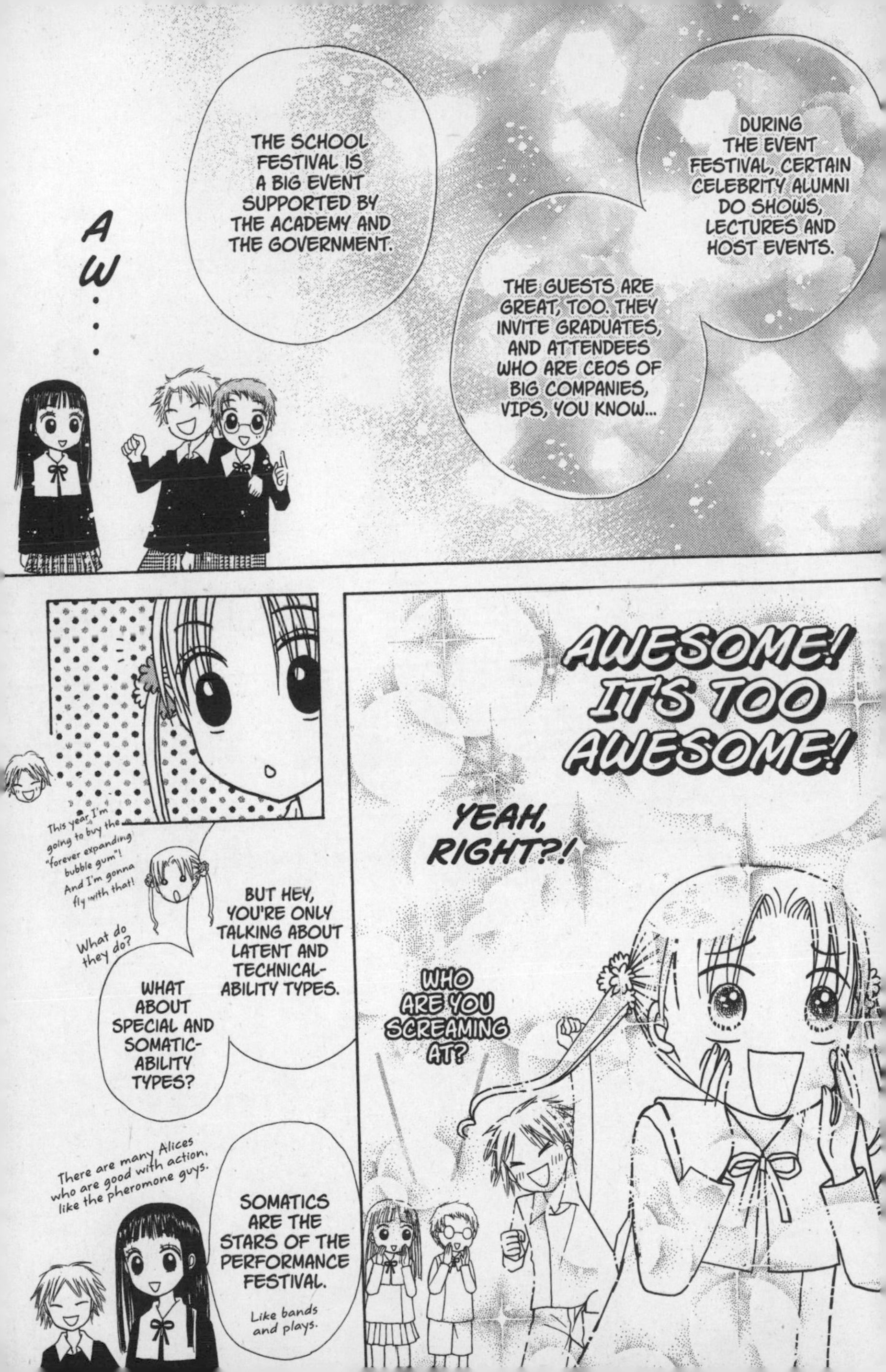
DURING THE EVENT FESTIVAL, CERTAIN CELEBRITY ALUMNI DO SHOWS, LECTURES AND HOST EVENTS.
THE GUESTS ARE GREAT, TOO. THEY INVITE GRADUATES, AND ATTENDEES WHO ARE CEOS OF BIG COMPANIES, VIPS, YOU KNOW...
THE SCHOOL FESTIVAL IS A BIG EVENT SUPPORTED BY THE ACADEMY AND THE GOVERNMENT.
AW...
AWESOME! IT'S TOO AWESOME!
YEAH, RIGHT?!
WHO ARE YOU SCREAMING AT?
This year, I'm going to buy the "forever expanding" bubble gum"! And I'm gonna fly with that!
BUT HEY, YOU'RE ONLY TALKING ABOUT LATENT AND TECHNICAL-ABILITY TYPES.
What do they do?
WHAT ABOUT SPECIAL AND SOMATIC-ABILITY TYPES?
There are many Alices who are good with action, like the pheromone guys.
SOMATICS ARE THE STARS OF THE PERFORMANCE FESTIVAL.
Like bands and plays.

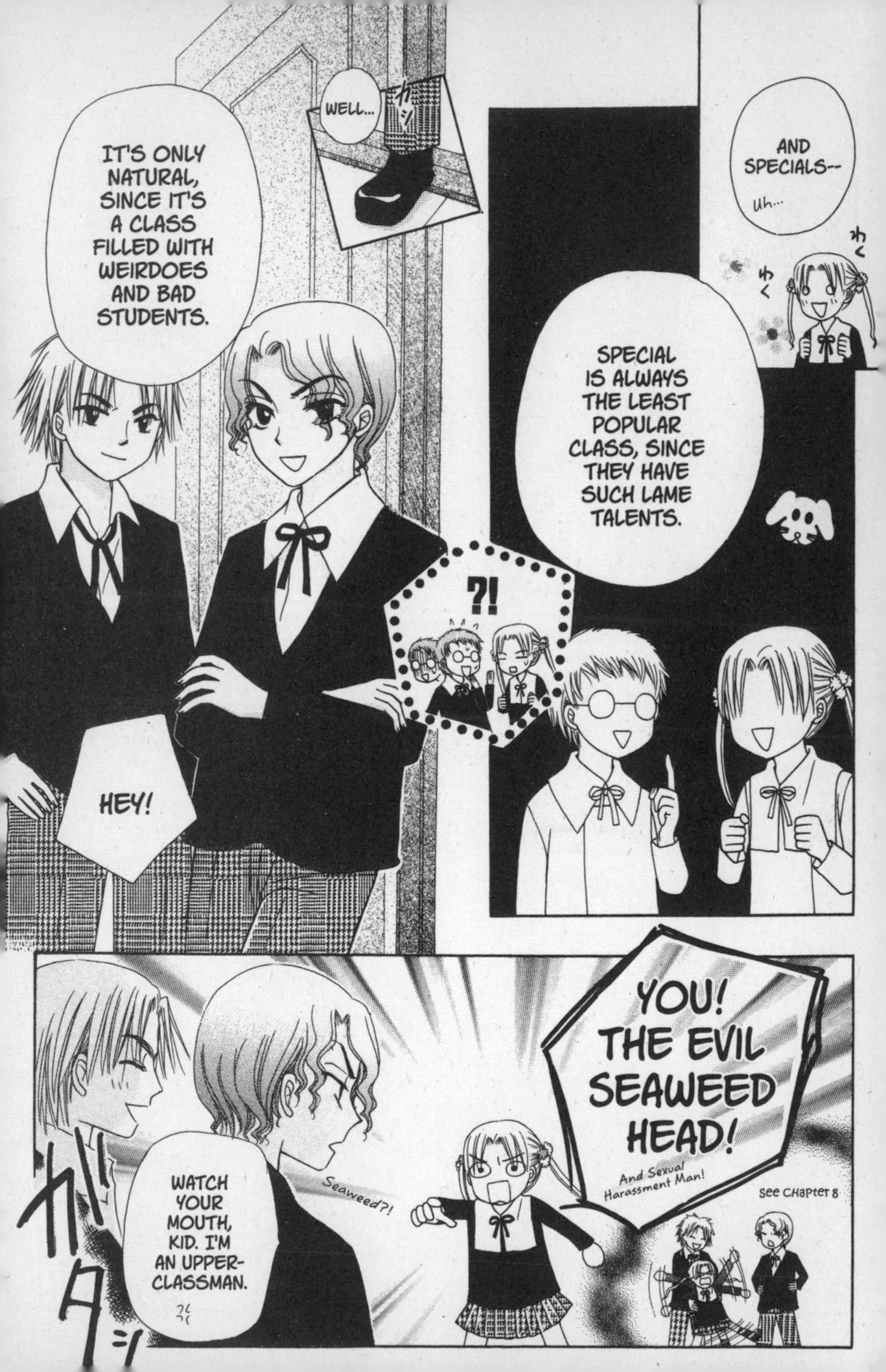
AND SPECIALS--
Uh...
SPECIAL IS ALWAYS THE LEAST POPULAR CLASS, SINCE THEY HAVE SUCH LAME TALENTS.
WELL...
IT'S ONLY NATURAL, SINCE IT'S A CLASS FILLED WITH WEIRDOES AND BAD STUDENTS.
?!
HEY!
YOU! THE EVIL SEAWEED HEAD!
And Sexual Harassment Man!
See Chapter 8
Seaweed?!
WATCH YOUR MOUTH, KID. I'M AN UPPER-CLASSMAN.

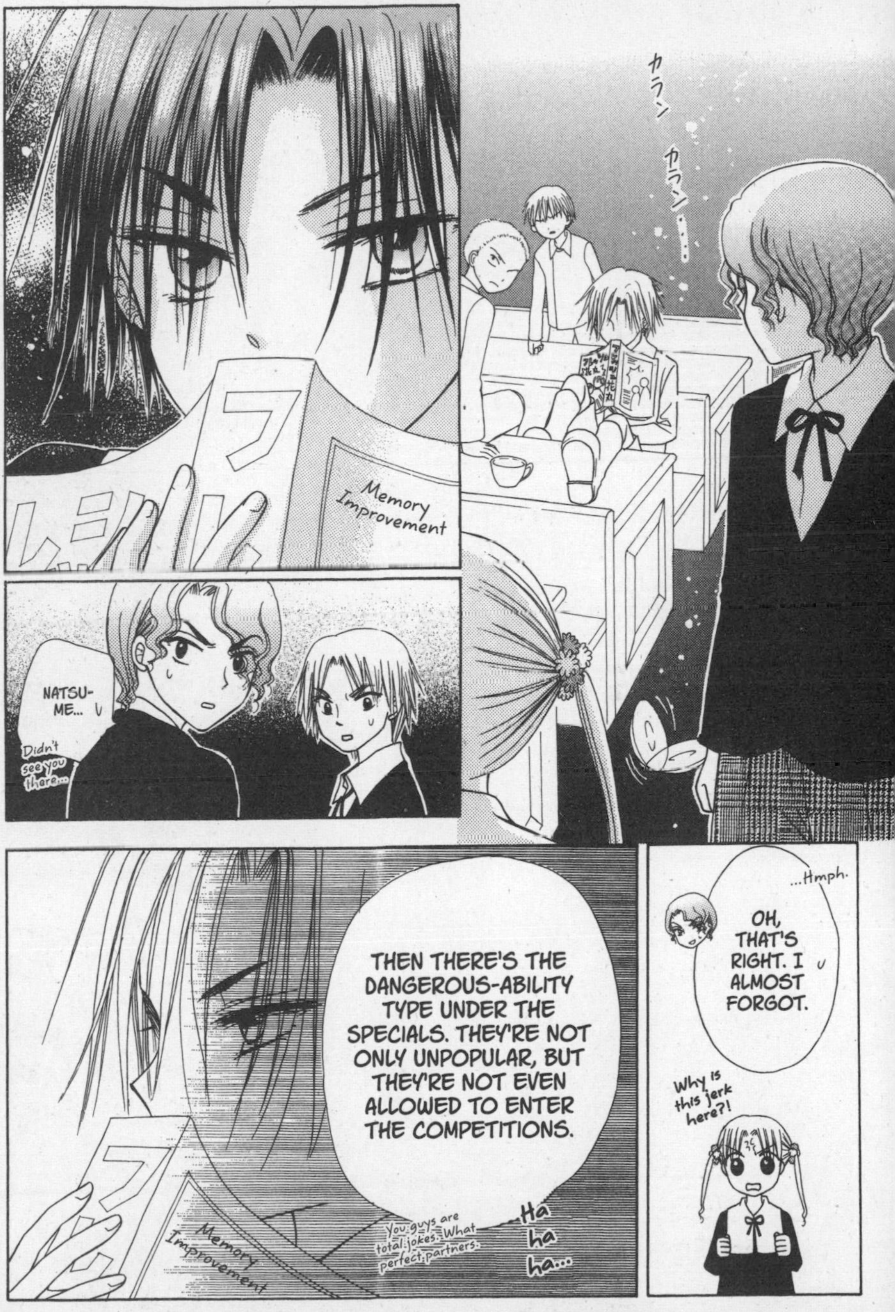
カラン
カラン・・・
Memory Improvement
NATSUME...
Didn't see you there...
...Hmph.
OH, THAT'S RIGHT. I ALMOST FORGOT.
Why is this jerk here?!
THEN THERE'S THE DANGEROUS-ABILITY TYPE UNDER THE SPECIALS. THEY'RE NOT ONLY UNPOPULAR, BUT THEY'RE NOT EVEN ALLOWED TO ENTER THE COMPETITIONS.
Ha ha ha...
You guys are total jokes. What perfect partners.
Memory Improvement

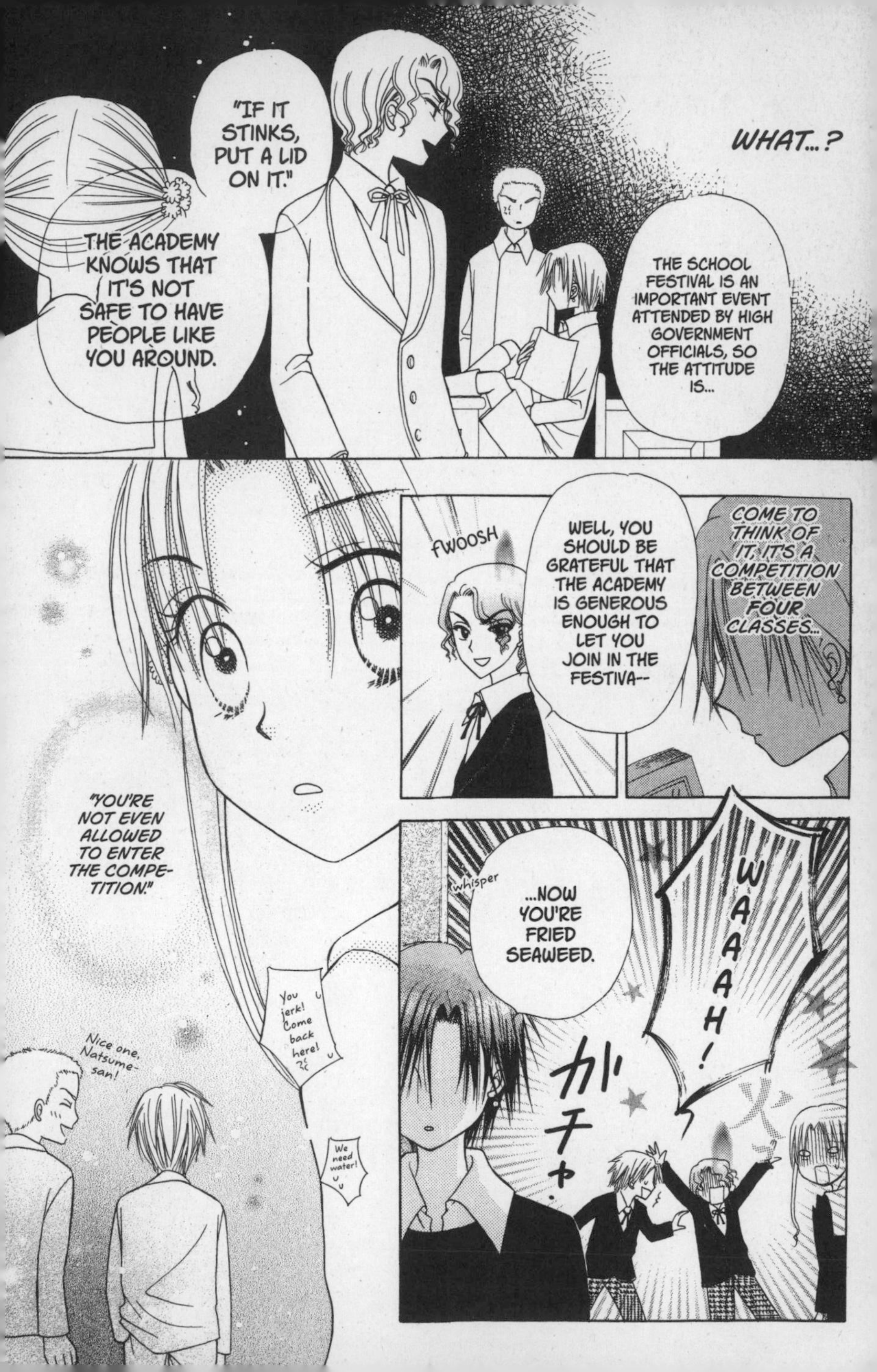
WHAT...?
THE SCHOOL FESTIVAL IS AN IMPORTANT EVENT ATTENDED BY HIGH GOVERNMENT OFFICIALS, SO THE ATTITUDE IS...
"IF IT STINKS, PUT A LID ON IT."
THE ACADEMY KNOWS THAT IT'S NOT SAFE TO HAVE PEOPLE LIKE YOU AROUND.
COME TO THINK OF IT, IT'S A COMPETITION BETWEEN FOUR CLASSES...
FWOOSH
WELL, YOU SHOULD BE GRATEFUL THAT THE ACADEMY IS GENEROUS ENOUGH TO LET YOU JOIN IN THE FESTIVA--
WAAAAH!
ガチャ
whisper
...NOW YOU'RE FRIED SEAWEED.
"YOU'RE NOT EVEN ALLOWED TO ENTER THE COMPETITION."
You jerk! Come back here!
We need water!
Nice one, Natsume-san!

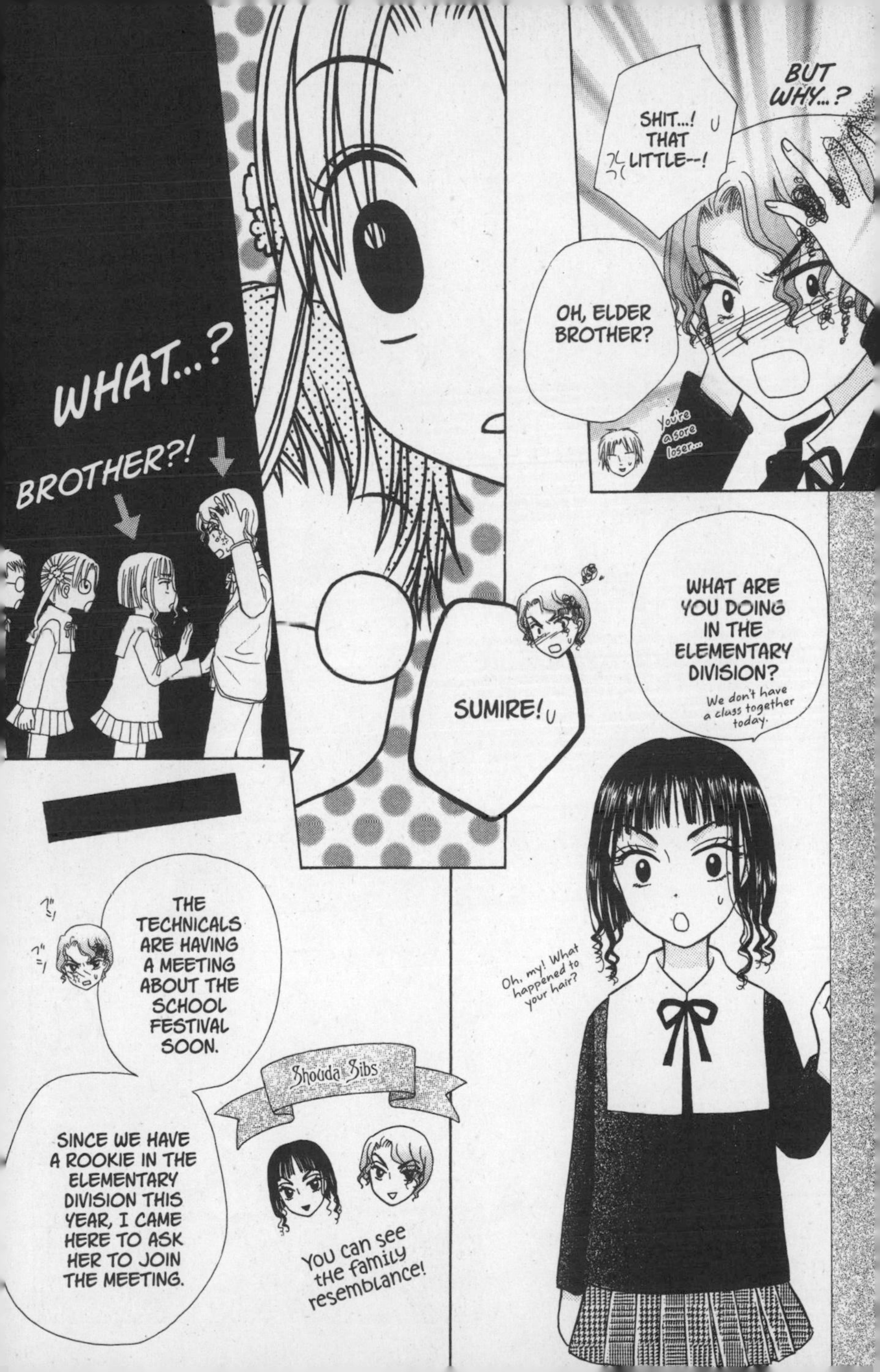
BUT WHY...?
SHIT...! THAT LITTLE--!
OH, ELDER BROTHER?
You're a sore loser...
SUMIRE!
WHAT...?
BROTHER?!
WHAT ARE YOU DOING IN THE ELEMENTARY DIVISION?
We don't have a class together today.
Oh, my! What happened to your hair?
[redacted]
THE TECHNICALS ARE HAVING A MEETING ABOUT THE SCHOOL FESTIVAL SOON.
SINCE WE HAVE A ROOKIE IN THE ELEMENTARY DIVISION THIS YEAR, I CAME HERE TO ASK HER TO JOIN THE MEETING.
Shouda Sibs
You can see the family resemblance!

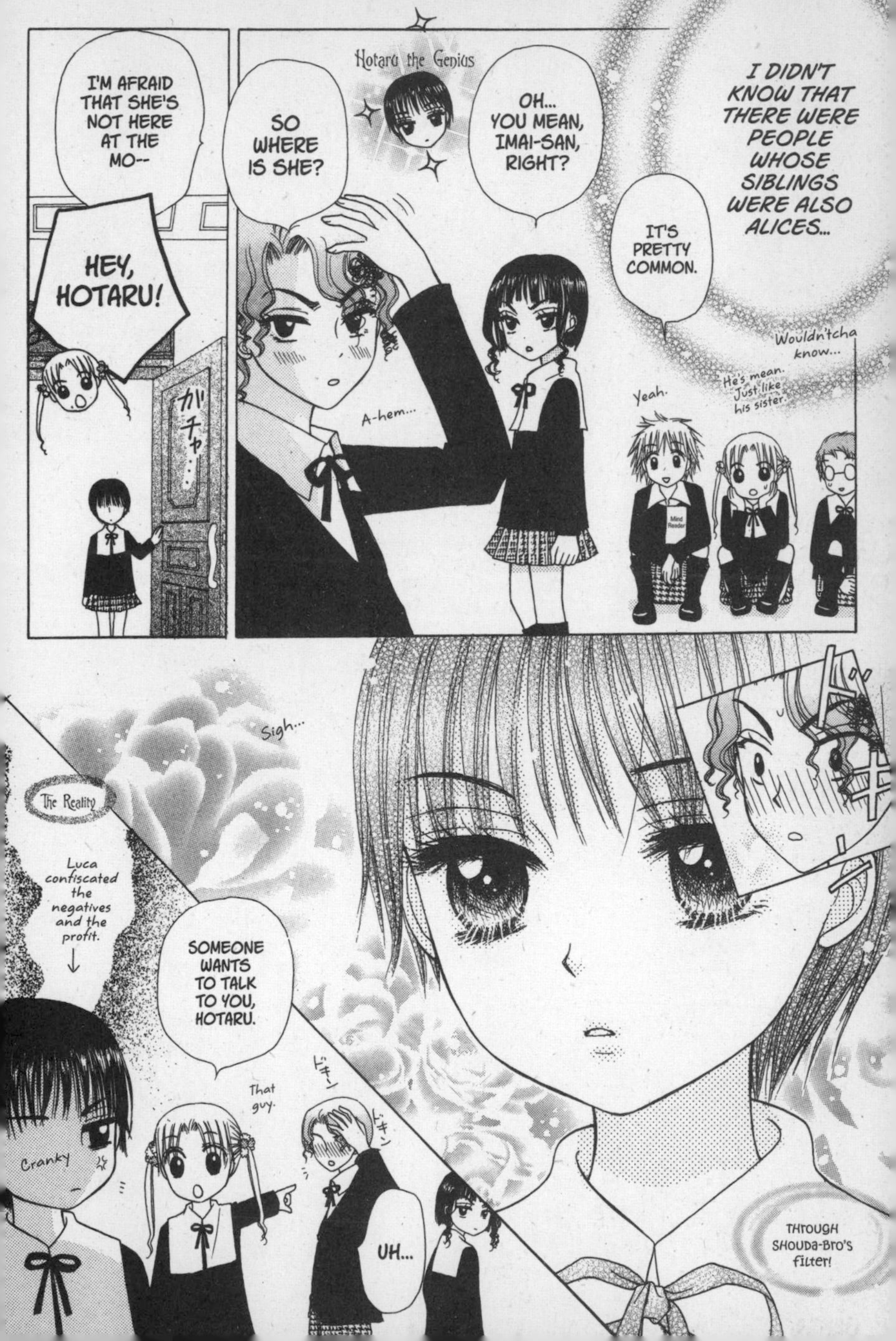
I DIDN'T KNOW THAT THERE WERE PEOPLE WHOSE SIBLINGS WERE ALSO ALICES...
IT'S PRETTY COMMON.
OH... YOU MEAN, IMAI-SAN, RIGHT?
Hotaru the Genius
SO WHERE IS SHE?
Wouldn'tcha know...
He's mean. Just like his sister.
Yeah.
A-hem...
Mind Reader
I'M AFRAID THAT SHE'S NOT HERE AT THE MO--
HEY, HOTARU!
ガチャ…
Sigh...
THROUGH SHOUDA-BRO'S filter!
The Reality
Luca confiscated the negatives and the profit.
↓
SOMEONE WANTS TO TALK TO YOU, HOTARU.
That guy.
ドキーン
ドキン
Cranky
UH...

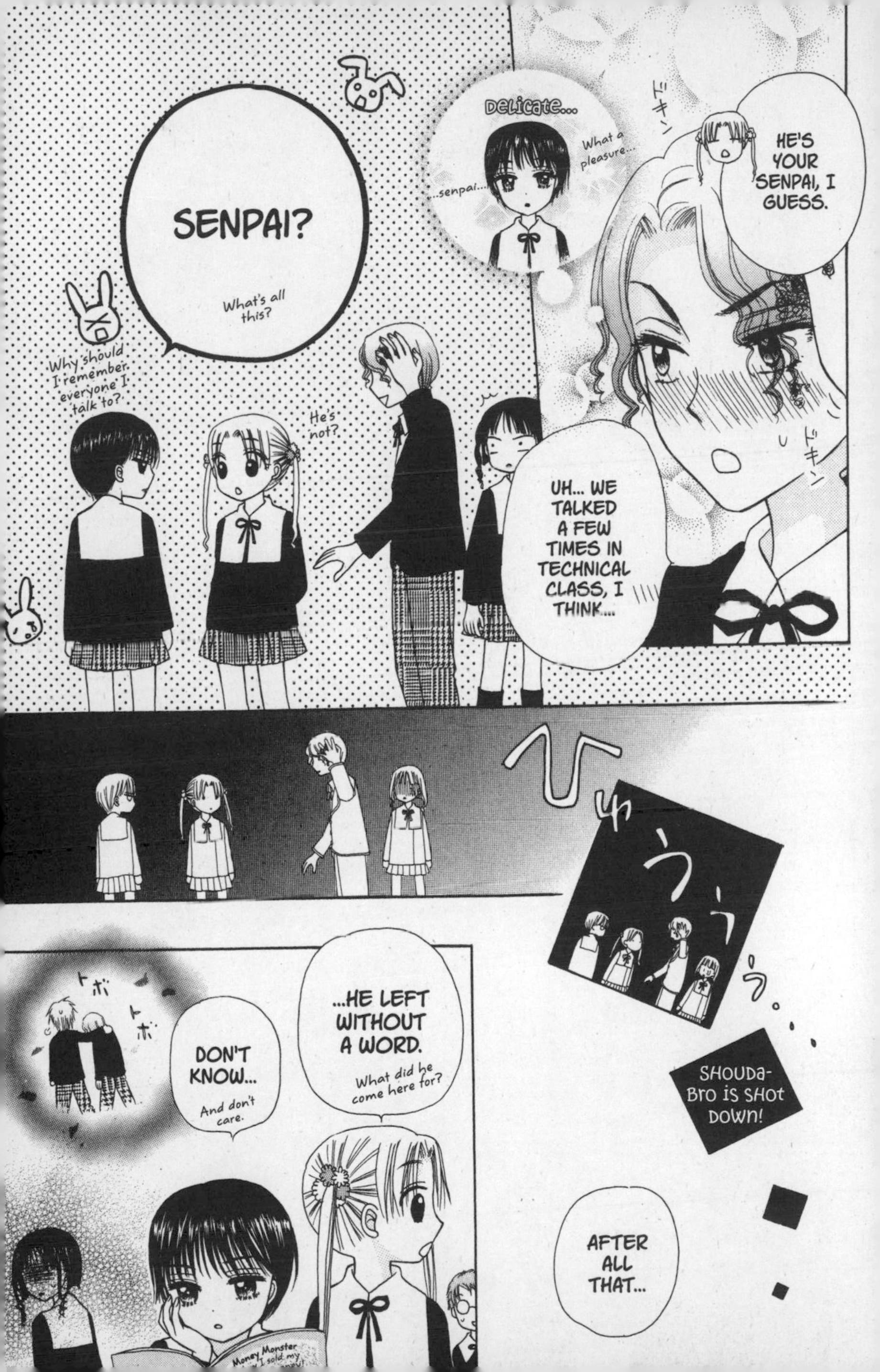
ドキン
HE'S YOUR SENPAI, I GUESS.
Delicate...
What a pleasure...
...senpai...
ドキン
SENPAI?
What's all this?
He's not?
Why should I remember everyone I talk to?
UH... WE TALKED A FEW TIMES IN TECHNICAL CLASS, I THINK...
ひゅううう
SHOUDA-Bro is SHOT DOWN!
AFTER ALL THAT...
...HE LEFT WITHOUT A WORD.
What did he come here for?
DON'T KNOW...
And don't care.
トボ
トボ
Money Monster

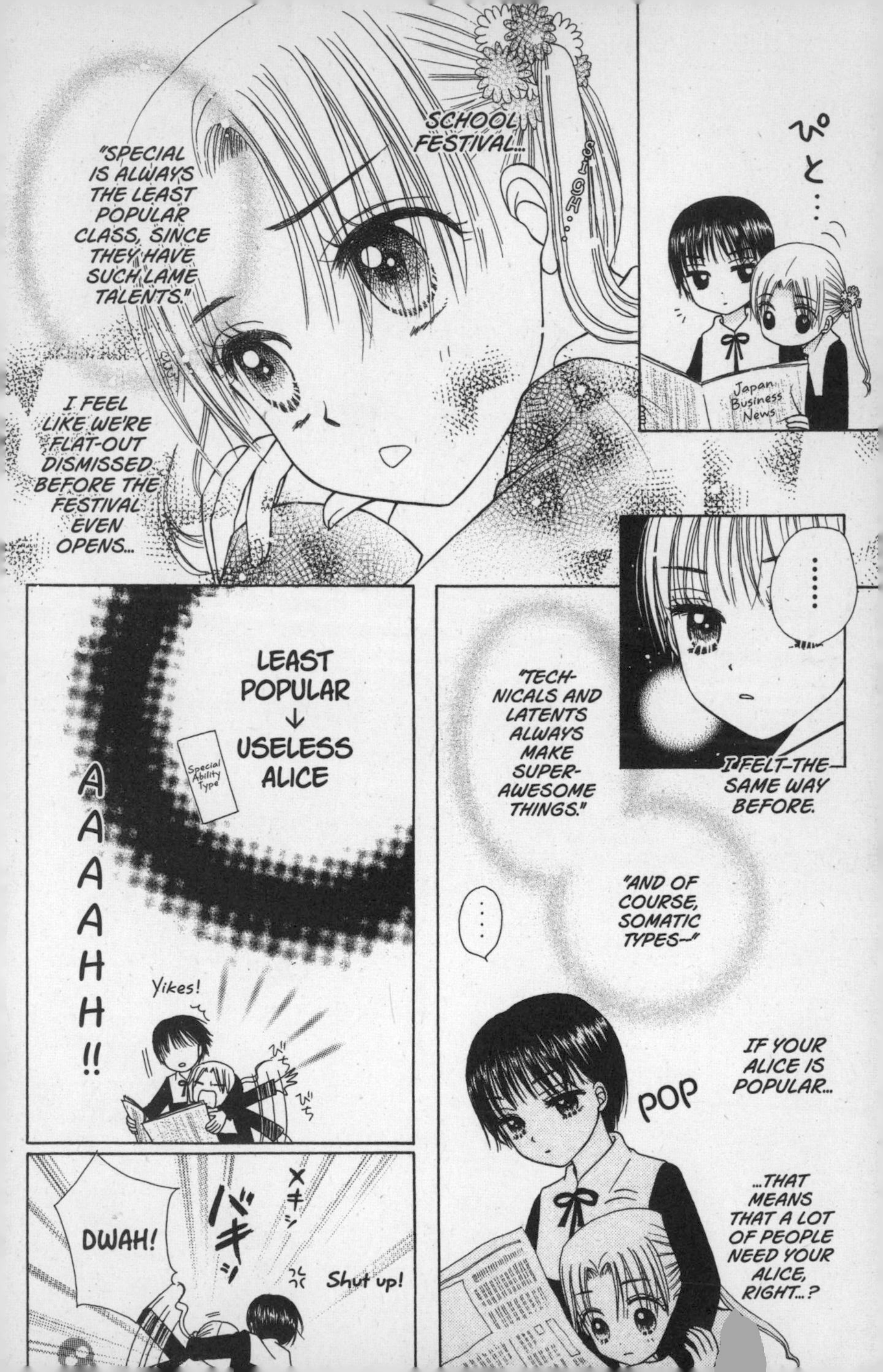
ぴと…
Japan Business News
SCHOOL FESTIVAL...
SIGH...
"SPECIAL IS ALWAYS THE LEAST POPULAR CLASS, SINCE THEY HAVE SUCH LAME TALENTS."
I FEEL LIKE WE'RE FLAT-OUT DISMISSED BEFORE THE FESTIVAL EVEN OPENS...
......
I FELT THE SAME WAY BEFORE.
"TECHNICALS AND LATENTS ALWAYS MAKE SUPER-AWESOME THINGS."
...
"AND OF COURSE, SOMATIC TYPES--"
POP
IF YOUR ALICE IS POPULAR...
...THAT MEANS THAT A LOT OF PEOPLE NEED YOUR ALICE, RIGHT...?
LEAST POPULAR ↓ USELESS ALICE
Special Ability Type
AAAAAHH!!
Yikes!
DWAH!
メキッ
バキッ
Shut up!

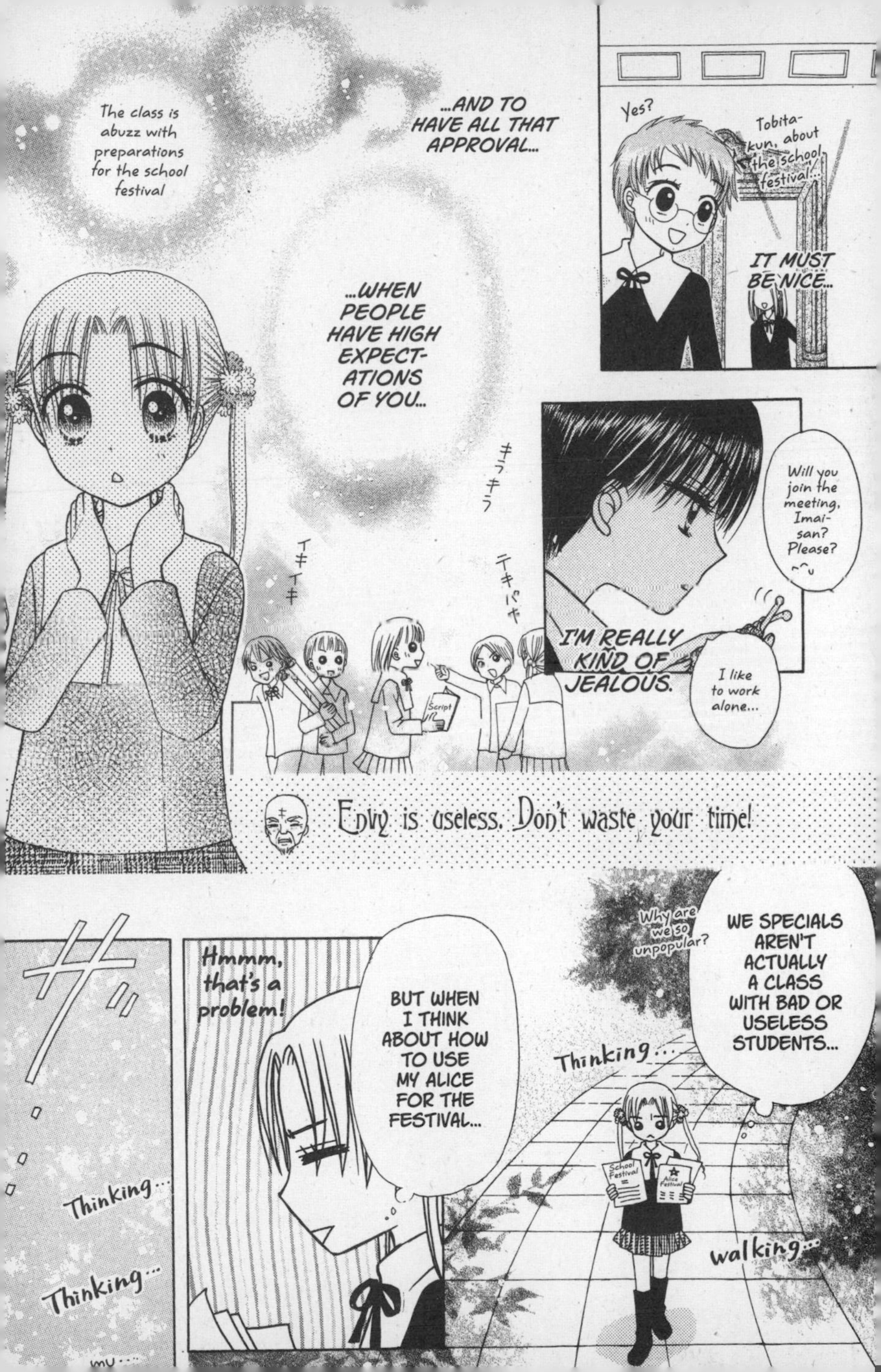
Tobita-kun, about the school festival!...
Yes?
IT MUST BE NICE...
Will you join the meeting, Imai-san? Please?
I like to work alone...
I'M REALLY KIND OF JEALOUS.
The class is abuzz with preparations for the school festival
...AND TO HAVE ALL THAT APPROVAL...
...WHEN PEOPLE HAVE HIGH EXPECTATIONS OF YOU...
キラキラ
テキパキ
イキイキ
Script
Envy is useless. Don't waste your time!
WE SPECIALS AREN'T ACTUALLY A CLASS WITH BAD OR USELESS STUDENTS...
Why are we so unpopular?
Thinking...
School Festival
Alice Festival
walking...
Hmmm, that's a problem!
BUT WHEN I THINK ABOUT HOW TO USE MY ALICE FOR THE FESTIVAL...
Thinking...
Thinking...
mu...

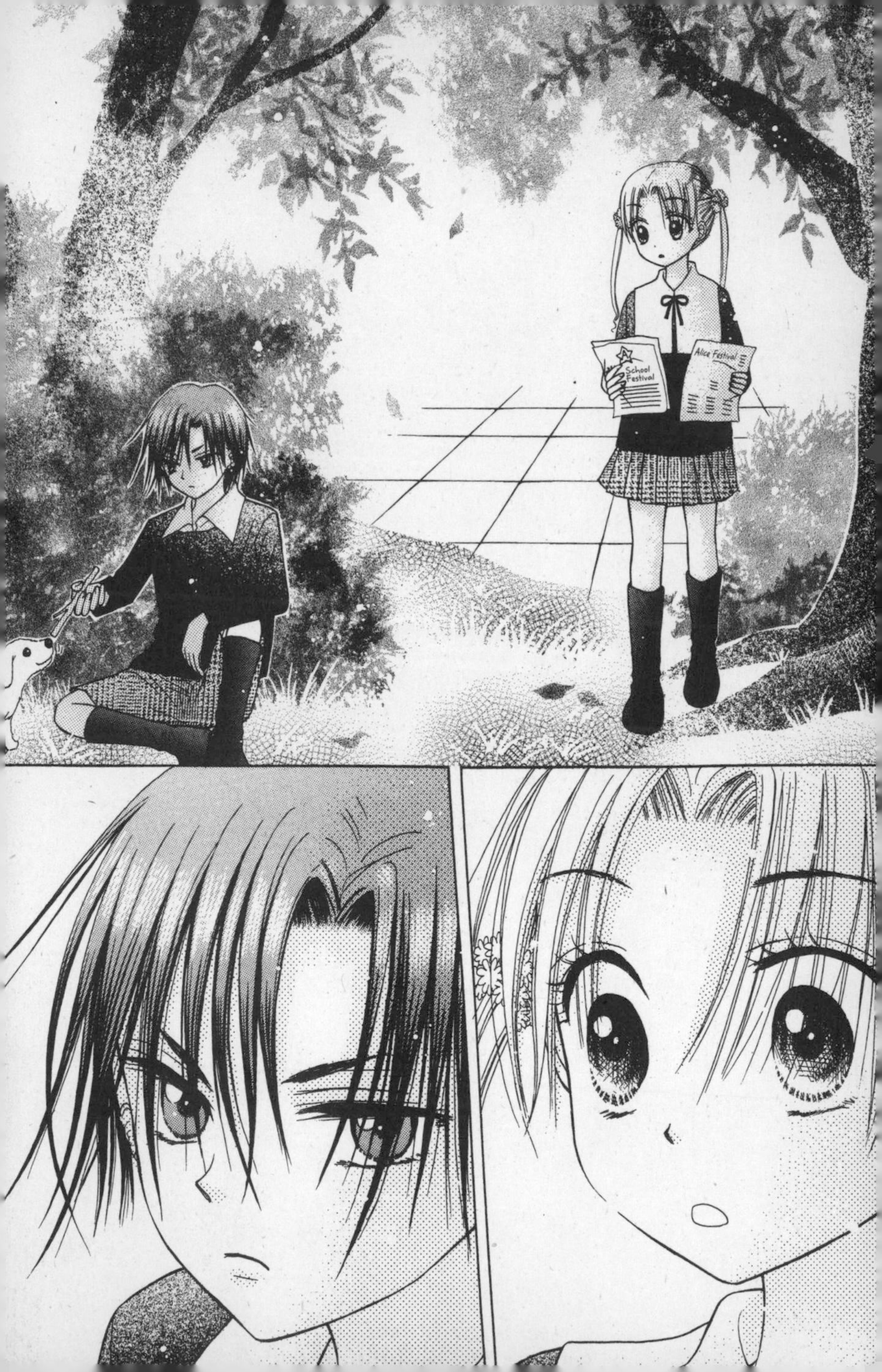
Alice Festival
School Festival

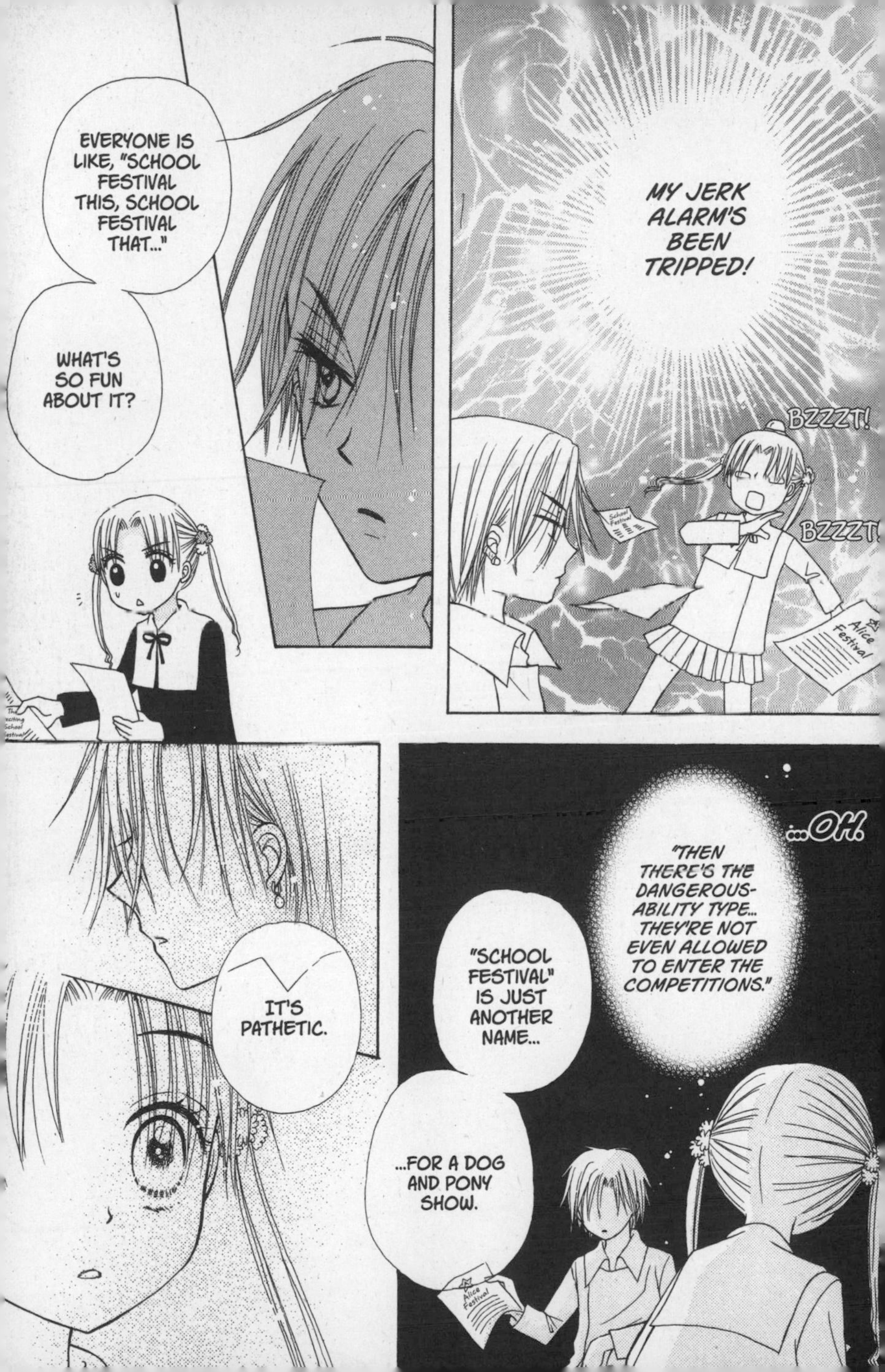
MY JERK ALARM'S BEEN TRIPPED!
BZZZT!
BZZZT!
School Festival
Alice Festival
EVERYONE IS LIKE, "SCHOOL FESTIVAL THIS, SCHOOL FESTIVAL THAT..."
WHAT'S SO FUN ABOUT IT?
...OH.
"THEN THERE'S THE DANGEROUS-ABILITY TYPE... THEY'RE NOT EVEN ALLOWED TO ENTER THE COMPETITIONS."
"SCHOOL FESTIVAL" IS JUST ANOTHER NAME...
...FOR A DOG AND PONY SHOW.
Alice Festival
IT'S PATHETIC.

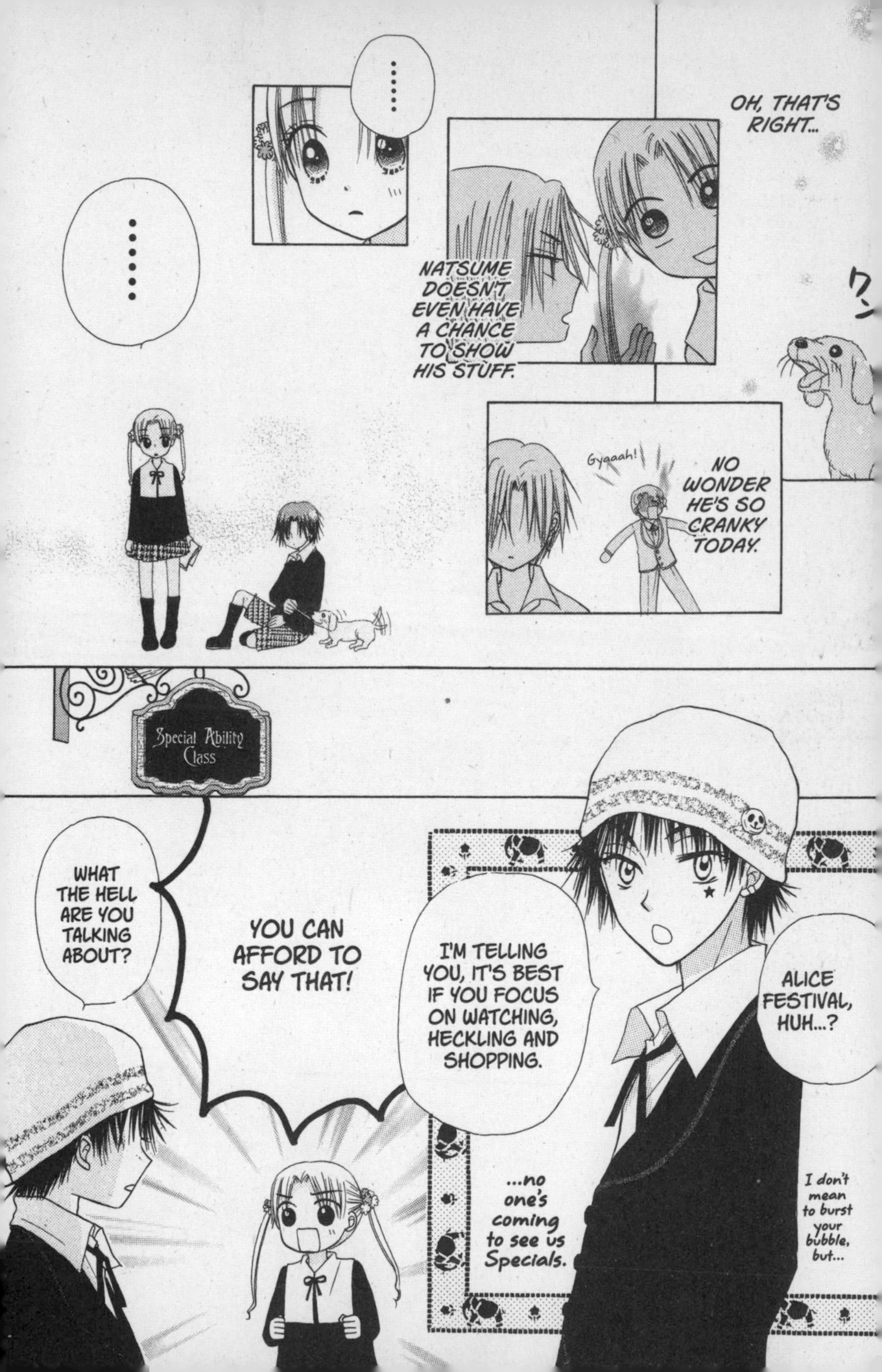
OH, THAT'S RIGHT...
ワン
NATSUME DOESN'T EVEN HAVE A CHANCE TO SHOW HIS STUFF.
......
NO WONDER HE'S SO CRANKY TODAY.
Gyaaah!
......
Special Ability Class
ALICE FESTIVAL, HUH...?
I don't mean to burst your bubble, but...
...no one's coming to see us Specials.
I'M TELLING YOU, IT'S BEST IF YOU FOCUS ON WATCHING, HECKLING AND SHOPPING.
YOU CAN AFFORD TO SAY THAT!
WHAT THE HELL ARE YOU TALKING ABOUT?

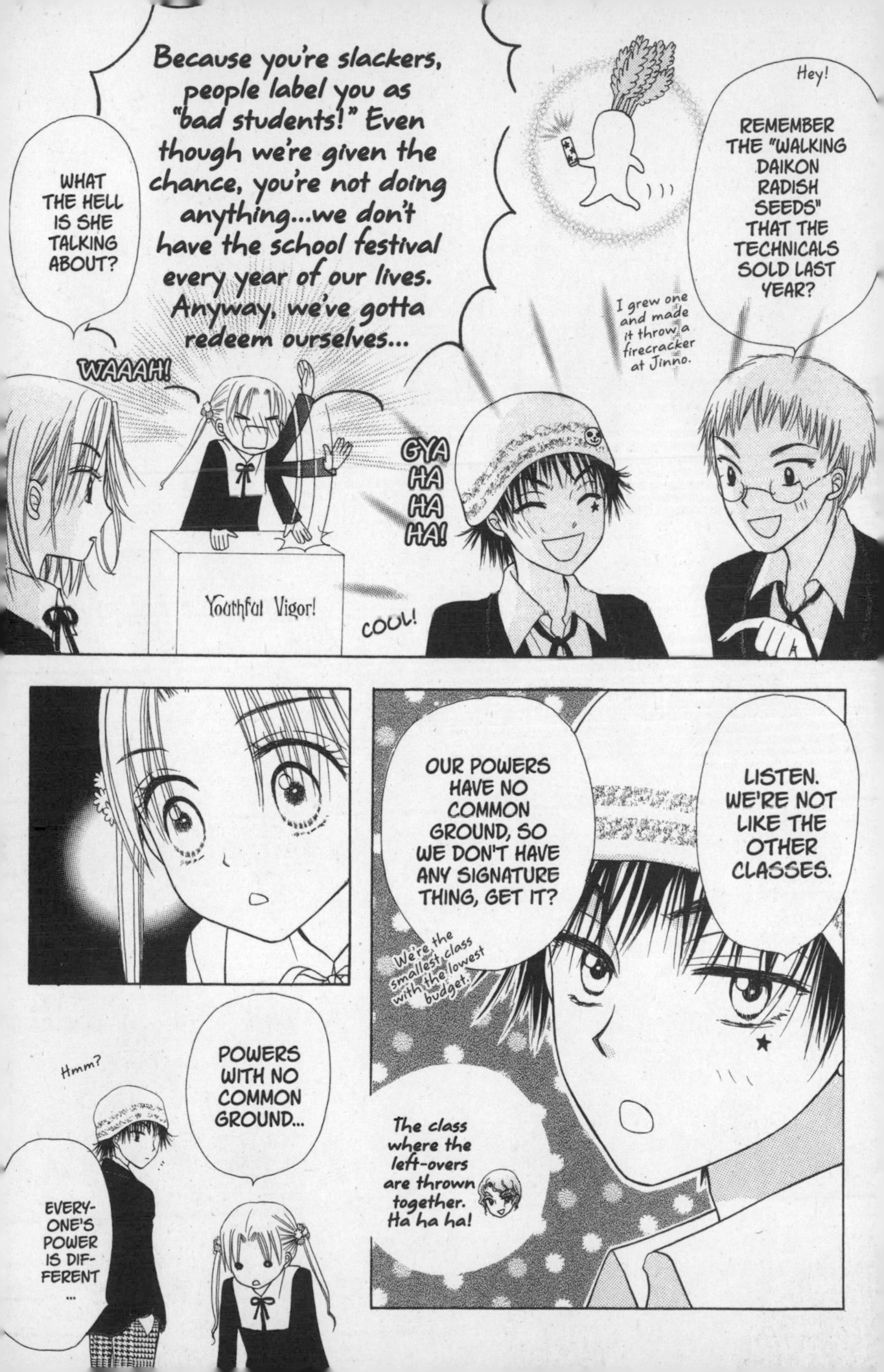
Hey!
REMEMBER THE "WALKING DAIKON RADISH SEEDS" THAT THE TECHNICALS SOLD LAST YEAR?
I grew one and made it throw a firecracker at Jinno.
Because you're slackers, people label you as "bad students!" Even though we're given the chance, you're not doing anything...we don't have the school festival every year of our lives. Anyway, we've gotta redeem ourselves...
WHAT THE HELL IS SHE TALKING ABOUT?
WAAAH!
GYA HA HA HA!
Youthful Vigor!
COOL!
LISTEN. WE'RE NOT LIKE THE OTHER CLASSES.
OUR POWERS HAVE NO COMMON GROUND, SO WE DON'T HAVE ANY SIGNATURE THING, GET IT?
We're the smallest class with the lowest budget.
The class where the left-overs are thrown together. Ha ha ha!
POWERS WITH NO COMMON GROUND...
Hmm?
EVERY-ONE'S POWER IS DIF-FERENT ...

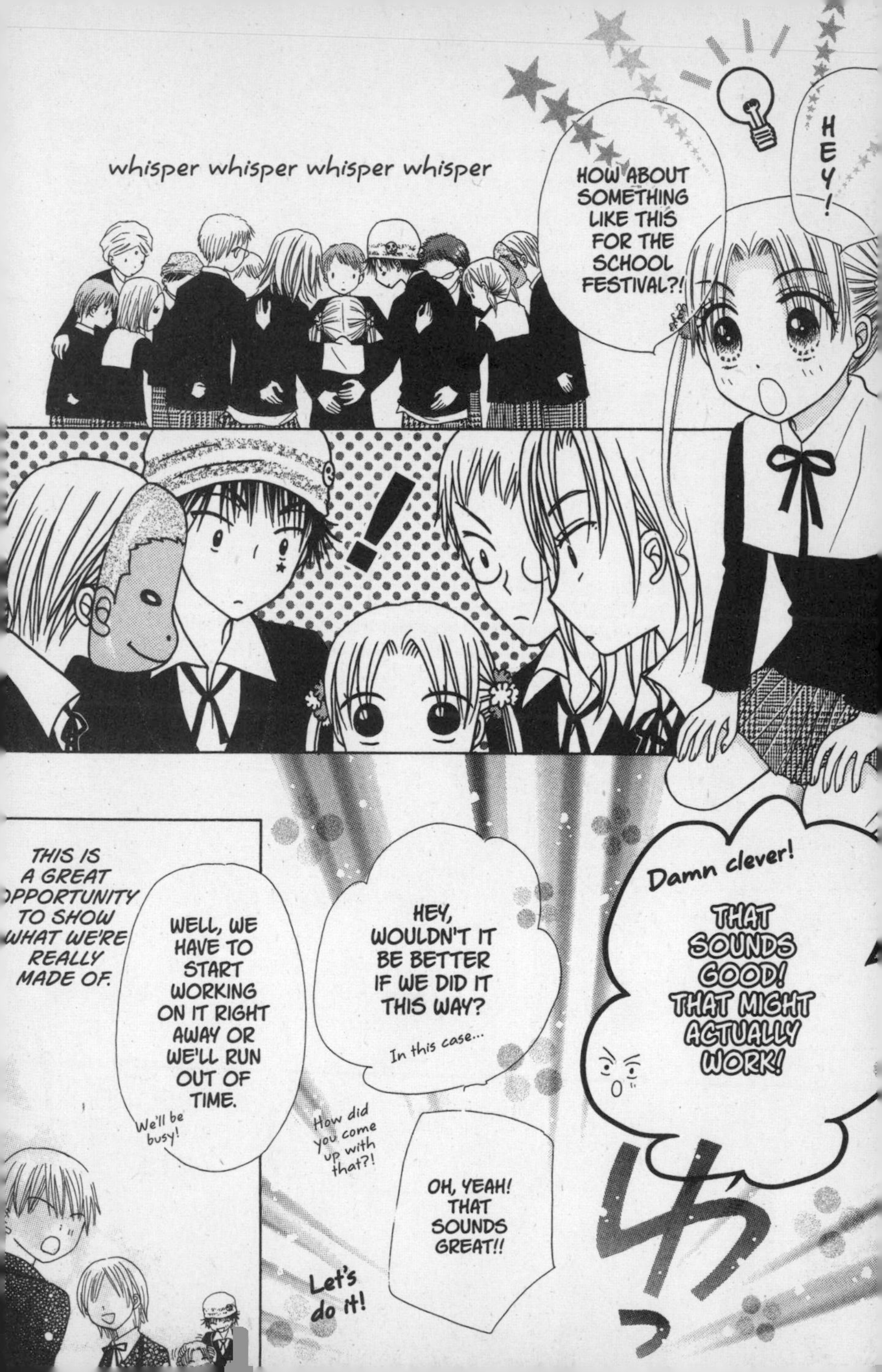
HEY!
HOW ABOUT SOMETHING LIKE THIS FOR THE SCHOOL FESTIVAL?!
whisper whisper whisper whisper
!
Damn clever!
THAT SOUNDS GOOD! THAT MIGHT ACTUALLY WORK!
HEY, WOULDN'T IT BE BETTER IF WE DID IT THIS WAY?
In this case...
OH, YEAH! THAT SOUNDS GREAT!!
How did you come up with that?!
Let's do it!
WELL, WE HAVE TO START WORKING ON IT RIGHT AWAY OR WE'LL RUN OUT OF TIME.
We'll be busy!
THIS IS A GREAT OPPORTUNITY TO SHOW WHAT WE'RE REALLY MADE OF.

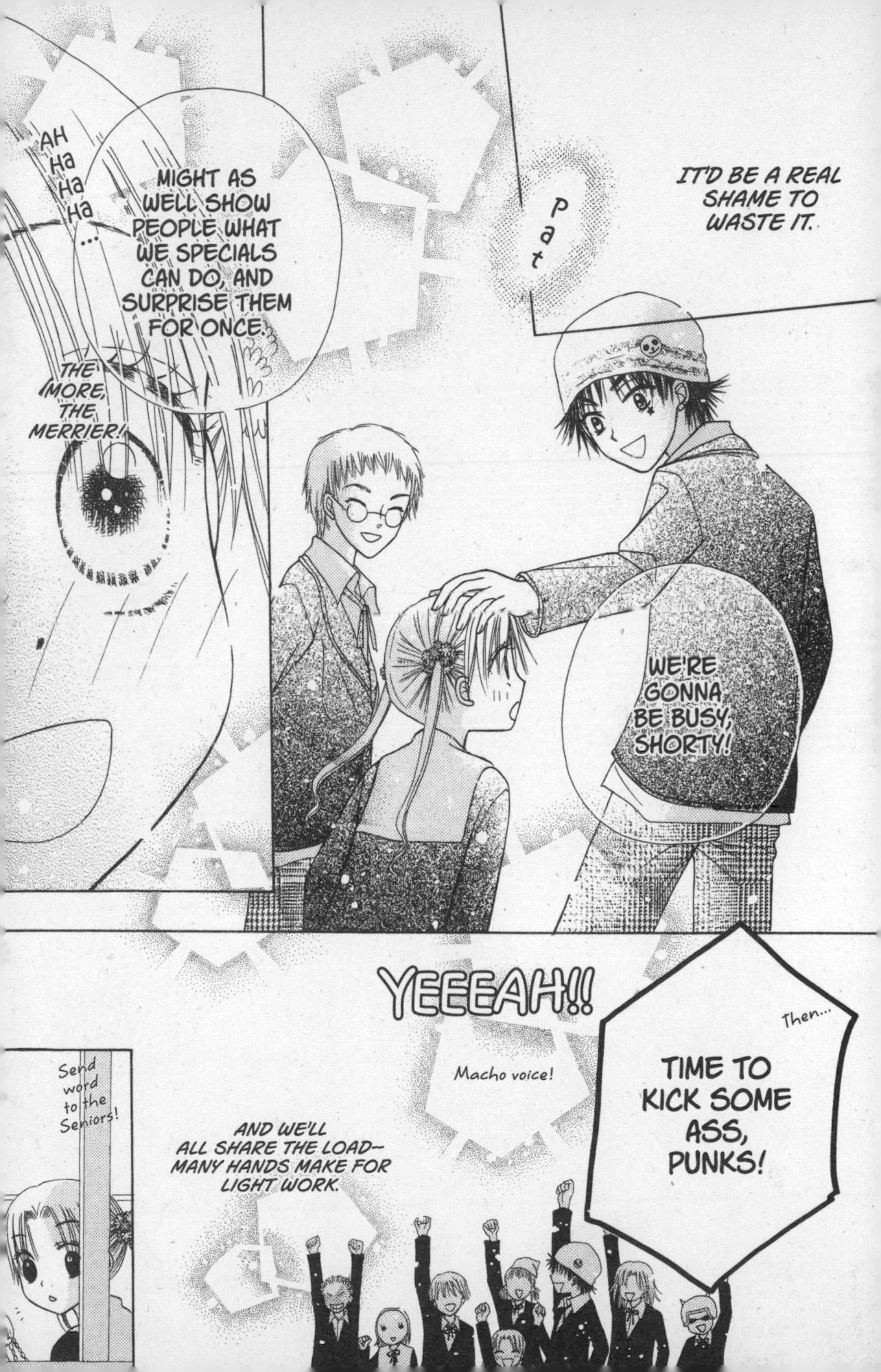

IT'D BE A REAL SHAME TO WASTE IT.
Pat
WE'RE GONNA BE BUSY, SHORTY!
MIGHT AS WELL SHOW PEOPLE WHAT WE SPECIALS CAN DO, AND SURPRISE THEM FOR ONCE.
AH Ha Ha Ha...
THE MORE, THE MERRIER!
YEEEAH!!
Then...
TIME TO KICK SOME ASS, PUNKS!
Macho voice!
AND WE'LL ALL SHARE THE LOAD–MANY HANDS MAKE FOR LIGHT WORK.
Send word to the Seniors!

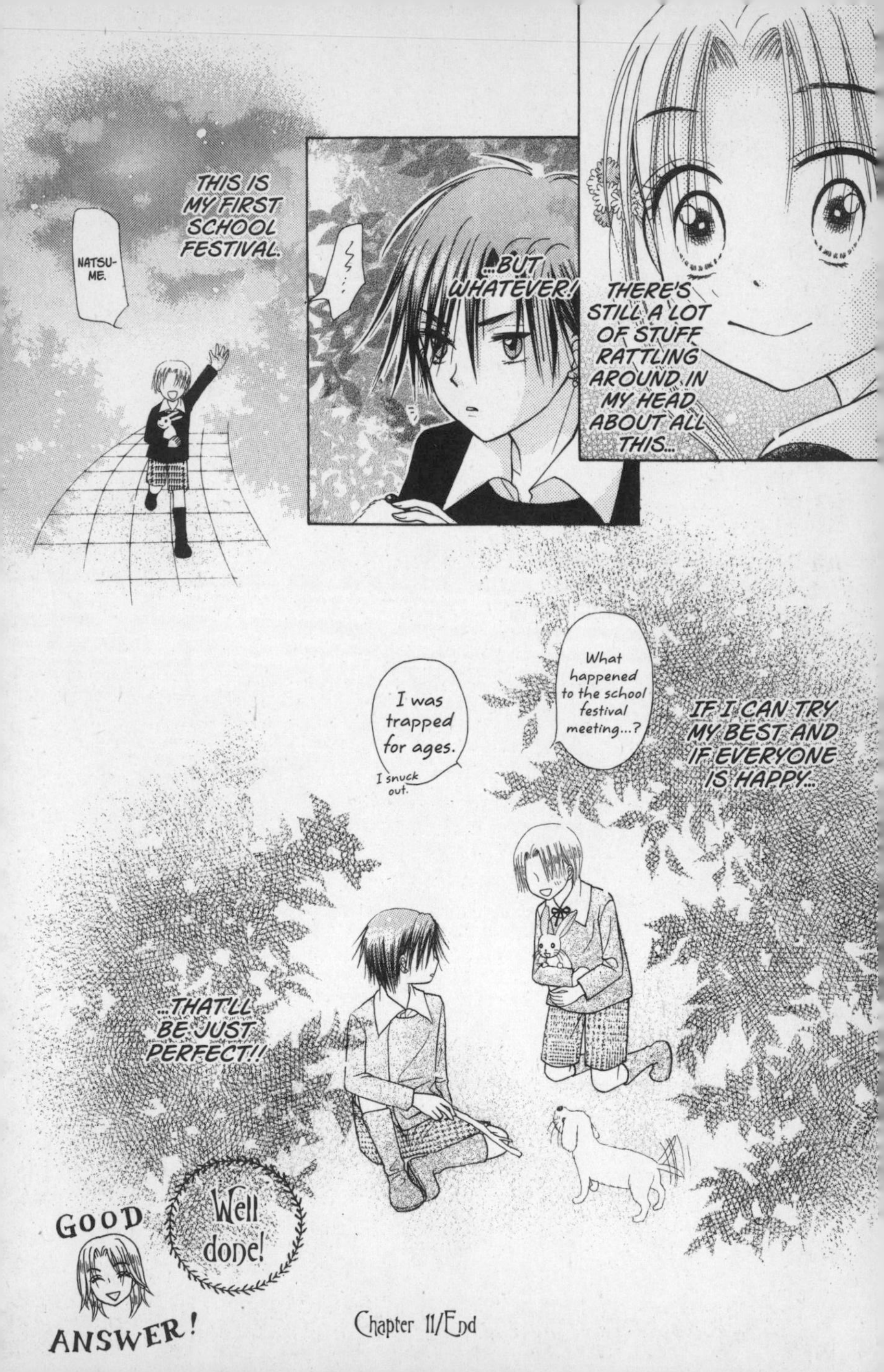
THERE'S STILL A LOT OF STUFF RATTLING AROUND IN MY HEAD ABOUT ALL THIS...
...BUT WHATEVER!
THIS IS MY FIRST SCHOOL FESTIVAL.
NATSU-ME.
IF I CAN TRY MY BEST AND IF EVERYONE IS HAPPY...
What happened to the school festival meeting...?
I was trapped for ages.
I snuck out.
...THAT'LL BE JUST PERFECT!!
Well done!
GOOD ANSWER!

Chapter 11/End

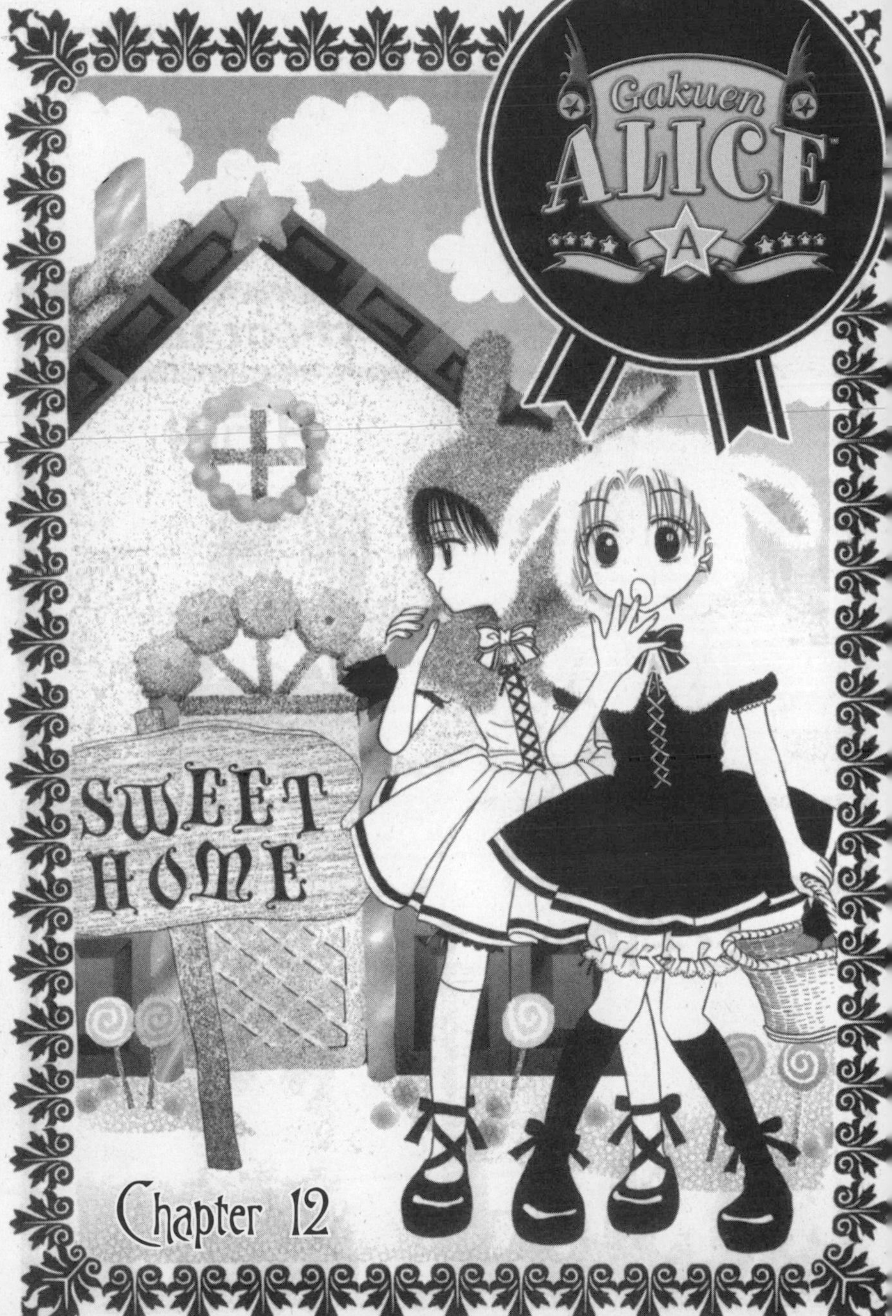
Gakuen ALICE
SWEET HOME
Chapter 12

THE STUDENTS AT ALICE ACADEMY ARE GIVEN AN ALLOWANCE EVERY MONTH, THE AMOUNT DEPENDING ON THEIR STAR RANKING.

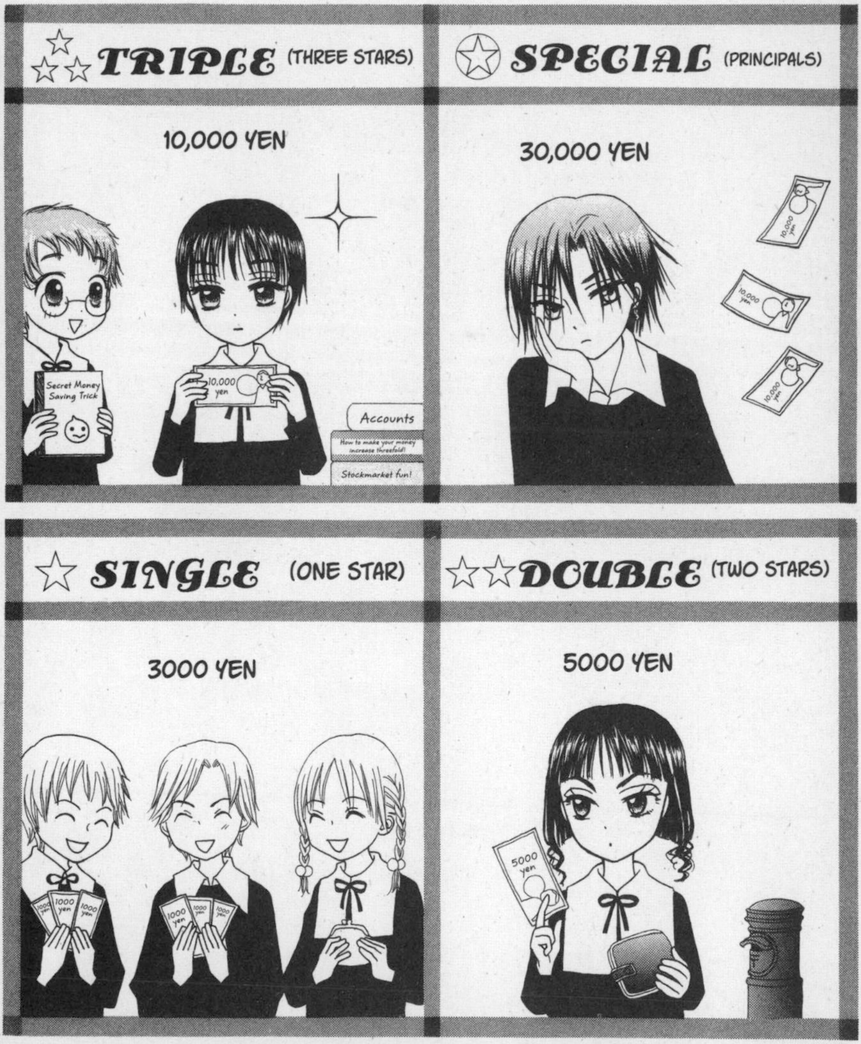

SPECIAL (PRINCIPALS)
30,000 YEN
10,000 yen
10,000 yen
10,000 yen
TRIPLE (THREE STARS)
10,000 YEN
10,000 yen
Accounts
How to make your money increase threefold!
Stockmarket fun!
Secret Money Saving Trick
DOUBLE (TWO STARS)
5000 YEN
5000 yen
SINGLE (ONE STAR)
3000 YEN
1000 yen
1000 yen
1000 yen
1000 yen
1000 yen
1000 yen

100 yen ≈ 1 dollar

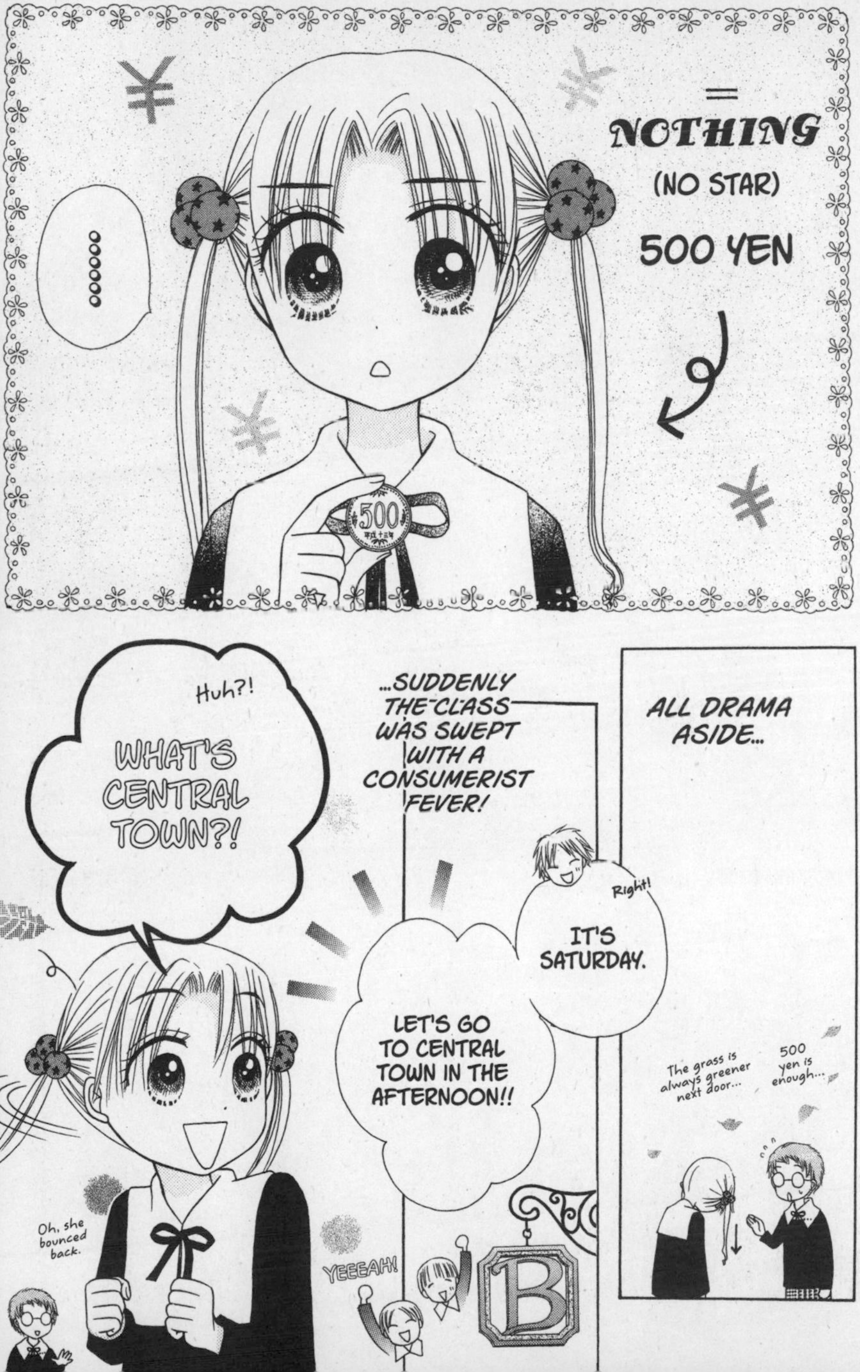
= NOTHING
(NO STAR)
500 YEN
.....
ALL DRAMA ASIDE...
500 yen is enough...
The grass is always greener next door...
...SUDDENLY THE CLASS WAS SWEPT WITH A CONSUMERIST FEVER!
Right!
IT'S SATURDAY.
LET'S GO TO CENTRAL TOWN IN THE AFTERNOON!!
YEEEAH!
Huh?!
WHAT'S CENTRAL TOWN?!
Oh, she bounced back.

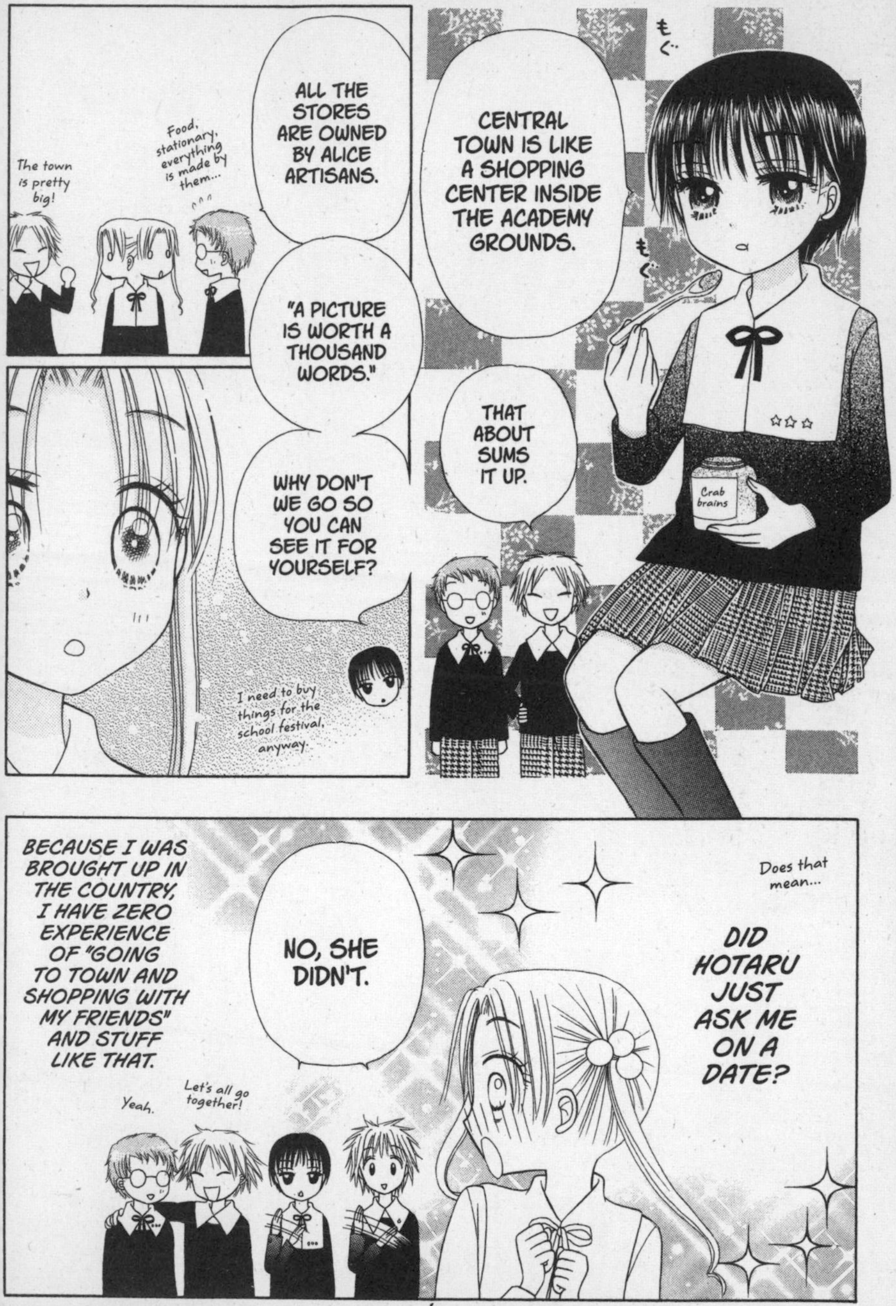
もぐ
CENTRAL TOWN IS LIKE A SHOPPING CENTER INSIDE THE ACADEMY GROUNDS.
もぐ
THAT ABOUT SUMS IT UP.
Crab brains
ALL THE STORES ARE OWNED BY ALICE ARTISANS.
Food, stationary, everything is made by them...
The town is pretty big!
"A PICTURE IS WORTH A THOUSAND WORDS."
WHY DON'T WE GO SO YOU CAN SEE IT FOR YOURSELF?
I need to buy things for the school festival, anyway.
Does that mean...
DID HOTARU JUST ASK ME ON A DATE?
NO, SHE DIDN'T.
BECAUSE I WAS BROUGHT UP IN THE COUNTRY, I HAVE ZERO EXPERIENCE OF "GOING TO TOWN AND SHOPPING WITH MY FRIENDS" AND STUFF LIKE THAT.
Let's all go together!
Yeah.

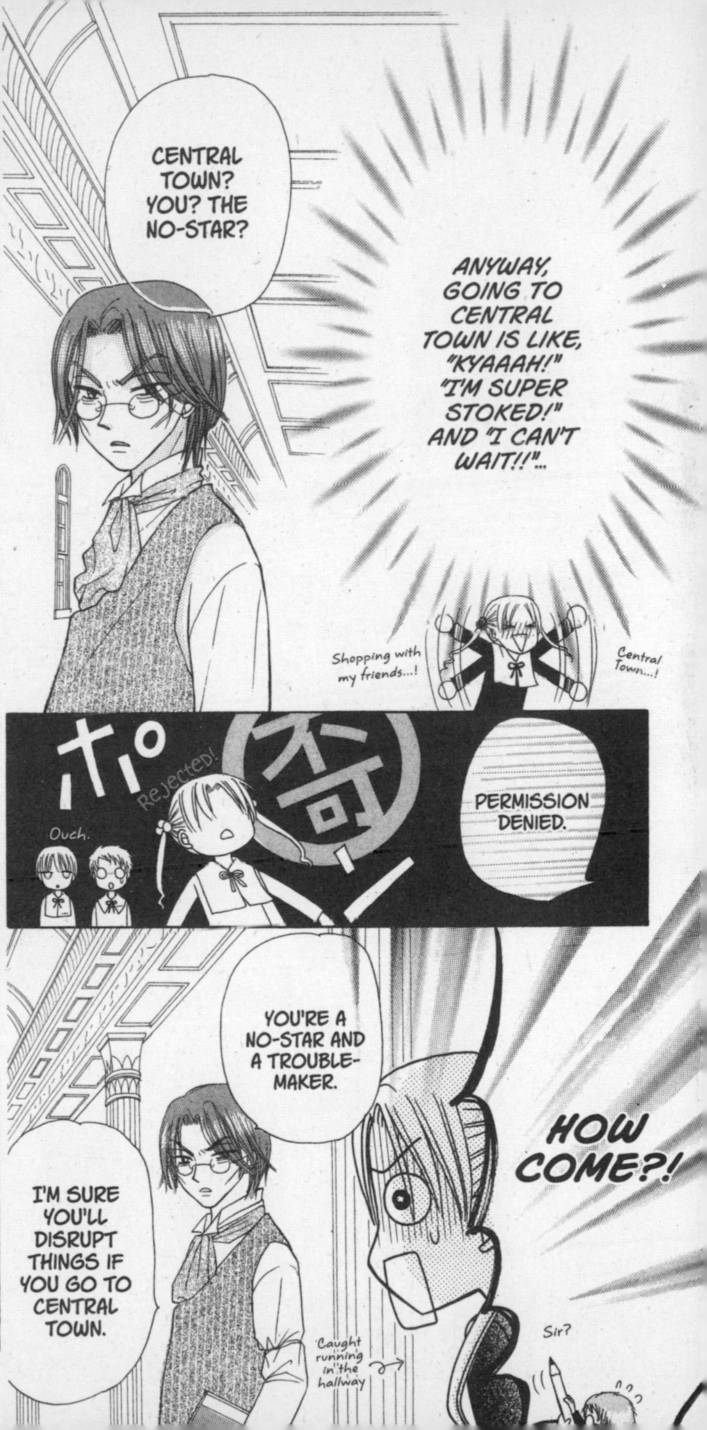
ANYWAY, GOING TO CENTRAL TOWN IS LIKE, "KYAAAH!" "I'M SUPER STOKED!" AND "I CAN'T WAIT!!"...
Central Town...!
Shopping with my friends...!
CENTRAL TOWN? YOU? THE NO-STAR?
PERMISSION DENIED.
Rejected!
Ouch.
HOW COME?!
Sir?
Caught running in the hallway
YOU'RE A NO-STAR AND A TROUBLE-MAKER.
I'M SURE YOU'LL DISRUPT THINGS IF YOU GO TO CENTRAL TOWN.

Read at your own discretion.

Higuchi's Room 2

PROFILE 5

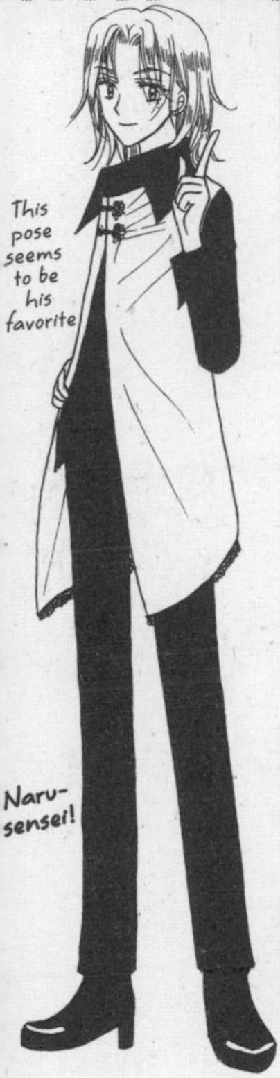
This pose seems to be his favorite
Naru-sensei!

Narumi-sensei
Born on Aug. 10
27 years old
Leo, Blood type O

Like Natsume, he is a mysterious person in *Gakuen Alice*. Many readers are wondering about the relationship between him and "that woman." He's one of the key players in the story, so I'd like to show you a chapter from his past someday. By the way, I don't know if it's fun or hard to pick his outfits... Somebody please design one for me!

Go to 3

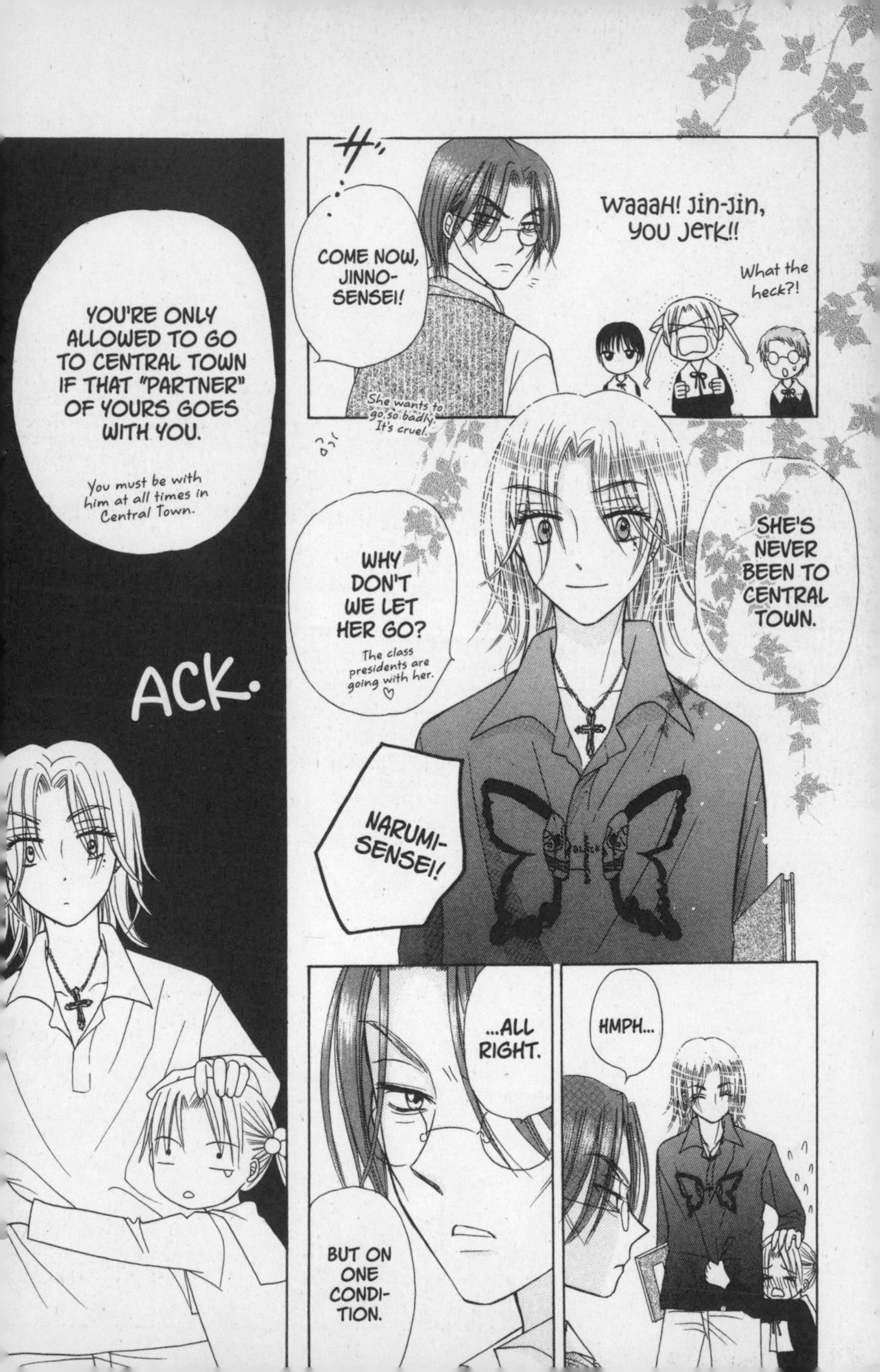
WAAAH! JIN-JIN, YOU JERK!!
What the heck?!
COME NOW, JINNO-SENSEI!
She wants to go so badly. It's cruel.
SHE'S NEVER BEEN TO CENTRAL TOWN.
WHY DON'T WE LET HER GO?
The class presidents are going with her. ♡
NARUMI-SENSEI!
HMPH...
...ALL RIGHT.
BUT ON ONE CONDITION.
YOU'RE ONLY ALLOWED TO GO TO CENTRAL TOWN IF THAT "PARTNER" OF YOURS GOES WITH YOU.
You must be with him at all times in Central Town.
ACK.

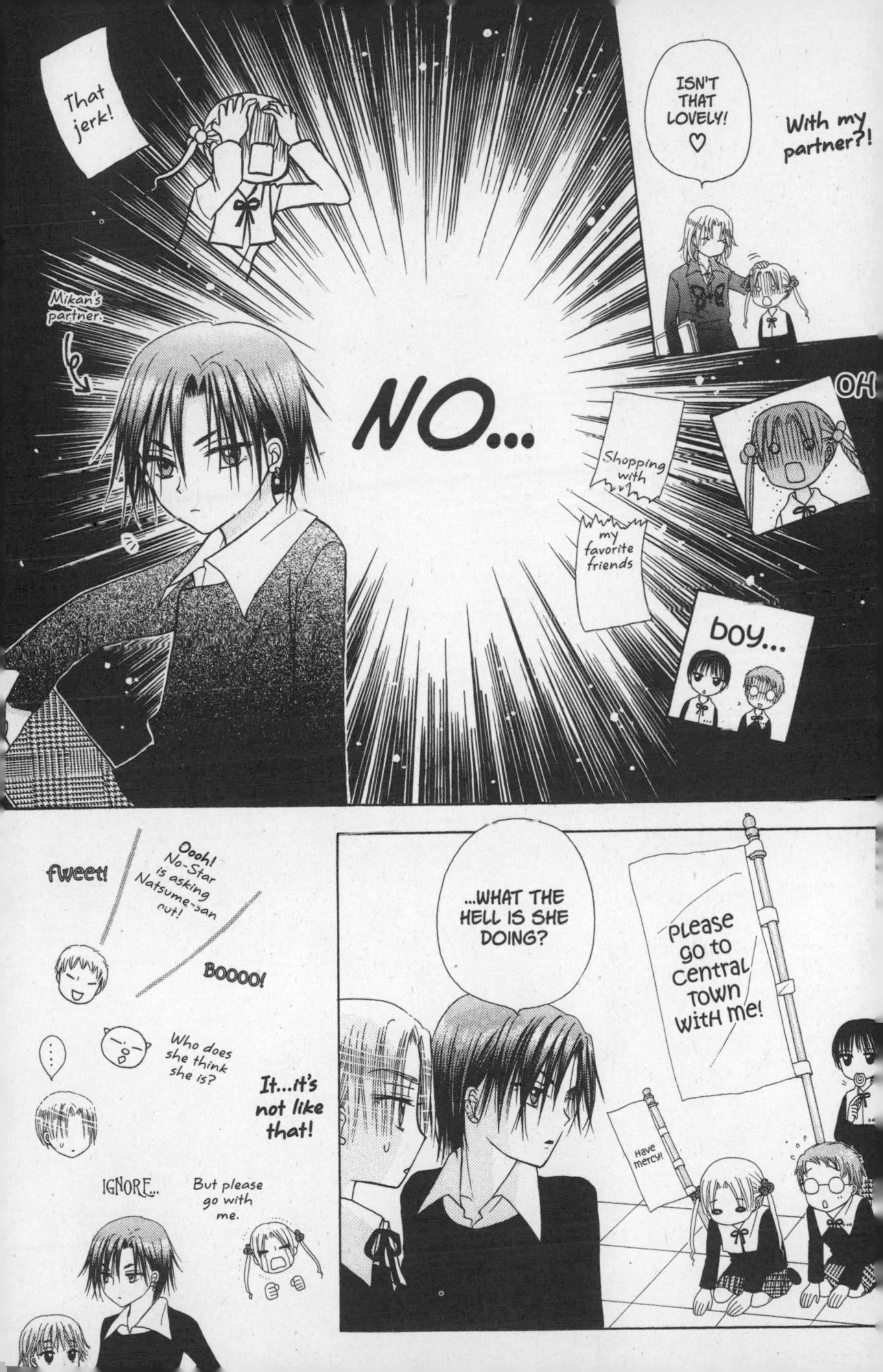
ISN'T THAT LOVELY! ♡
With my partner?!
OH
Shopping with
my favorite friends
boy...
NO...
That jerk!
Mikan's partner.
...WHAT THE HELL IS SHE DOING?
Please go to Central Town with me!
Have mercy!
Oooh! No-Star is asking Natsume-san out!
fweet!
BOOOO!
Who does she think she is?
...
It...it's not like that!
IGNORE...
But please go with me.

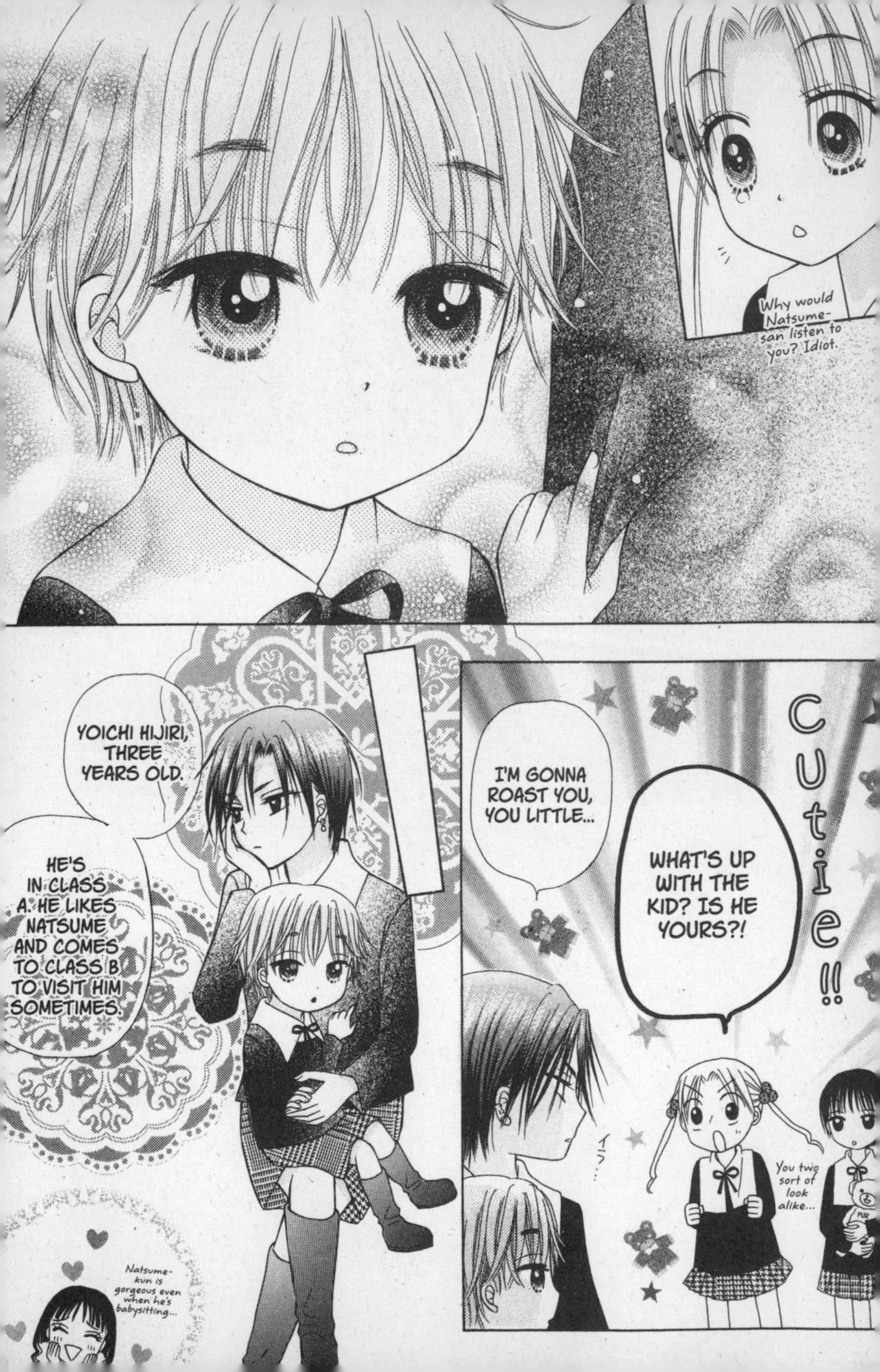
Why would Natsume-san listen to you? Idiot.
Cutie!!
WHAT'S UP WITH THE KID? IS HE YOURS?!
I'M GONNA ROAST YOU, YOU LITTLE...
You two sort of look alike...
イラ…
YOICHI HIJIRI, THREE YEARS OLD.
HE'S IN CLASS A. HE LIKES NATSUME AND COMES TO CLASS B TO VISIT HIM SOMETIMES.
Natsume-kun is gorgeous even when he's babysitting...

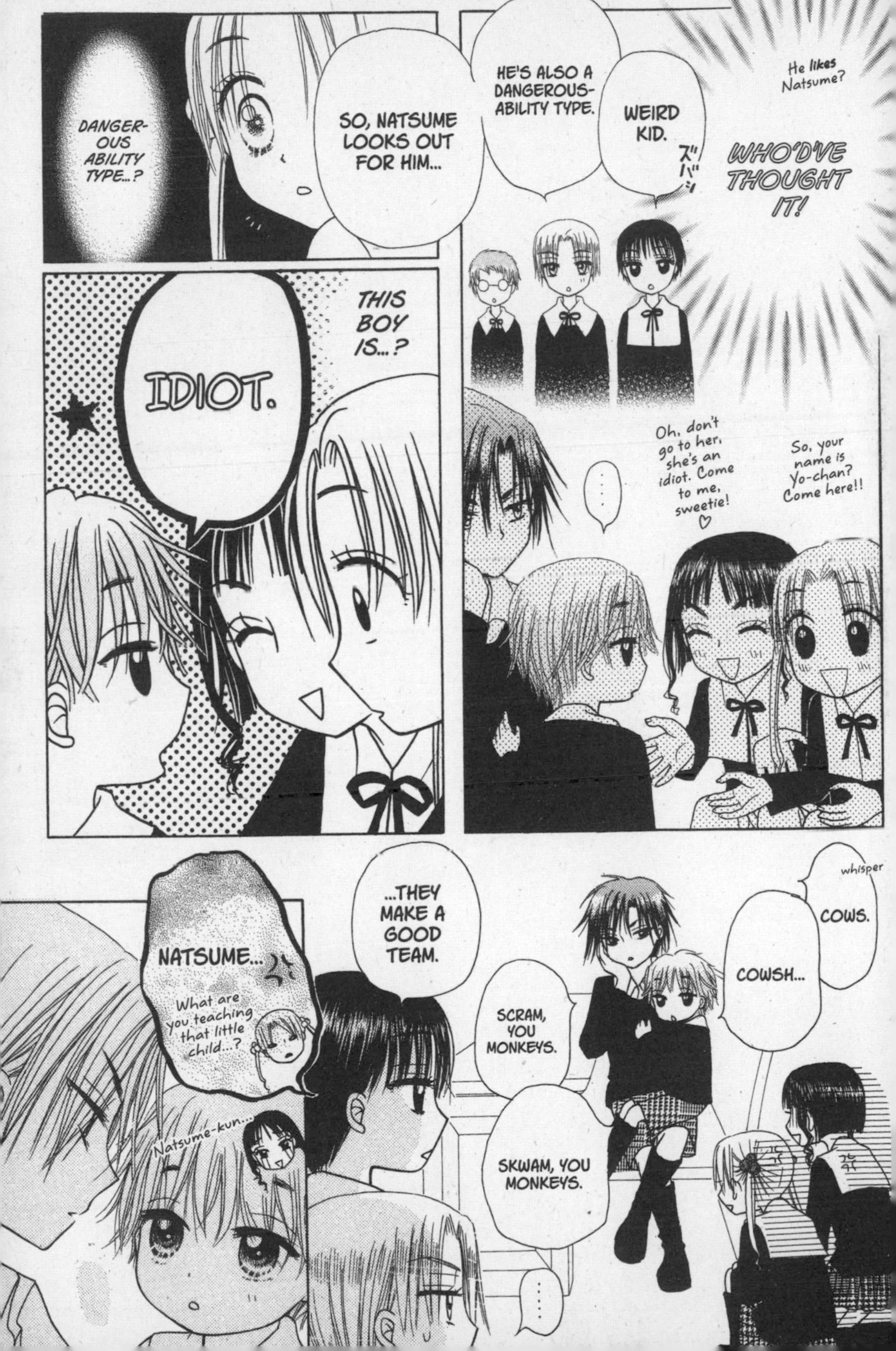
He likes Natsume?
WHO'D'VE THOUGHT IT!
WEIRD KID.
ズバッ
HE'S ALSO A DANGEROUS-ABILITY TYPE.
So, your name is Yo-chan? Come here!!
Oh, don't go to her, she's an idiot. Come to me, sweetie! ♡
. . . .
SO, NATSUME LOOKS OUT FOR HIM...
DANGEROUS ABILITY TYPE...?
THIS BOY IS...?
IDIOT.
whisper
COWS.
COWSH...
SCRAM, YOU MONKEYS.
SKWAM, YOU MONKEYS.
...THEY MAKE A GOOD TEAM.
. . . . .
NATSUME...
What are you teaching that little child...?
Natsume-kun...

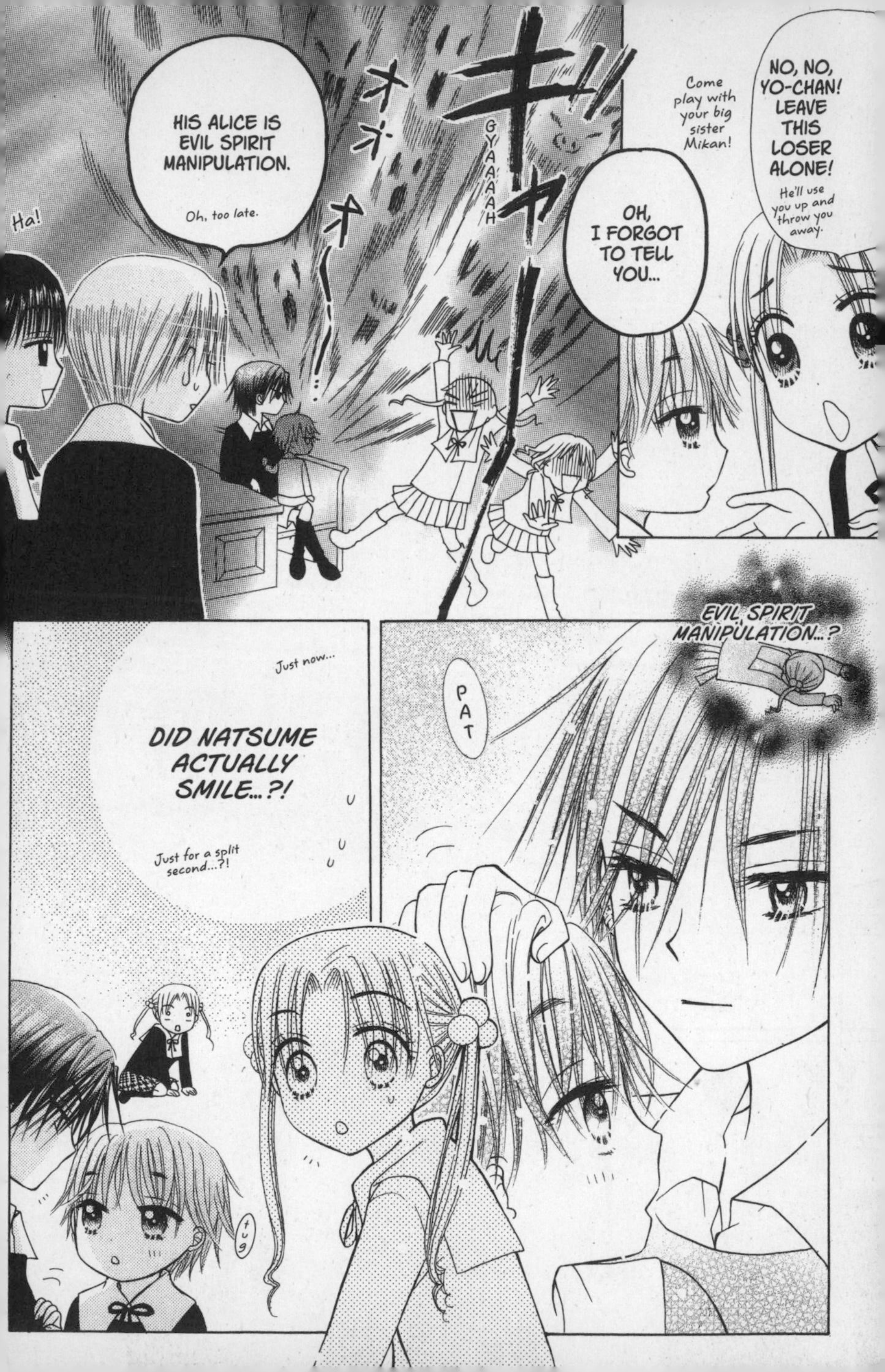
NO, NO, YO-CHAN! LEAVE THIS LOSER ALONE!
He'll use you up and throw you away.
Come play with your big sister Mikan!
OH, I FORGOT TO TELL YOU...
GYAAAAAH
HIS ALICE IS EVIL SPIRIT MANIPULATION.
Oh, too late.
Ha!
EVIL SPIRIT MANIPULATION...?
PAT
Just now...
DID NATSUME ACTUALLY SMILE...?!
Just for a split second...?!
tug

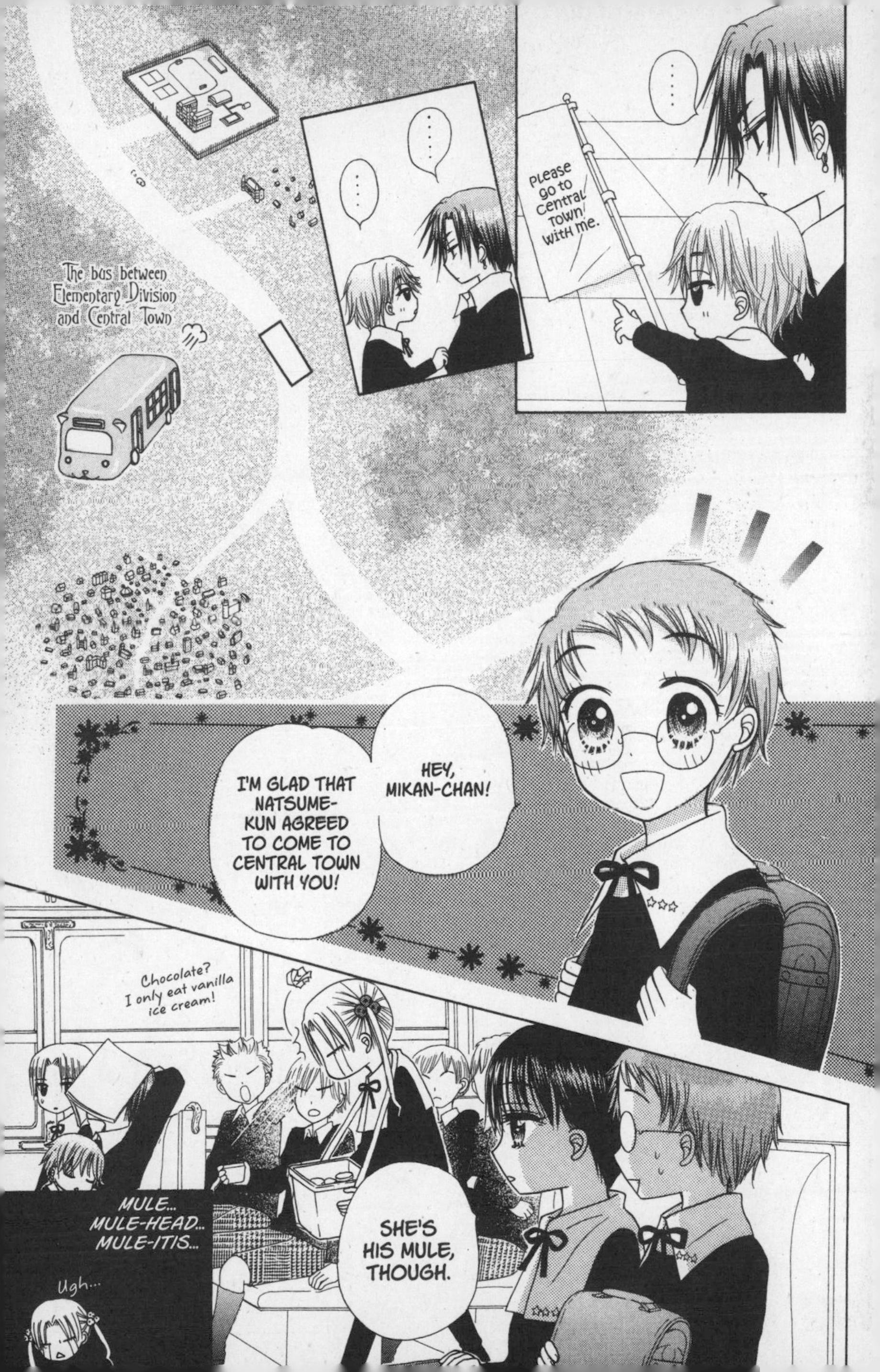
...
Please go to Central Town with me.
...
...
The bus between Elementary Division and Central Town
HEY, MIKAN-CHAN!
I'M GLAD THAT NATSUME-KUN AGREED TO COME TO CENTRAL TOWN WITH YOU!
SHE'S HIS MULE, THOUGH.
Chocolate? I only eat vanilla ice cream!
MULE... MULE-HEAD... MULE-ITIS...
Ugh...

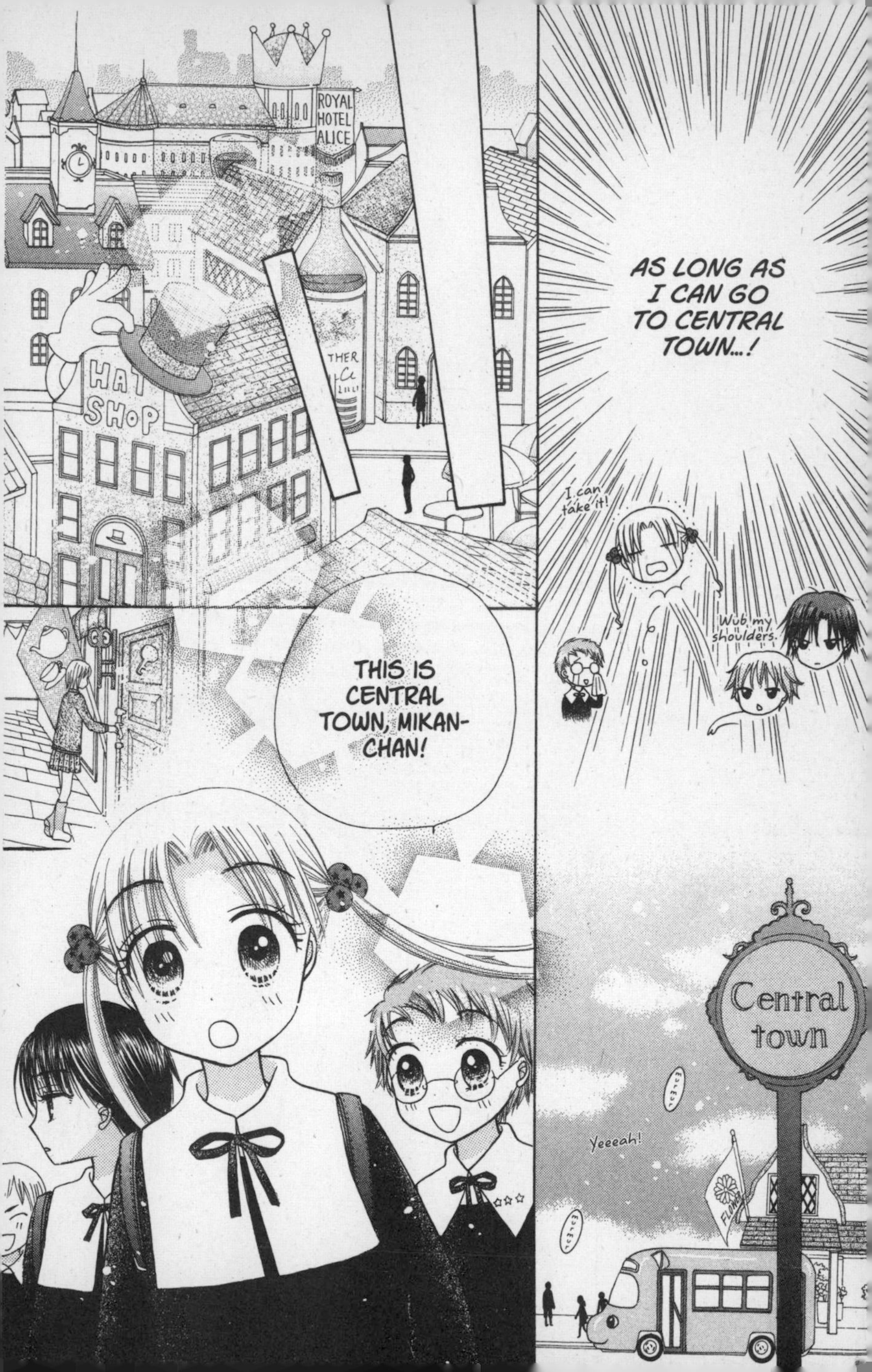
AS LONG AS I CAN GO TO CENTRAL TOWN...!
I can take it!
Wub my shoulders.
Central town
Yeeeah!
ROYAL HOTEL ALICE
HAT SHOP
THIS IS CENTRAL TOWN, MIKAN-CHAN!

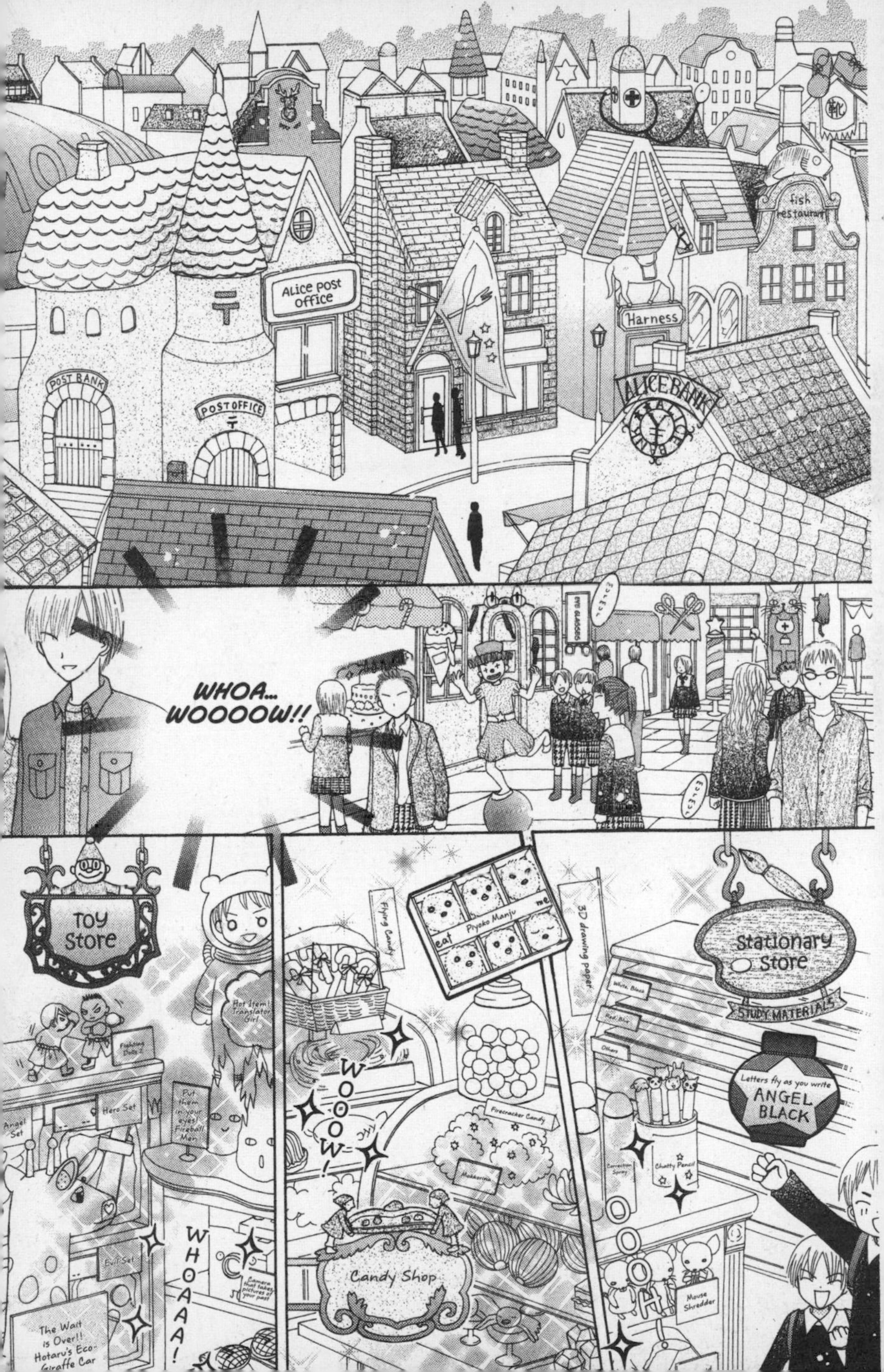
fish restaurant
Harness
ALICE BANK
Alice post office
POST BANK
POST OFFICE
EYE GLASSES
WHOA... WOOOOW!!
Stationary Store
STUDY MATERIALS
White, Black
Red, Blue
Others
Letters fly as you write
ANGEL BLACK
Correction Spray
Chatty Pencil
Mouse Shredder
3D drawing paper
Piyoko Manju
eat me
Flying Candy
Firecracker Candy
WOOOOW!
Candy Shop
Toy Store
Hot Item! Translator Girl
Hero Set
Angel Set
Put them in your eyes! Fireball Man
Evil Set
Camera that takes pictures of your past
WHOAAAA!
The Wait is Over!! Hotaru's Eco-Giraffe Car

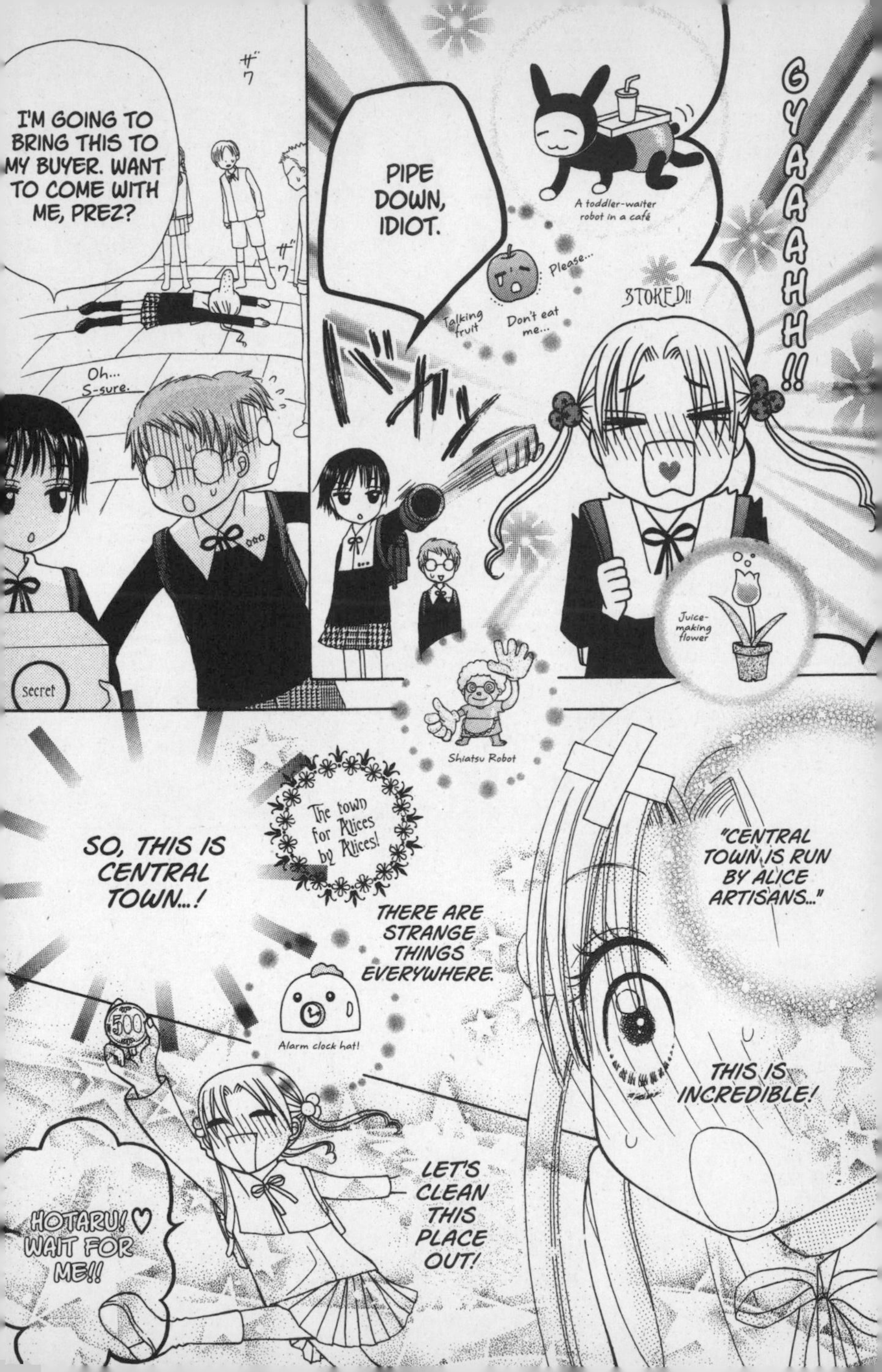
GYAAAAHH!!
STOKED!!
A toddler-waiter robot in a café
Please...
Don't eat me...
Talking fruit
Juice-making flower
PIPE DOWN, IDIOT.
I'M GOING TO BRING THIS TO MY BUYER. WANT TO COME WITH ME, PREZ?
Oh... S-sure.
secret
Shiatsu Robot
THIS IS INCREDIBLE!
"CENTRAL TOWN IS RUN BY ALICE ARTISANS..."
The town for Alices by Alices!
SO, THIS IS CENTRAL TOWN...!
THERE ARE STRANGE THINGS EVERYWHERE.
Alarm clock hat!
500
LET'S CLEAN THIS PLACE OUT!
HOTARU! ♥ WAIT FOR ME!!

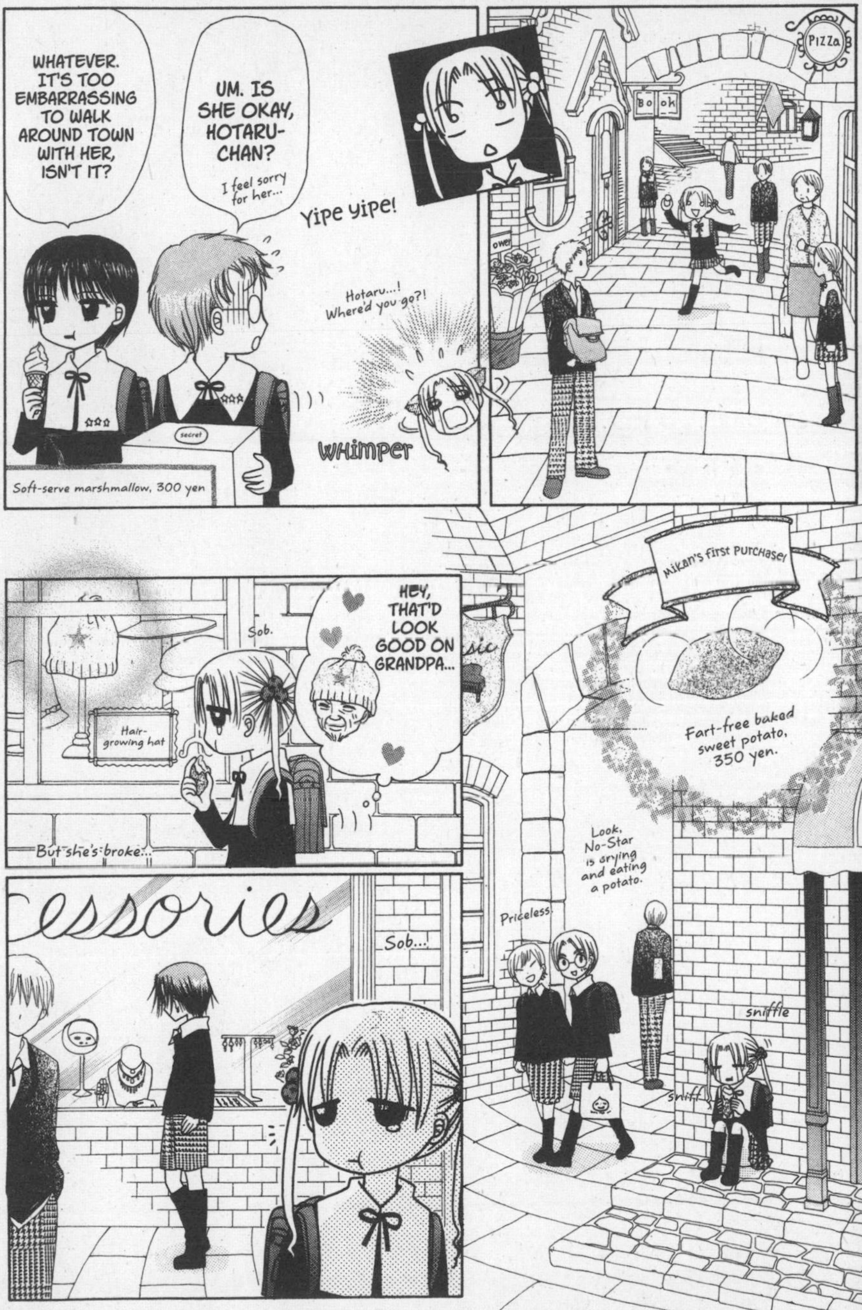
PIZZa
Book
Yipe yipe!
UM. IS SHE OKAY, HOTARU-CHAN?
I feel sorry for her...
WHATEVER. IT'S TOO EMBARRASSING TO WALK AROUND TOWN WITH HER, ISN'T IT?
Hotaru...! Where'd you go?!
Whimper
Soft-serve marshmallow, 300 yen
Mikan's first purchase!
Fart-free baked sweet potato, 350 yen.
Look, No-Star is crying and eating a potato.
Priceless.
sniffle
sniff
HEY, THAT'D LOOK GOOD ON GRANDPA...
Sob.
Hair-growing hat
But she's broke...
essories
Sob...

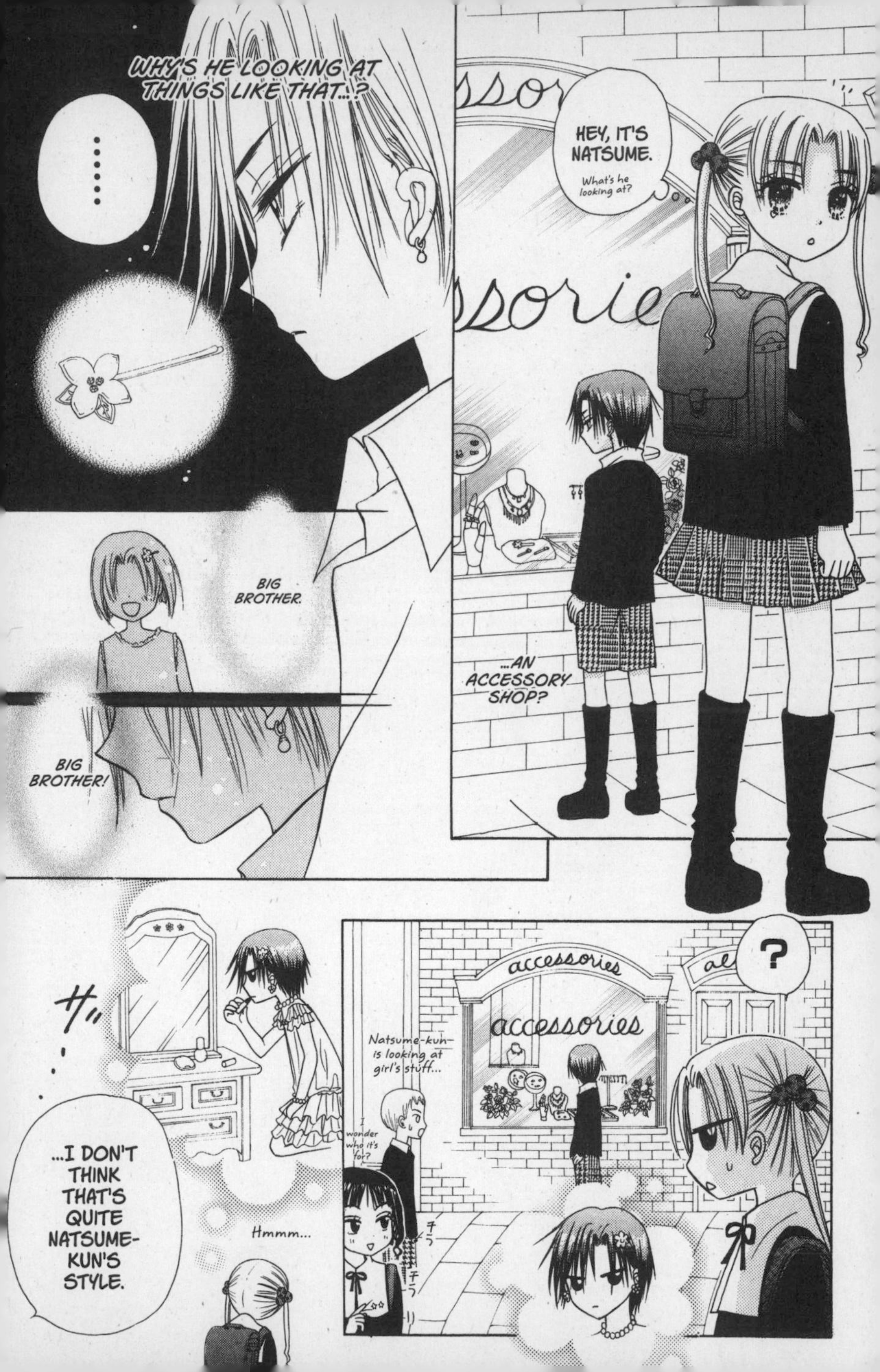

HEY, IT'S NATSUME.
What's he looking at?
...AN ACCESSORY SHOP?
accessories
WHY'S HE LOOKING AT THINGS LIKE THAT...?
......
BIG BROTHER.
BIG BROTHER!
?
accessories
accessories
Natsume-kun is looking at girl's stuff...
I wonder who it's for?
Hmmm...
...I DON'T THINK THAT'S QUITE NATSUME-KUN'S STYLE.

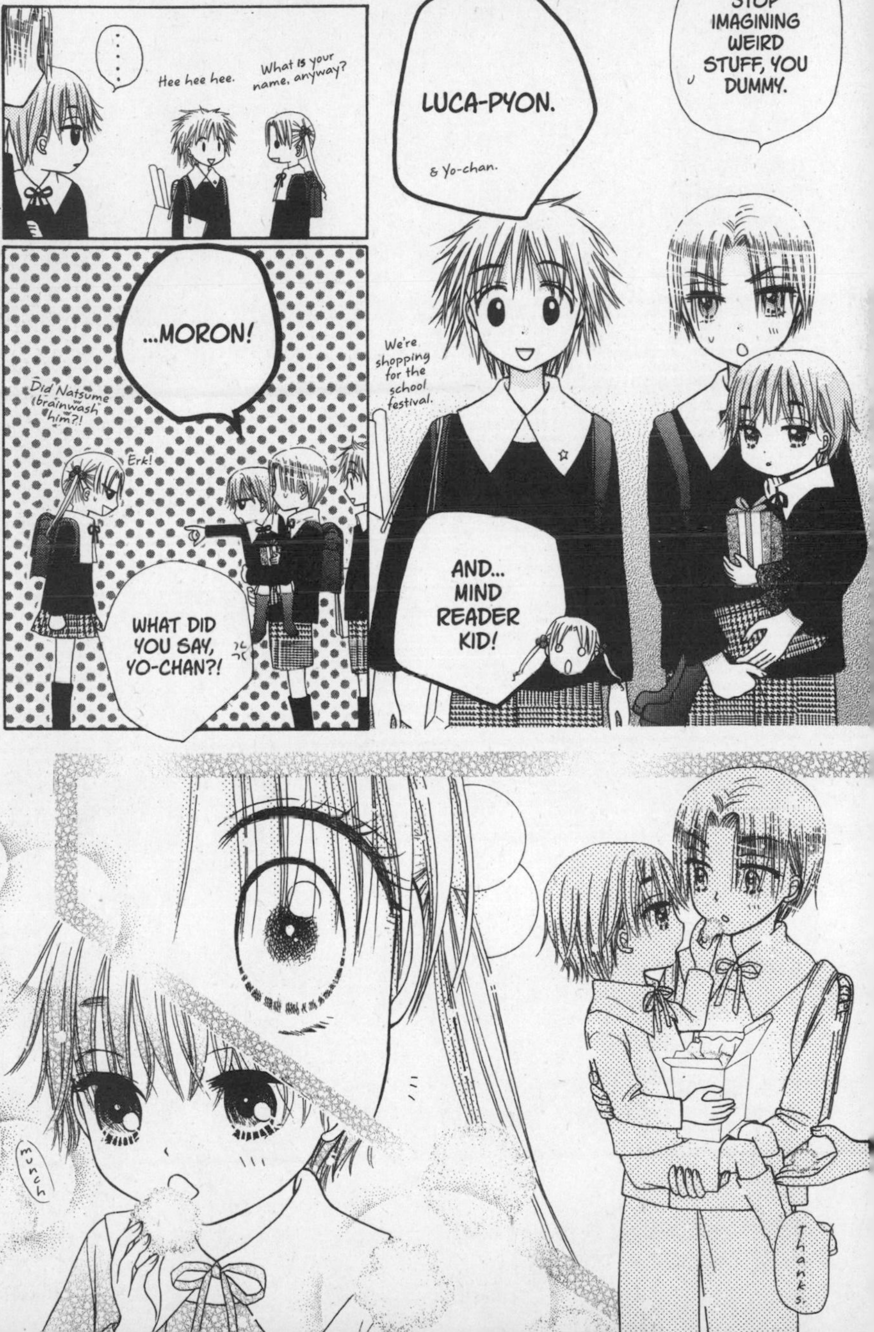
STOP IMAGINING WEIRD STUFF, YOU DUMMY.
LUCA-PYON.
& Yo-chan.
We're shopping for the school festival.
AND... MIND READER KID!
. . . . .
Hee hee hee.
What is your name, anyway?
...MORON!
Did Natsume brainwash him?!
Erk!
WHAT DID YOU SAY, YO-CHAN?!
Thanks.
munch

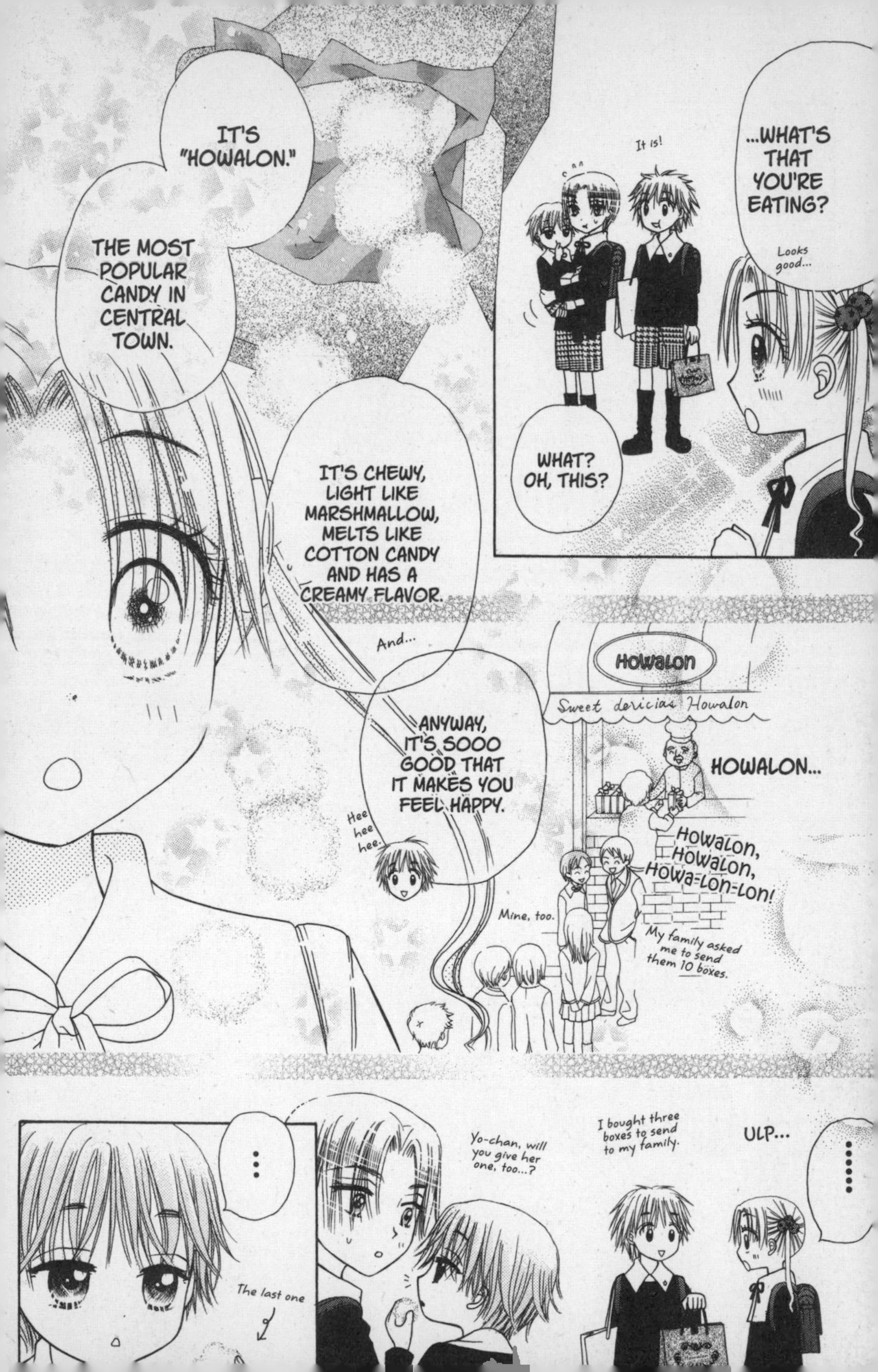
...WHAT'S THAT YOU'RE EATING?
Looks good...
It is!
WHAT? OH, THIS?
Howalon
Sweet dericias Howalon
HOWALON...
Howalon, Howalon, Howa-lon-lon!
My family asked me to send them 10 boxes.
Mine, too.
IT'S "HOWALON."
THE MOST POPULAR CANDY IN CENTRAL TOWN.
IT'S CHEWY, LIGHT LIKE MARSHMALLOW, MELTS LIKE COTTON CANDY AND HAS A CREAMY FLAVOR.
And...
ANYWAY, IT'S SOOO GOOD THAT IT MAKES YOU FEEL HAPPY.
Hee hee hee.
......
ULP...
I bought three boxes to send to my family.
Yo-chan, will you give her one, too...?
...
The last one

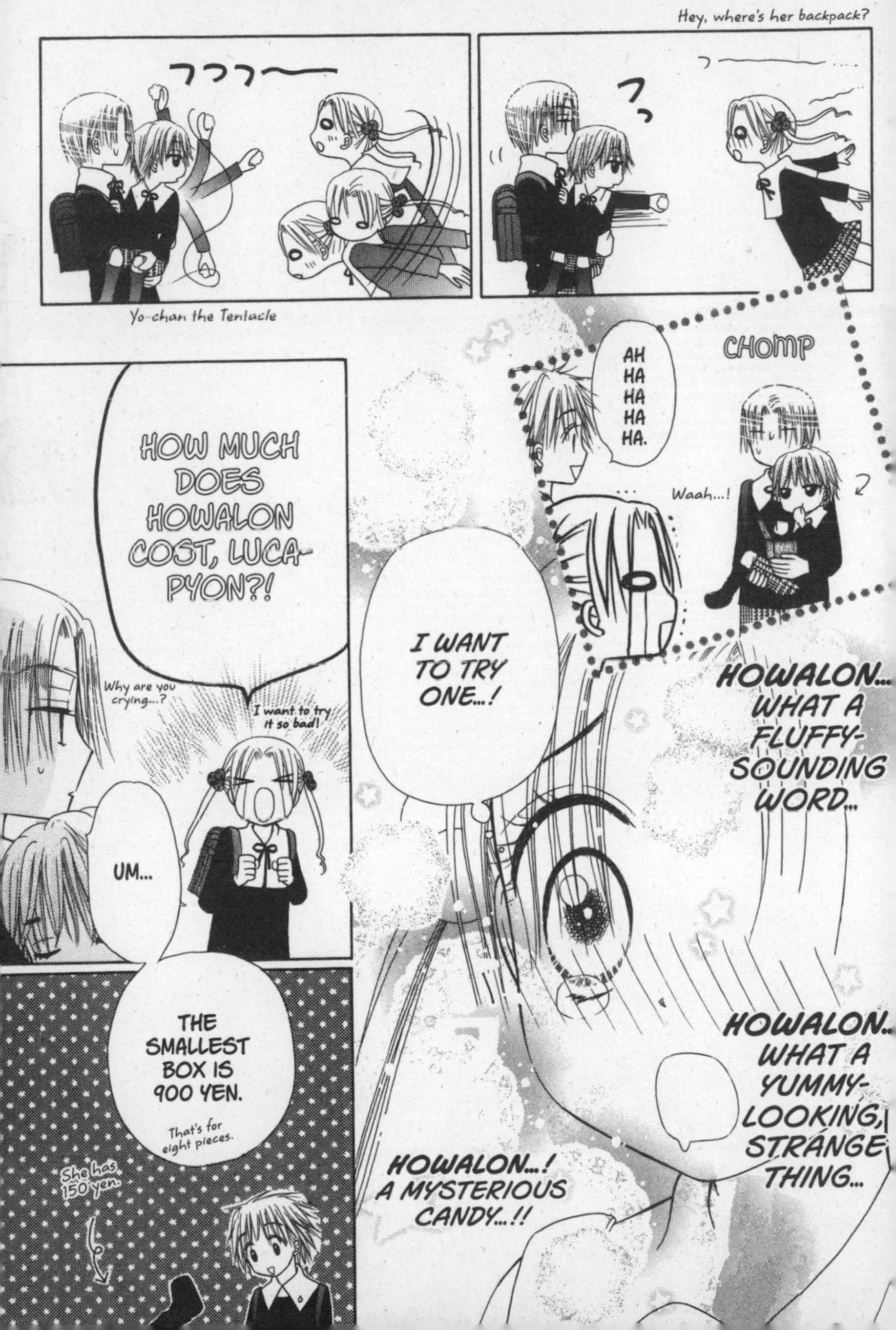
Hey, where's her backpack?
Yo-chan the Tentacle
CHOMP
Waah...!
AH HA HA HA HA.
...
I WANT TO TRY ONE...!
HOWALON... WHAT A FLUFFY-SOUNDING WORD...
HOWALON... WHAT A YUMMY-LOOKING, STRANGE THING...
HOWALON...! A MYSTERIOUS CANDY...!!
HOW MUCH DOES HOWALON COST, LUCA-PYON?!
I want to try it so bad!
Why are you crying...?
UM...
THE SMALLEST BOX IS 900 YEN.
That's for eight pieces.
She has 150 yen.

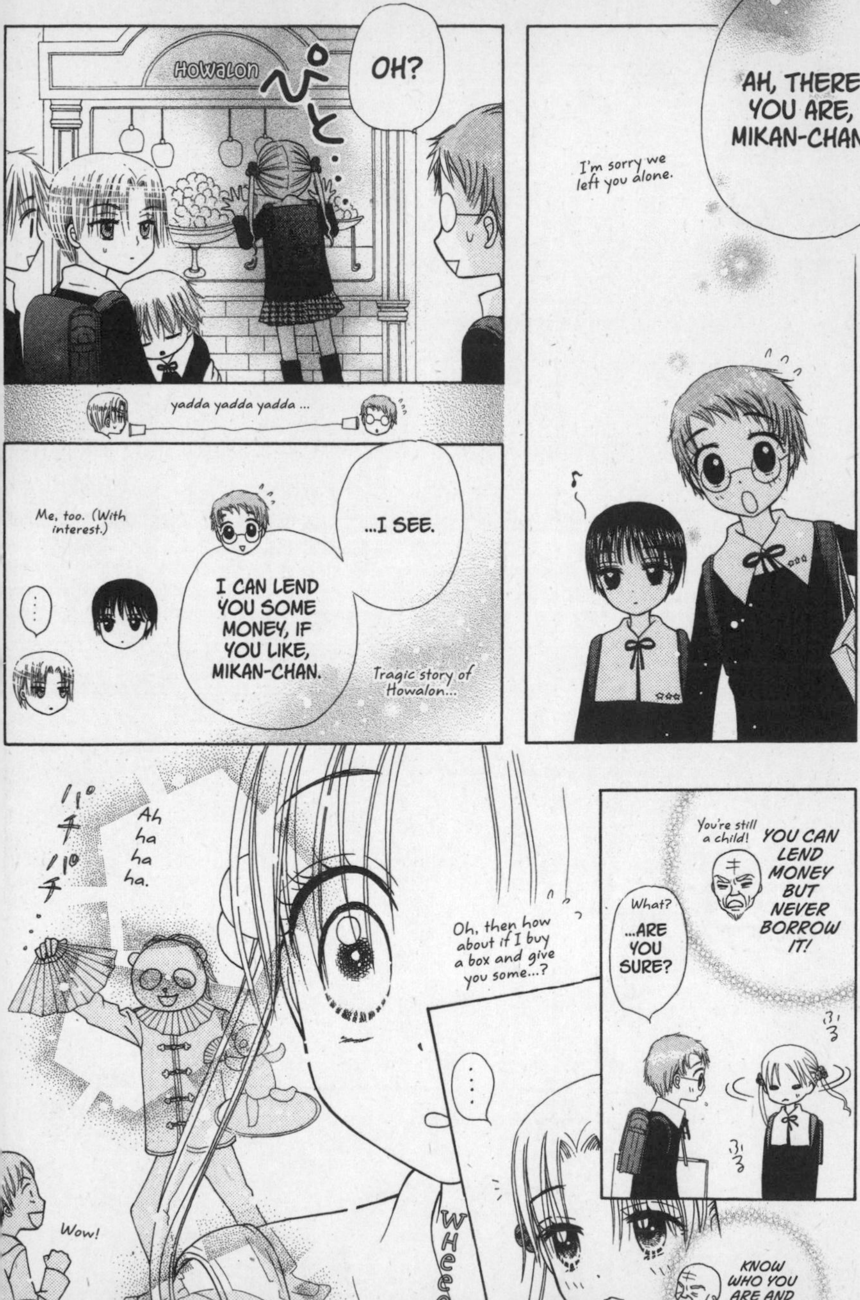
AH, THERE YOU ARE, MIKAN-CHAN.
I'm sorry we left you alone.
Howalon
ぺと…
OH?
yadda yadda yadda ...
...I SEE.
I CAN LEND YOU SOME MONEY, IF YOU LIKE, MIKAN-CHAN.
Tragic story of Howalon...
Me, too. (With interest.)
...
You're still a child!
YOU CAN LEND MONEY BUT NEVER BORROW IT!
What?
...ARE YOU SURE?
ふる
ふる
KNOW WHO YOU ARE AND YOUR WORTH!
Oh, then how about if I buy a box and give you some...?
....
Wheee!
Ah ha ha ha.
パチパチ
Wow!

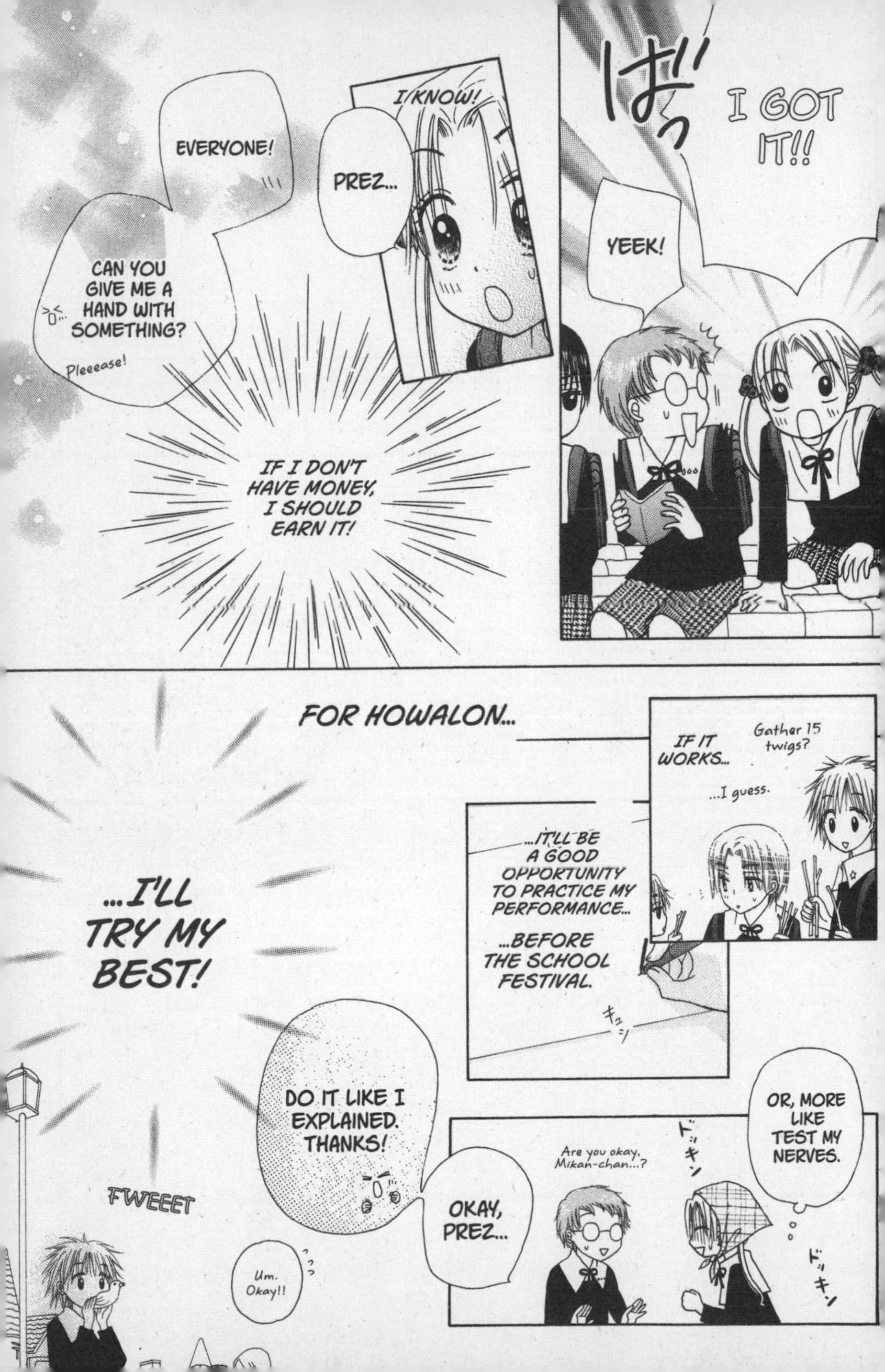
ぱっ
I GOT IT!!
YEEK!
I KNOW!
PREZ...
EVERYONE!
CAN YOU GIVE ME A HAND WITH SOMETHING?
Pleeease!
IF I DON'T HAVE MONEY, I SHOULD EARN IT!
FOR HOWALON...
IF IT WORKS...
Gather 15 twigs?
...I guess.
...IT'LL BE A GOOD OPPORTUNITY TO PRACTICE MY PERFORMANCE...
...BEFORE THE SCHOOL FESTIVAL.
キュッ
OR, MORE LIKE TEST MY NERVES.
ドッキン
ドッキン
Are you okay, Mikan-chan...?
...I'LL TRY MY BEST!
DO IT LIKE I EXPLAINED. THANKS!
OKAY, PREZ...
Um. Okay!!
FWEEEET

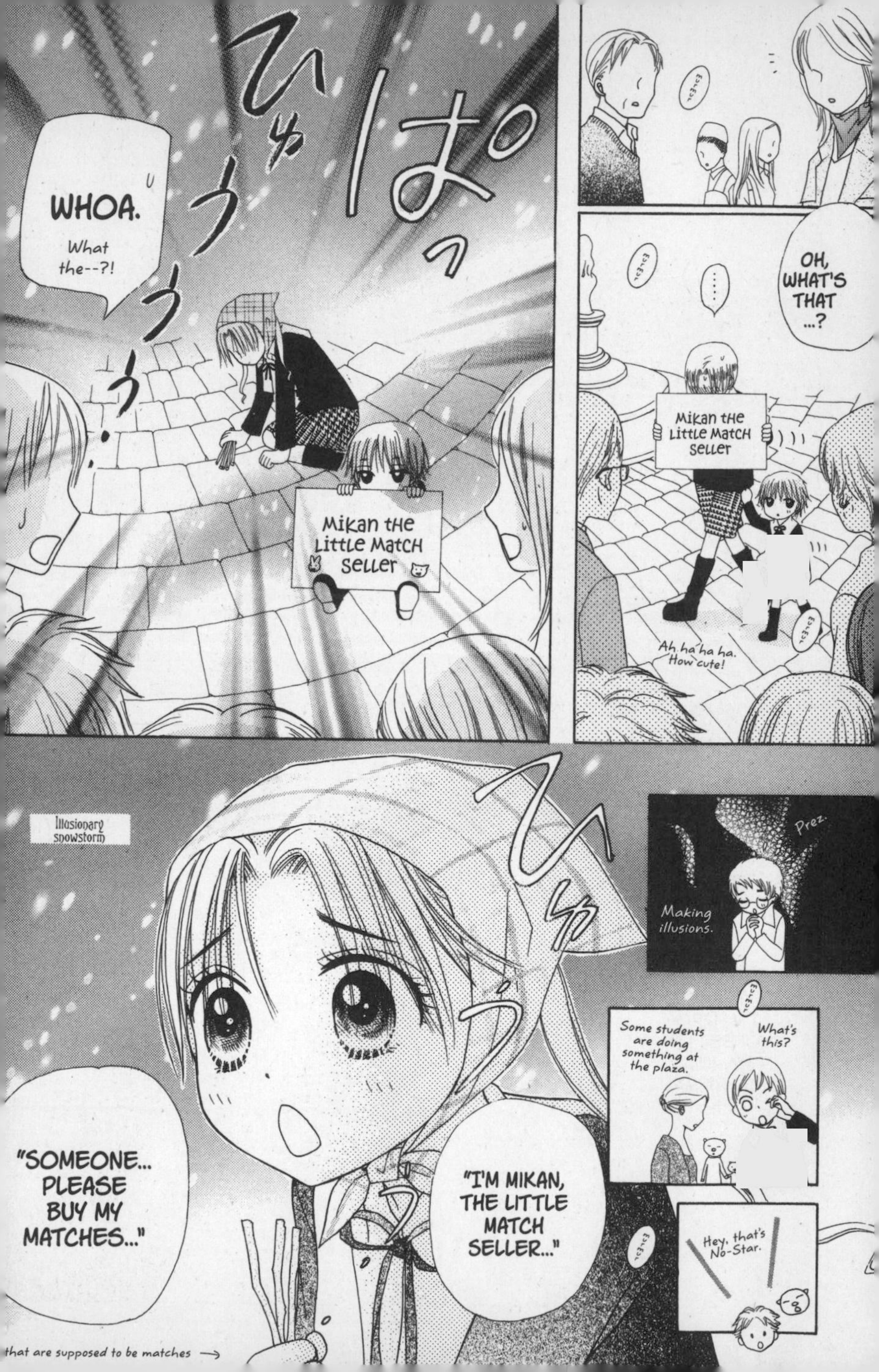
OH, WHAT'S THAT ...?
...
Mikan the Little Match Seller
Ah ha ha ha. How cute!
ぱっ
ひゅううう
WHOA. What the--?!
Mikan the Little Match Seller
Prez.
Making illusions.
Some students are doing something at the plaza.
What's this?
Hey, that's No-Star.
Illusionary snowstorm
ひゅう
"I'M MIKAN, THE LITTLE MATCH SELLER..."
"SOMEONE... PLEASE BUY MY MATCHES..."
that are supposed to be matches →

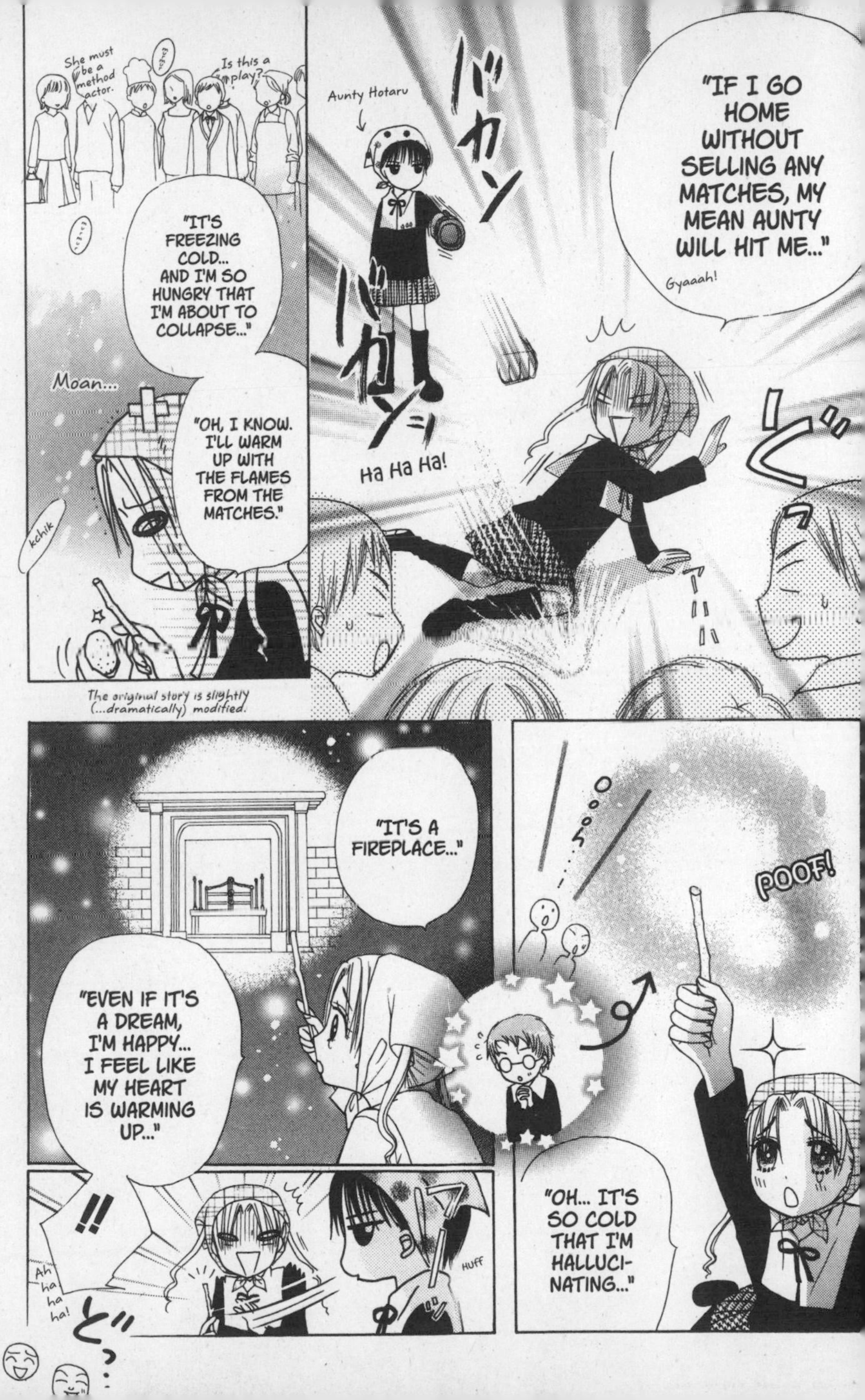
"IF I GO HOME WITHOUT SELLING ANY MATCHES, MY MEAN AUNTY WILL HIT ME..."
Gyaaah!
Aunty Hotaru
Ha Ha Ha!
She must be a method actor.
Is this a play?
"IT'S FREEZING COLD... AND I'M SO HUNGRY THAT I'M ABOUT TO COLLAPSE..."
Moan...
"OH, I KNOW. I'LL WARM UP WITH THE FLAMES FROM THE MATCHES."
kchik
The original story is slightly (...dramatically) modified.
POOF!
"OH... IT'S SO COLD THAT I'M HALLUCINATING..."
"IT'S A FIREPLACE..."
"EVEN IF IT'S A DREAM, I'M HAPPY... I FEEL LIKE MY HEART IS WARMING UP..."
HUFF
Ah ha ha ha!

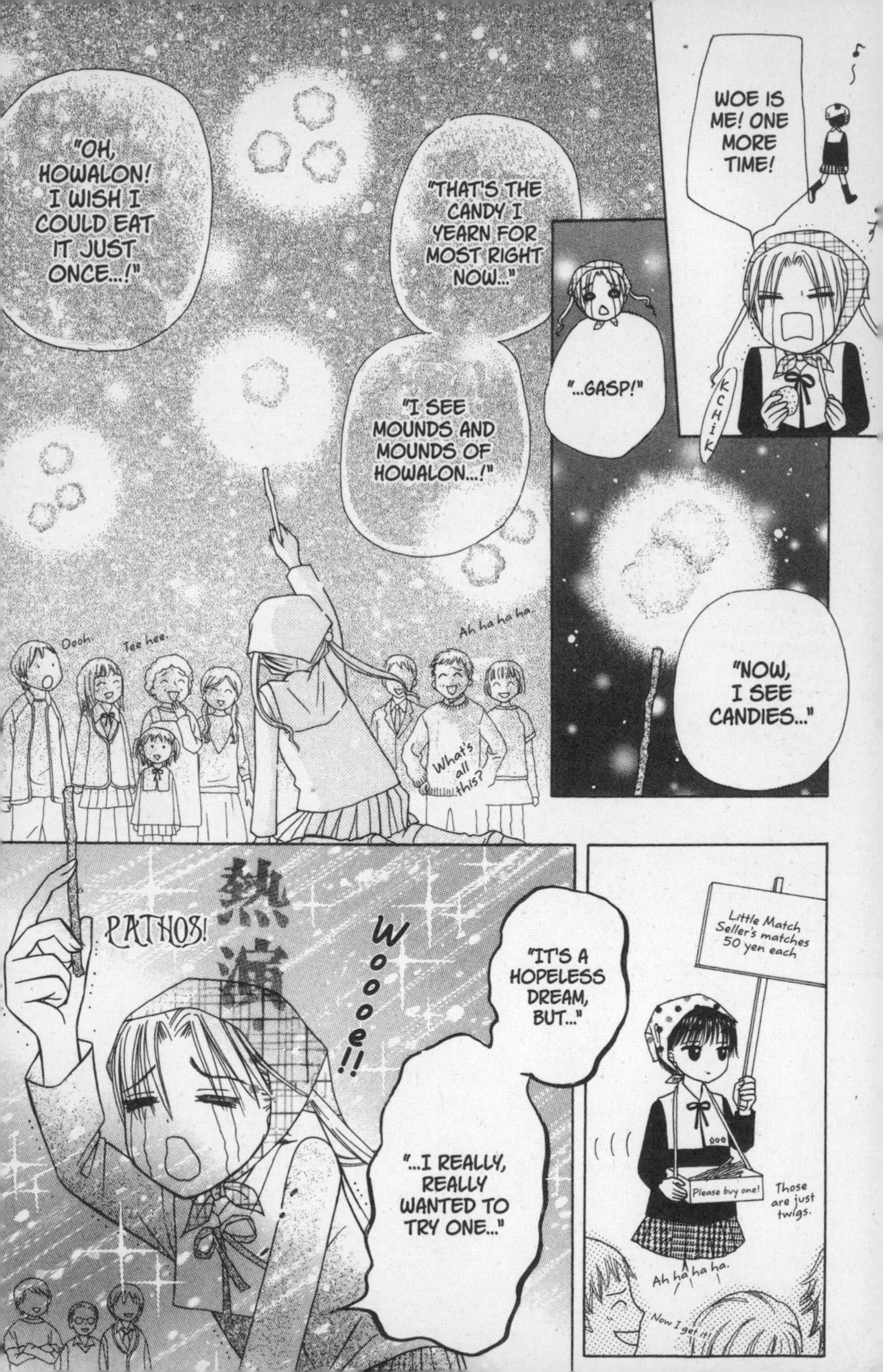
WOE IS ME! ONE MORE TIME!
KCHIK
"...GASP!"
"NOW, I SEE CANDIES..."
"I SEE MOUNDS AND MOUNDS OF HOWALON...!"
"THAT'S THE CANDY I YEARN FOR MOST RIGHT NOW..."
"OH, HOWALON! I WISH I COULD EAT IT JUST ONCE...!"
Ah ha ha ha.
What's all this?
Tee hee.
Oooh.
Little Match Seller's matches 50 yen each
Please buy one!
Those are just twigs.
Ah ha ha ha.
Now I get it!
"IT'S A HOPELESS DREAM, BUT..."
"...I REALLY, REALLY WANTED TO TRY ONE..."
Woooe!!
熱演
PATHOS!

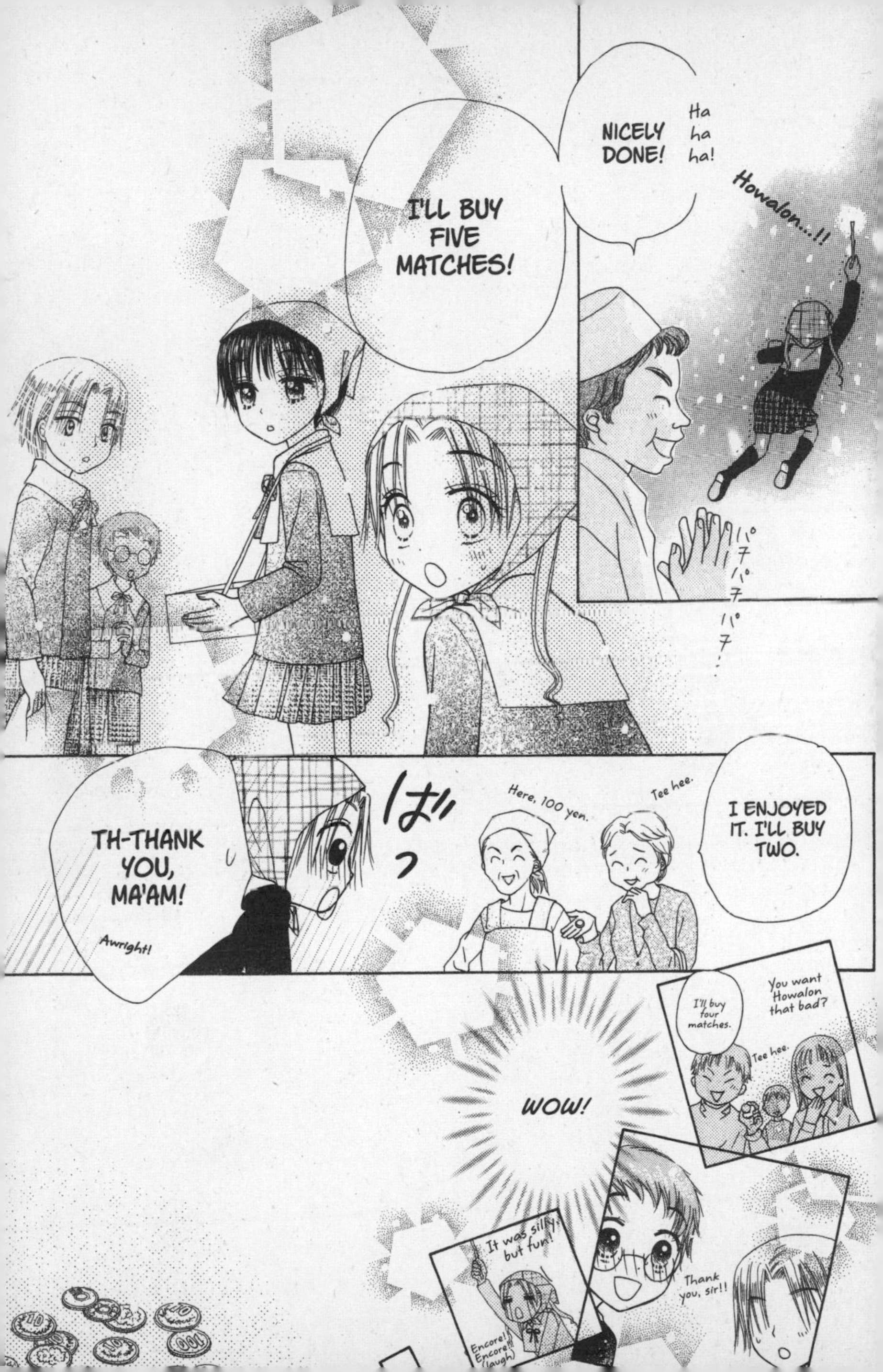

NICELY DONE!
Ha ha ha!
Howalon...!!
パフパフパフ…
I'LL BUY FIVE MATCHES!
I ENJOYED IT. I'LL BUY TWO.
Tee hee.
Here, 100 yen.
ばっ
TH-THANK YOU, MA'AM!
Awright!
You want Howalon that bad?
I'll buy four matches.
Tee hee.
WOW!
Thank you, sir!!
It was silly, but fun!
Encore! Encore! (laugh)

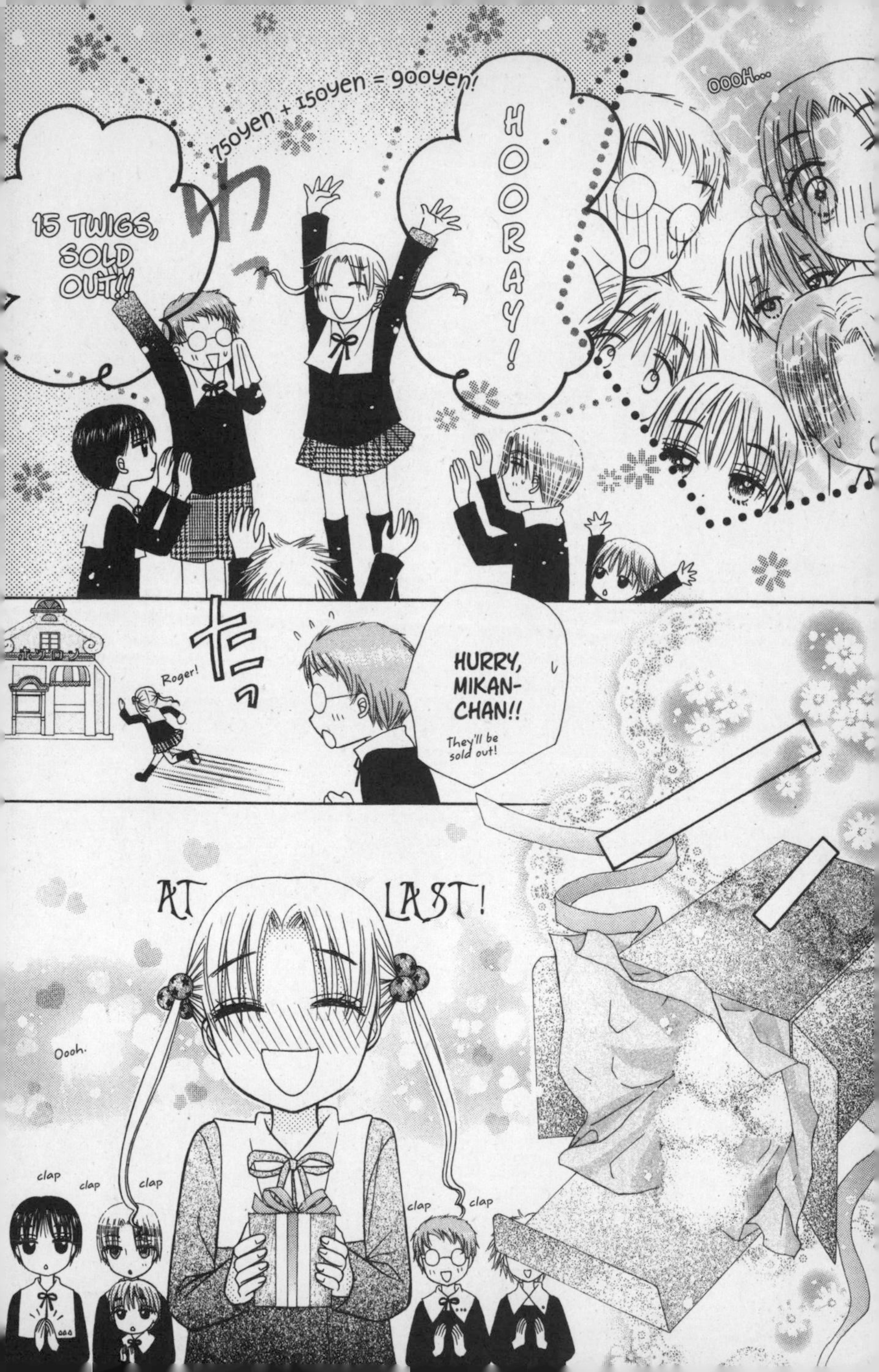
OOOH...
HOORAY!
750yen + 150yen = 900yen!
15 TWIGS, SOLD OUT!!
HURRY, MIKAN-CHAN!!
They'll be sold out!
Roger!
AT LAST!
Oooh.
clap
clap
clap
clap
clap

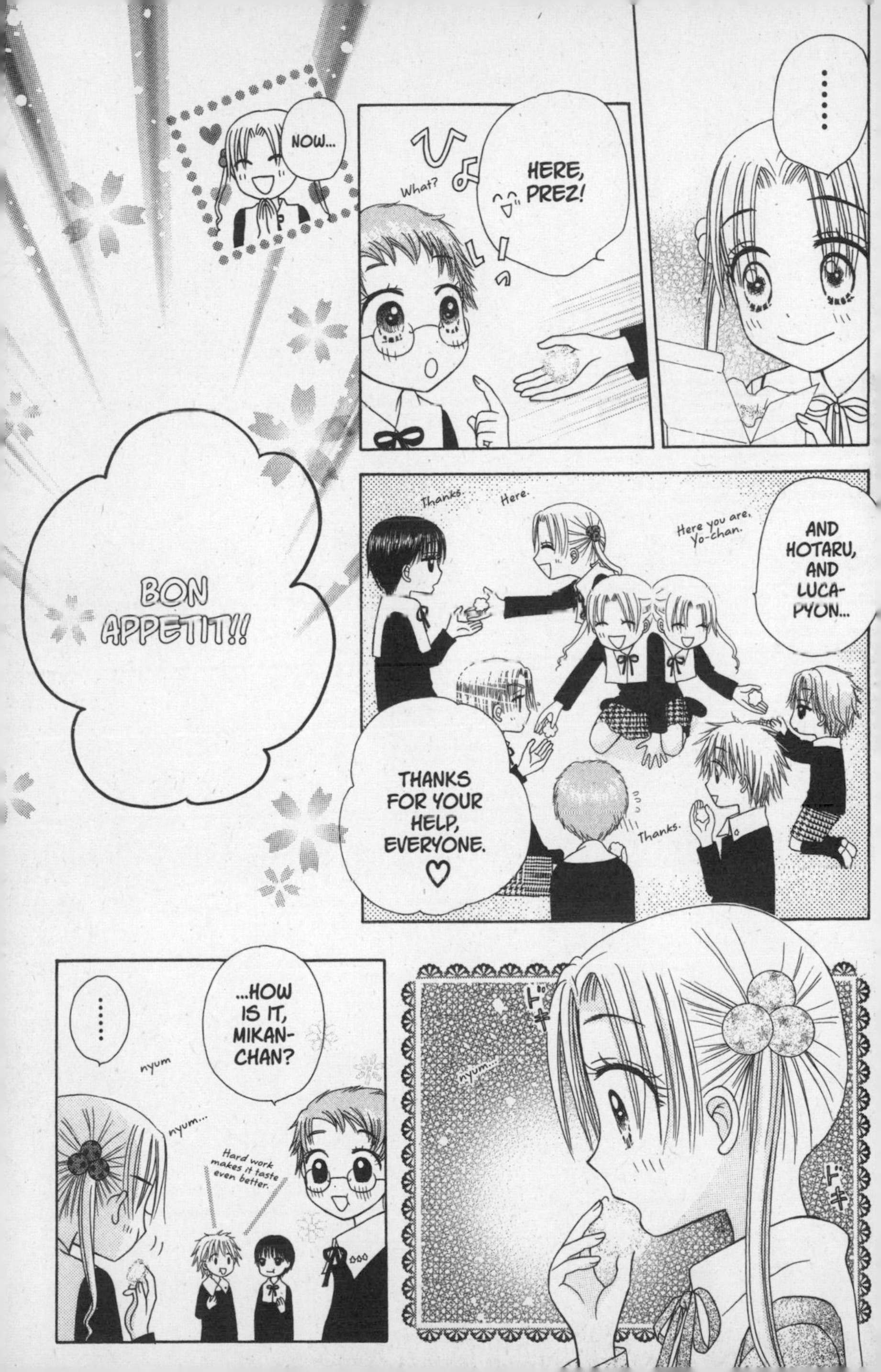
......
HERE, PREZ!
What?
NOW...
BON APPETIT!!
AND HOTARU, AND LUCA-PYON...
Here you are, Yo-chan.
Here.
Thanks.
THANKS FOR YOUR HELP, EVERYONE. ♡
Thanks.
ドキ
nyum...
ドキ
...HOW IS IT, MIKAN-CHAN?
......
nyum
nyum...
Hard work makes it taste even better.

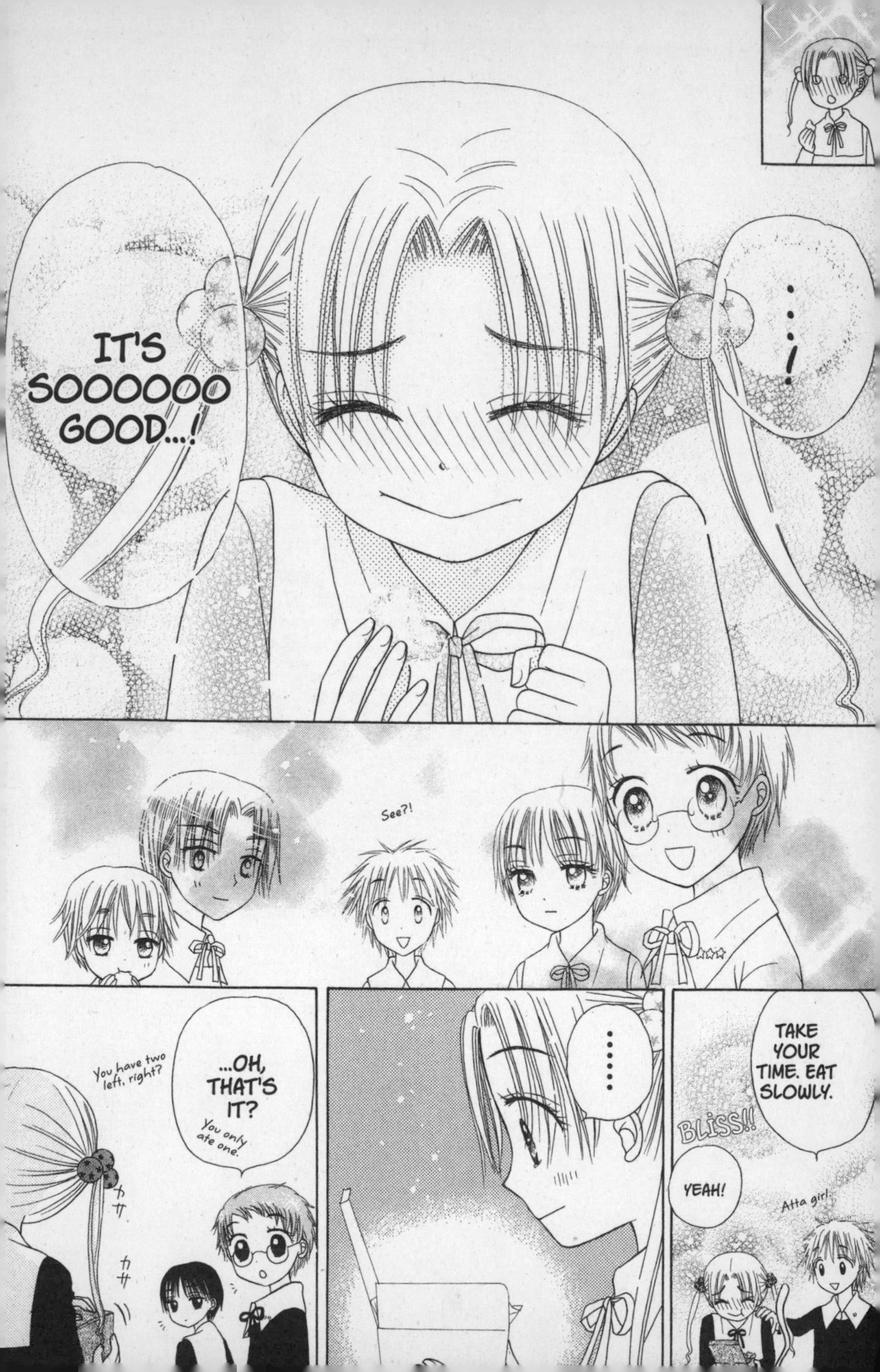
...!
IT'S SOOOOOO GOOD...!
See?!
TAKE YOUR TIME. EAT SLOWLY.
BLISS!!
YEAH!
Atta girl.
......
...OH, THAT'S IT?
You only ate one.
You have two left, right?
カサ
カサ

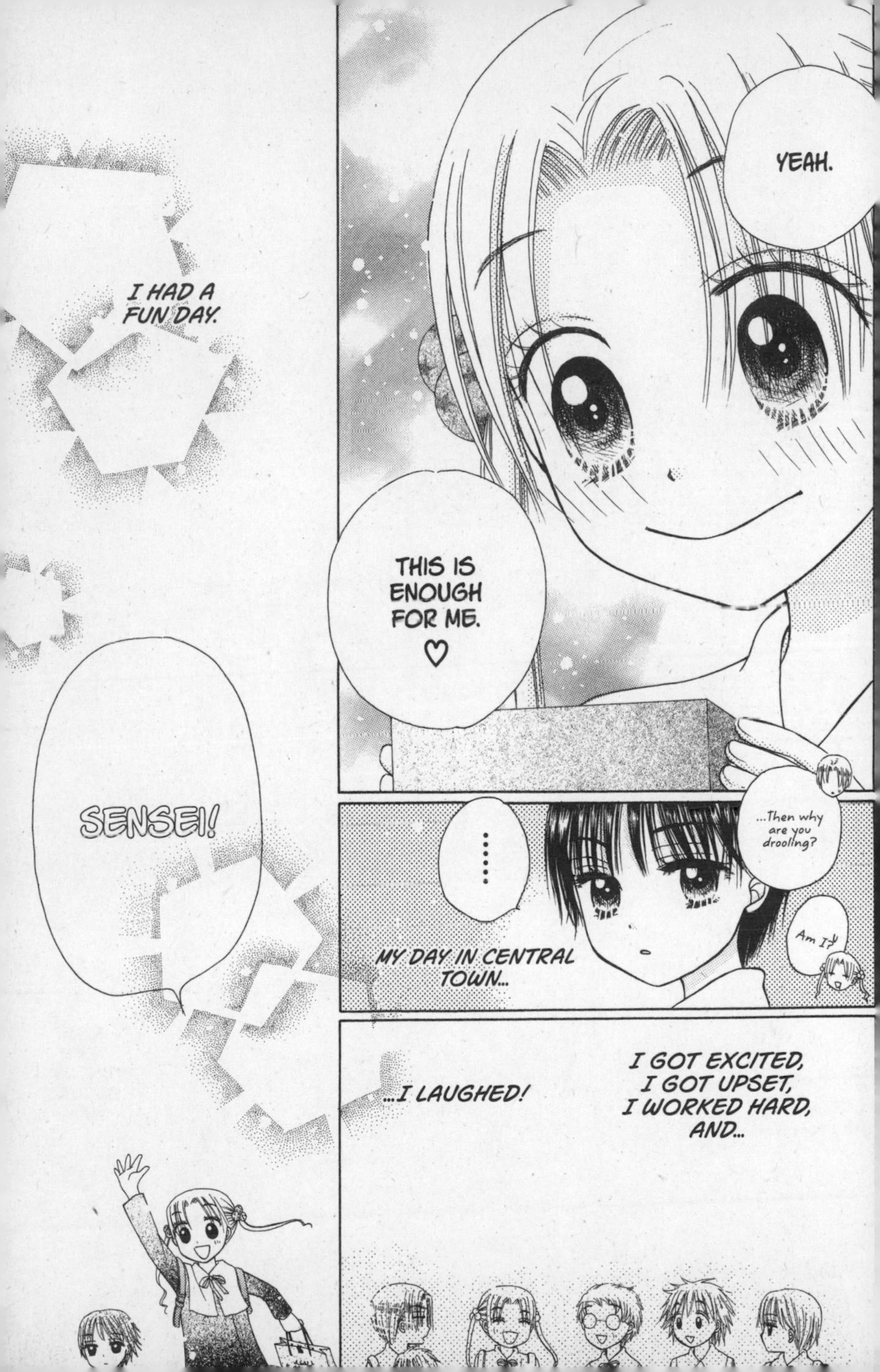
YEAH.
THIS IS ENOUGH FOR ME. ♡
...Then why are you drooling?
Am I?
......
MY DAY IN CENTRAL TOWN...
I GOT EXCITED, I GOT UPSET, I WORKED HARD, AND...
...I LAUGHED!
I HAD A FUN DAY.
SENSEI!

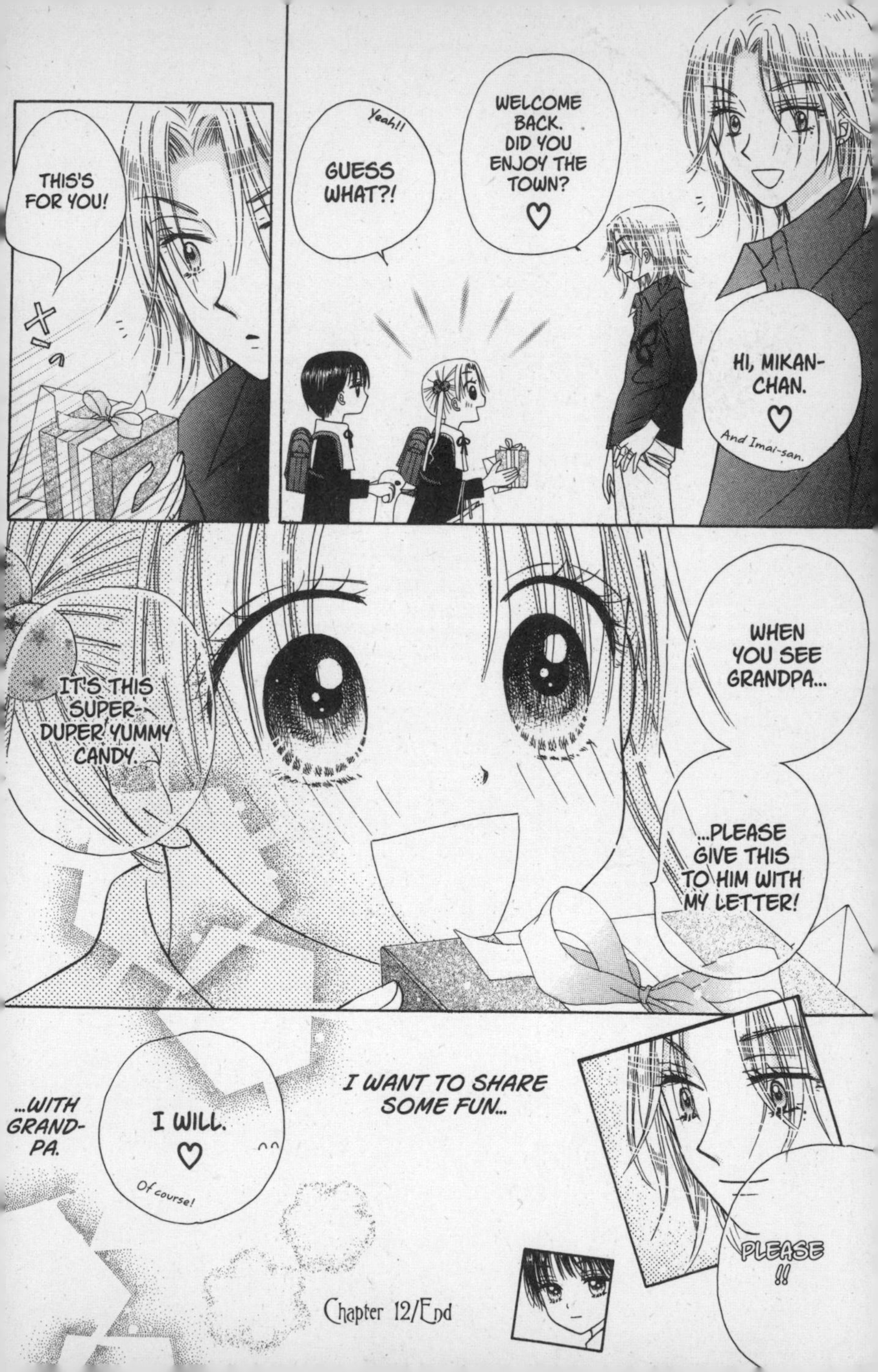
HI, MIKAN-CHAN. ♡
And Imai-san.
WELCOME BACK. DID YOU ENJOY THE TOWN? ♡
Yeah!!
GUESS WHAT?!
THIS'S FOR YOU!
WHEN YOU SEE GRANDPA...
...PLEASE GIVE THIS TO HIM WITH MY LETTER!
IT'S THIS SUPER-DUPER YUMMY CANDY.
PLEASE!!
I WANT TO SHARE SOME FUN...
I WILL. ♡
Of course!
...WITH GRANDPA.

Chapter 12/End

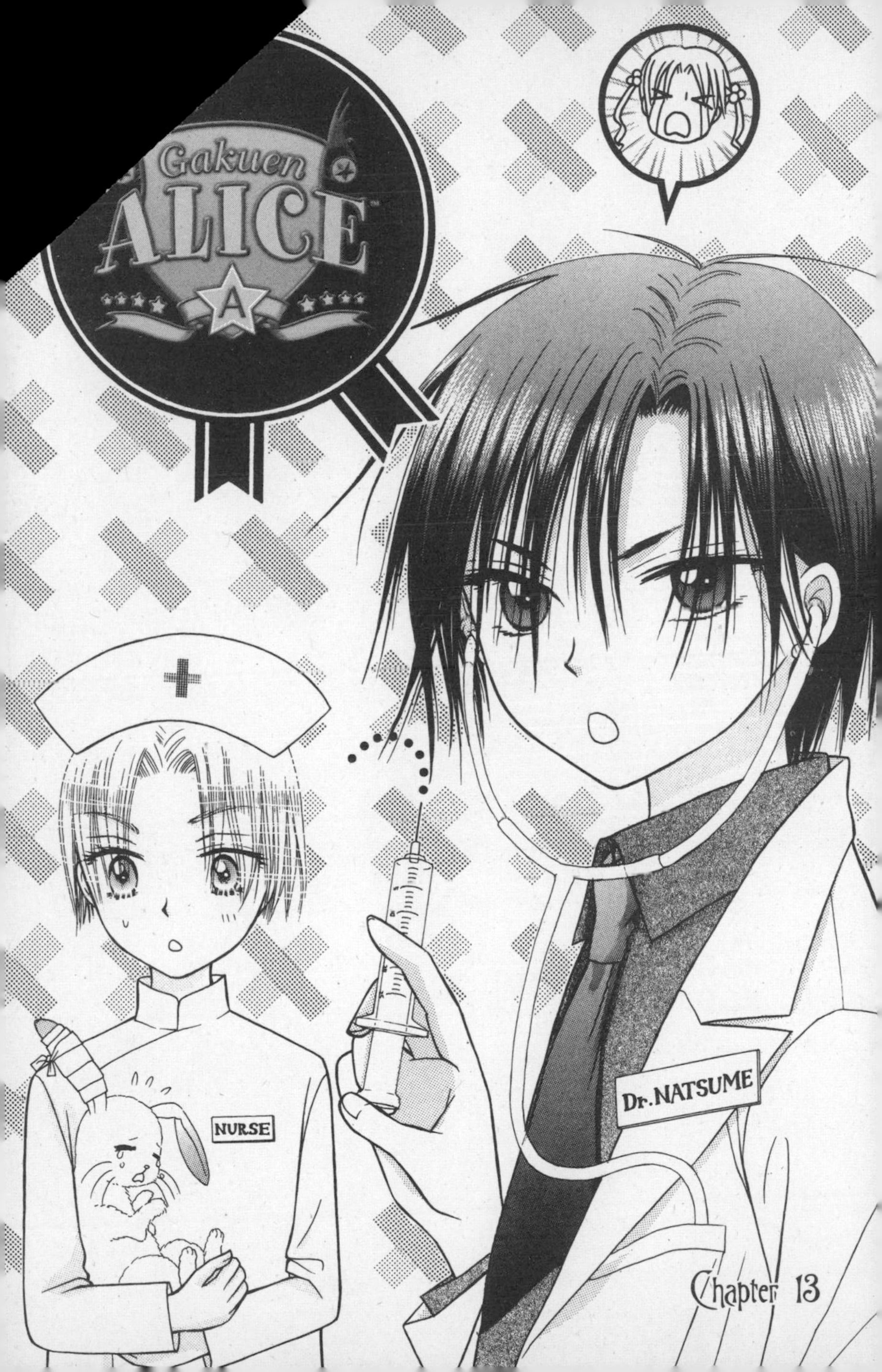
Gakuen ALICE
A
NURSE
Dr. NATSUME
Chapter 13

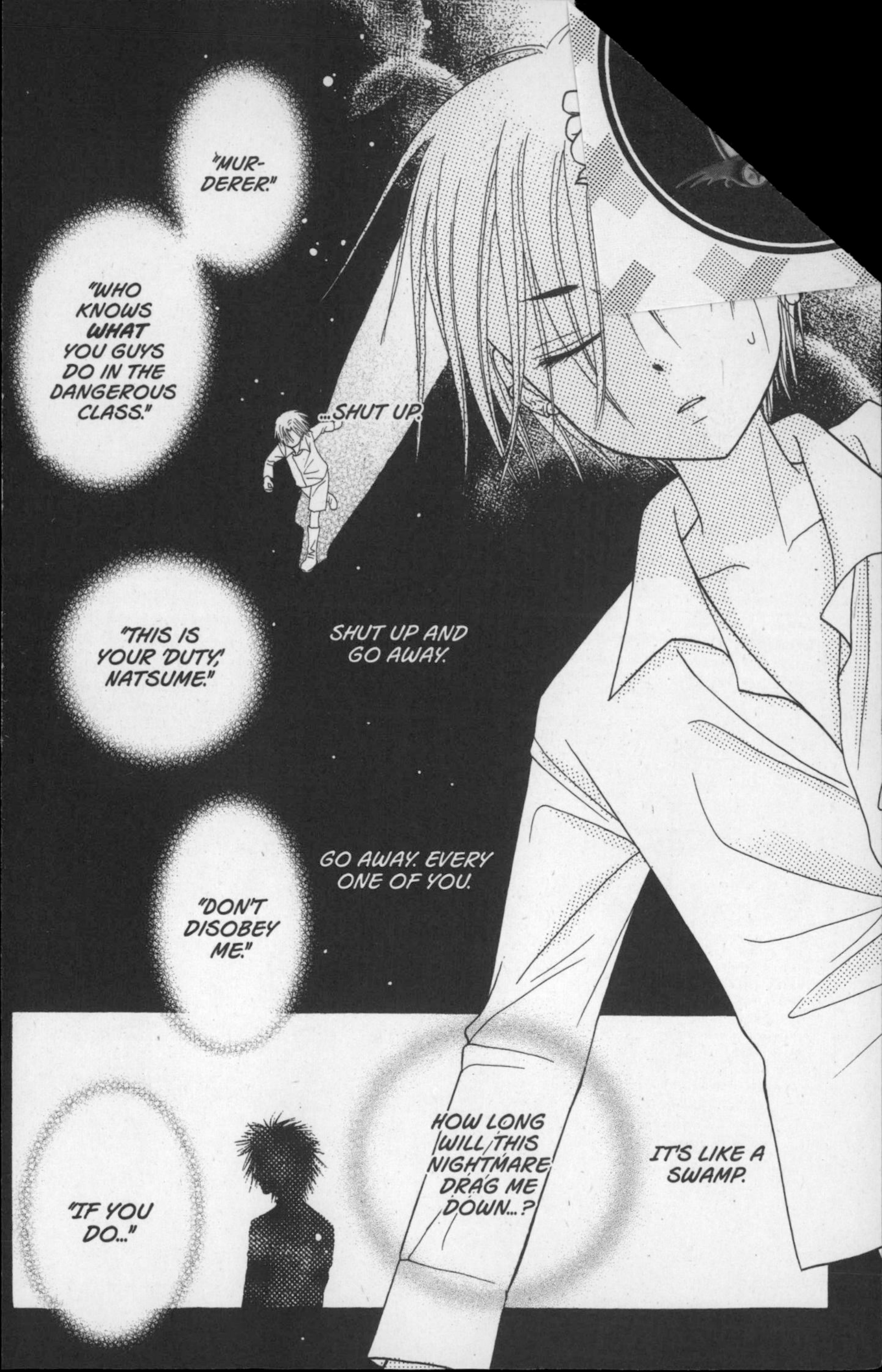
"MUR-DERER."
"WHO KNOWS WHAT YOU GUYS DO IN THE DANGEROUS CLASS."
...SHUT UP.
SHUT UP AND GO AWAY.
"THIS IS YOUR 'DUTY,' NATSUME."
GO AWAY. EVERY ONE OF YOU.
"DON'T DISOBEY ME."
IT'S LIKE A SWAMP.
HOW LONG WILL THIS NIGHTMARE DRAG ME DOWN...?
"IF YOU DO..."

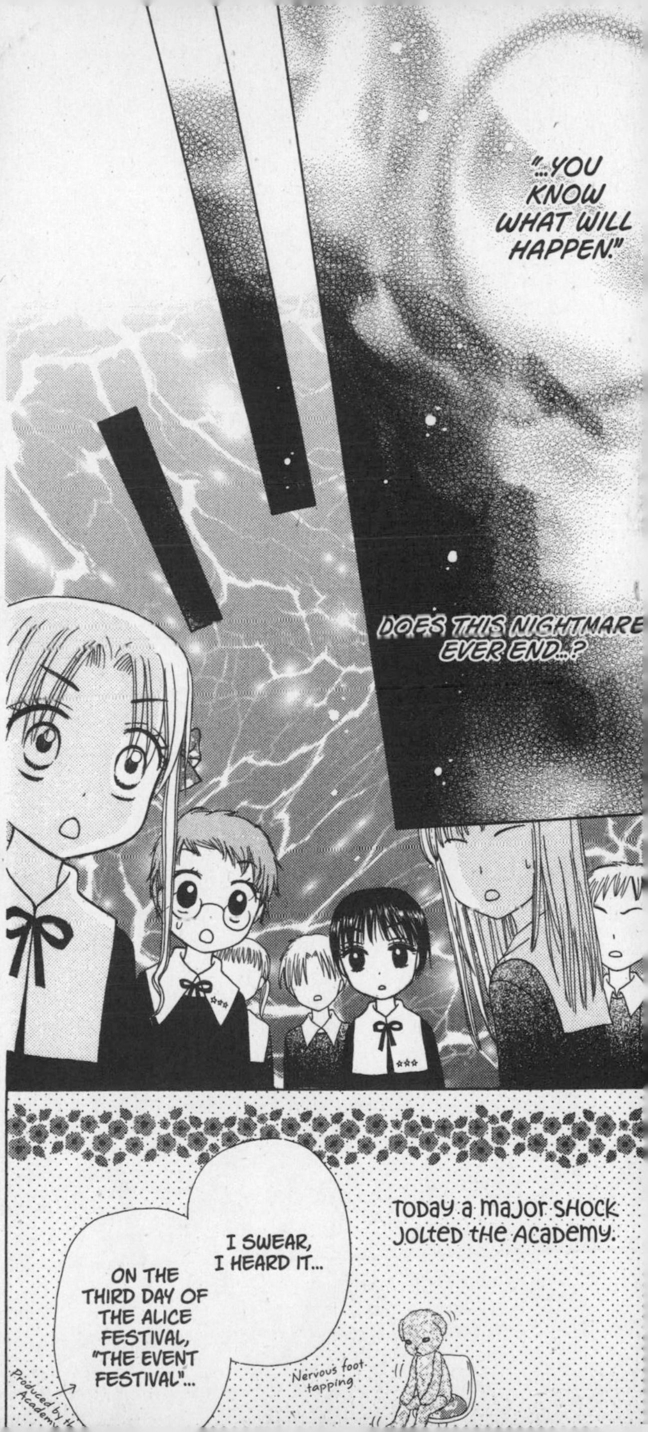

"...YOU KNOW WHAT WILL HAPPEN."
DOES THIS NIGHTMARE EVER END...?
TODAY A MAJOR SHOCK JOLTED THE ACADEMY.
I SWEAR, I HEARD IT...
ON THE THIRD DAY OF THE ALICE FESTIVAL, "THE EVENT FESTIVAL"...
Nervous foot tapping

Read at your own discretion.

Higuchi's Room 3

PROFILE 6

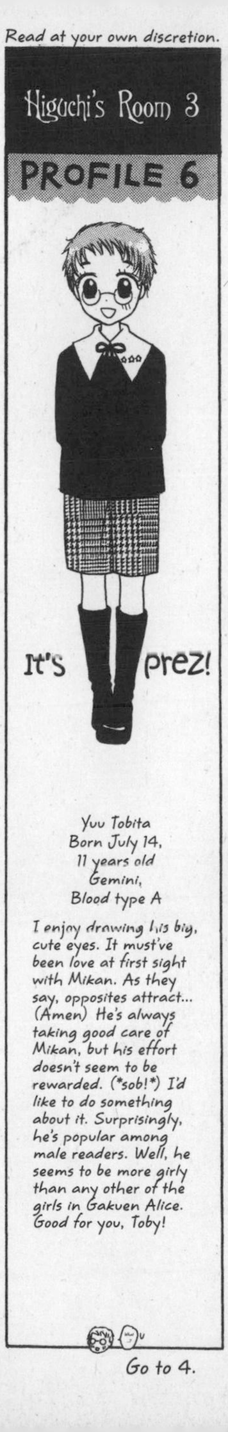

It's prez!

Yuu Tobita
Born July 14,
11 years old
Gemini,
Blood type A

I enjoy drawing his big, cute eyes. It must've been love at first sight with Mikan. As they say, opposites attract... (Amen) He's always taking good care of Mikan, but his effort doesn't seem to be rewarded. (*sob!*) I'd like to do something about it. Surprisingly, he's popular among male readers. Well, he seems to be more girly than any other of the girls in Gakuen Alice. Good for you, Toby!

Go to 4.

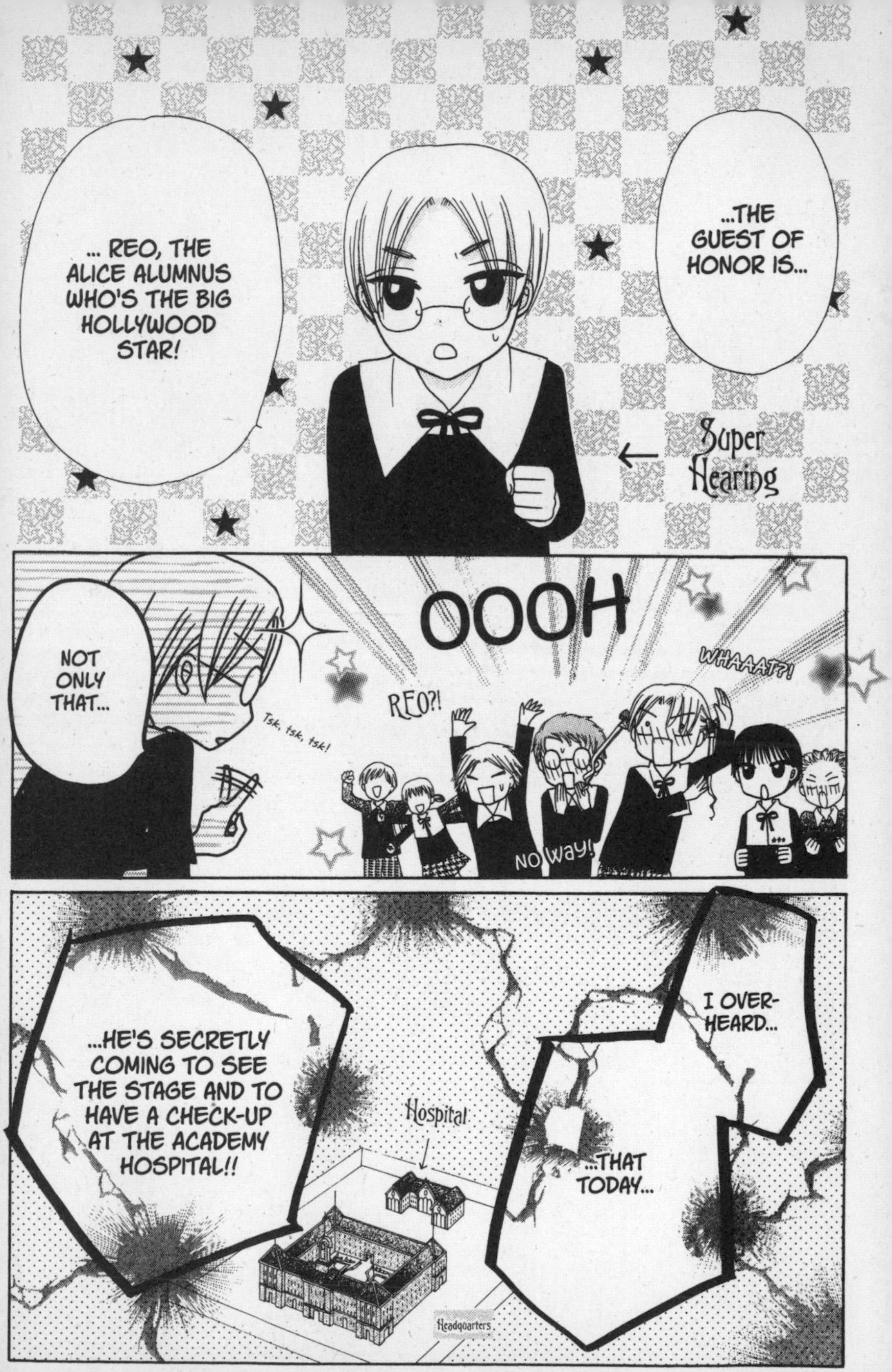
...THE GUEST OF HONOR IS...
Super Hearing
... REO, THE ALICE ALUMNUS WHO'S THE BIG HOLLYWOOD STAR!
WHAAAT?!
OOOH
REO?!
NO WAY!
Tsk, tsk, tsk!
NOT ONLY THAT...
I OVER-HEARD...
...THAT TODAY...
Hospital
Headquarters
...HE'S SECRETLY COMING TO SEE THE STAGE AND TO HAVE A CHECK-UP AT THE ACADEMY HOSPITAL!!

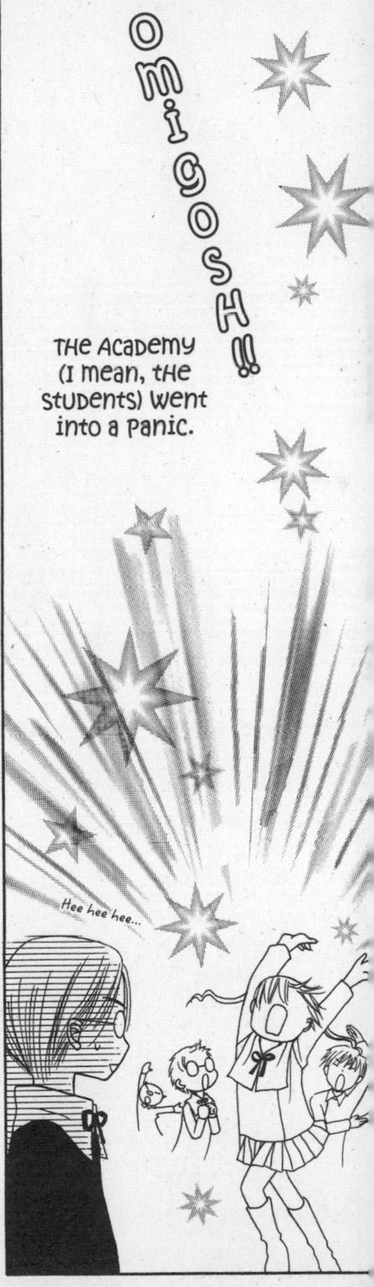
OMIGOSH!!
The Academy (I mean, the students) went into a panic.
Hee hee hee...

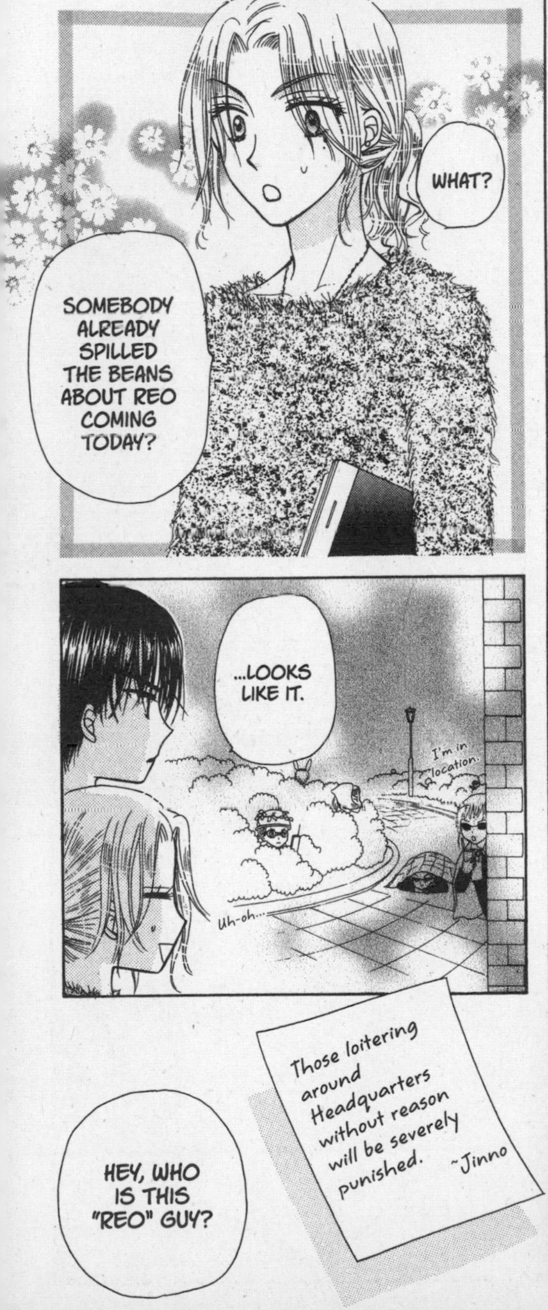
WHAT?
SOMEBODY ALREADY SPILLED THE BEANS ABOUT REO COMING TODAY?
...LOOKS LIKE IT.
I'm in location.
Uh-oh...
Those loitering around Headquarters without reason will be severely punished. ~Jinno
HEY, WHO IS THIS "REO" GUY?

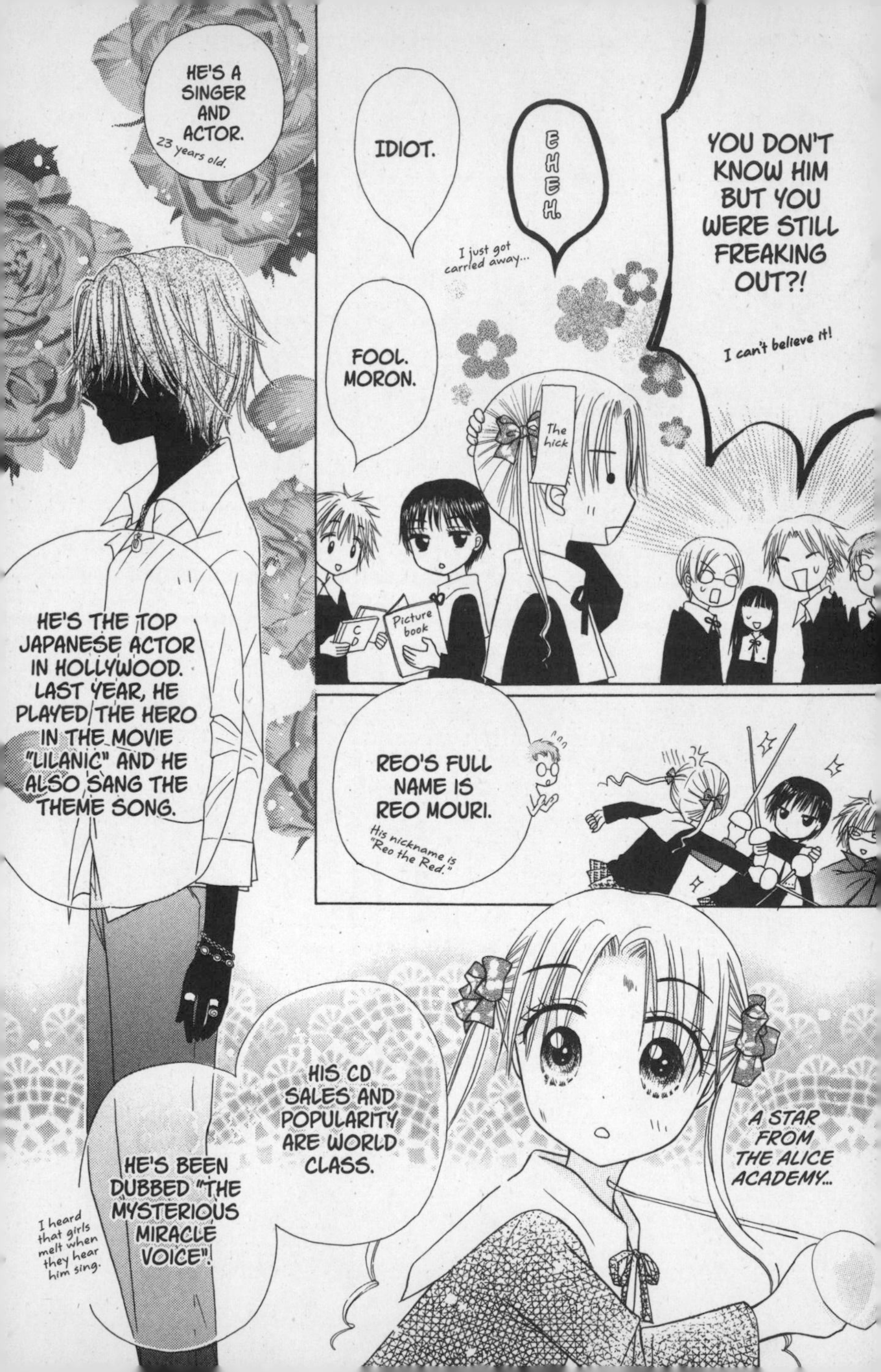
YOU DON'T KNOW HIM BUT YOU WERE STILL FREAKING OUT?!
I can't believe it!
EHEH.
I just got carried away...
IDIOT.
FOOL. MORON.
The hick
CD
Picture book
REO'S FULL NAME IS REO MOURI.
His nickname is "Reo the Red."
HE'S A SINGER AND ACTOR.
23 years old.
HE'S THE TOP JAPANESE ACTOR IN HOLLYWOOD. LAST YEAR, HE PLAYED THE HERO IN THE MOVIE "LILANIC" AND HE ALSO SANG THE THEME SONG.
A STAR FROM THE ALICE ACADEMY...
HIS CD SALES AND POPULARITY ARE WORLD CLASS.
HE'S BEEN DUBBED "THE MYSTERIOUS MIRACLE VOICE"!
I heard that girls melt when they hear him sing.

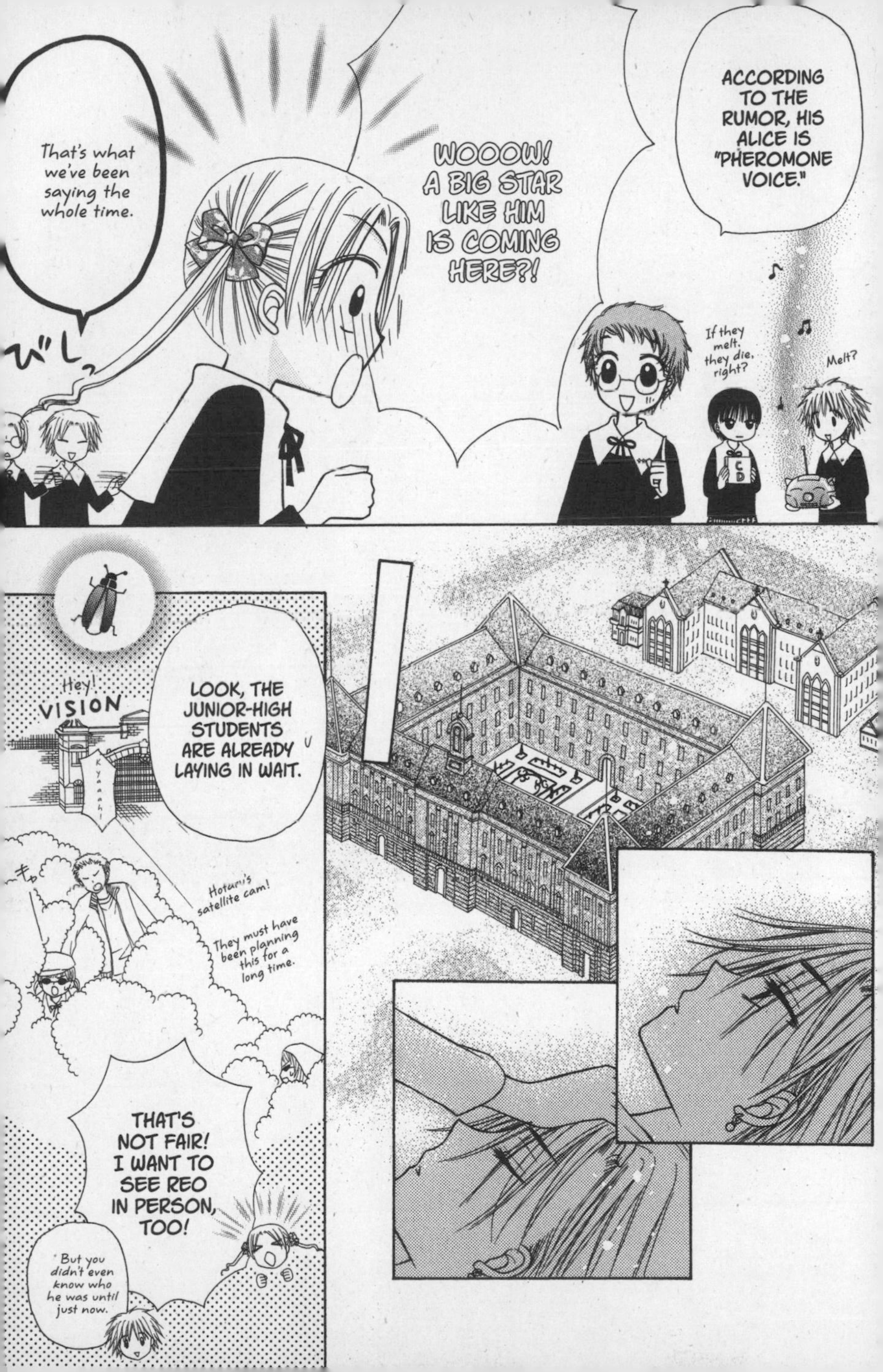
ACCORDING TO THE RUMOR, HIS ALICE IS "PHEROMONE VOICE."
Melt?
If they melt, they die, right?
WOOOW! A BIG STAR LIKE HIM IS COMING HERE?!
That's what we've been saying the whole time.
びし
LOOK, THE JUNIOR-HIGH STUDENTS ARE ALREADY LAYING IN WAIT.
Hey! VISION
Kyaaah!
Hotaru's satellite cam!
They must have been planning this for a long time.
THAT'S NOT FAIR! I WANT TO SEE REO IN PERSON, TOO!
But you didn't even know who he was until just now.

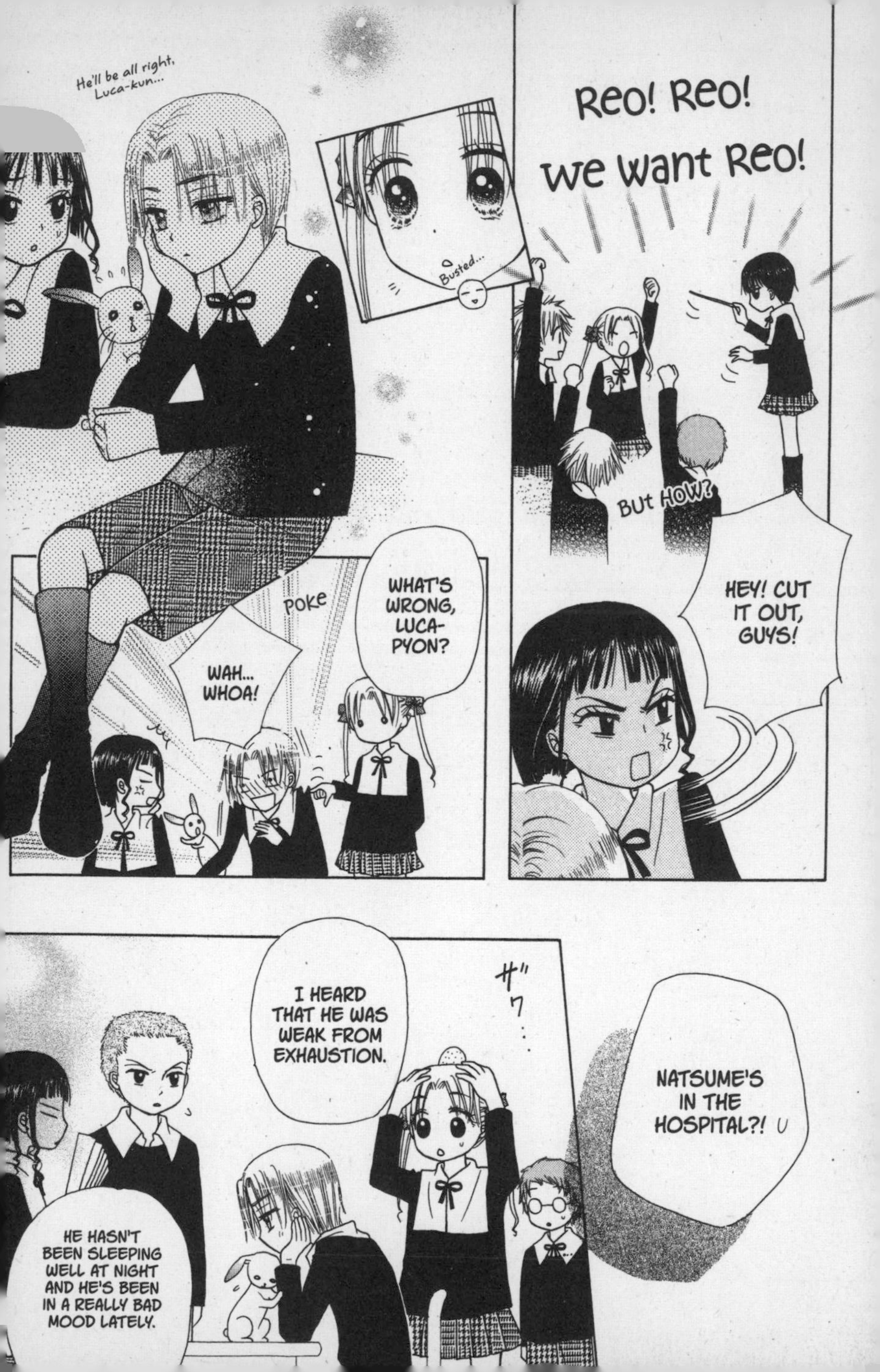
Reo! Reo! We want Reo!
But HOW?
HEY! CUT IT OUT, GUYS!
He'll be all right, Luca-kun...
Busted...
WHAT'S WRONG, LUCA-PYON?
POKE
WAH... WHOA!
NATSUME'S IN THE HOSPITAL?!
ザワ
I HEARD THAT HE WAS WEAK FROM EXHAUSTION.
HE HASN'T BEEN SLEEPING WELL AT NIGHT AND HE'S BEEN IN A REALLY BAD MOOD LATELY.

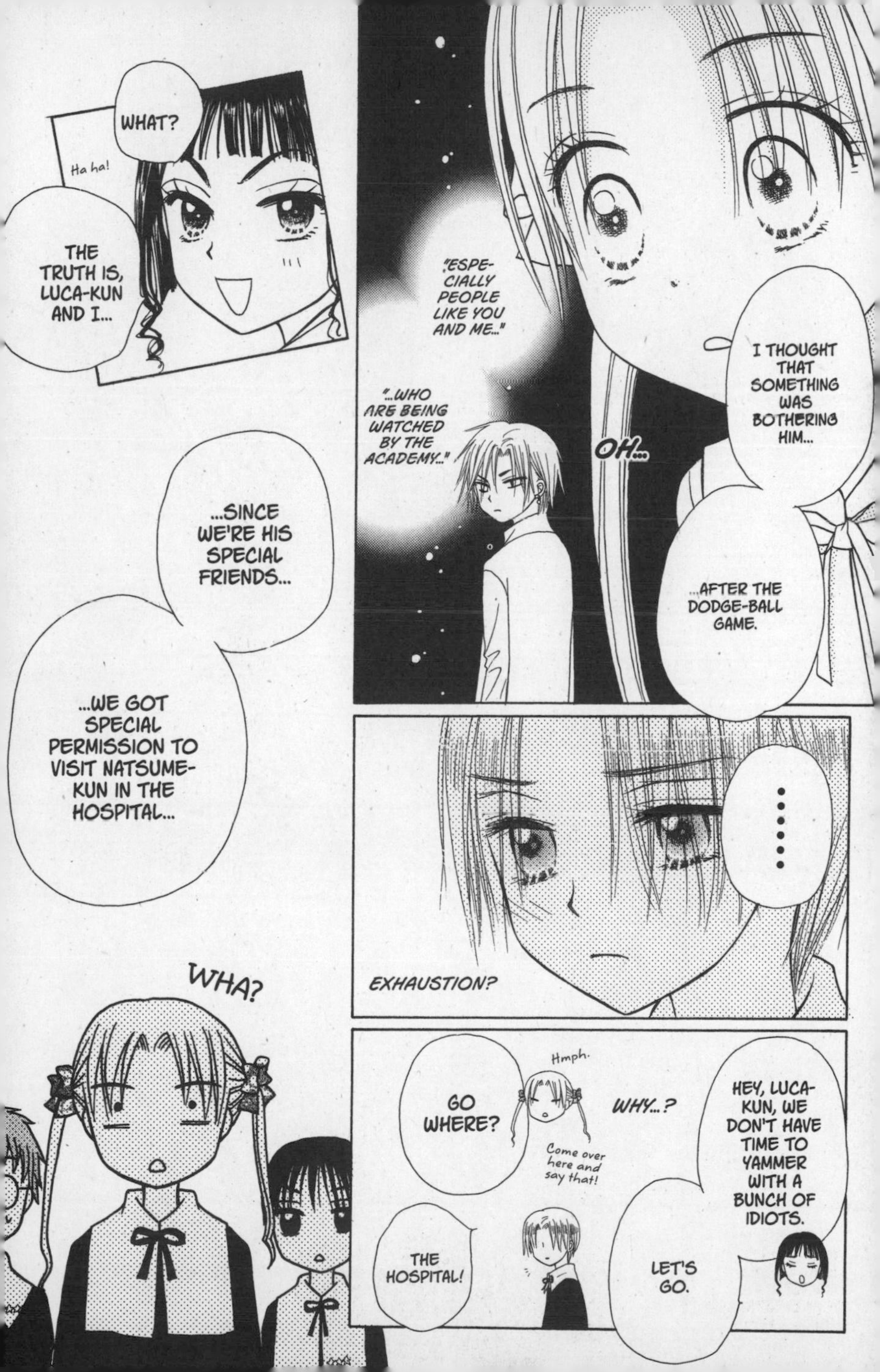
I THOUGHT THAT SOMETHING WAS BOTHERING HIM...
...AFTER THE DODGE-BALL GAME.
OH...
"ESPE-CIALLY PEOPLE LIKE YOU AND ME..."
"...WHO ARE BEING WATCHED BY THE ACADEMY..."
......
EXHAUSTION?
HEY, LUCA-KUN, WE DON'T HAVE TIME TO YAMMER WITH A BUNCH OF IDIOTS.
LET'S GO.
WHY...?
Hmph.
Come over here and say that!
GO WHERE?
THE HOSPITAL!
WHAT?
Ha ha!
THE TRUTH IS, LUCA-KUN AND I...
...SINCE WE'RE HIS SPECIAL FRIENDS...
...WE GOT SPECIAL PERMISSION TO VISIT NATSUME-KUN IN THE HOSPITAL...
WHA?

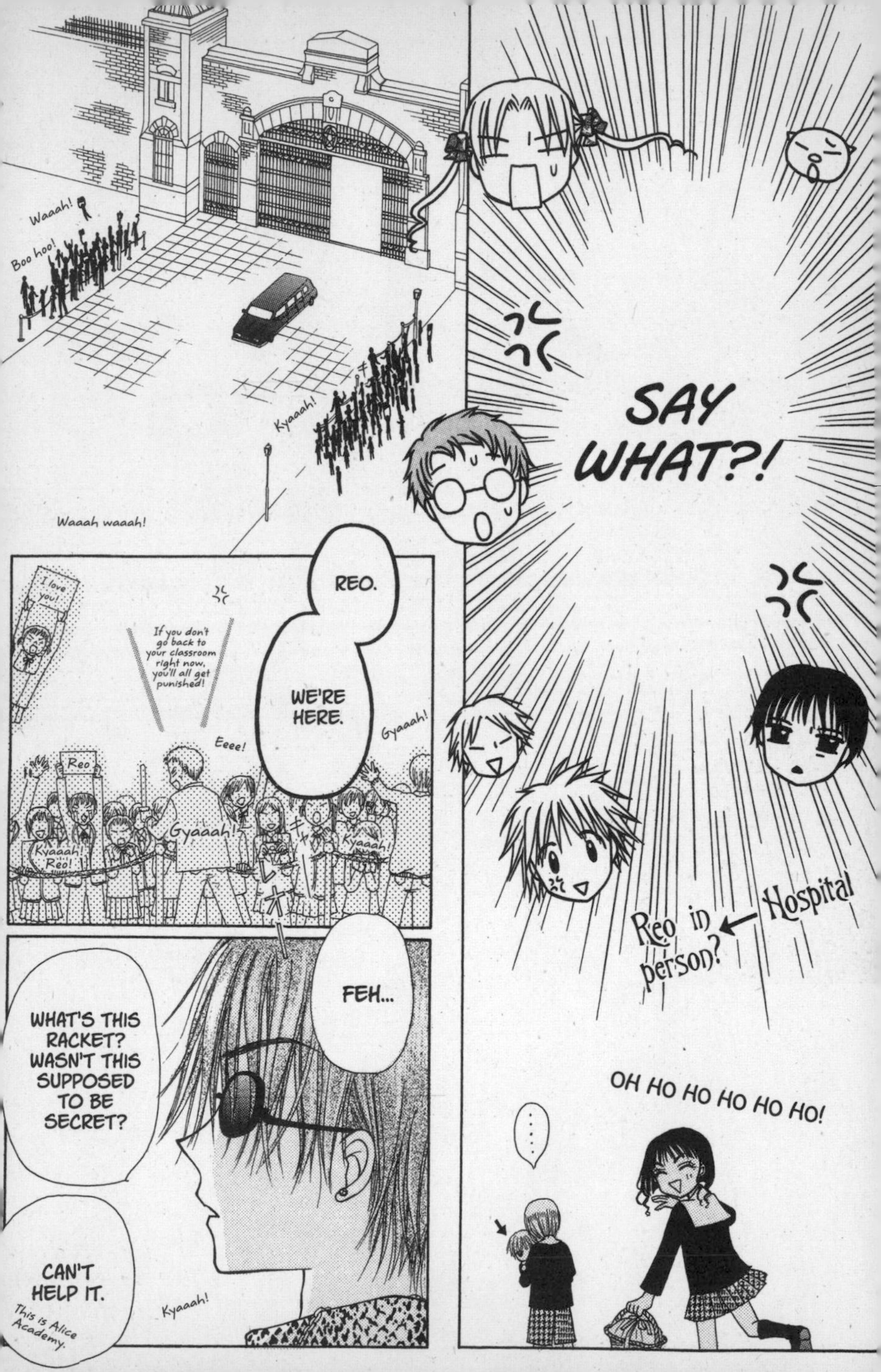
SAY WHAT?!
Hospital
Reo in person?
OH HO HO HO HO HO!
......
Waaah!
Boo hoo!
Kyaaah!
Waaah waaah!
REO.
WE'RE HERE.
Gyaaah!
If you don't go back to your classroom right now, you'll all get punished!
I love you!
Eeee!
Reo
Kyaaah!
Gyaaah!
Kyaaah! Reo!
FEH...
WHAT'S THIS RACKET? WASN'T THIS SUPPOSED TO BE SECRET?
Kyaaah!
CAN'T HELP IT.
This is Alice Academy.

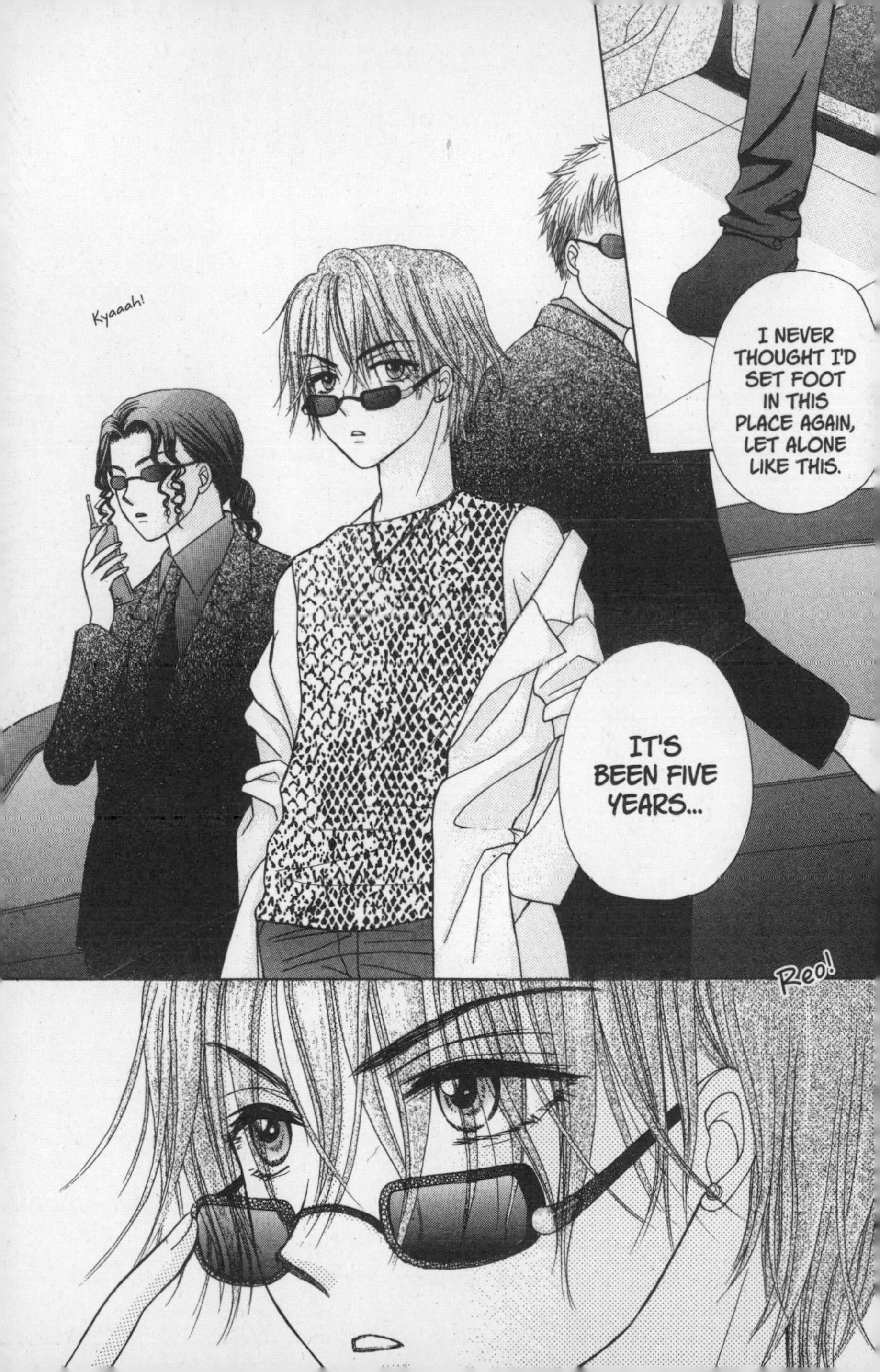
I NEVER THOUGHT I'D SET FOOT IN THIS PLACE AGAIN, LET ALONE LIKE THIS.
IT'S BEEN FIVE YEARS...
Kyaaah!
Reo!

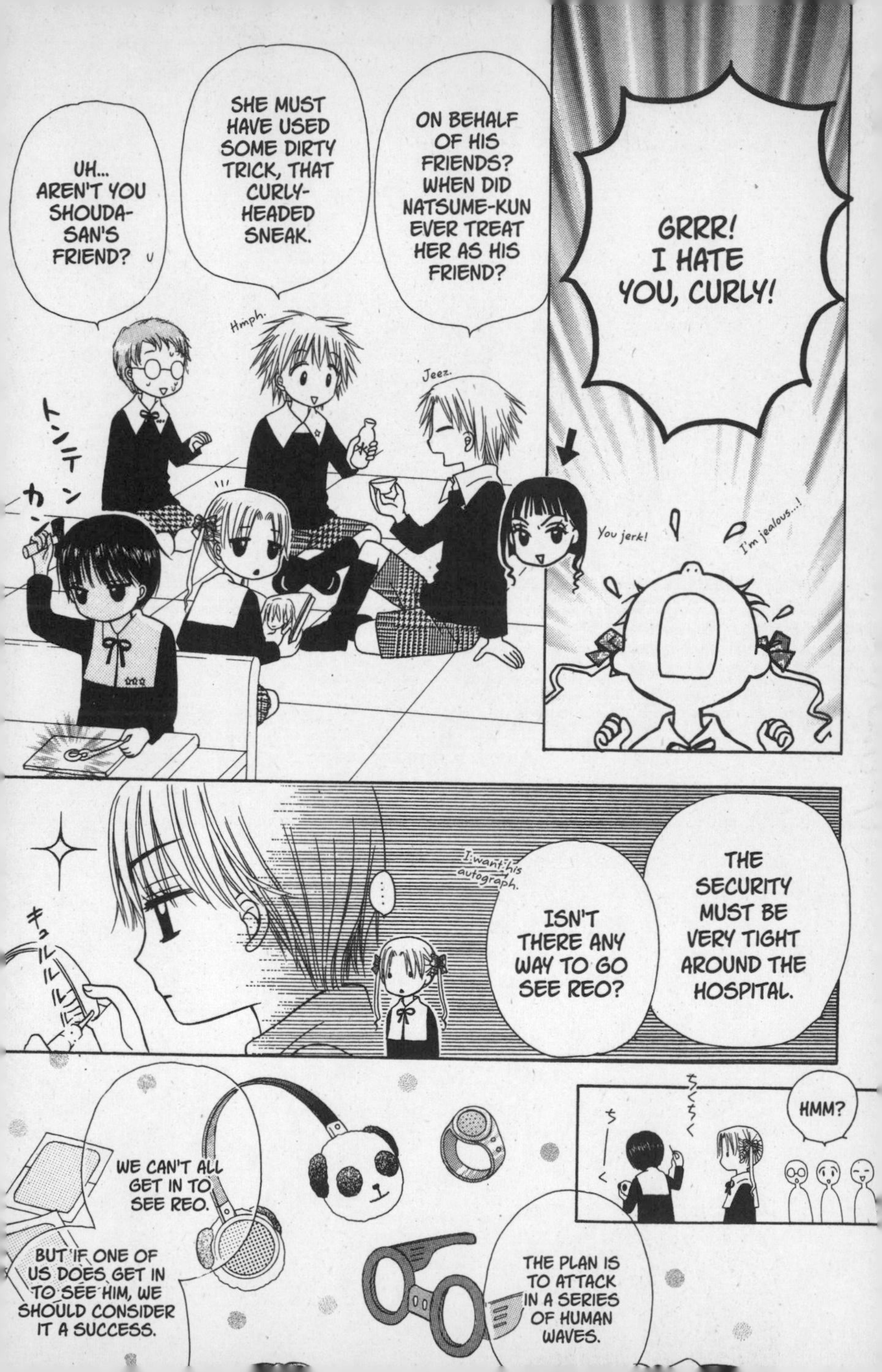
GRRR! I HATE YOU, CURLY!
You jerk!
I'm jealous...!
ON BEHALF OF HIS FRIENDS? WHEN DID NATSUME-KUN EVER TREAT HER AS HIS FRIEND?
SHE MUST HAVE USED SOME DIRTY TRICK, THAT CURLY-HEADED SNEAK.
UH... AREN'T YOU SHOUDA-SAN'S FRIEND?
Hmph.
Jeez.
トンテンカン
THE SECURITY MUST BE VERY TIGHT AROUND THE HOSPITAL.
ISN'T THERE ANY WAY TO GO SEE REO?
I want his autograph.
...
キュルルル
HMM?
ちくちく
ち一く
THE PLAN IS TO ATTACK IN A SERIES OF HUMAN WAVES.
WE CAN'T ALL GET IN TO SEE REO.
BUT IF ONE OF US DOES GET IN TO SEE HIM, WE SHOULD CONSIDER IT A SUCCESS.

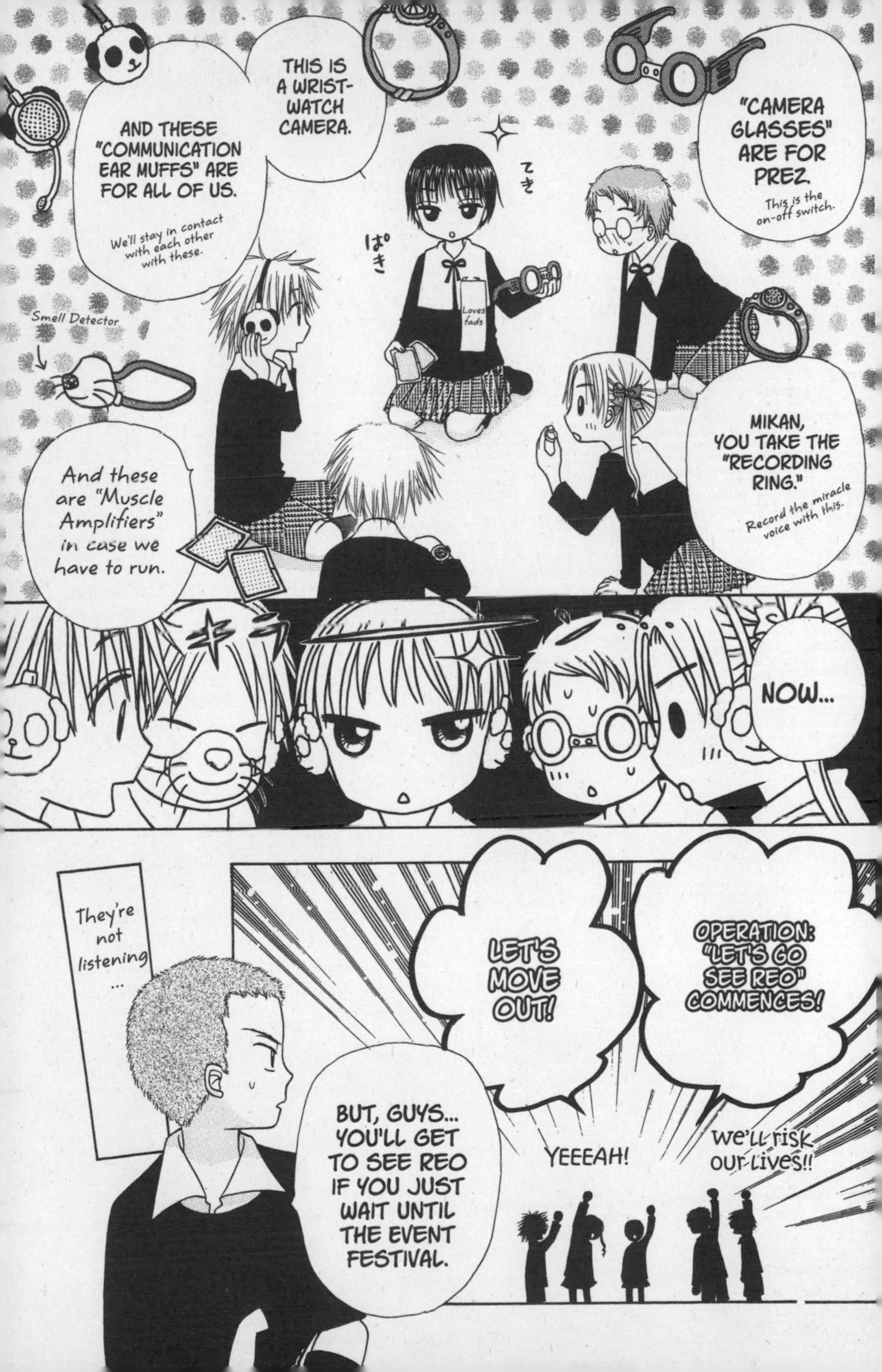
"CAMERA GLASSES" ARE FOR PREZ.
This is the on-off switch.
THIS IS A WRIST-WATCH CAMERA.
てき
ぱき
AND THESE "COMMUNICATION EAR MUFFS" ARE FOR ALL OF US.
We'll stay in contact with each other with these.
Loves fads
MIKAN, YOU TAKE THE "RECORDING RING."
Record the miracle voice with this.
Smell Detector
And these are "Muscle Amplifiers" in case we have to run.
NOW...
OPERATION: "LET'S GO SEE REO" COMMENCES!
LET'S MOVE OUT!
We'll risk our lives!!
YEEEAH!
BUT, GUYS... YOU'LL GET TO SEE REO IF YOU JUST WAIT UNTIL THE EVENT FESTIVAL.
They're not listening ...

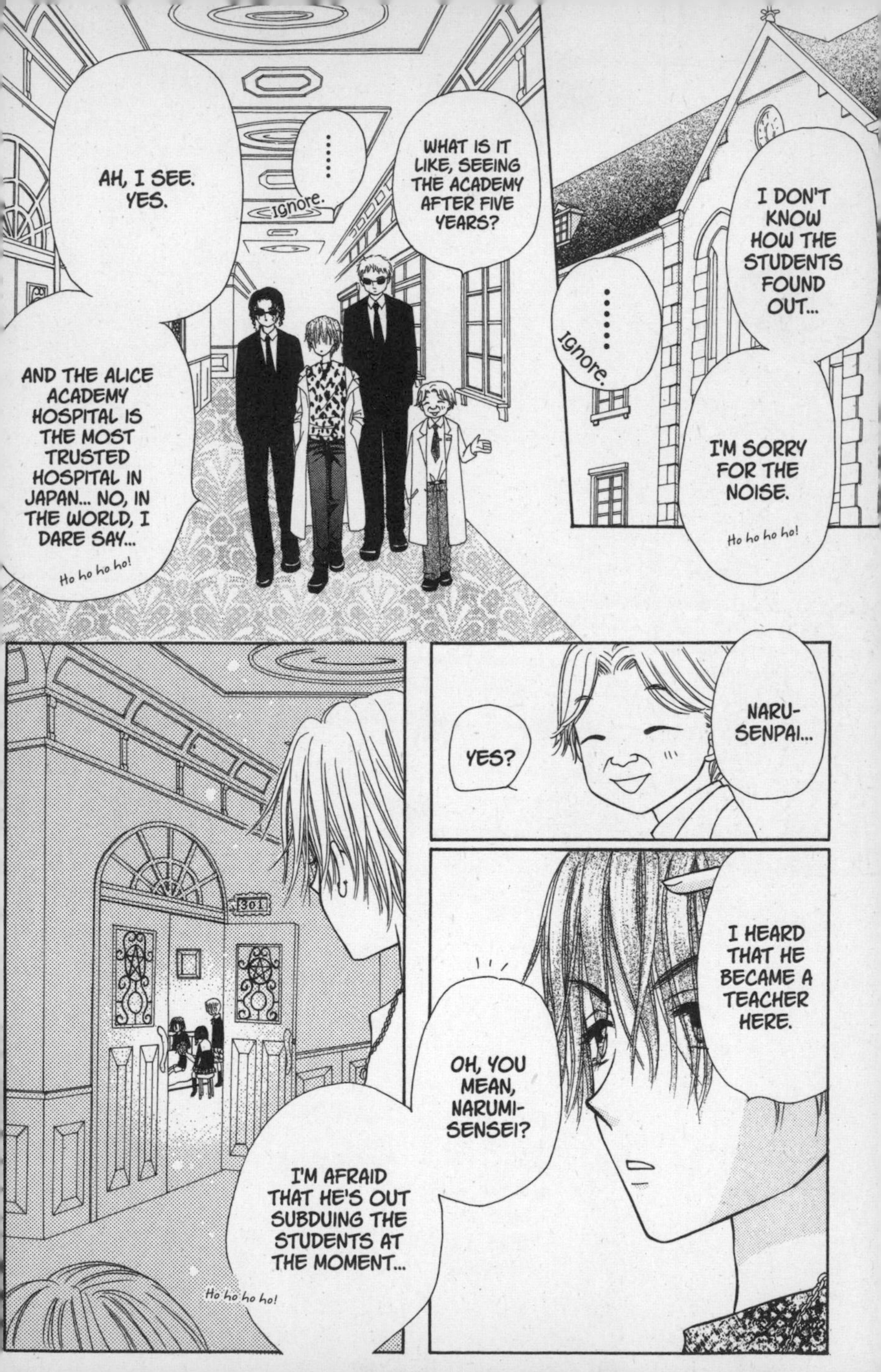
I DON'T KNOW HOW THE STUDENTS FOUND OUT...
......
Ignore.
I'M SORRY FOR THE NOISE.
Ho ho ho ho!
WHAT IS IT LIKE, SEEING THE ACADEMY AFTER FIVE YEARS?
......
Ignore.
AH, I SEE. YES.
AND THE ALICE ACADEMY HOSPITAL IS THE MOST TRUSTED HOSPITAL IN JAPAN... NO, IN THE WORLD, I DARE SAY...
Ho ho ho ho!
NARU-SENPAI...
YES?
I HEARD THAT HE BECAME A TEACHER HERE.
OH, YOU MEAN, NARUMI-SENSEI?
I'M AFRAID THAT HE'S OUT SUBDUING THE STUDENTS AT THE MOMENT...
Ho ho ho ho!
301

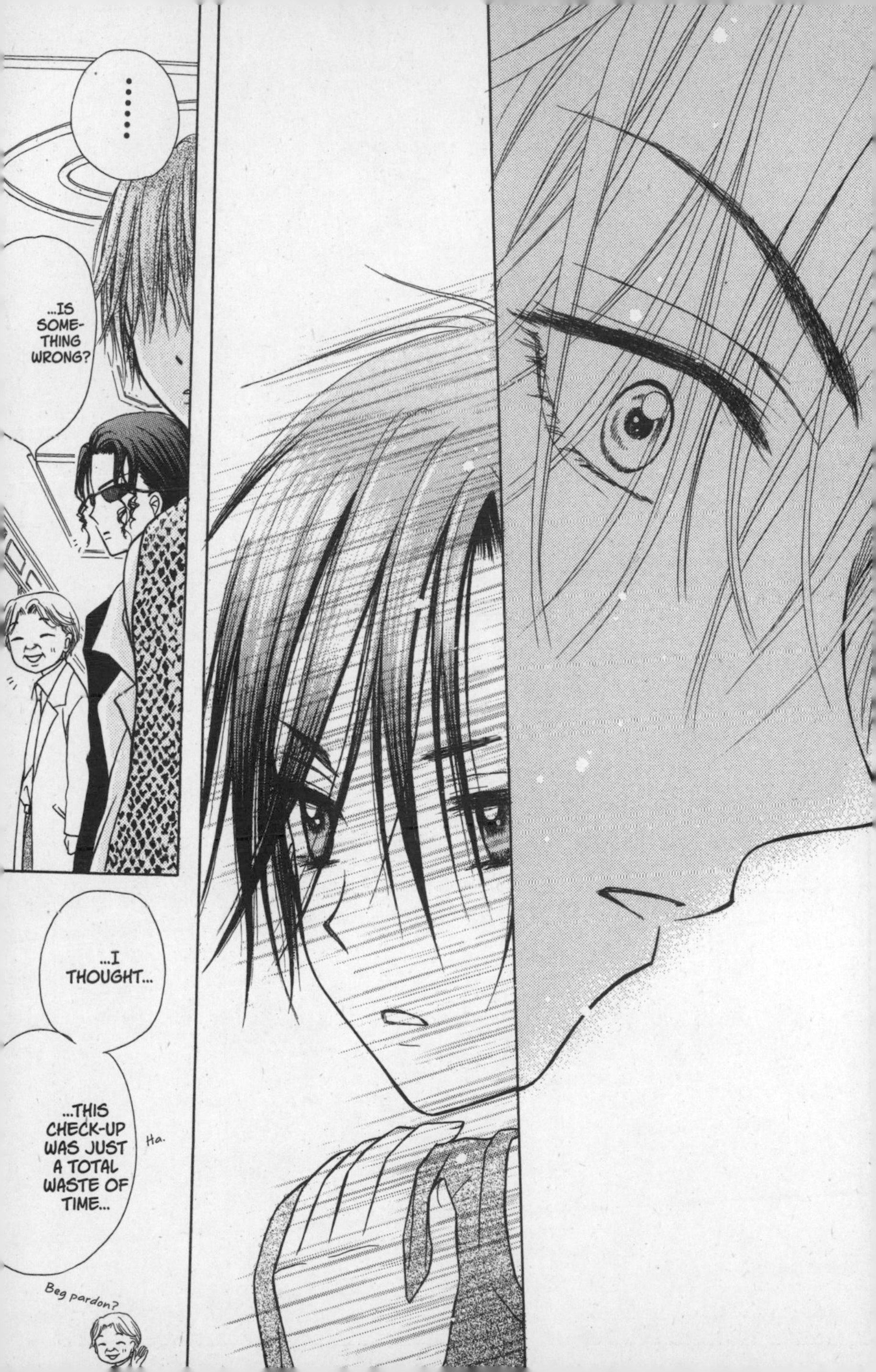
......
...IS SOMETHING WRONG?
...I THOUGHT...
...THIS CHECK-UP WAS JUST A TOTAL WASTE OF TIME...
Ha.
Beg pardon?

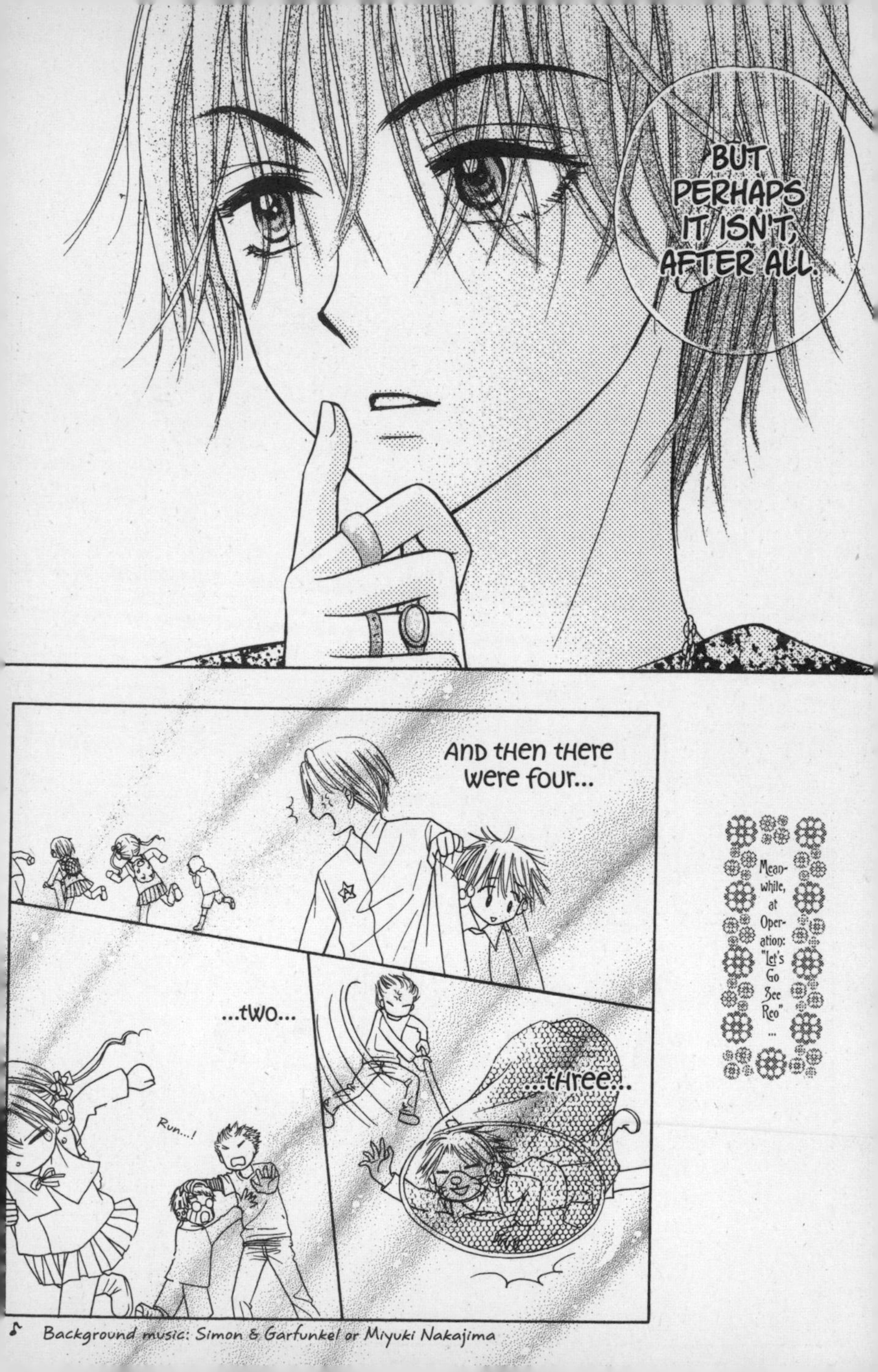
BUT PERHAPS IT ISN'T, AFTER ALL.
Meanwhile, at Operation: "Let's Go See Reo"...
And then there were four...
...three...
...two...
Run...!

♪ Background music: Simon & Garfunkel or Miyuki Nakajima

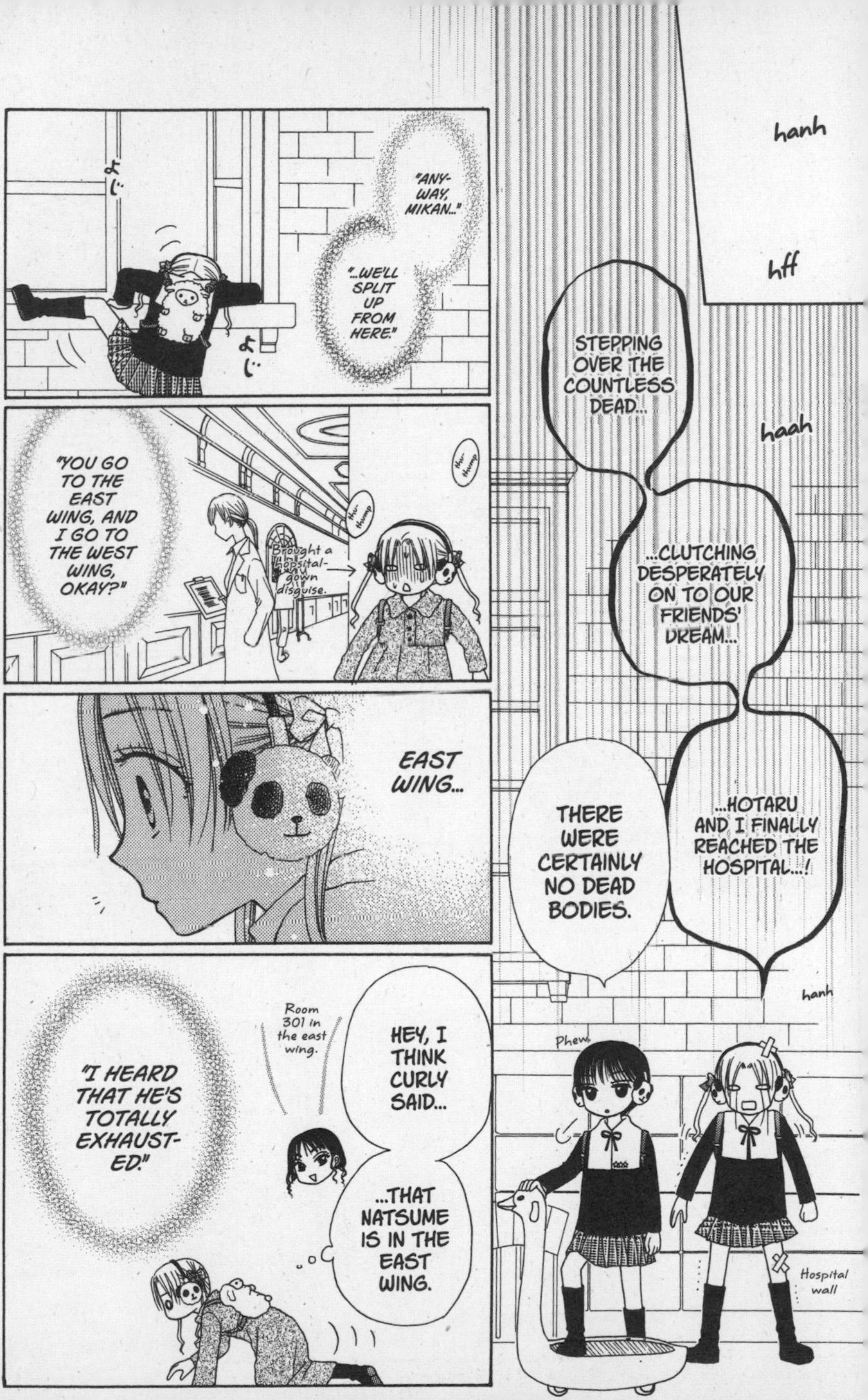
hanh
hff
STEPPING OVER THE COUNTLESS DEAD...
haah
...CLUTCHING DESPERATELY ON TO OUR FRIENDS' DREAM...
...HOTARU AND I FINALLY REACHED THE HOSPITAL...!
THERE WERE CERTAINLY NO DEAD BODIES.
hanh
Phew
Hospital wall
"ANY-WAY, MIKAN..."
"...WE'LL SPLIT UP FROM HERE."
よじ
よじ
Hu-Hump
Hu-Hump
Brought a hopsital-gown disguise.
"YOU GO TO THE EAST WING, AND I GO TO THE WEST WING, OKAY?"
EAST WING...
HEY, I THINK CURLY SAID...
...THAT NATSUME IS IN THE EAST WING.
Room 301 in the east wing.
"I HEARD THAT HE'S TOTALLY EXHAUSTED."

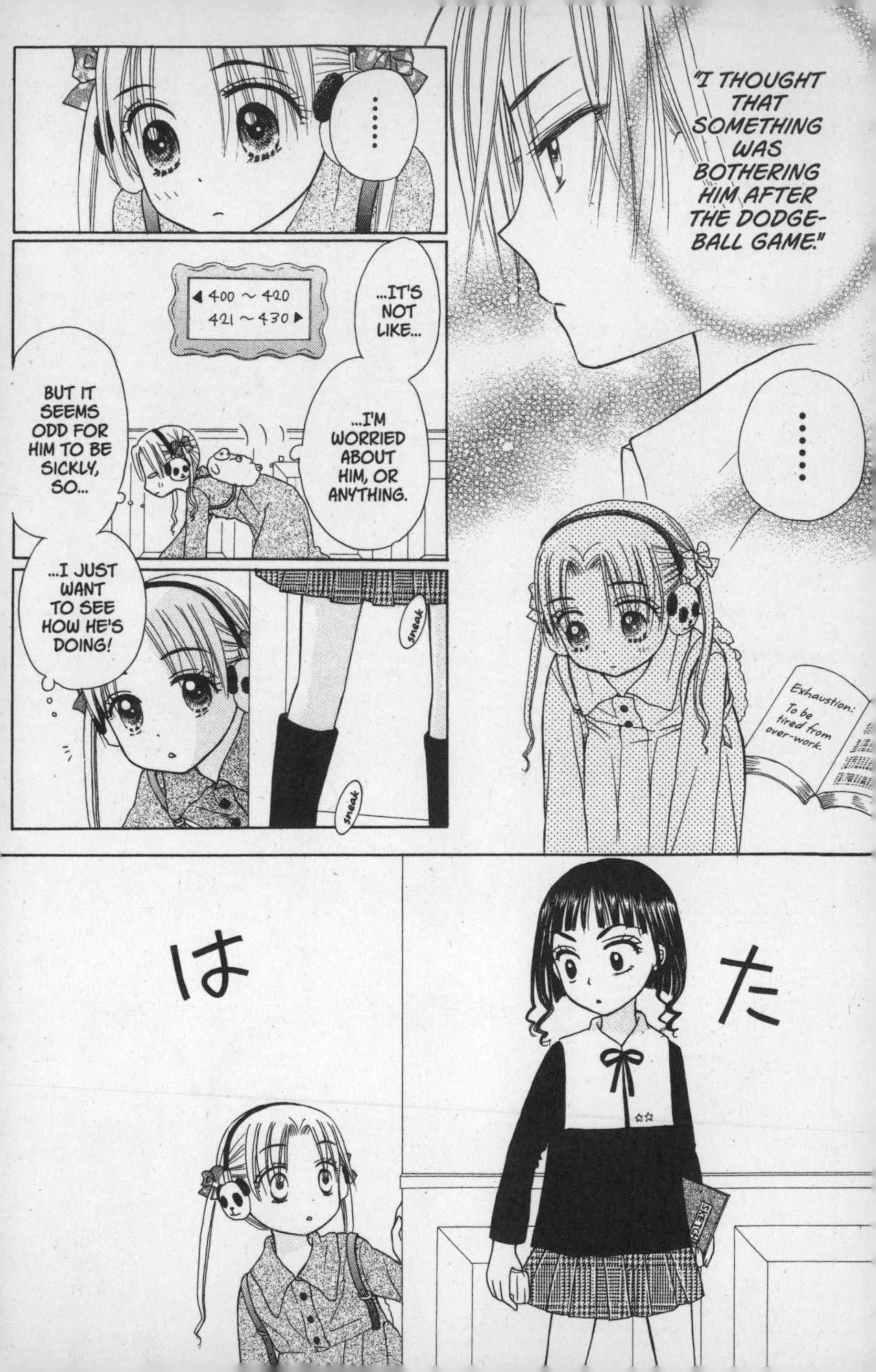
"I THOUGHT THAT SOMETHING WAS BOTHERING HIM AFTER THE DODGE-BALL GAME."
......
Exhaustion: To be tired from over-work.
......
400 ~ 420
421 ~ 430
...IT'S NOT LIKE...
...I'M WORRIED ABOUT HIM, OR ANYTHING.
BUT IT SEEMS ODD FOR HIM TO BE SICKLY, SO...
sneak
sneak
...I JUST WANT TO SEE HOW HE'S DOING!
た
は

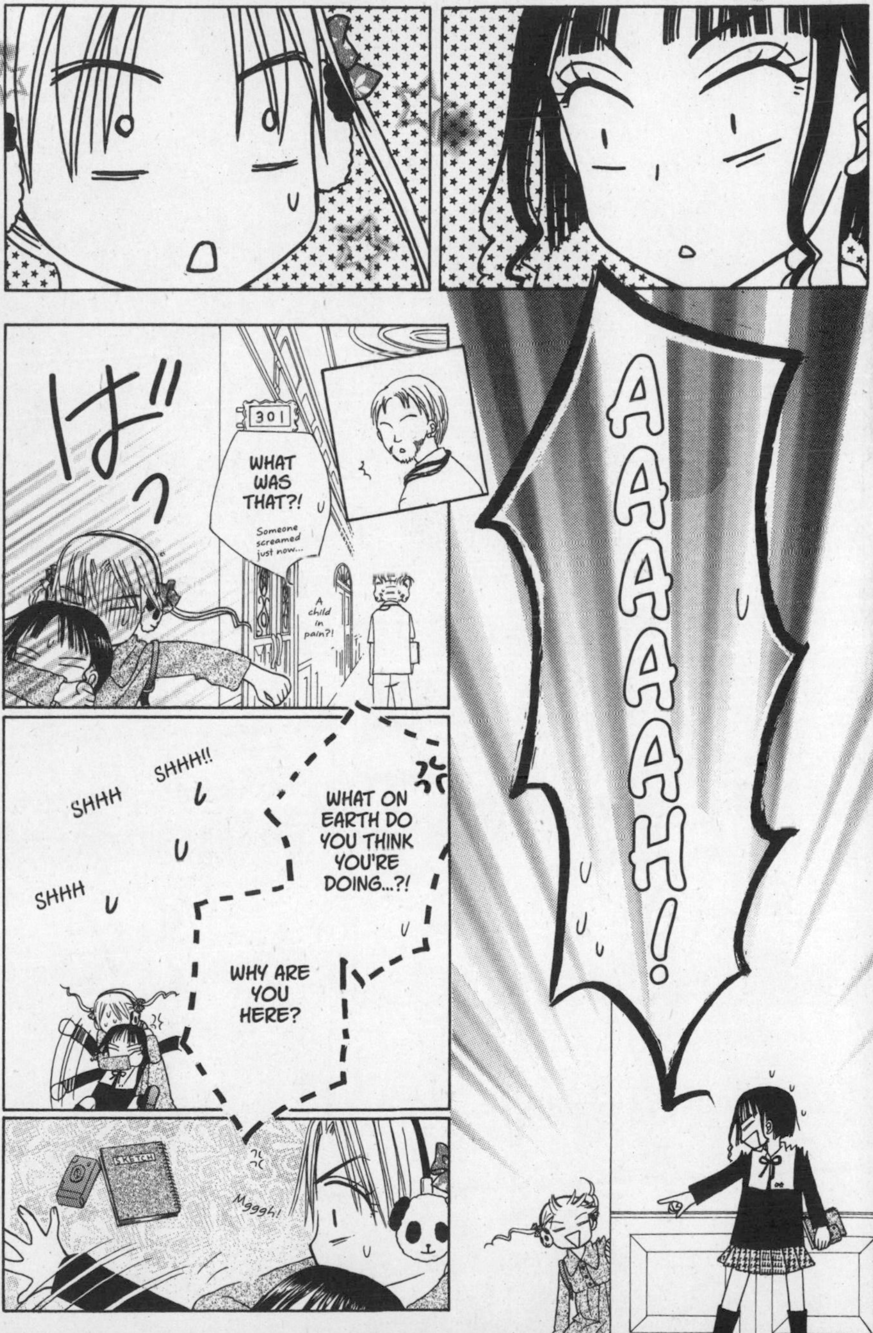
AAAAAAH!
301
WHAT WAS THAT?!
Someone screamed just now...
A child in pain?!
ばっ
WHAT ON EARTH DO YOU THINK YOU'RE DOING...?!
WHY ARE YOU HERE?
SHHH!!
SHHH
SHHH
SKETCH
Mgggh!

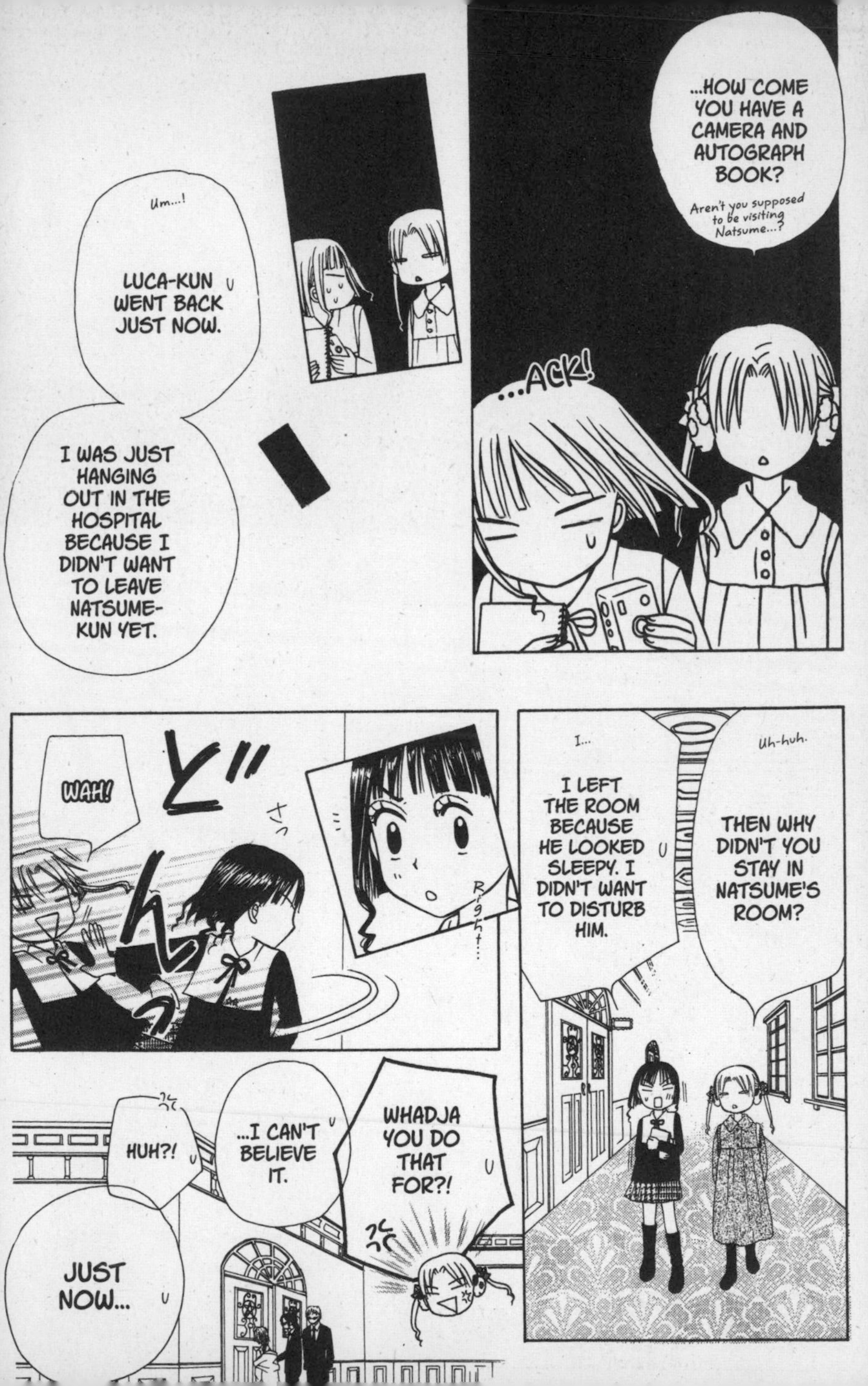
...HOW COME YOU HAVE A CAMERA AND AUTOGRAPH BOOK?
Aren't you supposed to be visiting Natsume...?
...ACK!
Um...!
LUCA-KUN WENT BACK JUST NOW.
I WAS JUST HANGING OUT IN THE HOSPITAL BECAUSE I DIDN'T WANT TO LEAVE NATSUME-KUN YET.
Uh-huh.
THEN WHY DIDN'T YOU STAY IN NATSUME'S ROOM?
I...
I LEFT THE ROOM BECAUSE HE LOOKED SLEEPY. I DIDN'T WANT TO DISTURB HIM.
Right...
WAH!
WHADJA YOU DO THAT FOR?!
...I CAN'T BELIEVE IT.
HUH?!
JUST NOW...

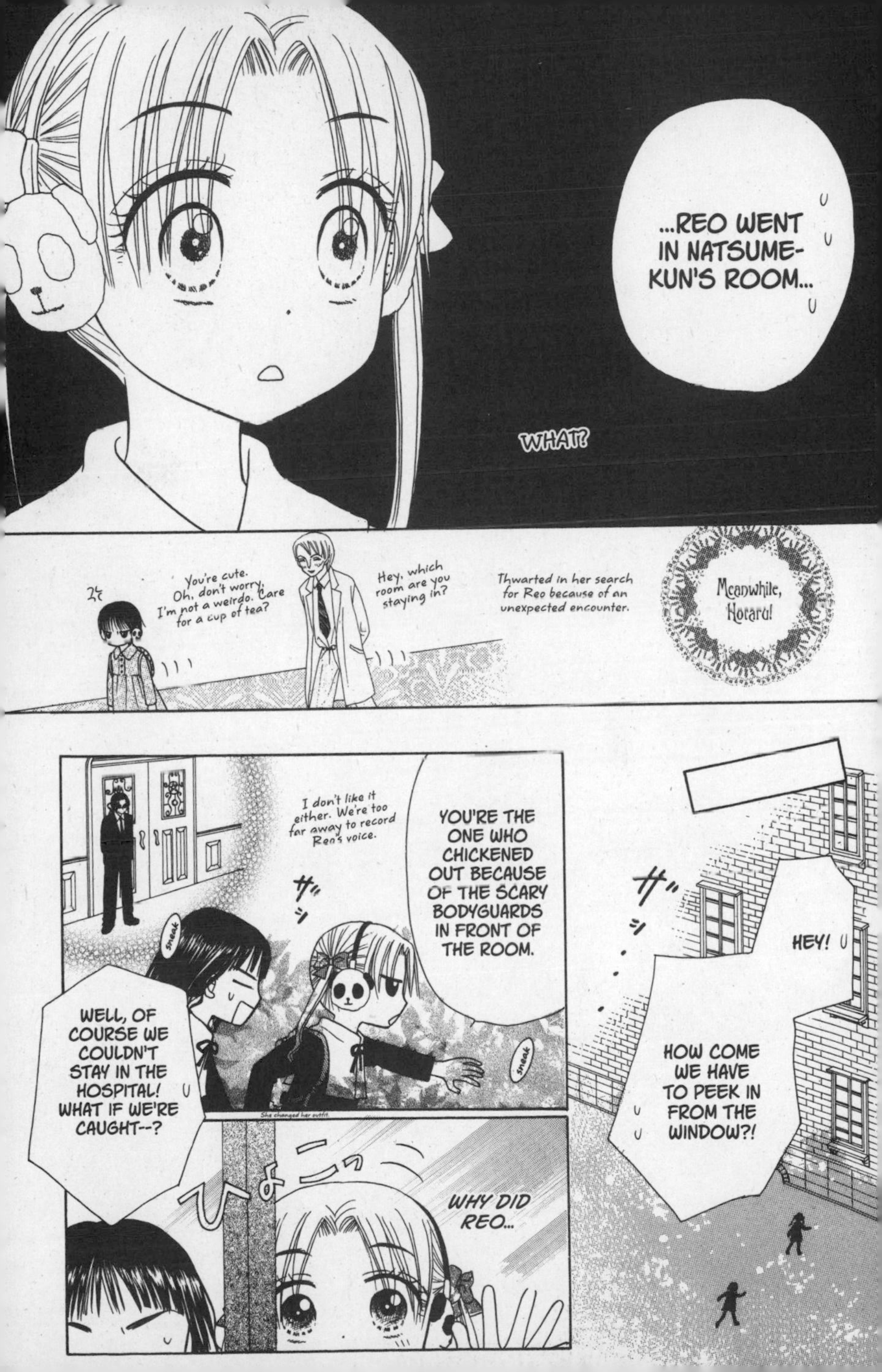

...REO WENT IN NATSUME-KUN'S ROOM...
WHAT?
Meanwhile, Hotaru!
Thwarted in her search for Reo because of an unexpected encounter.
Hey, which room are you staying in?
You're cute. Oh, don't worry. I'm not a weirdo. Care for a cup of tea?
HEY!
HOW COME WE HAVE TO PEEK IN FROM THE WINDOW?!
YOU'RE THE ONE WHO CHICKENED OUT BECAUSE OF THE SCARY BODYGUARDS IN FRONT OF THE ROOM.
I don't like it either. We're too far away to record Reo's voice.
sneak
sneak
WELL, OF COURSE WE COULDN'T STAY IN THE HOSPITAL! WHAT IF WE'RE CAUGHT--?
She changed her outfit.
WHY DID REO...

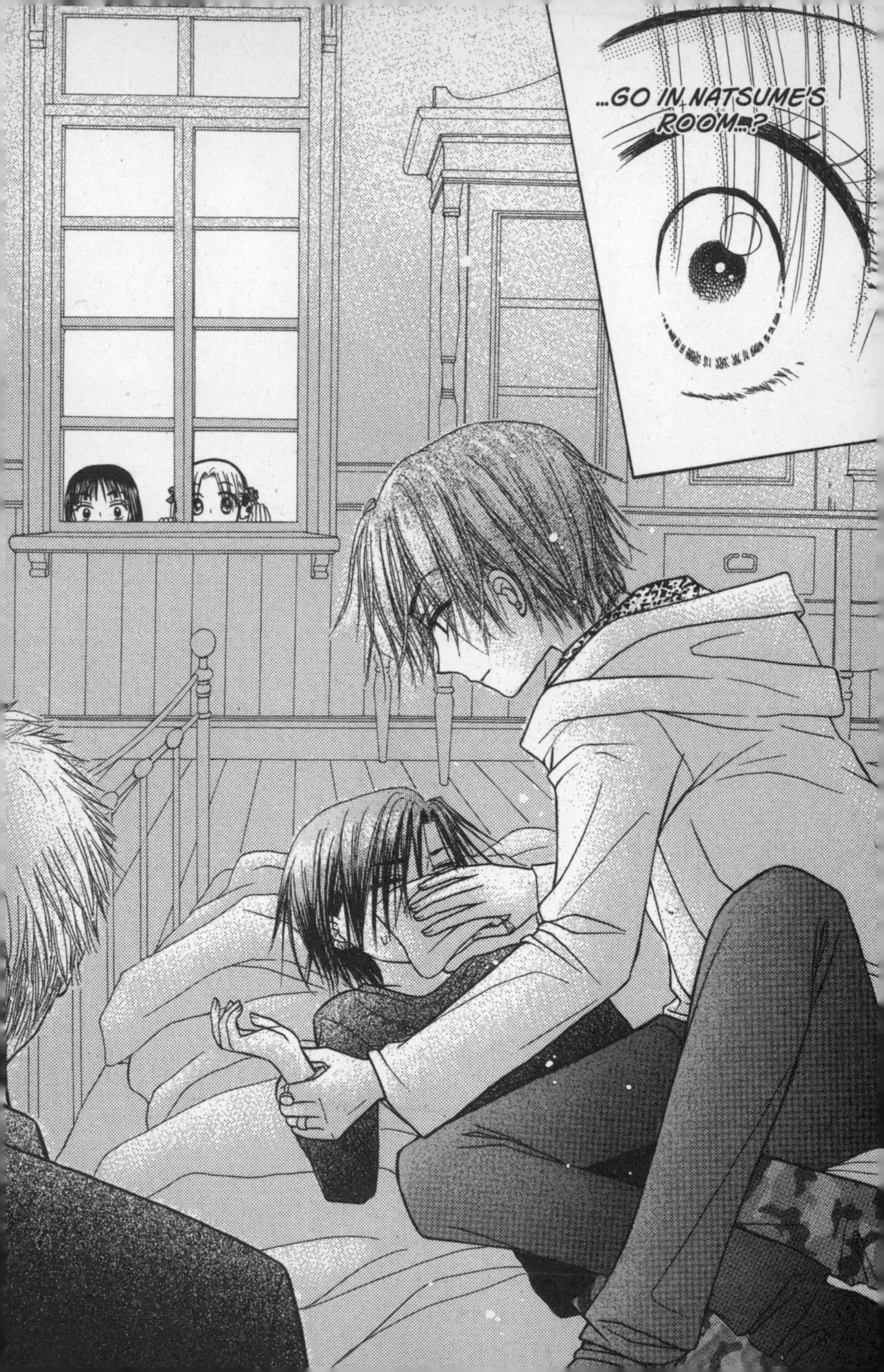
...GO IN NATSUME'S ROOM...?

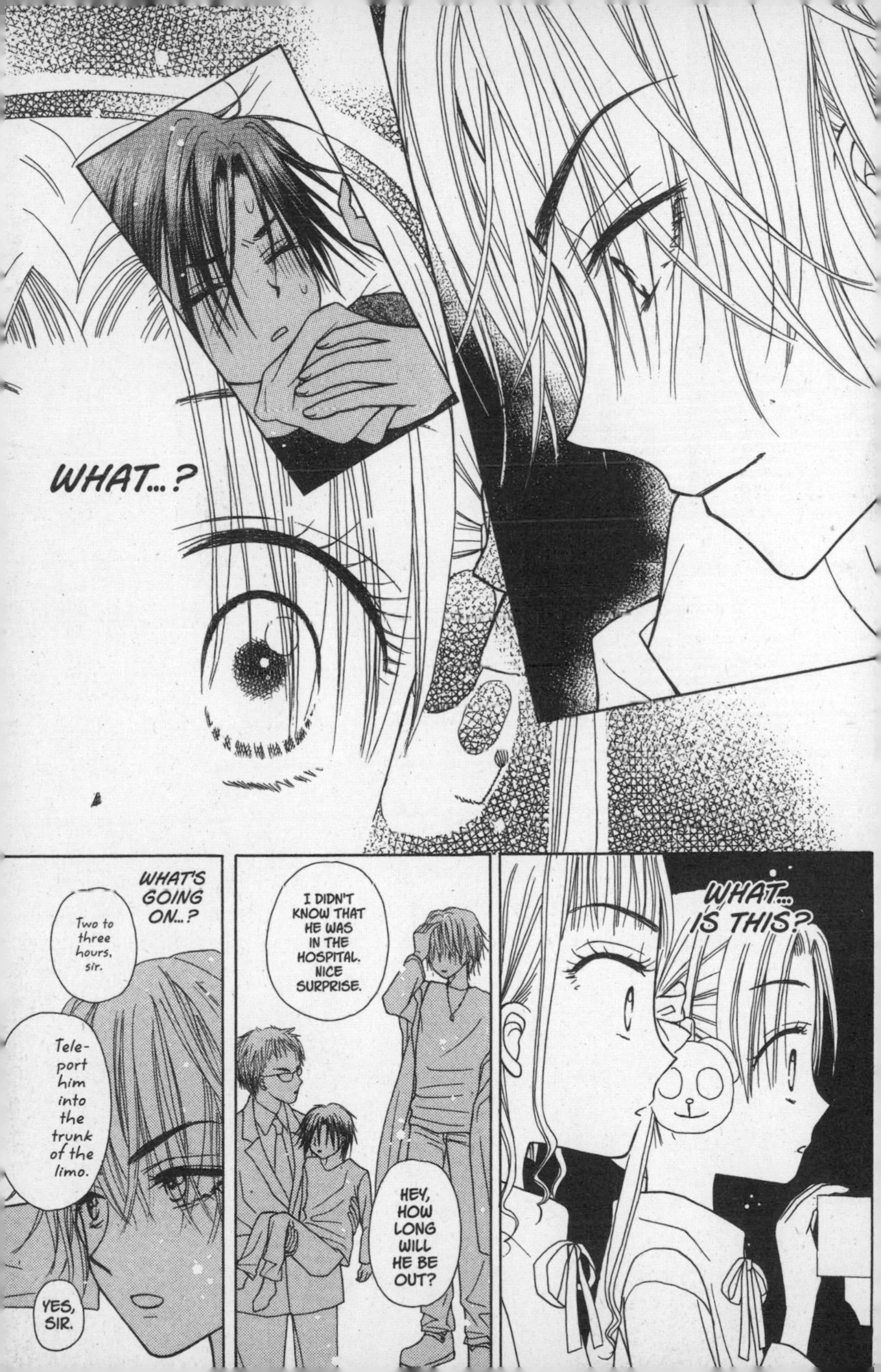
WHAT...?
WHAT... IS THIS?
I DIDN'T KNOW THAT HE WAS IN THE HOSPITAL. NICE SURPRISE.
HEY, HOW LONG WILL HE BE OUT?
WHAT'S GOING ON...?
Two to three hours, sir.
Tele-port him into the trunk of the limo.
YES, SIR.

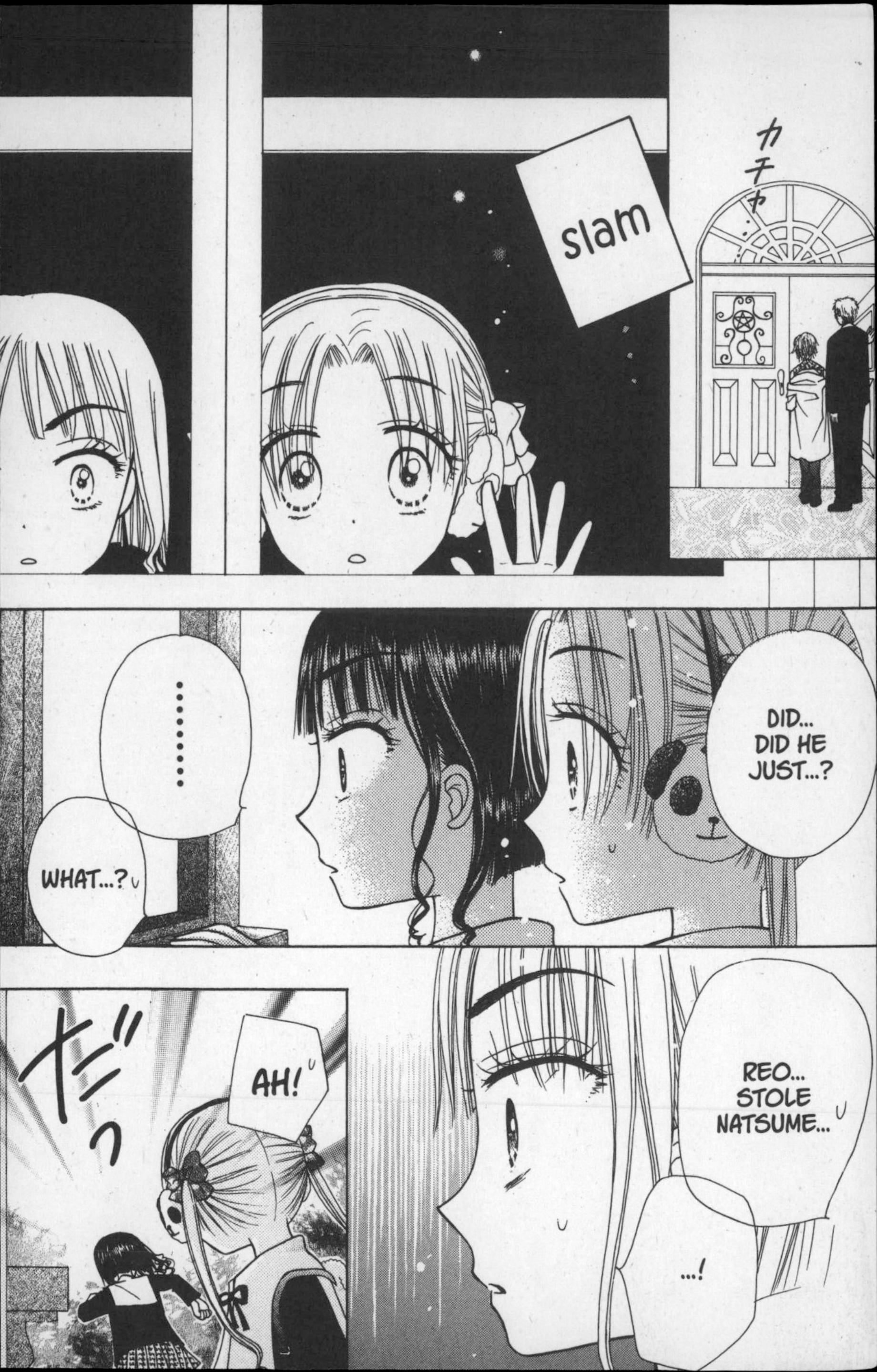
カチャ
slam
DID... DID HE JUST...?
......
WHAT...?
REO... STOLE NATSUME...
...!
AH!

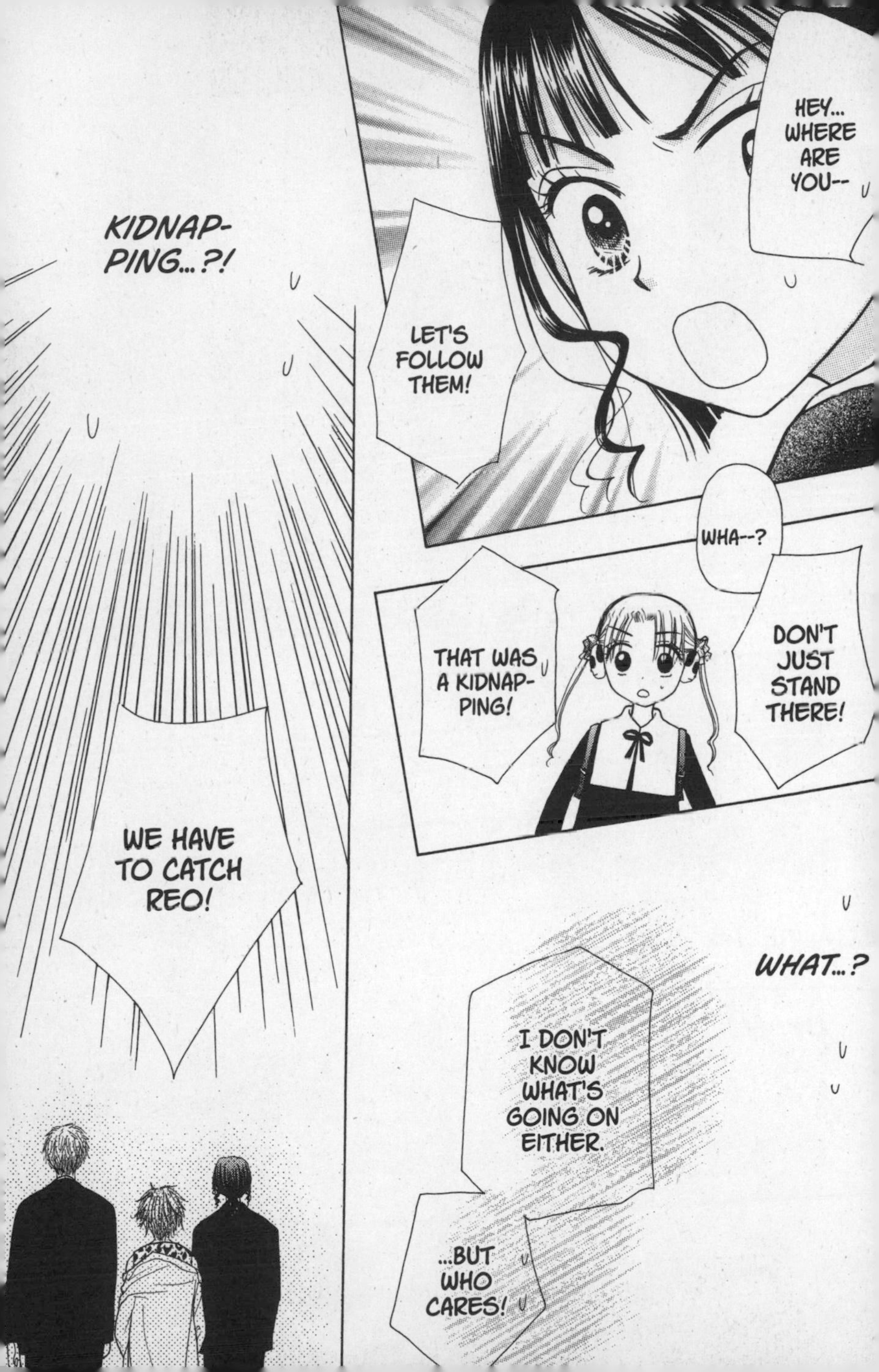
HEY... WHERE ARE YOU--
LET'S FOLLOW THEM!
WHA--?
DON'T JUST STAND THERE!
THAT WAS A KIDNAP-PING!
WHAT...?
I DON'T KNOW WHAT'S GOING ON EITHER.
...BUT WHO CARES!
KIDNAP-PING...?!
WE HAVE TO CATCH REO!

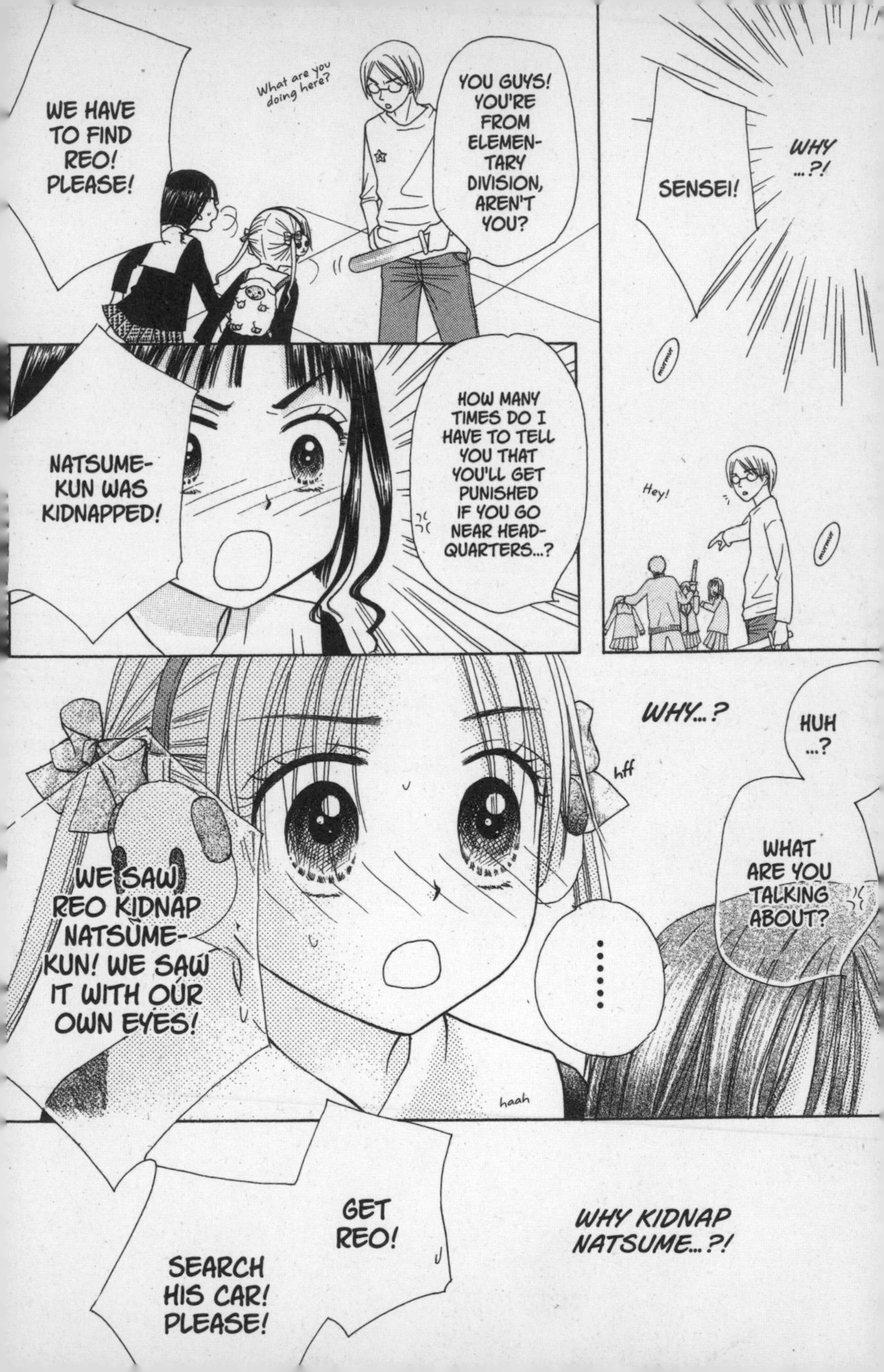
SENSEI!
WHY ...?!
murmur
Hey!
murmur
YOU GUYS! YOU'RE FROM ELEMENTARY DIVISION, AREN'T YOU?
What are you doing here?
WE HAVE TO FIND REO! PLEASE!
HOW MANY TIMES DO I HAVE TO TELL YOU THAT YOU'LL GET PUNISHED IF YOU GO NEAR HEADQUARTERS...?
NATSUME-KUN WAS KIDNAPPED!
WHY...?
HUH ...?
WHAT ARE YOU TALKING ABOUT?
hff
......
WE SAW REO KIDNAP NATSUME-KUN! WE SAW IT WITH OUR OWN EYES!
haah
WHY KIDNAP NATSUME...?!
GET REO!
SEARCH HIS CAR! PLEASE!

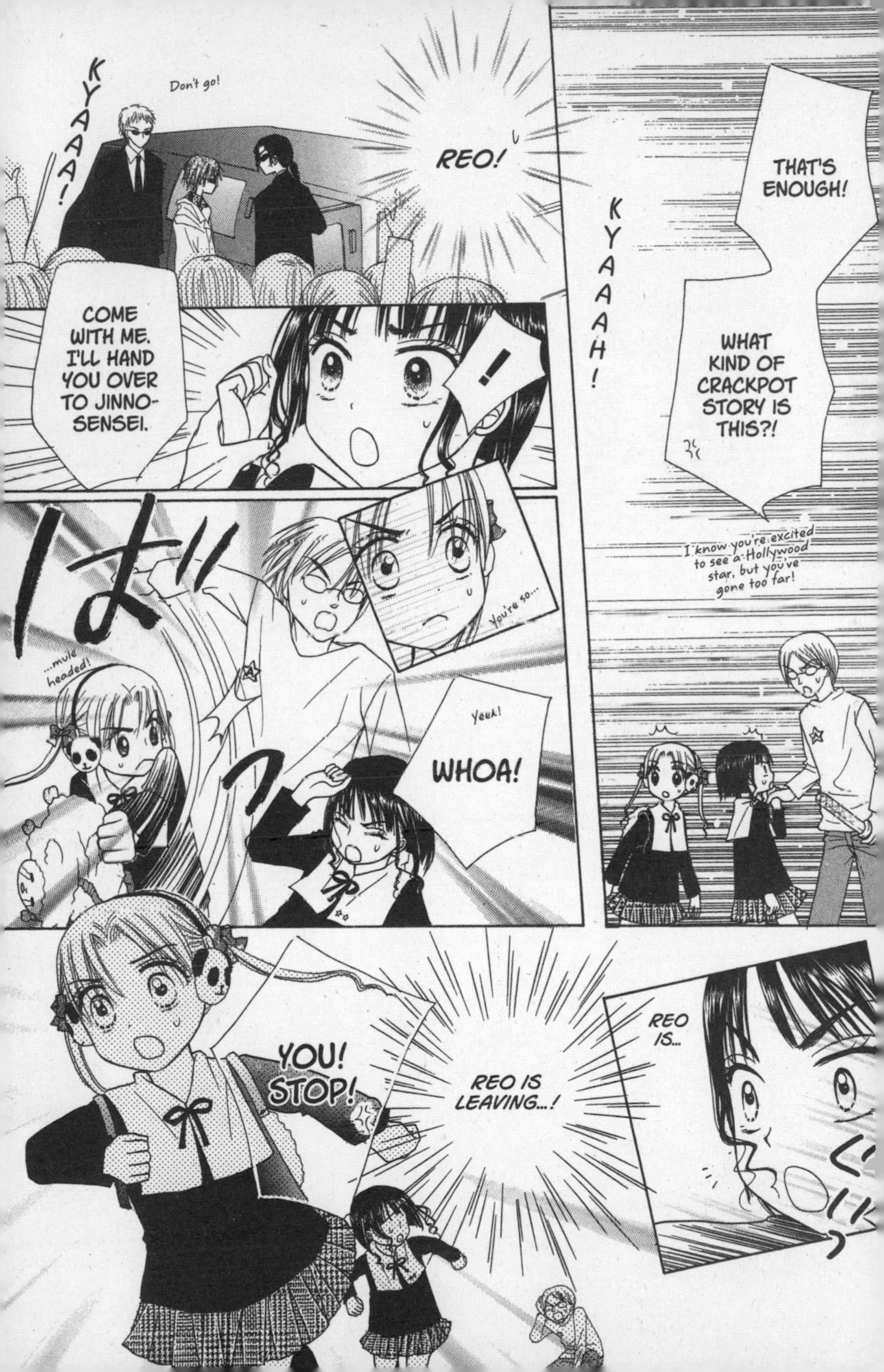
THAT'S ENOUGH!
WHAT KIND OF CRACKPOT STORY IS THIS?!
KYAAAAH!
I know you're excited to see a Hollywood star, but you've gone too far!
REO!
Don't go!
KYAAAA!
!
COME WITH ME. I'LL HAND YOU OVER TO JINNO-SENSEI.
You're so...
Yeek!
WHOA!
...mule headed!
REO IS...
REO IS LEAVING...!
YOU! STOP!

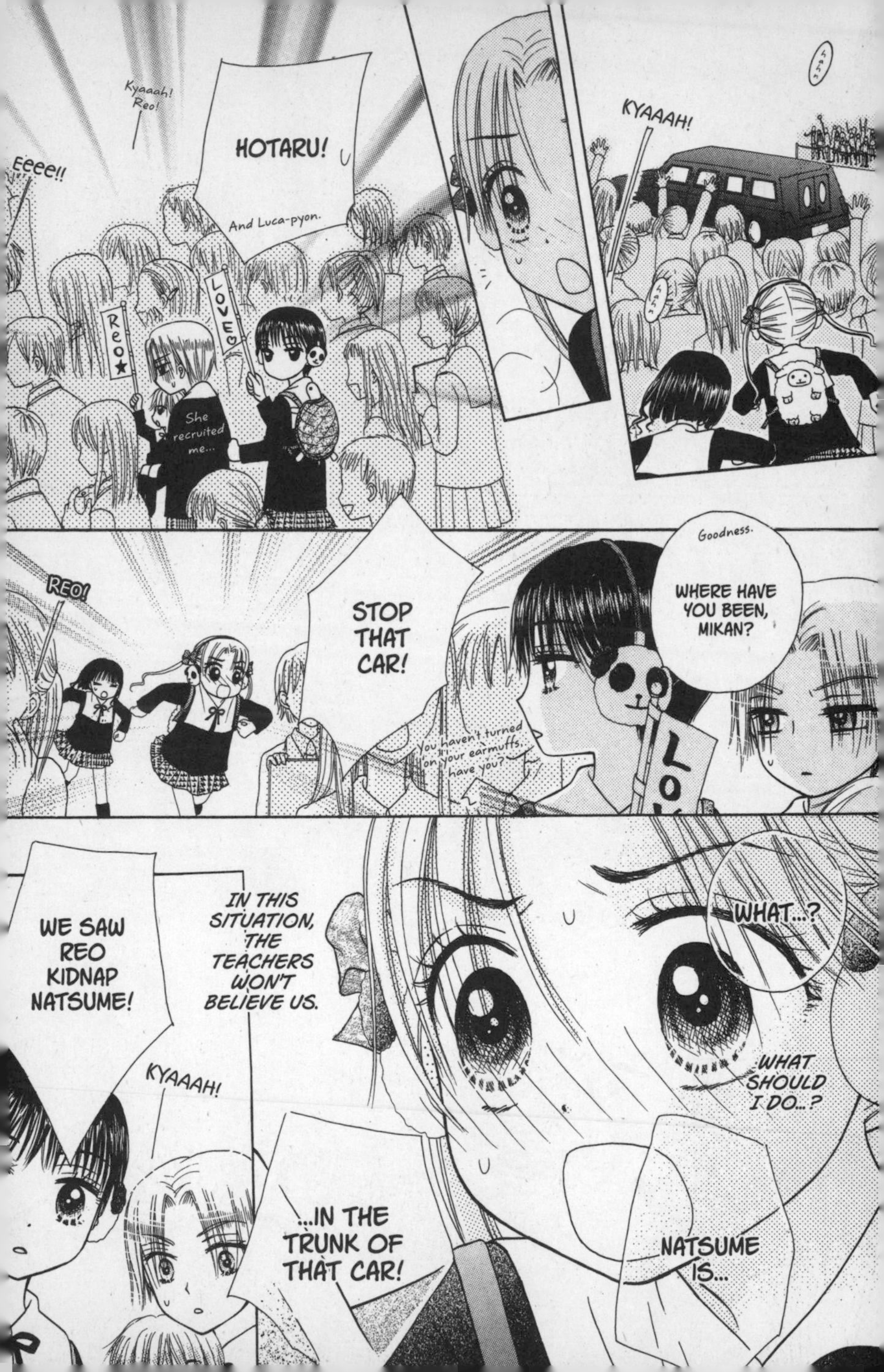
KYAAAH!
HOTARU!
And Luca-pyon.
Kyaaah! Reo!
Eeee!!
Reo★
LOVE♡
She recruited me...
Goodness.
WHERE HAVE YOU BEEN, MIKAN?
You haven't turned on your earmuffs, have you?
STOP THAT CAR!
REO!
WHAT...?
WHAT SHOULD I DO...?
NATSUME IS...
...IN THE TRUNK OF THAT CAR!
IN THIS SITUATION, THE TEACHERS WON'T BELIEVE US.
WE SAW REO KIDNAP NATSUME!
KYAAAH!

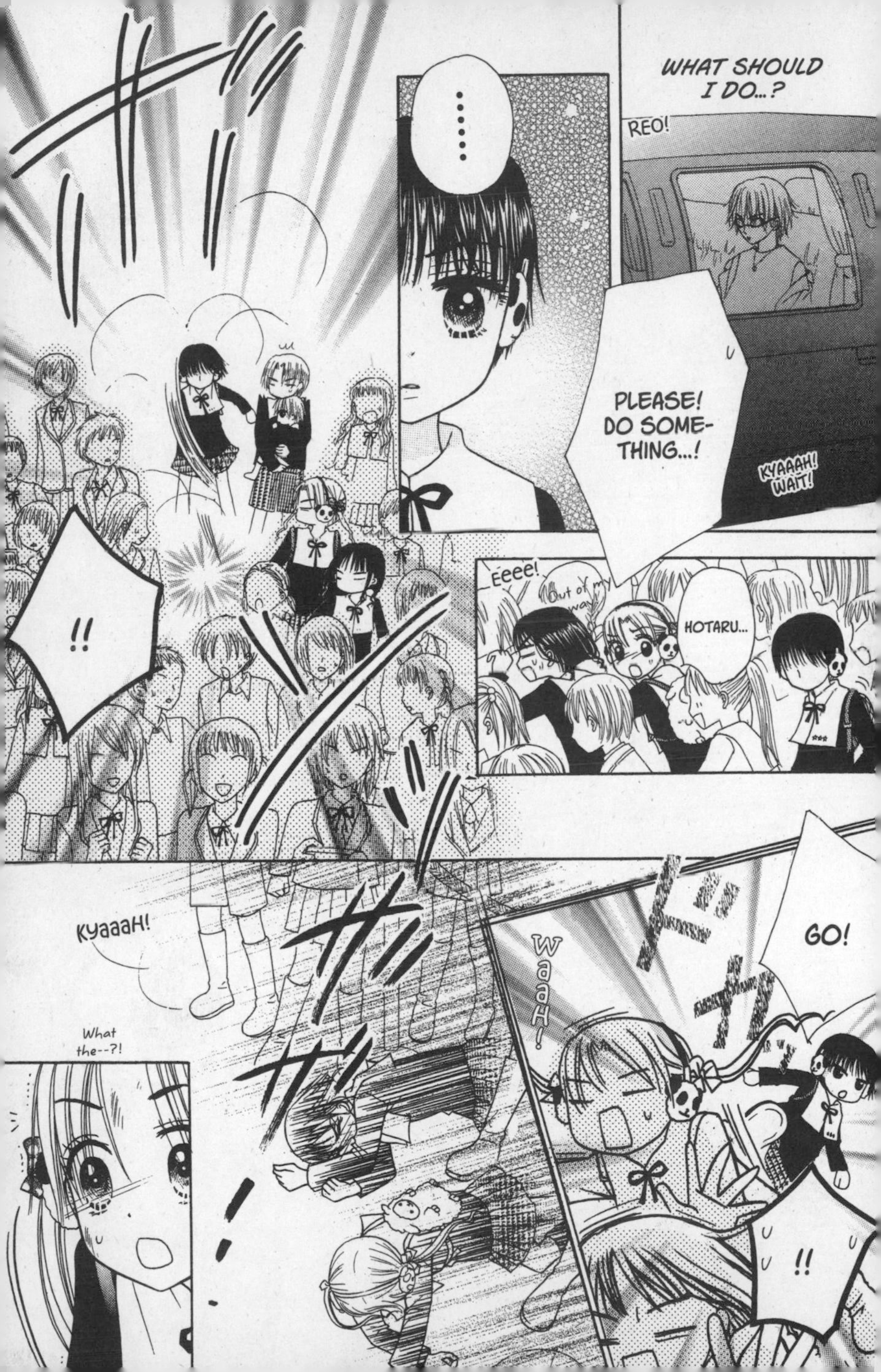
WHAT SHOULD I DO...?
REO!
PLEASE! DO SOME-THING...!
KYAAAH! WAIT!
......
Eeee!
Out of my way
HOTARU...
!!
GO!
WaaaH!
!!
KyaaaH!
What the--?!

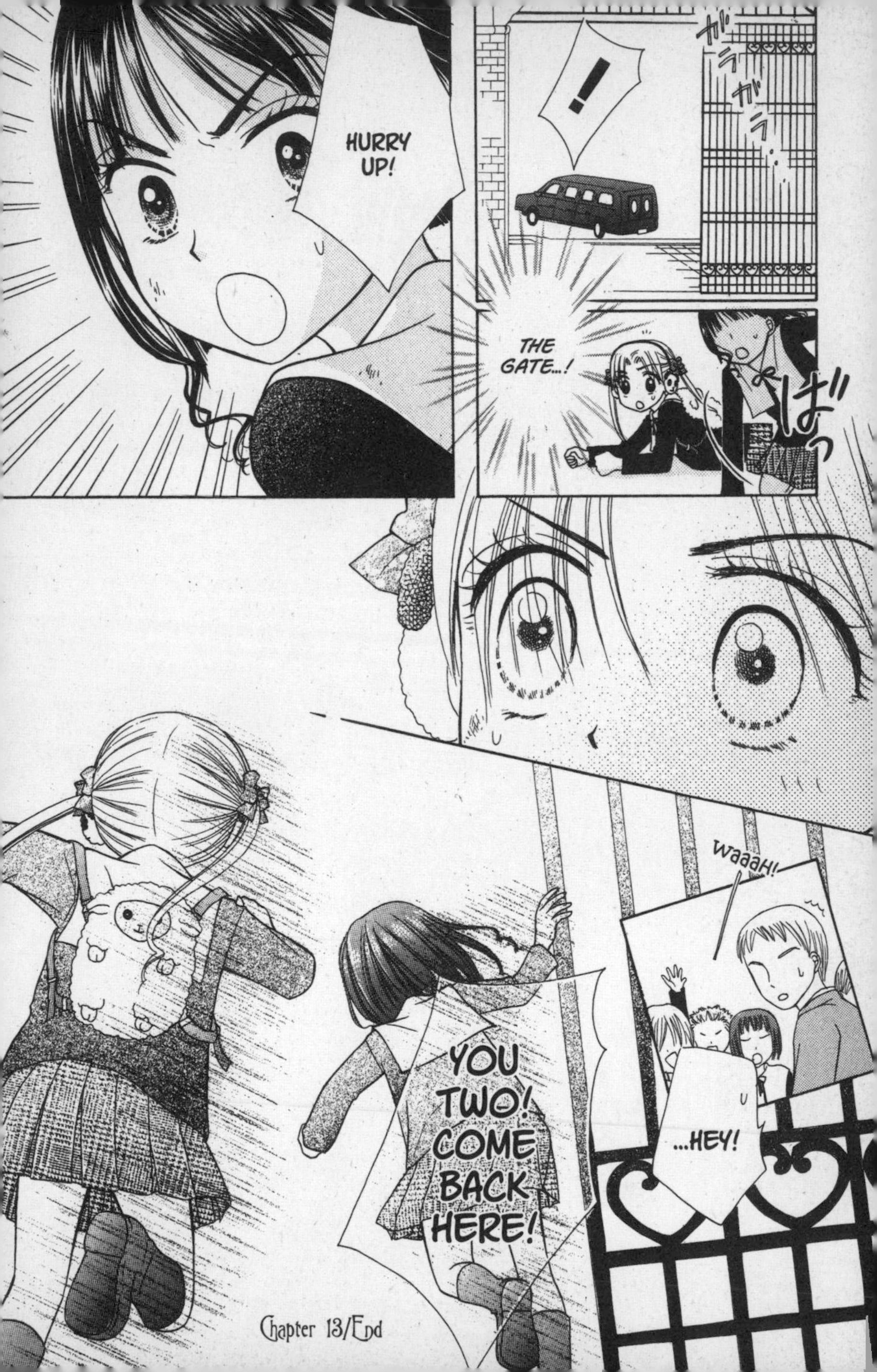
!
ガラガラ
THE GATE...!
ばっ
HURRY UP!
WAAAH!
...HEY!
YOU TWO! COME BACK HERE!

Chapter 13/End

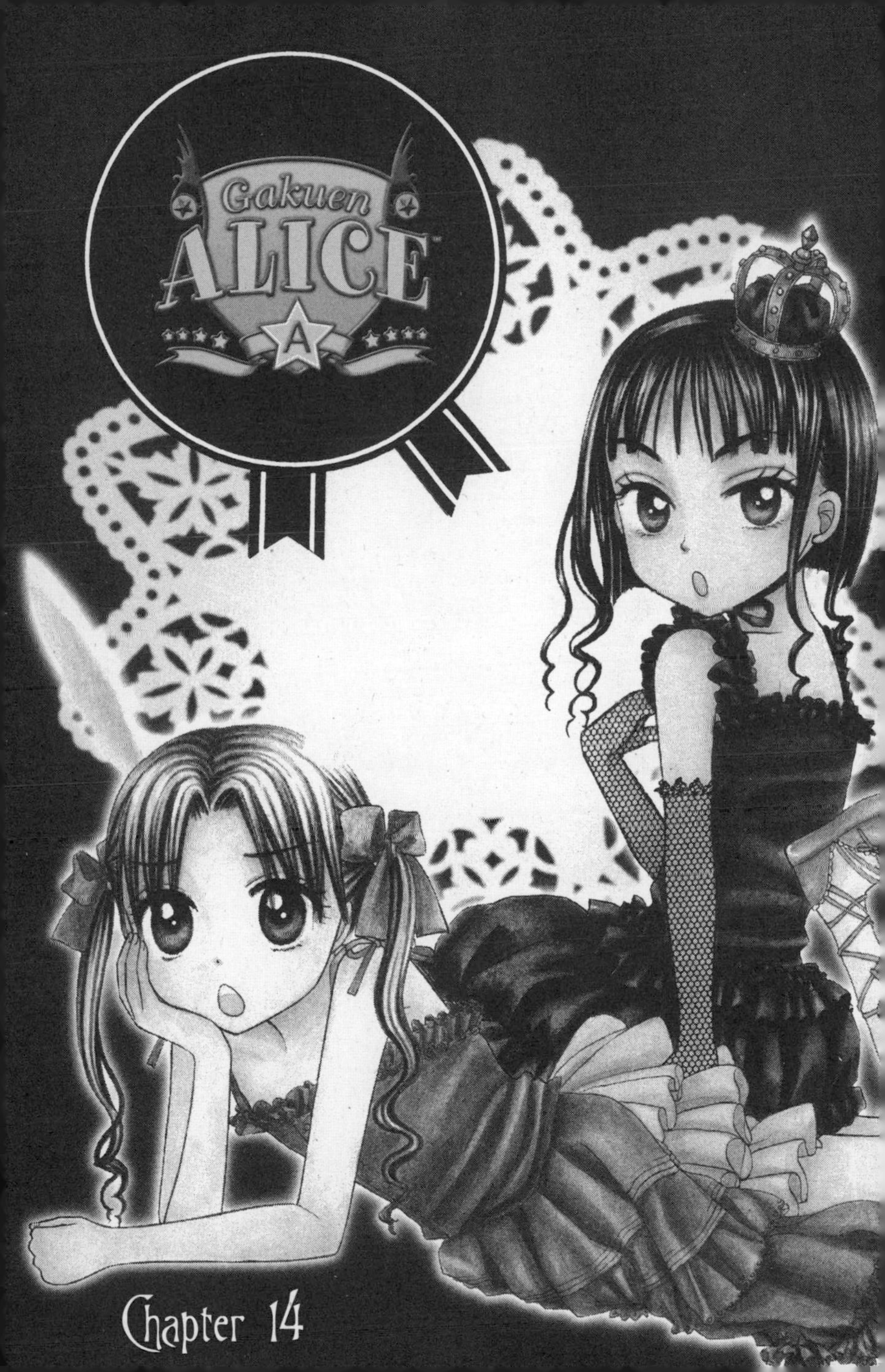
Gakuen
ALICE
Chapter 14

THANKS

Thank you for reading!

SPECIAL THANKS

Tomoe-san, Kari-san, Ishitani-san, Takano-san,
my family, friends, editor
and
You!

SEE YOU AGAIN

I hope to
continue
making manga
you enjoy.

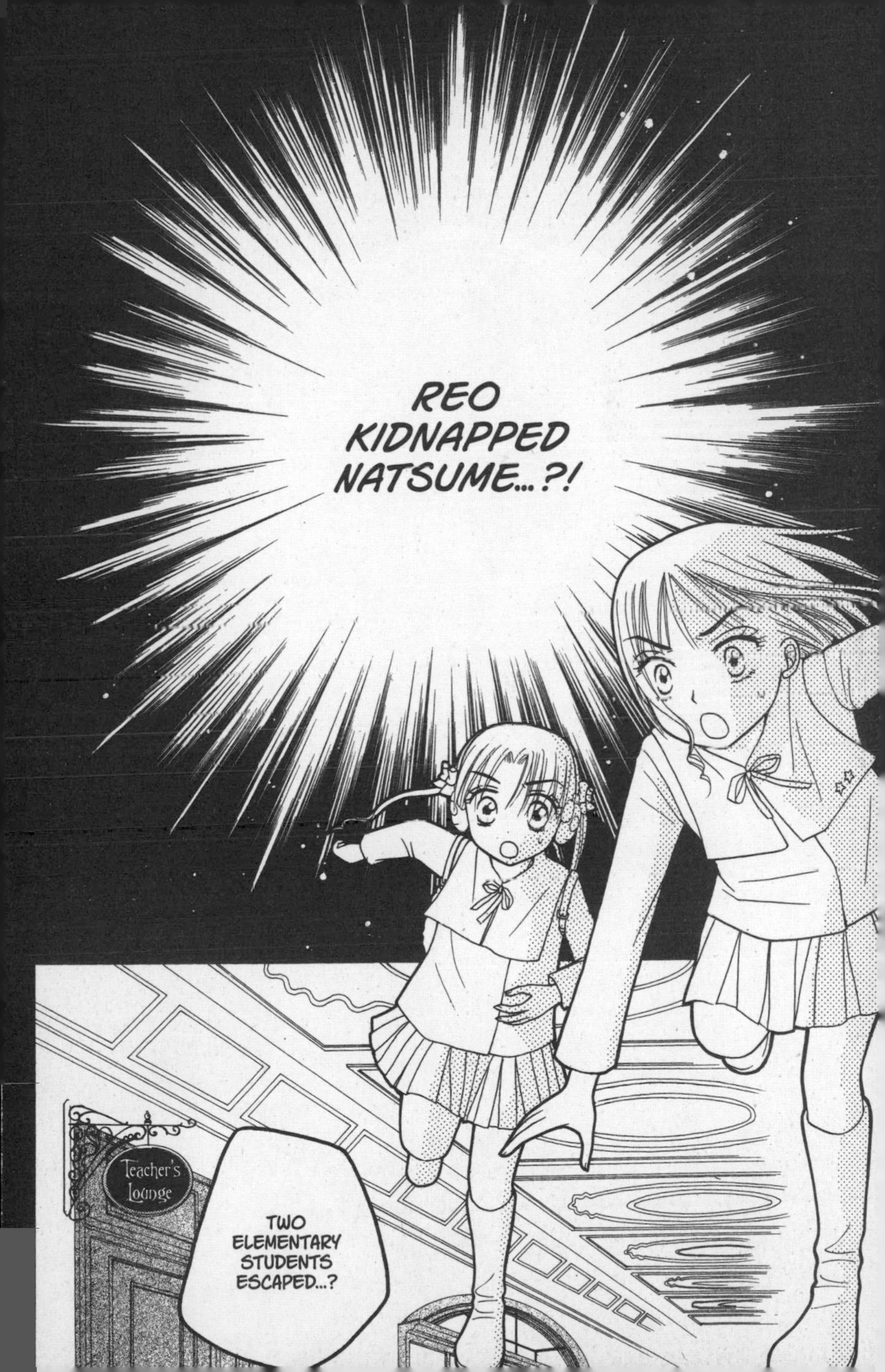
REO KIDNAPPED NATSUME...?!
Teacher's Lounge
TWO ELEMENTARY STUDENTS ESCAPED...?

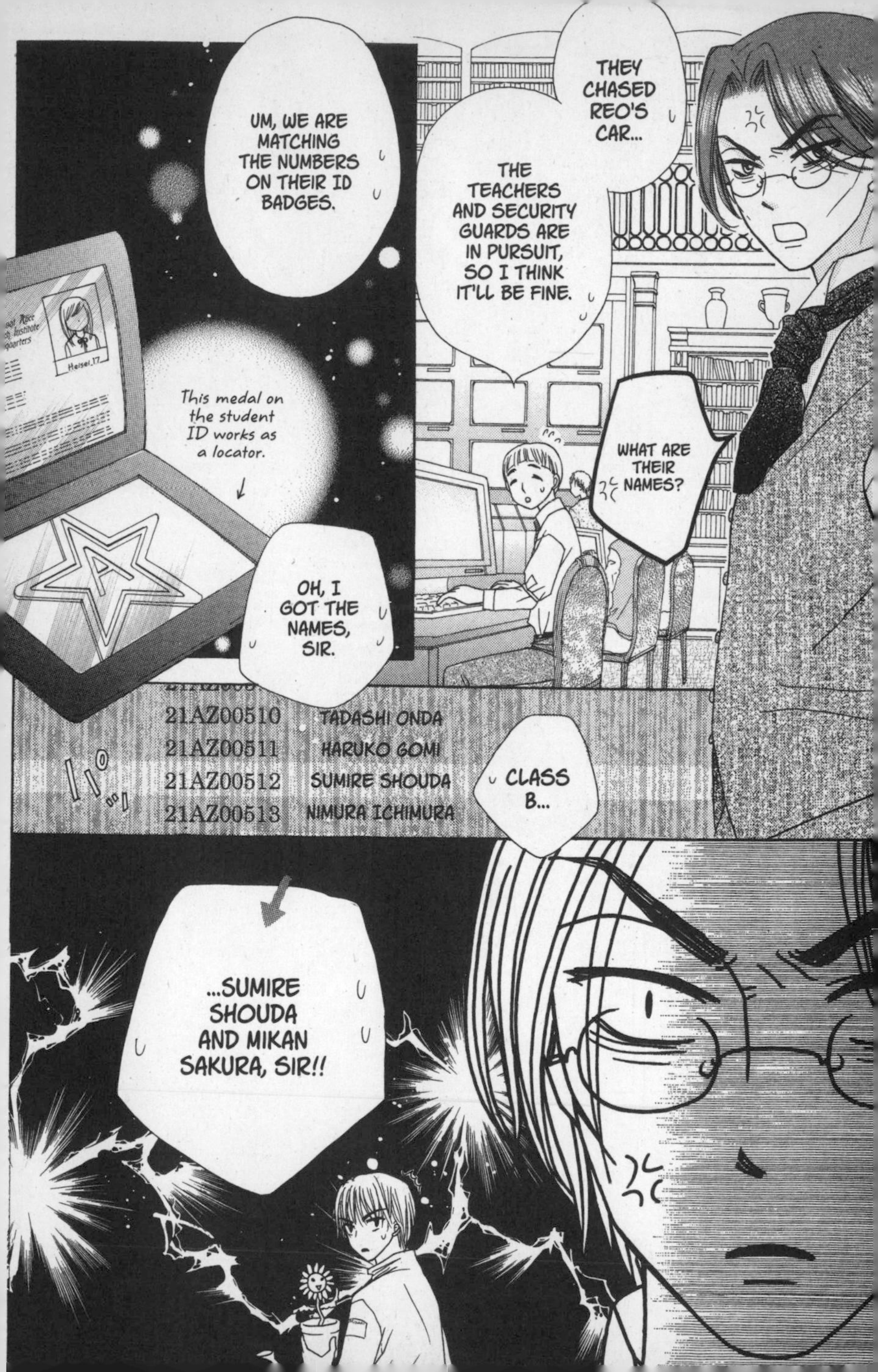
THEY CHASED REO'S CAR...
THE TEACHERS AND SECURITY GUARDS ARE IN PURSUIT, SO I THINK IT'LL BE FINE.
WHAT ARE THEIR NAMES?
UM, WE ARE MATCHING THE NUMBERS ON THEIR ID BADGES.
This medal on the student ID works as a locator.
OH, I GOT THE NAMES, SIR.
21AZ00510 TADASHI ONDA
21AZ00511 HARUKO GOMI
21AZ00512 SUMIRE SHOUDA
21AZ00513 NIMURA ICHIMURA
CLASS B...
...SUMIRE SHOUDA AND MIKAN SAKURA, SIR!!

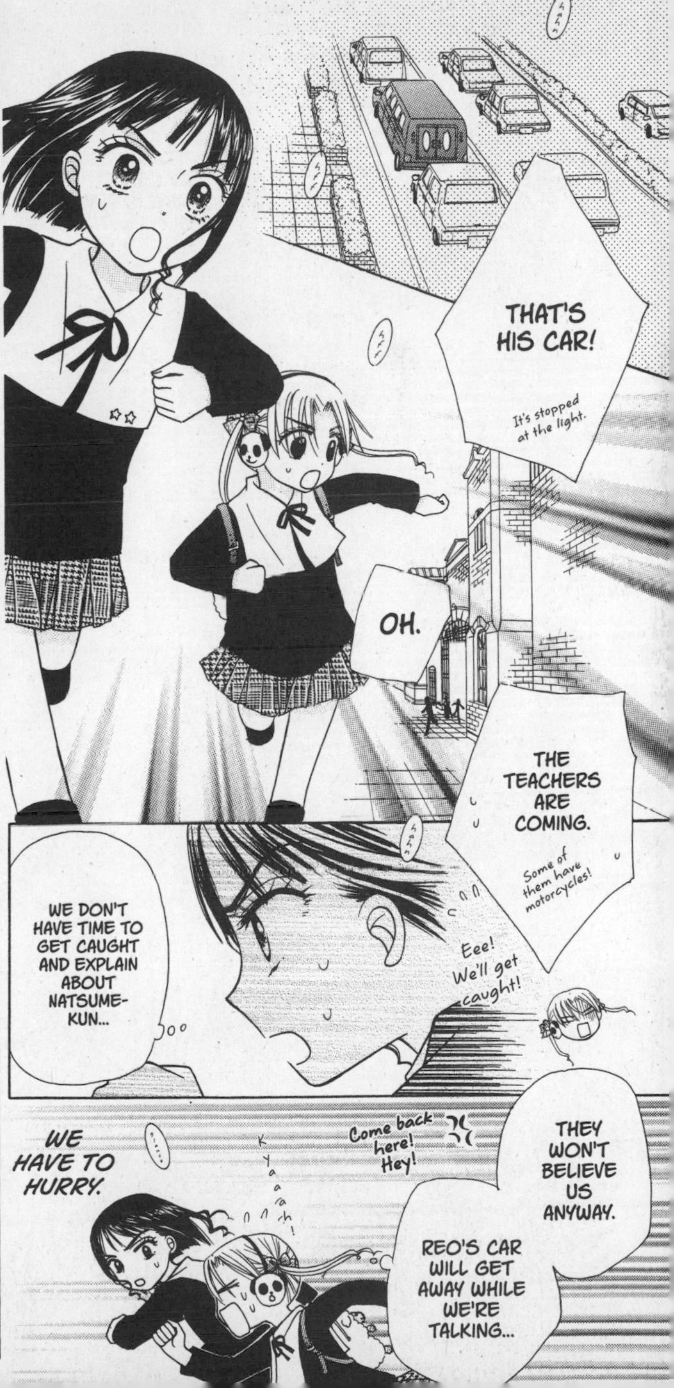
THAT'S HIS CAR!
It's stopped at the light.
OH.
THE TEACHERS ARE COMING.
Some of them have motorcycles!
Eee! We'll get caught!
WE DON'T HAVE TIME TO GET CAUGHT AND EXPLAIN ABOUT NATSUME-KUN...
THEY WON'T BELIEVE US ANYWAY.
REO'S CAR WILL GET AWAY WHILE WE'RE TALKING...
Come back here! Hey!
Kyaaah!
WE HAVE TO HURRY.

Higuchi's Room 4

PROFILE 7

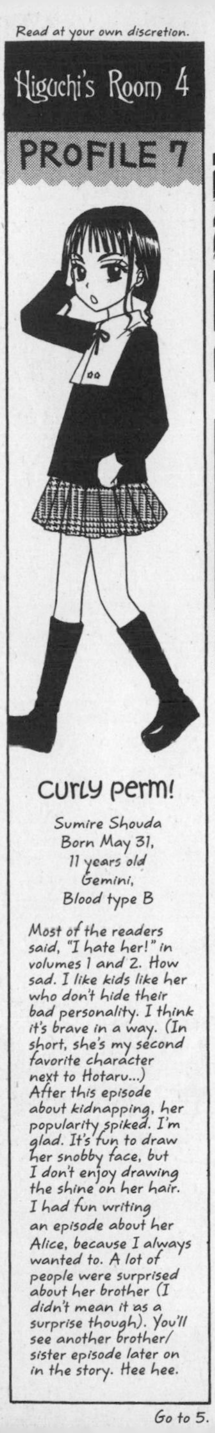

Curly perm!

Sumire Shouda
Born May 31,
11 years old
Gemini,
Blood type B

Most of the readers said, "I hate her!" in volumes 1 and 2. How sad. I like kids like her who don't hide their bad personality. I think it's brave in a way. (In short, she's my second favorite character next to Hotaru...) After this episode about kidnapping, her popularity spiked. I'm glad. It's fun to draw her snobby face, but I don't enjoy drawing the shine on her hair. I had fun writing an episode about her Alice, because I always wanted to. A lot of people were surprised about her brother (I didn't mean it as a surprise though). You'll see another brother/sister episode later on in the story. Hee hee.

Go to 5.

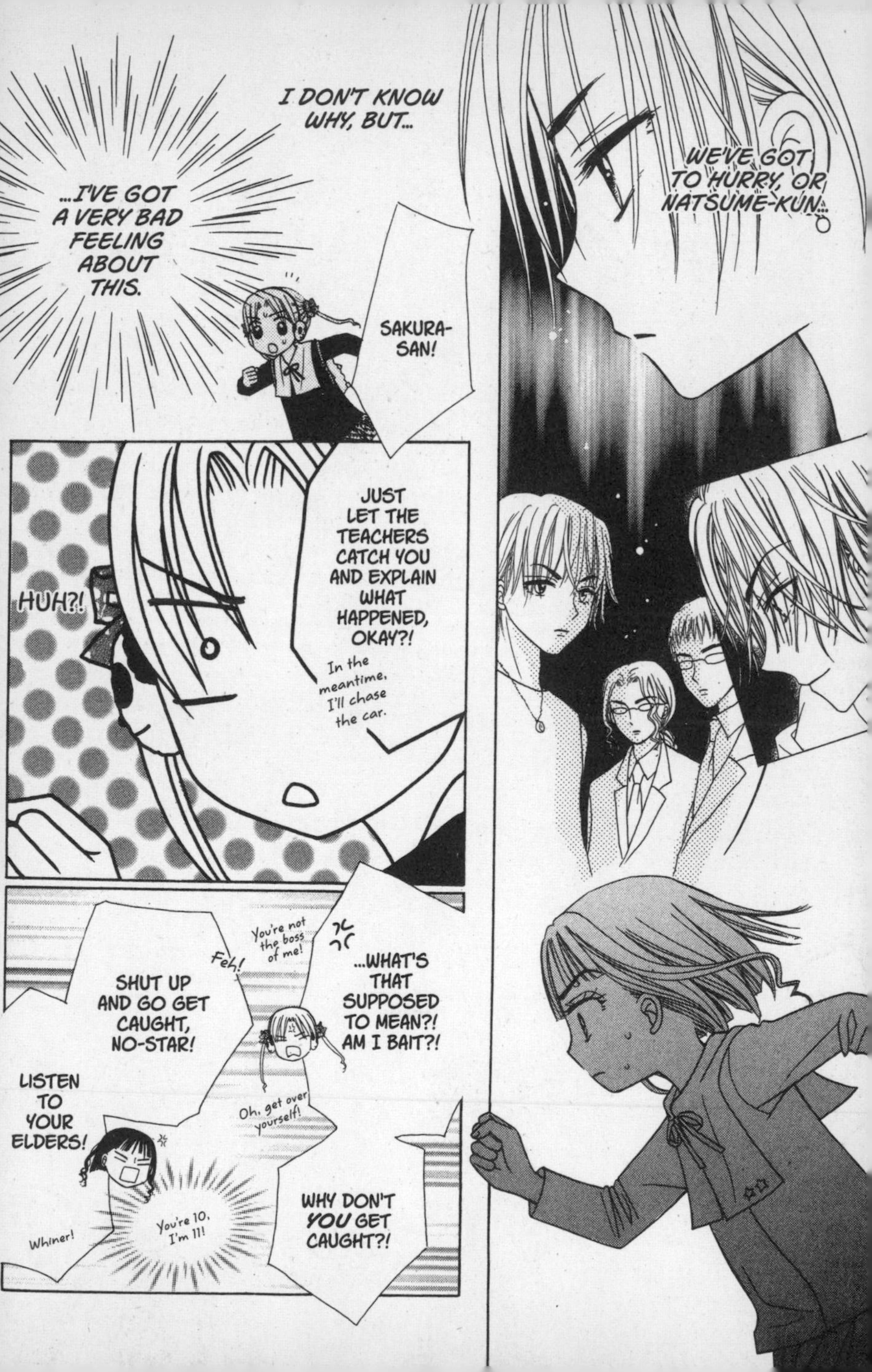
WE'VE GOT TO HURRY, OR NATSUME-KUN...
I DON'T KNOW WHY, BUT...
...I'VE GOT A VERY BAD FEELING ABOUT THIS.
SAKURA-SAN!
JUST LET THE TEACHERS CATCH YOU AND EXPLAIN WHAT HAPPENED, OKAY?!
In the meantime, I'll chase the car.
HUH?!
...WHAT'S THAT SUPPOSED TO MEAN?! AM I BAIT?!
You're not the boss of me!
Feh!
SHUT UP AND GO GET CAUGHT, NO-STAR!
Oh, get over yourself!
WHY DON'T YOU GET CAUGHT?!
LISTEN TO YOUR ELDERS!
You're 10, I'm 11!
Whiner!

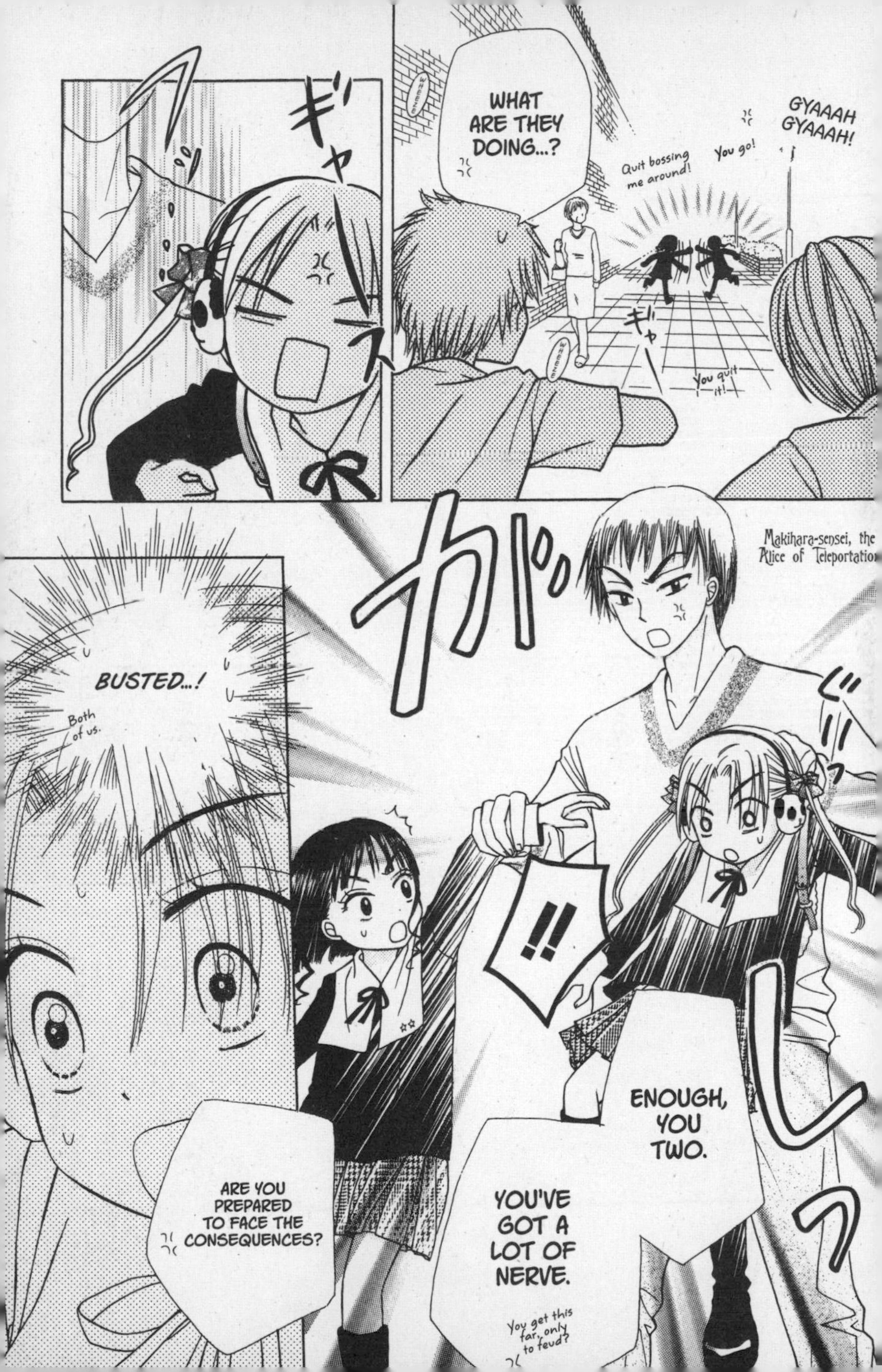
WHAT ARE THEY DOING...?
Quit bossing me around!
You go!
GYAAAH GYAAAH!
You quit it!
Makihara-sensei, the Alice of Teleportation
!!
ENOUGH, YOU TWO.
YOU'VE GOT A LOT OF NERVE.
You get this far, only to feud?
BUSTED...!
Both of us.
ARE YOU PREPARED TO FACE THE CONSEQUENCES?

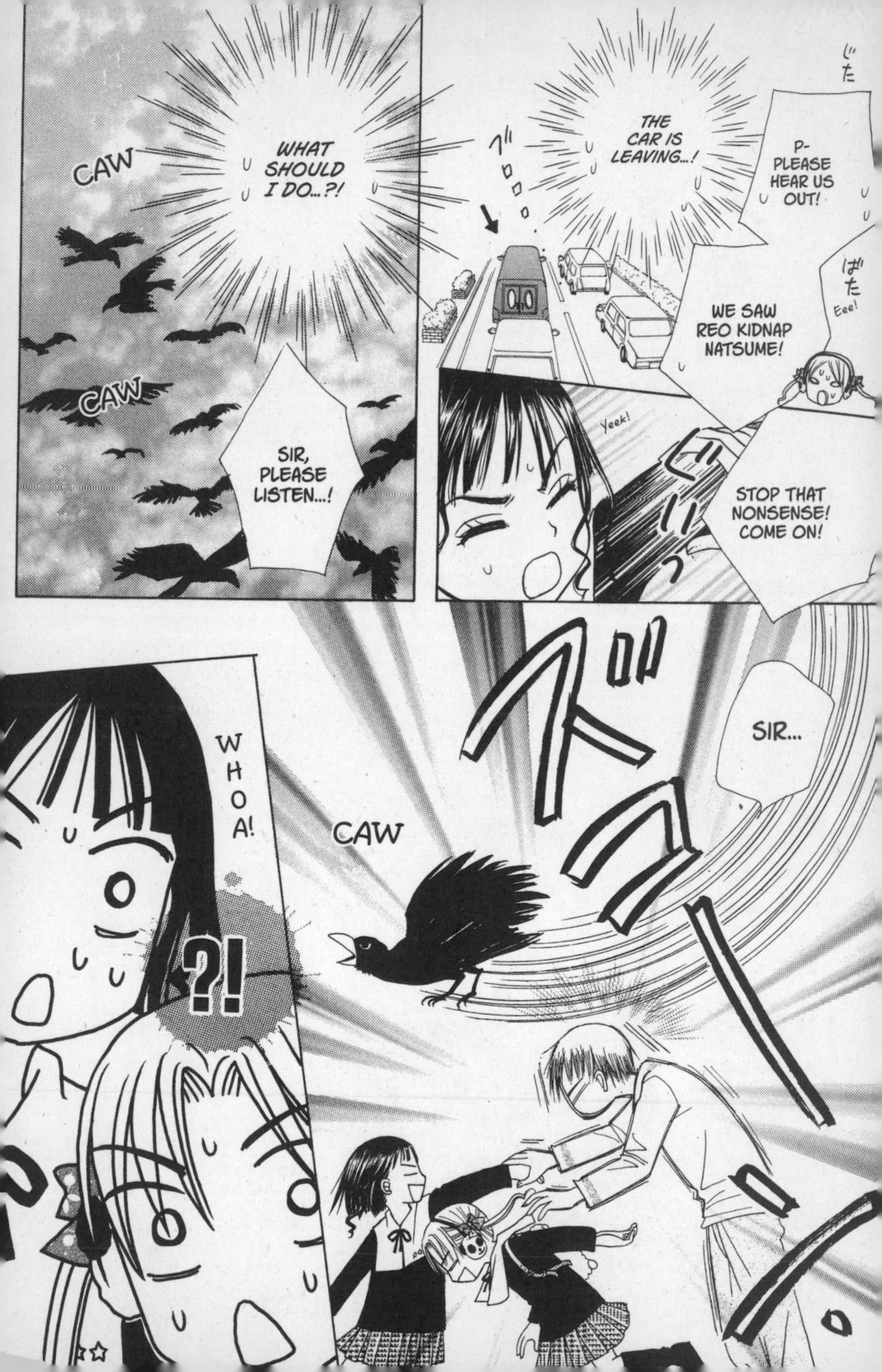
じた
P-PLEASE HEAR US OUT!
THE CAR IS LEAVING...!
ばた
Eee!
WE SAW REO KIDNAP NATSUME!
STOP THAT NONSENSE! COME ON!
Yeek!
WHAT SHOULD I DO...?!
CAW
CAW
SIR, PLEASE LISTEN...!
SIR...
CAW
WHOA!
?!

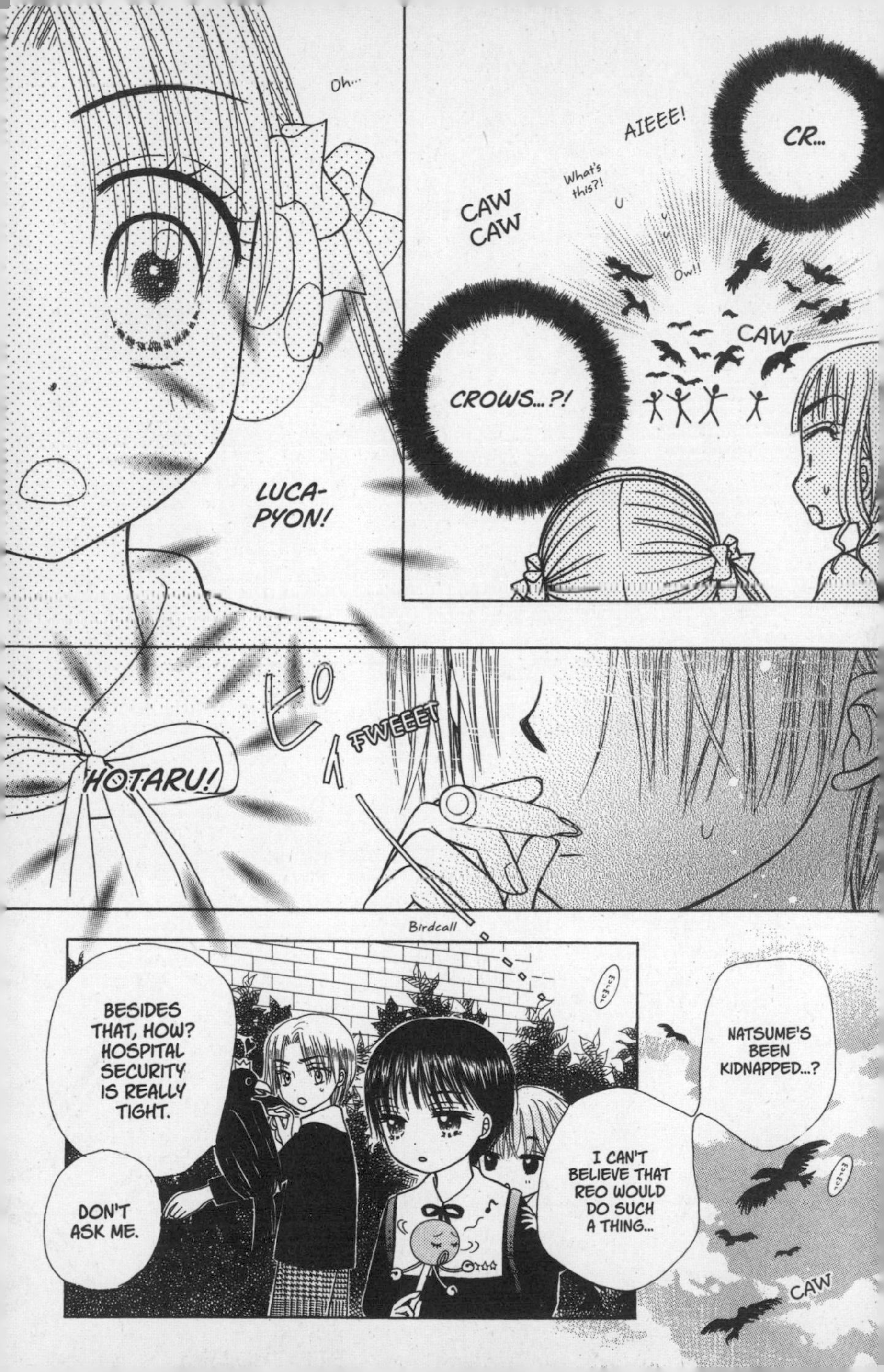
CR...
AIEEE!
What's this?!
CAW CAW
Ow!!
CAW
CROWS...?!
FWEEET
Birdcall
Oh...
LUCA-PYON!
HOTARU!
NATSUME'S BEEN KIDNAPPED...?
I CAN'T BELIEVE THAT REO WOULD DO SUCH A THING...
BESIDES THAT, HOW? HOSPITAL SECURITY IS REALLY TIGHT.
DON'T ASK ME.
CAW

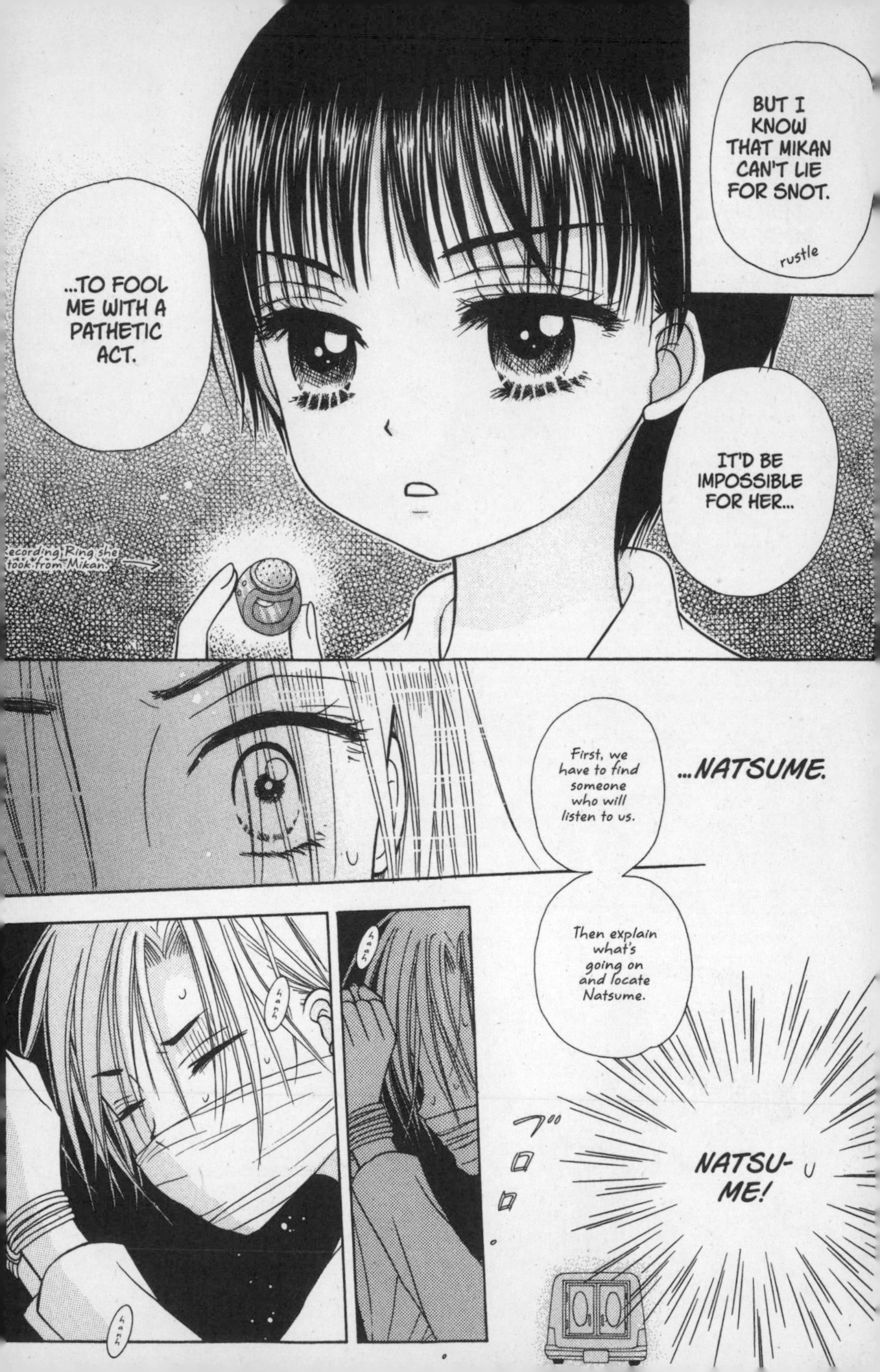
BUT I KNOW THAT MIKAN CAN'T LIE FOR SNOT.
rustle
IT'D BE IMPOSSIBLE FOR HER...
...TO FOOL ME WITH A PATHETIC ACT.
ecording Ring she took from Mikan.
...NATSUME.
First, we have to find someone who will listen to us.
Then explain what's going on and locate Natsume.
NATSU-ME!

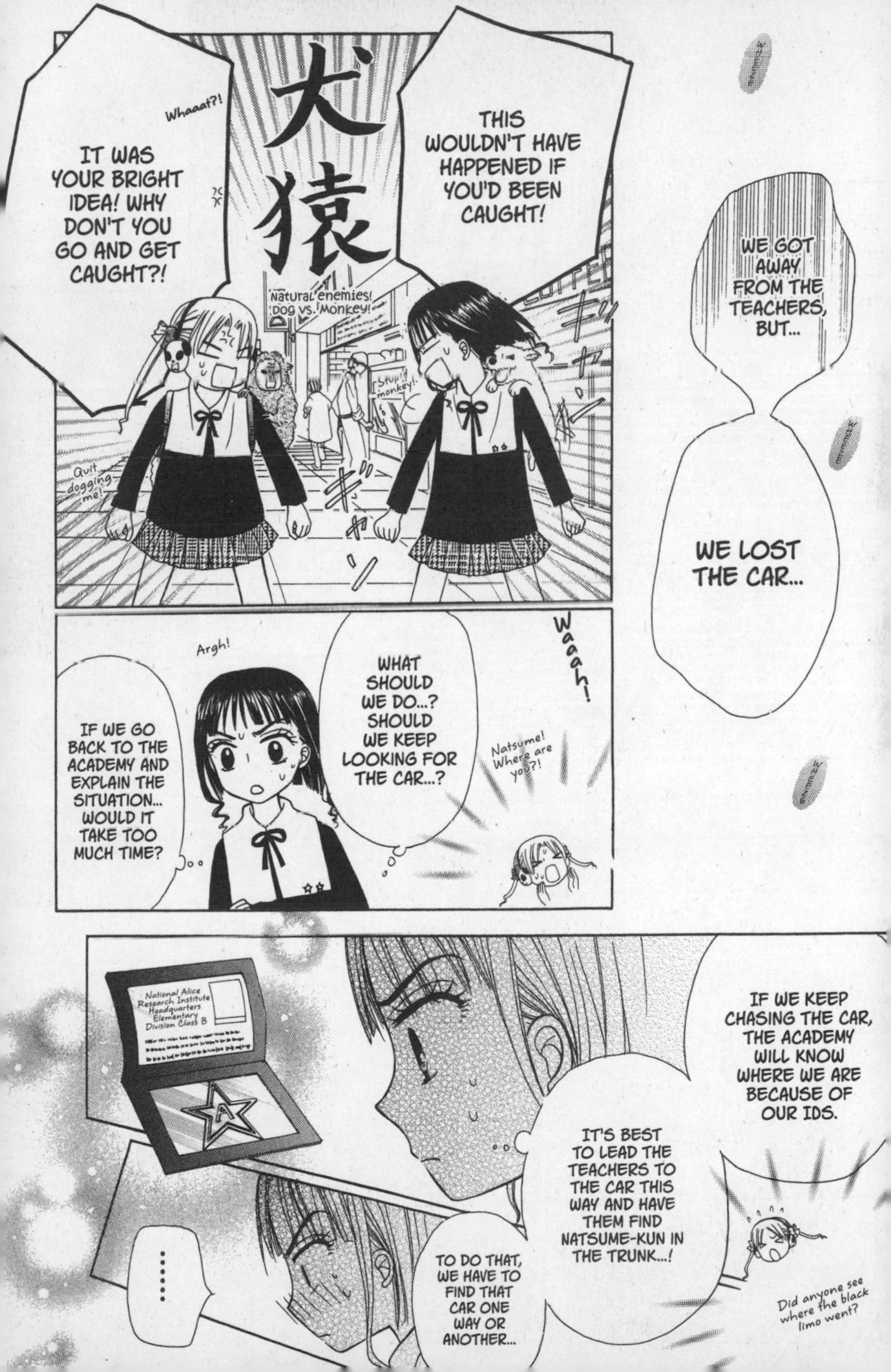
WE GOT AWAY FROM THE TEACHERS, BUT...
WE LOST THE CAR...
THIS WOULDN'T HAVE HAPPENED IF YOU'D BEEN CAUGHT!
犬猿
Whaaat?!
IT WAS YOUR BRIGHT IDEA! WHY DON'T YOU GO AND GET CAUGHT?!
Natural enemies! Dog vs. Monkey!
Stupid monkey!
Quit dogging me!
Waaah!
Natsume! Where are you?!
WHAT SHOULD WE DO...? SHOULD WE KEEP LOOKING FOR THE CAR...?
Argh!
IF WE GO BACK TO THE ACADEMY AND EXPLAIN THE SITUATION... WOULD IT TAKE TOO MUCH TIME?
IF WE KEEP CHASING THE CAR, THE ACADEMY WILL KNOW WHERE WE ARE BECAUSE OF OUR IDS.
Did anyone see where the black limo went?
IT'S BEST TO LEAD THE TEACHERS TO THE CAR THIS WAY AND HAVE THEM FIND NATSUME-KUN IN THE TRUNK...!
TO DO THAT, WE HAVE TO FIND THAT CAR ONE WAY OR ANOTHER...
......
National Alice Research Institute Headquarters Elementary Division Class B

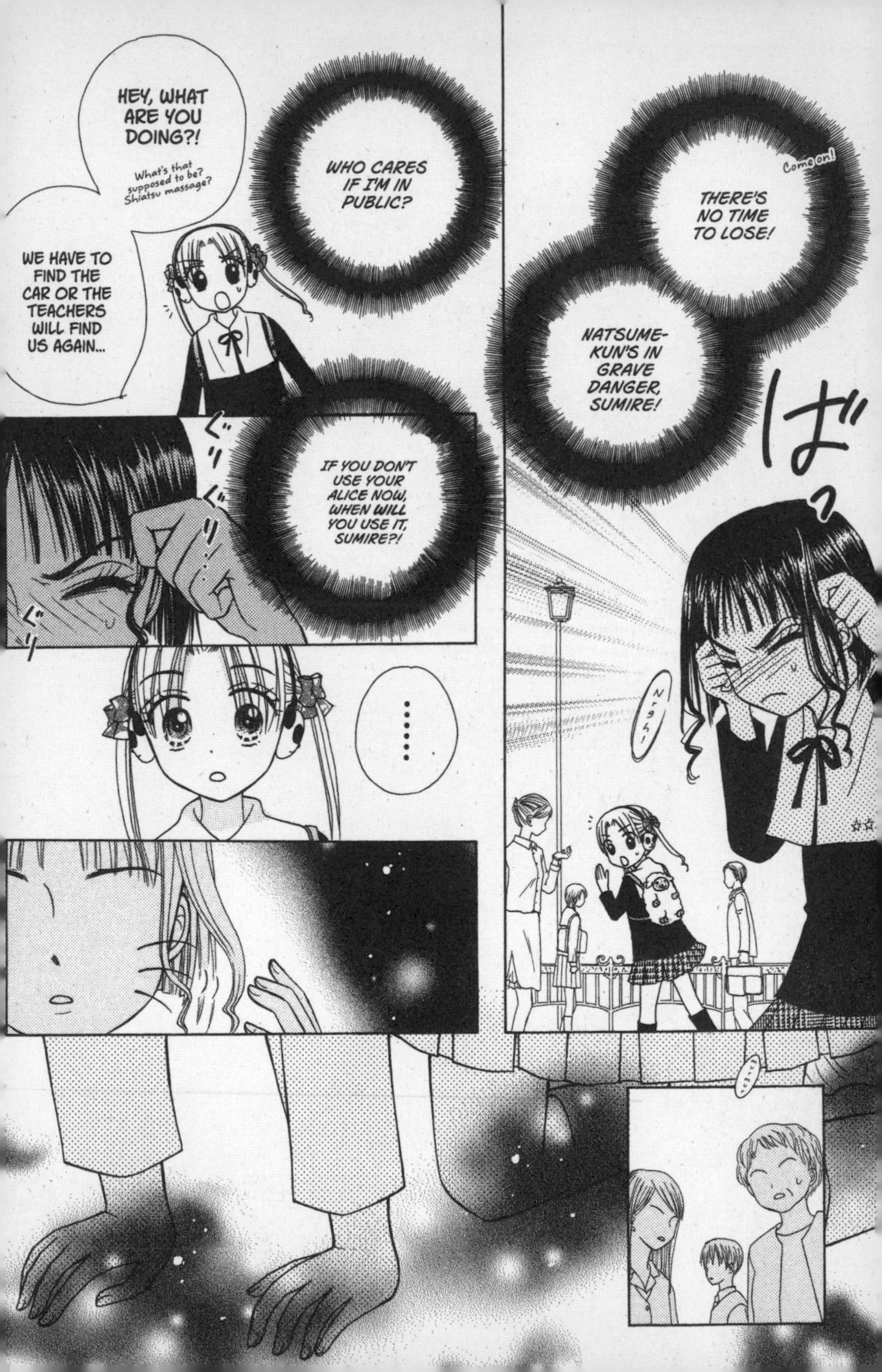

Come on!
THERE'S NO TIME TO LOSE!
NATSUME-KUN'S IN GRAVE DANGER, SUMIRE!
ば
HEY, WHAT ARE YOU DOING?!
What's that supposed to be? Shiatsu massage?
WE HAVE TO FIND THE CAR OR THE TEACHERS WILL FIND US AGAIN...
WHO CARES IF I'M IN PUBLIC?
IF YOU DON'T USE YOUR ALICE NOW, WHEN WILL YOU USE IT, SUMIRE?!
......

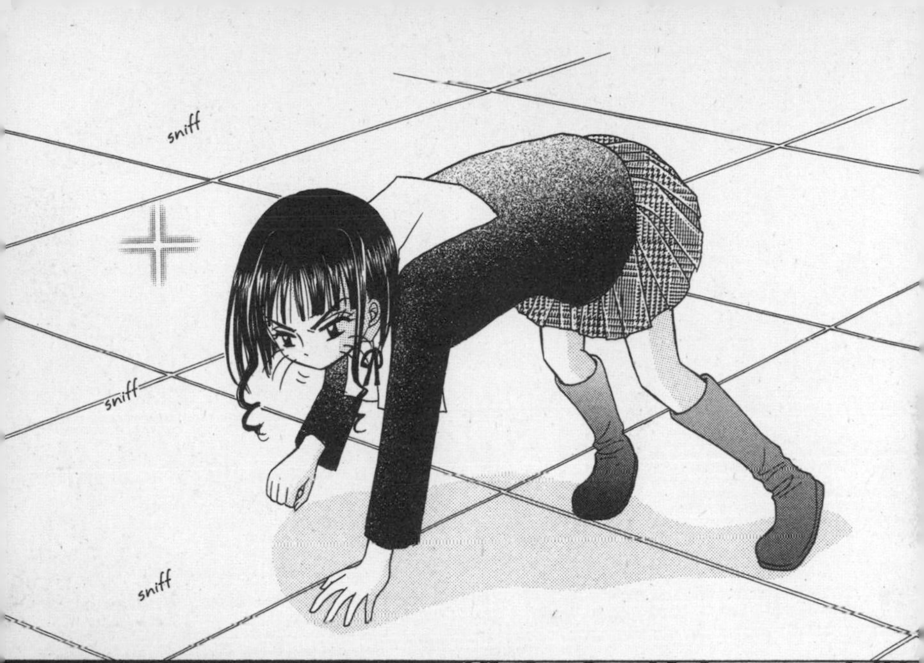
sniff
sniff
sniff
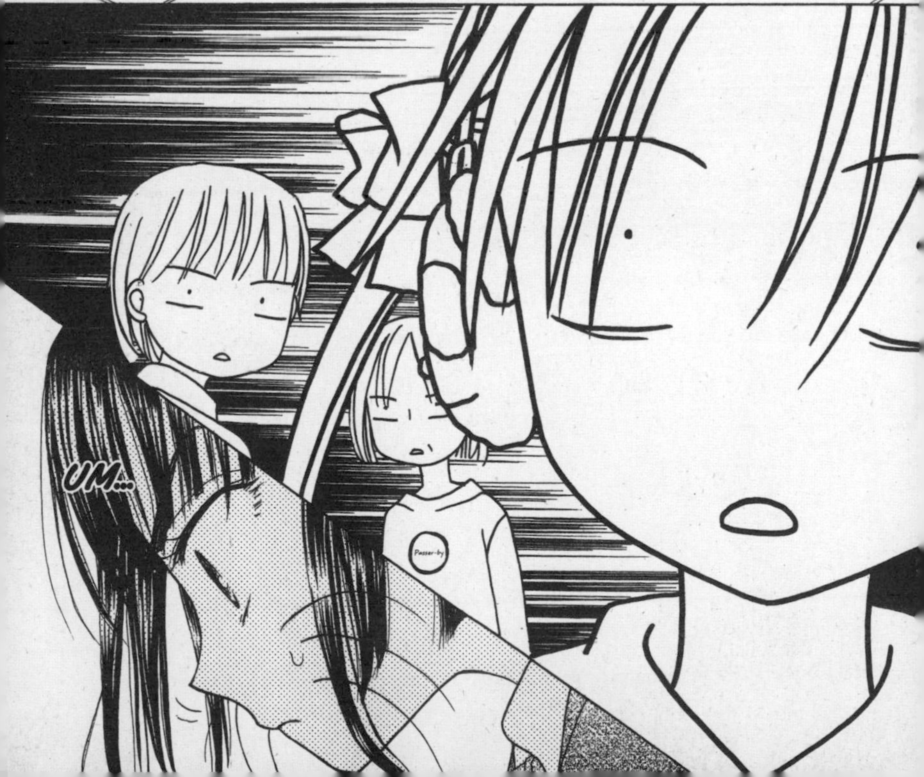
UM...
Passer-by

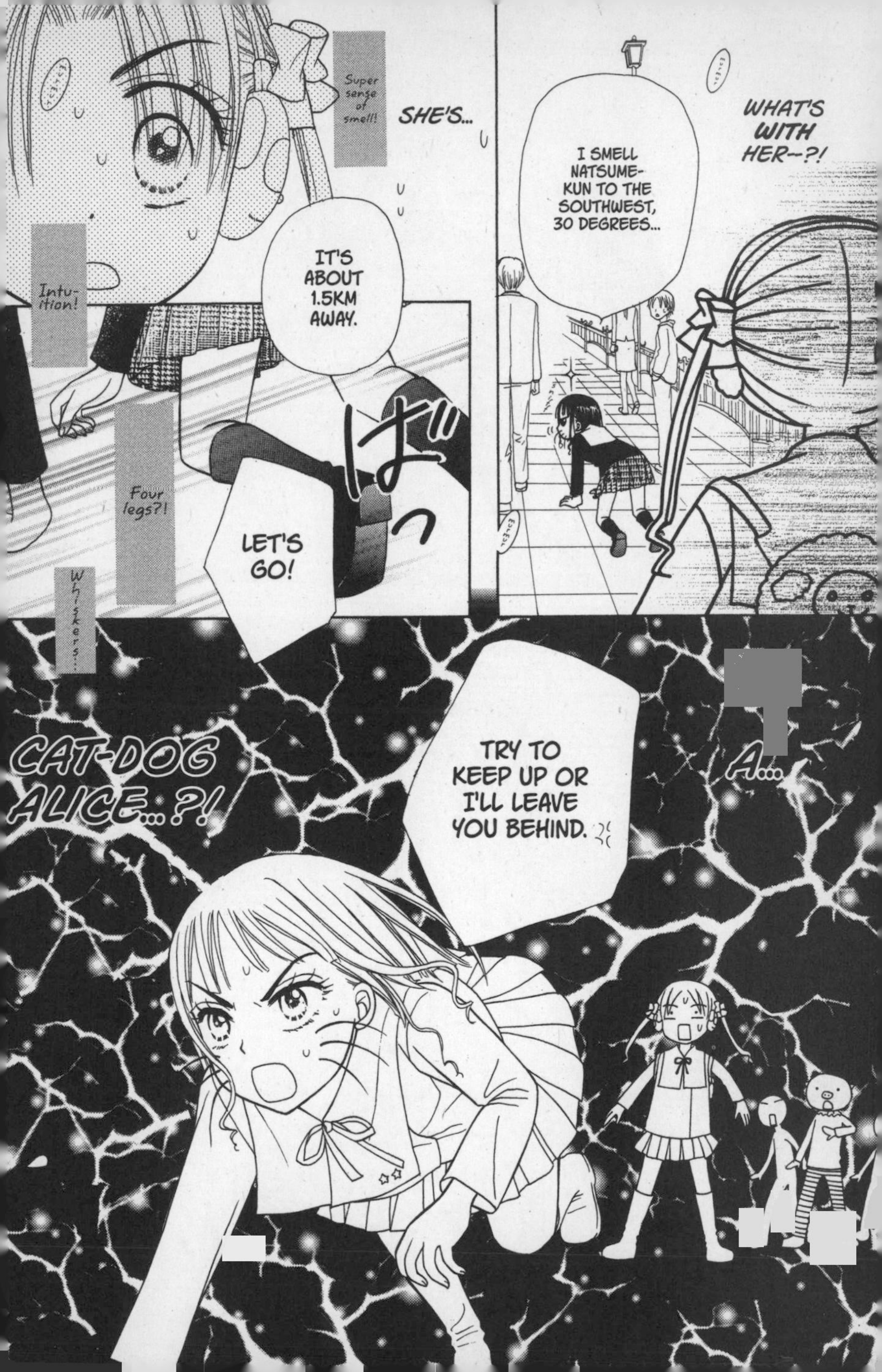
WHAT'S WITH HER--?!
I SMELL NATSUME-KUN TO THE SOUTHWEST, 30 DEGREES...
SHE'S...
Super sense of smell!
IT'S ABOUT 1.5KM AWAY.
Intu-ition!
Four legs?!
LET'S GO!
Whiskers...
A...
TRY TO KEEP UP OR I'LL LEAVE YOU BEHIND.
CAT-DOG ALICE...?!

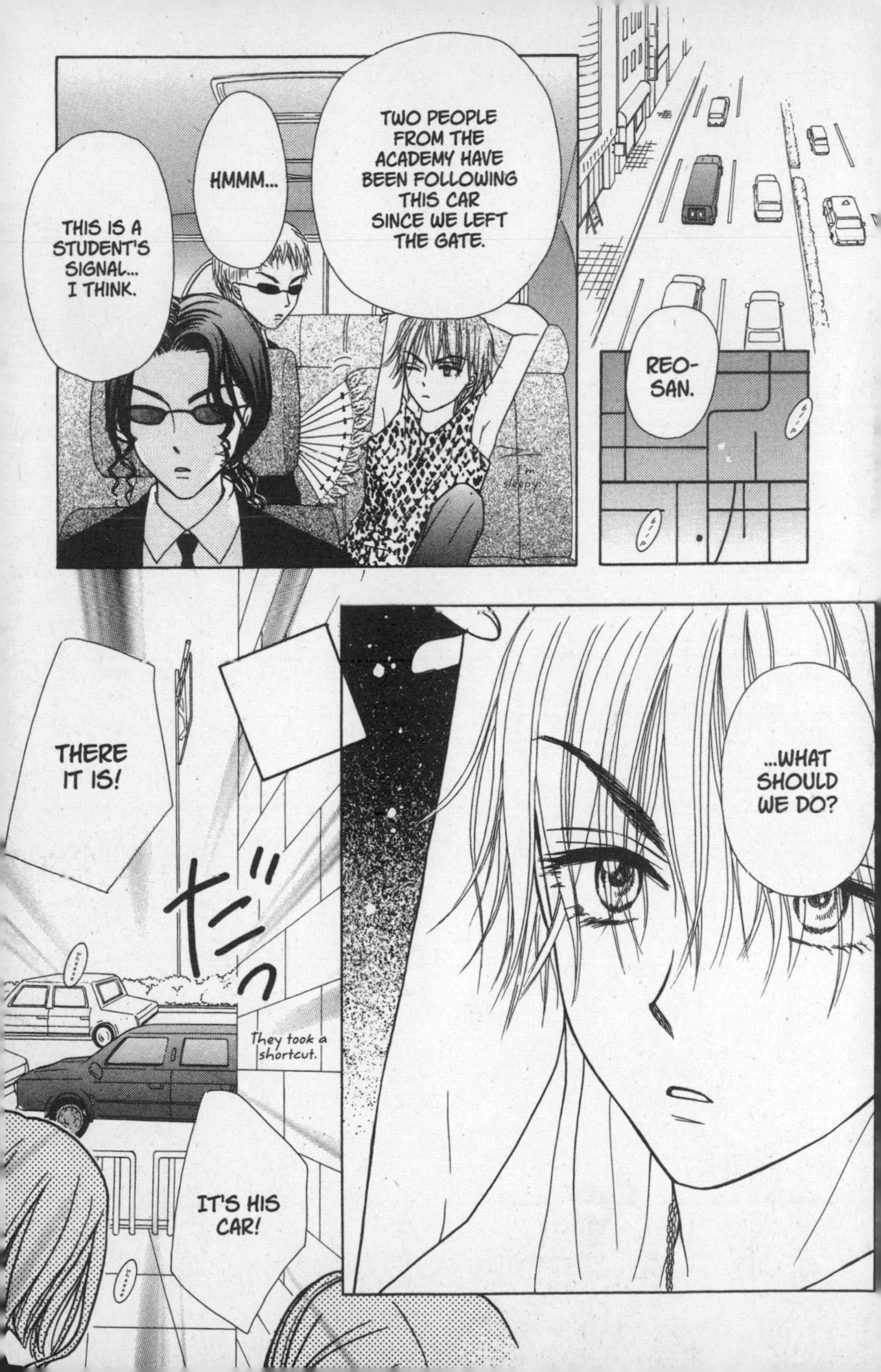
REO-SAN.
grip
grip
TWO PEOPLE FROM THE ACADEMY HAVE BEEN FOLLOWING THIS CAR SINCE WE LEFT THE GATE.
HMMM...
THIS IS A STUDENT'S SIGNAL... I THINK.
I'm sleepy.
...WHAT SHOULD WE DO?
THERE IT IS!
They took a shortcut.
IT'S HIS CAR!

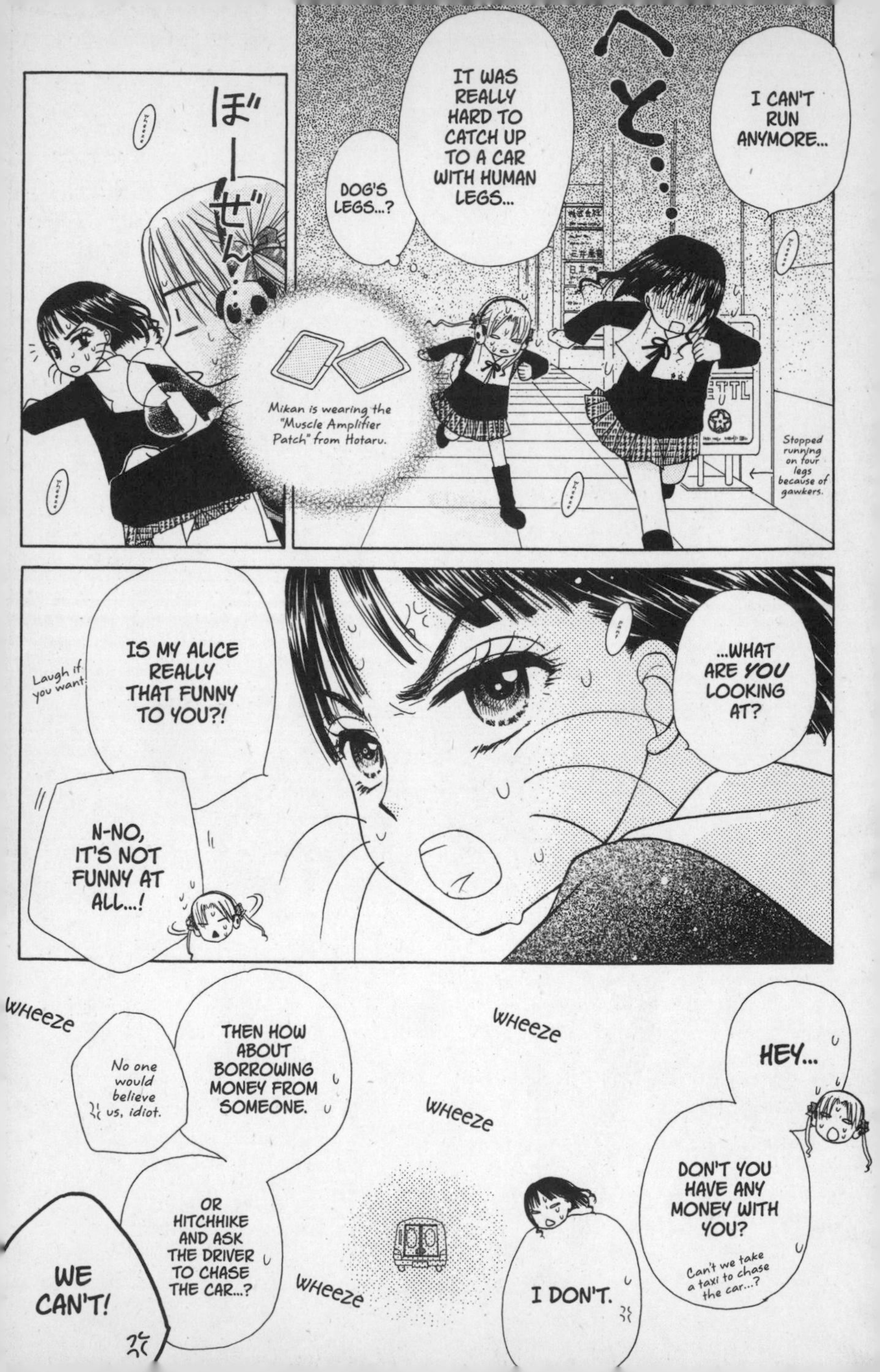
I CAN'T RUN ANYMORE...
へと・・・
IT WAS REALLY HARD TO CATCH UP TO A CAR WITH HUMAN LEGS...
DOG'S LEGS...?
Mikan is wearing the "Muscle Amplifier Patch" from Hotaru.
Stopped running on four legs because of gawkers.
ぼーぜん
...WHAT ARE YOU LOOKING AT?
IS MY ALICE REALLY THAT FUNNY TO YOU?!
Laugh if you want.
N-NO, IT'S NOT FUNNY AT ALL...!
HEY...
DON'T YOU HAVE ANY MONEY WITH YOU?
Can't we take a taxi to chase the car...?
WHEEZE
I DON'T.
WHEEZE
THEN HOW ABOUT BORROWING MONEY FROM SOMEONE.
WHEEZE
No one would believe us, idiot.
OR HITCHHIKE AND ASK THE DRIVER TO CHASE THE CAR...?
WHEEZE
WE CAN'T!

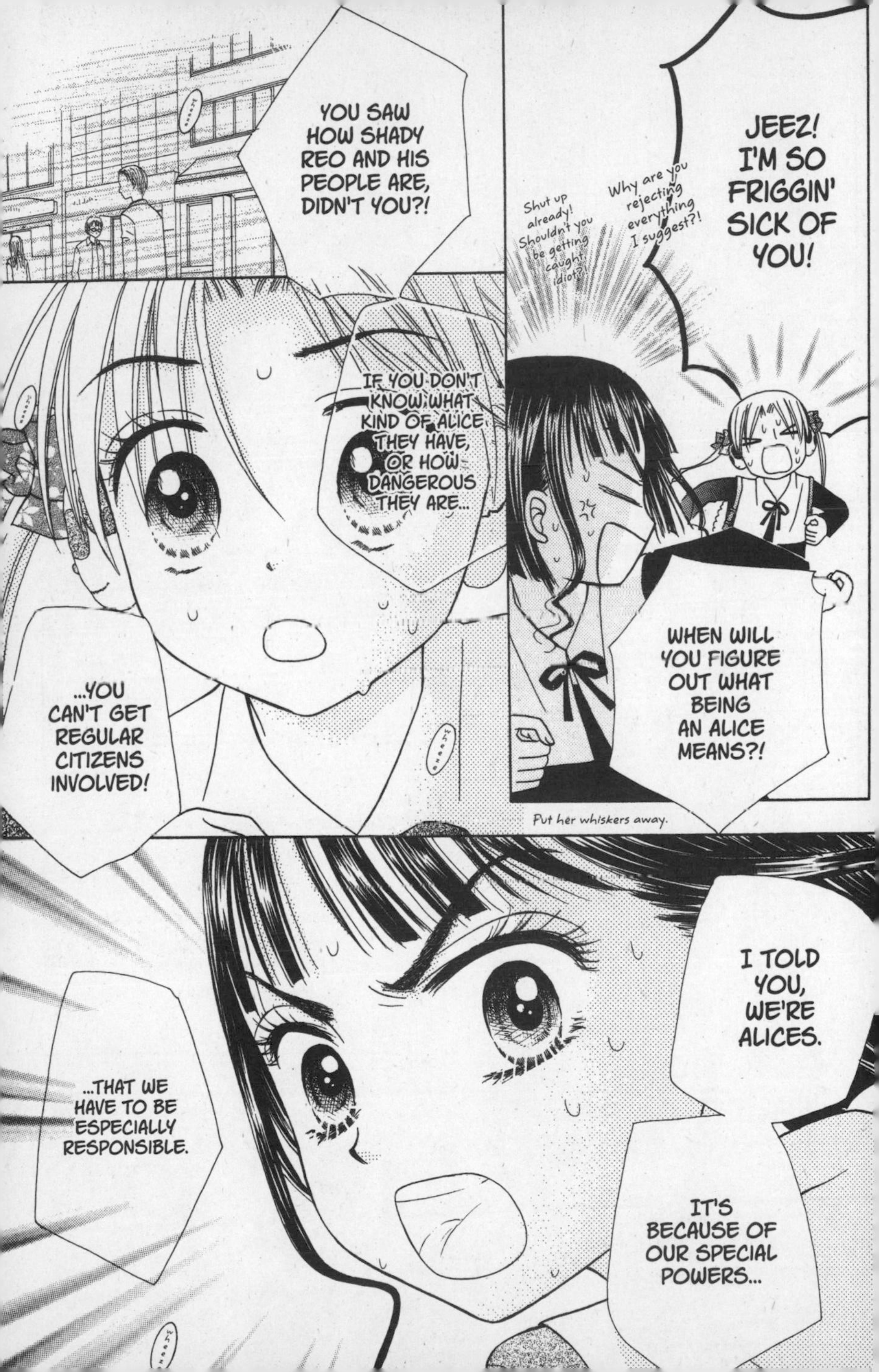
JEEZ! I'M SO FRIGGIN' SICK OF YOU!
Why are you rejecting everything I suggest?!
Shut up already! Shouldn't you be getting caught idiot?!
WHEN WILL YOU FIGURE OUT WHAT BEING AN ALICE MEANS?!
Put her whiskers away.
YOU SAW HOW SHADY REO AND HIS PEOPLE ARE, DIDN'T YOU?!
IF YOU DON'T KNOW WHAT KIND OF ALICE THEY HAVE, OR HOW DANGEROUS THEY ARE...
...YOU CAN'T GET REGULAR CITIZENS INVOLVED!
I TOLD YOU, WE'RE ALICES.
IT'S BECAUSE OF OUR SPECIAL POWERS...
...THAT WE HAVE TO BE ESPECIALLY RESPONSIBLE.

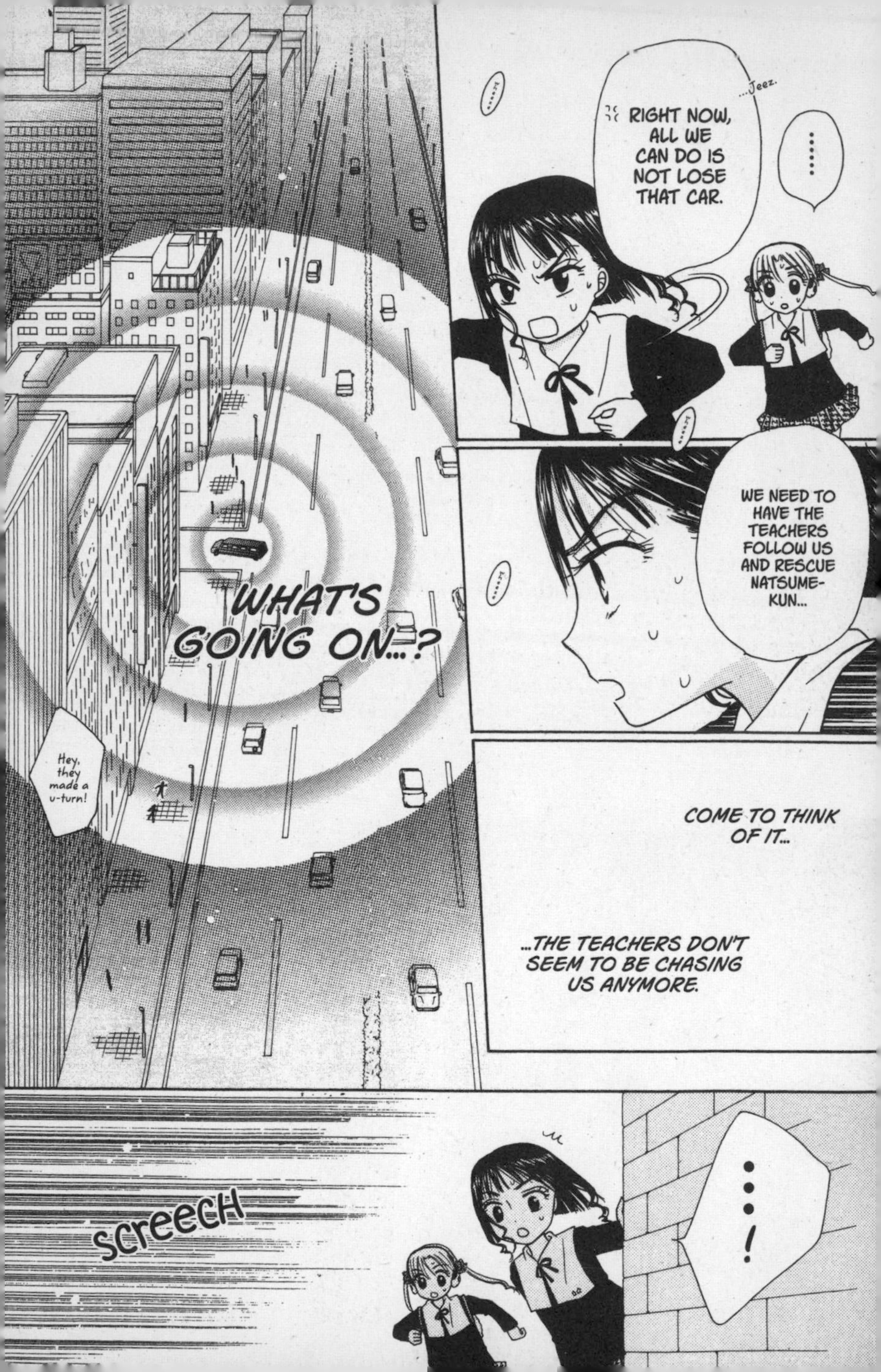
......
...Jeez.
RIGHT NOW, ALL WE CAN DO IS NOT LOSE THAT CAR.
......
......
WE NEED TO HAVE THE TEACHERS FOLLOW US AND RESCUE NATSUME-KUN...
......
COME TO THINK OF IT...
...THE TEACHERS DON'T SEEM TO BE CHASING US ANYMORE.
WHAT'S GOING ON...?
Hey, they made a u-turn!
...!
screech

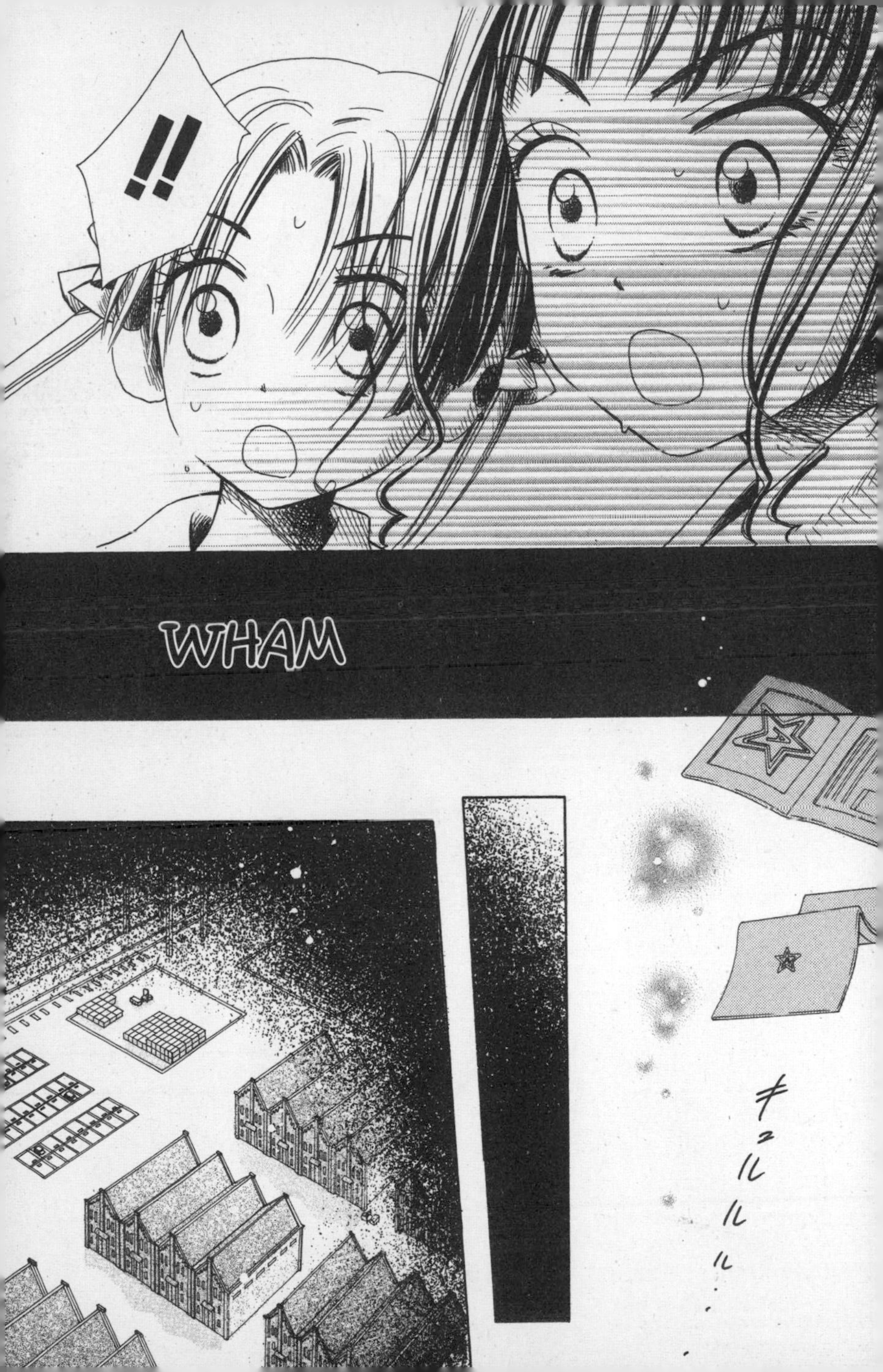
!!
WHAM
キュルルル‥

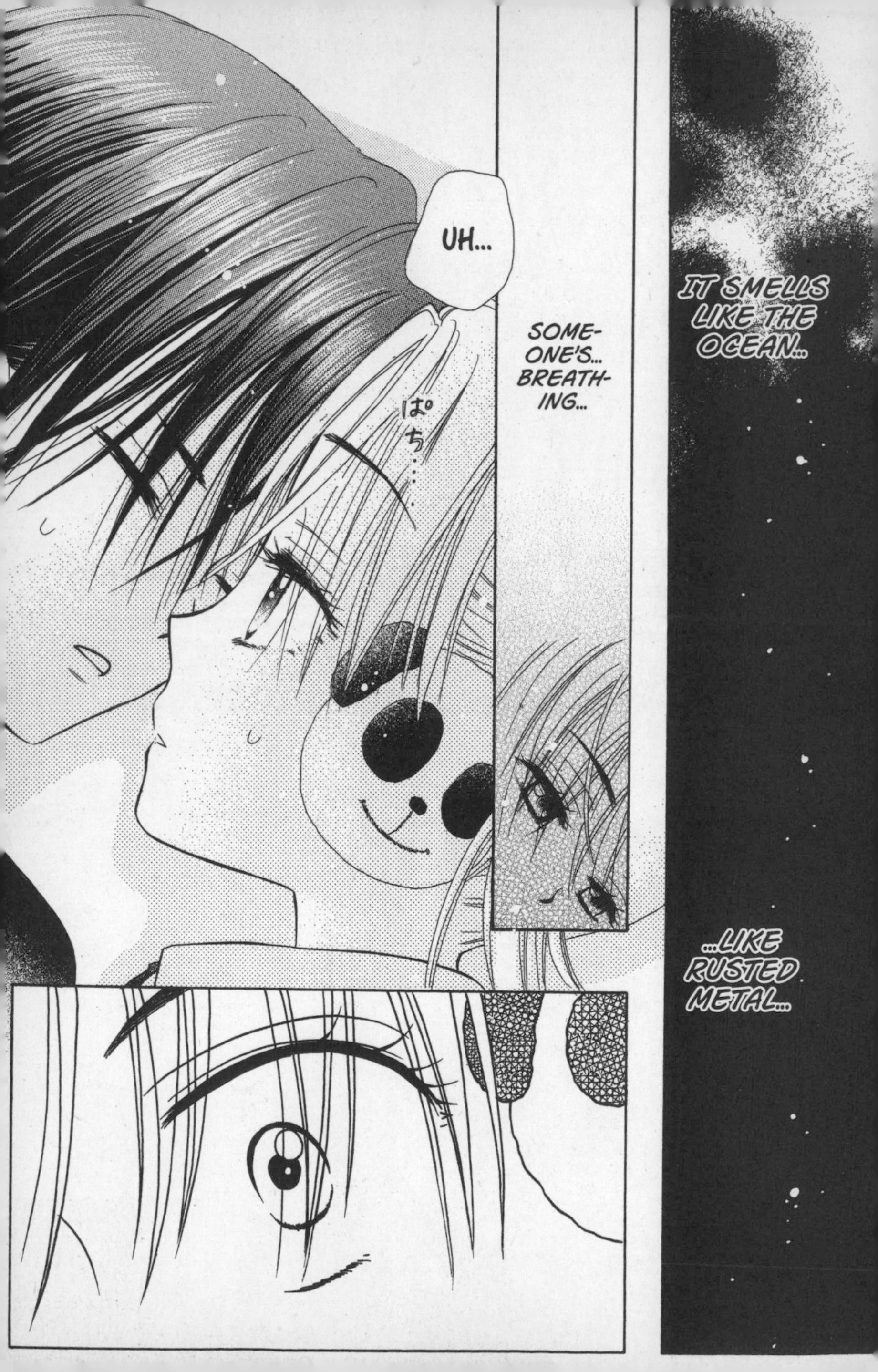
IT SMELLS LIKE THE OCEAN...
...LIKE RUSTED METAL...
SOME-ONE'S... BREATH-ING...
UH...
ぱち…

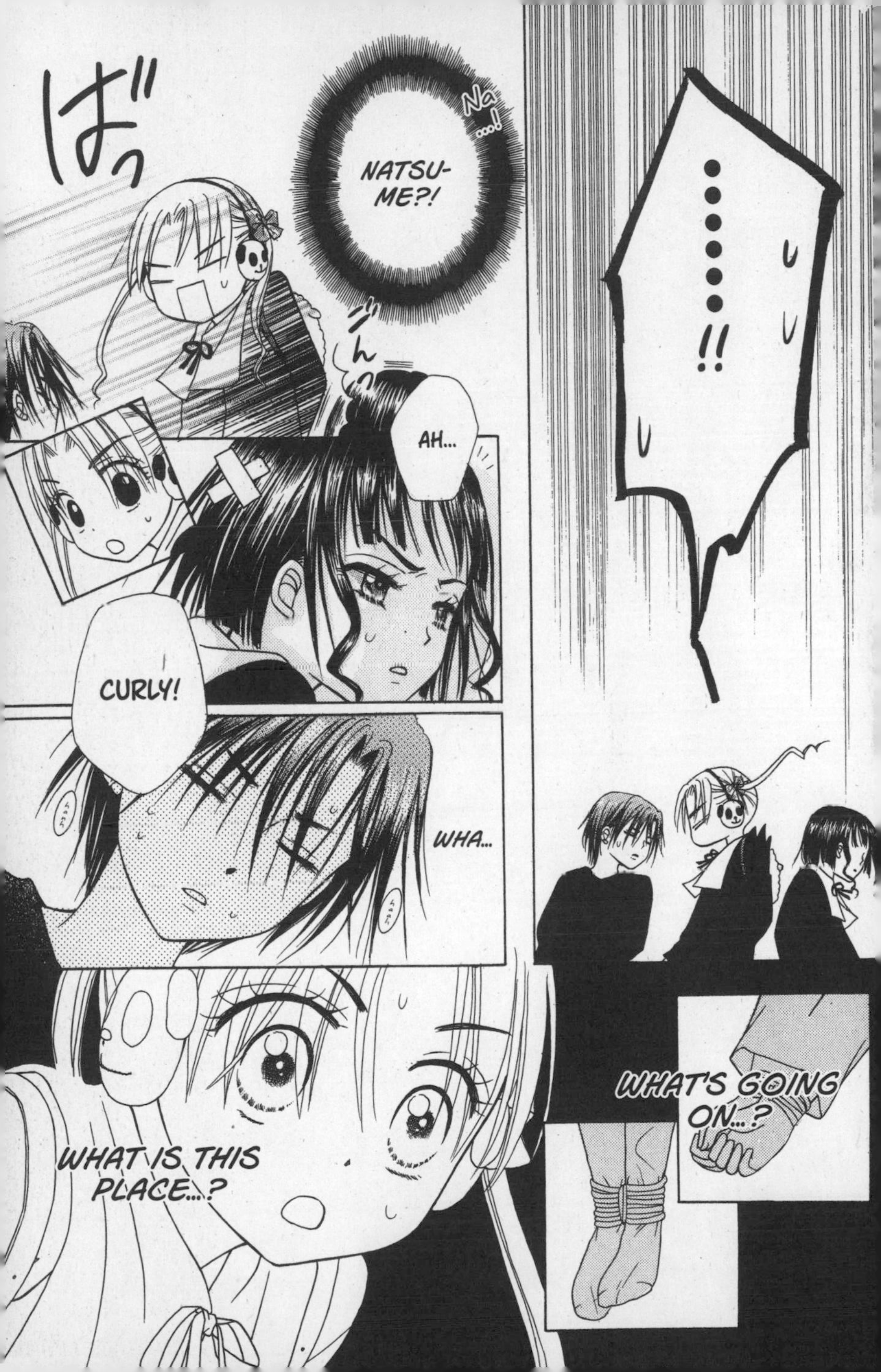
......!!
WHAT'S GOING ON...?
ばっ
Na...!
NATSU-ME?!
AH...
CURLY!
WHA...
WHAT IS THIS PLACE...?

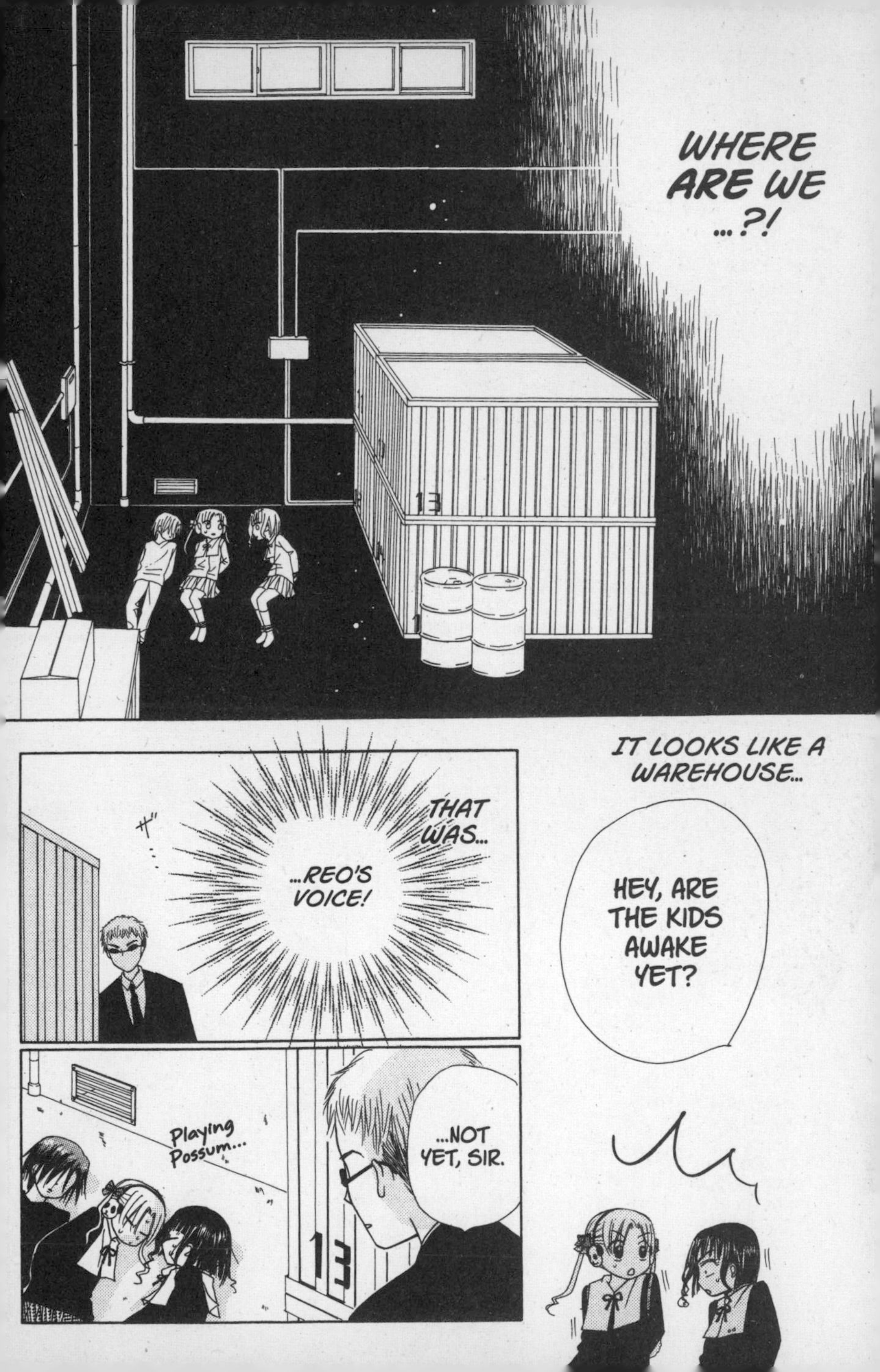
WHERE ARE WE ...?!
IT LOOKS LIKE A WAREHOUSE...
HEY, ARE THE KIDS AWAKE YET?
THAT WAS...
...REO'S VOICE!
...NOT YET, SIR.
Playing Possum...

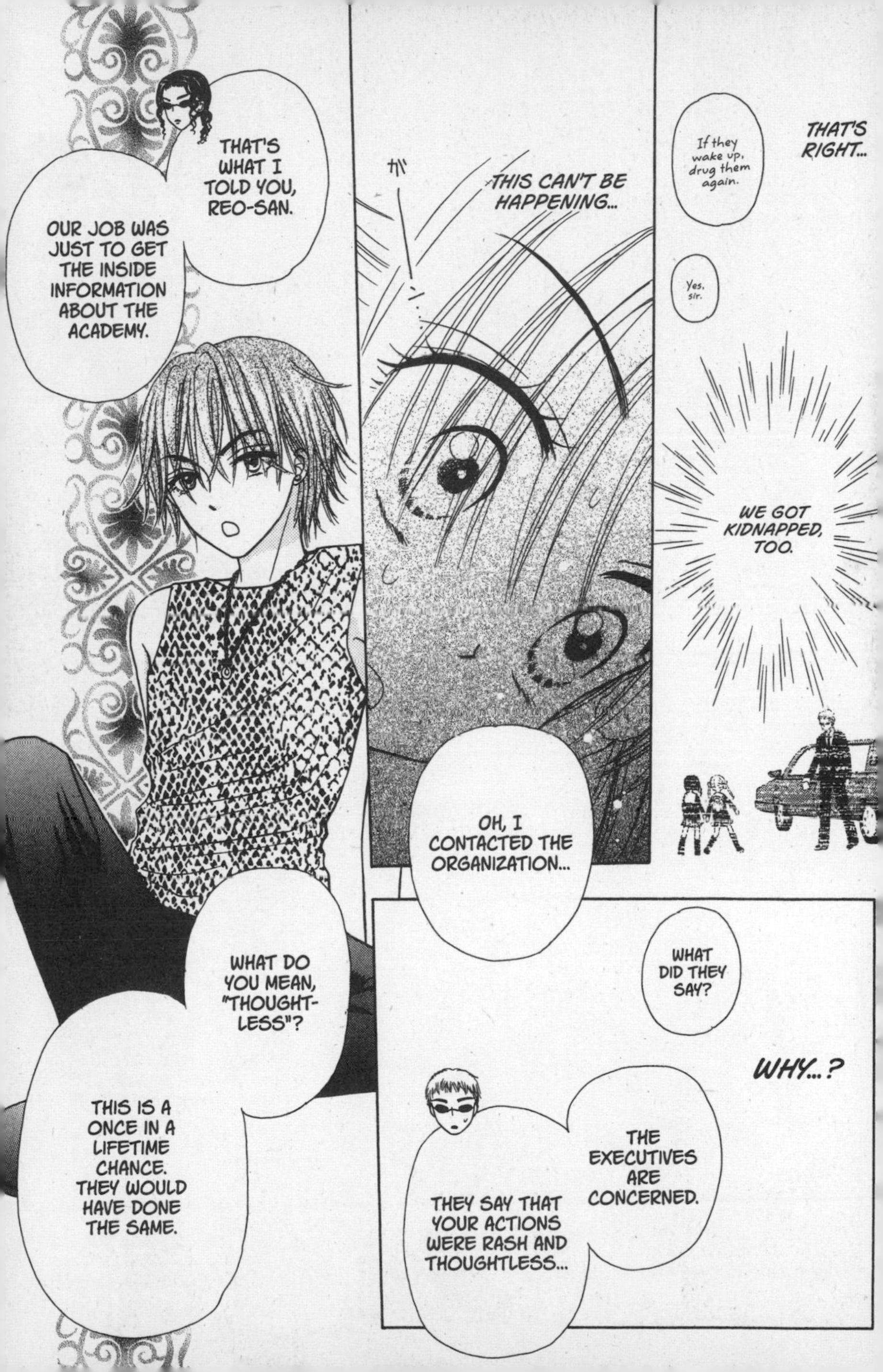
THAT'S RIGHT...
If they wake up, drug them again.
Yes, sir.
WE GOT KIDNAPPED, TOO.
ガ
THIS CAN'T BE HAPPENING...
OH, I CONTACTED THE ORGANIZATION...
WHAT DID THEY SAY?
WHY...?
THE EXECUTIVES ARE CONCERNED.
THEY SAY THAT YOUR ACTIONS WERE RASH AND THOUGHTLESS...
THAT'S WHAT I TOLD YOU, REO-SAN.
OUR JOB WAS JUST TO GET THE INSIDE INFORMATION ABOUT THE ACADEMY.
WHAT DO YOU MEAN, "THOUGHT-LESS"?
THIS IS A ONCE IN A LIFETIME CHANCE. THEY WOULD HAVE DONE THE SAME.

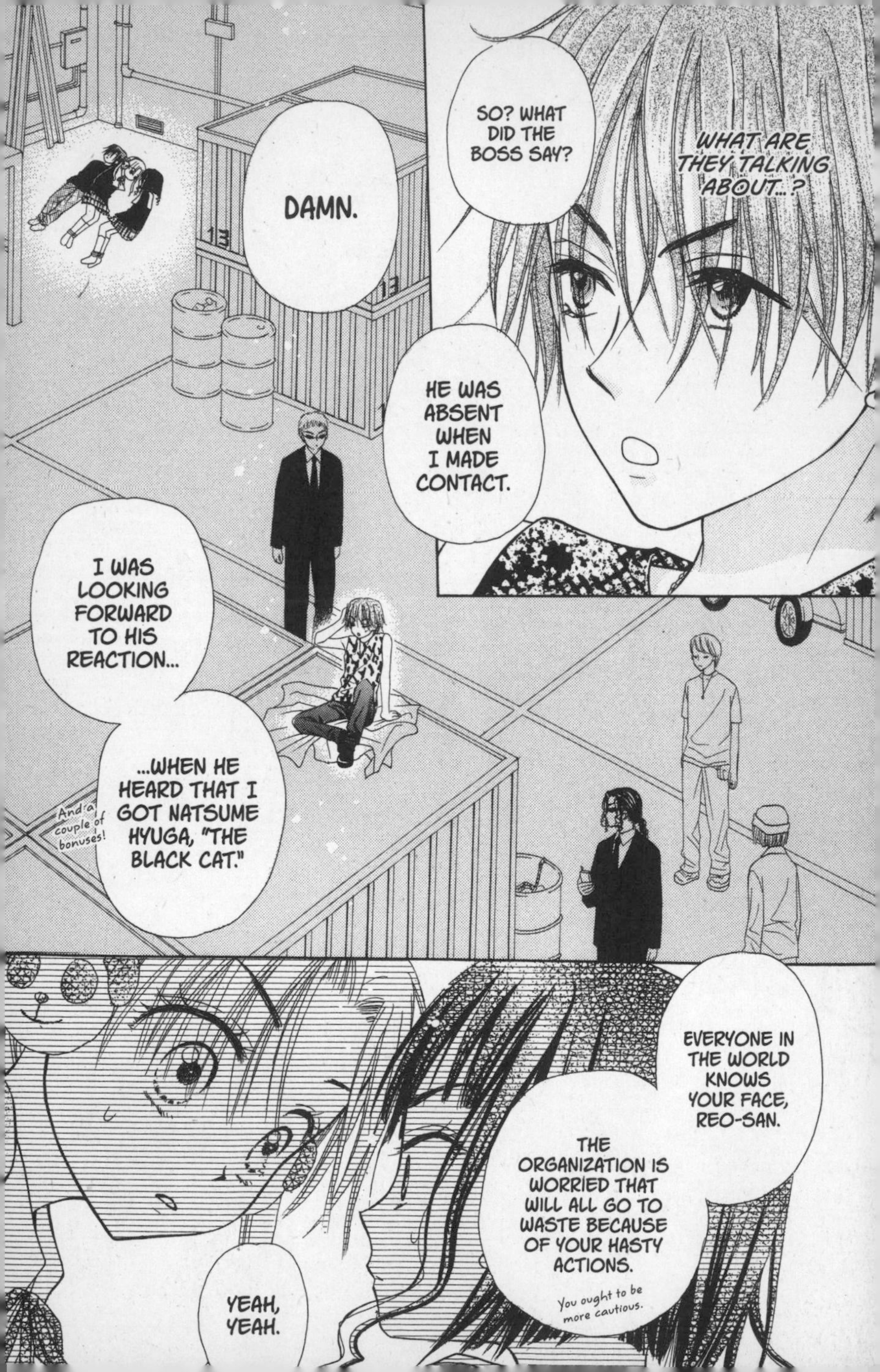
SO? WHAT DID THE BOSS SAY?
WHAT ARE THEY TALKING ABOUT...?
HE WAS ABSENT WHEN I MADE CONTACT.
DAMN.
I WAS LOOKING FORWARD TO HIS REACTION...
...WHEN HE HEARD THAT I GOT NATSUME HYUGA, "THE BLACK CAT."
And a couple of bonuses!
EVERYONE IN THE WORLD KNOWS YOUR FACE, REO-SAN.
THE ORGANIZATION IS WORRIED THAT WILL ALL GO TO WASTE BECAUSE OF YOUR HASTY ACTIONS.
You ought to be more cautious.
YEAH, YEAH.

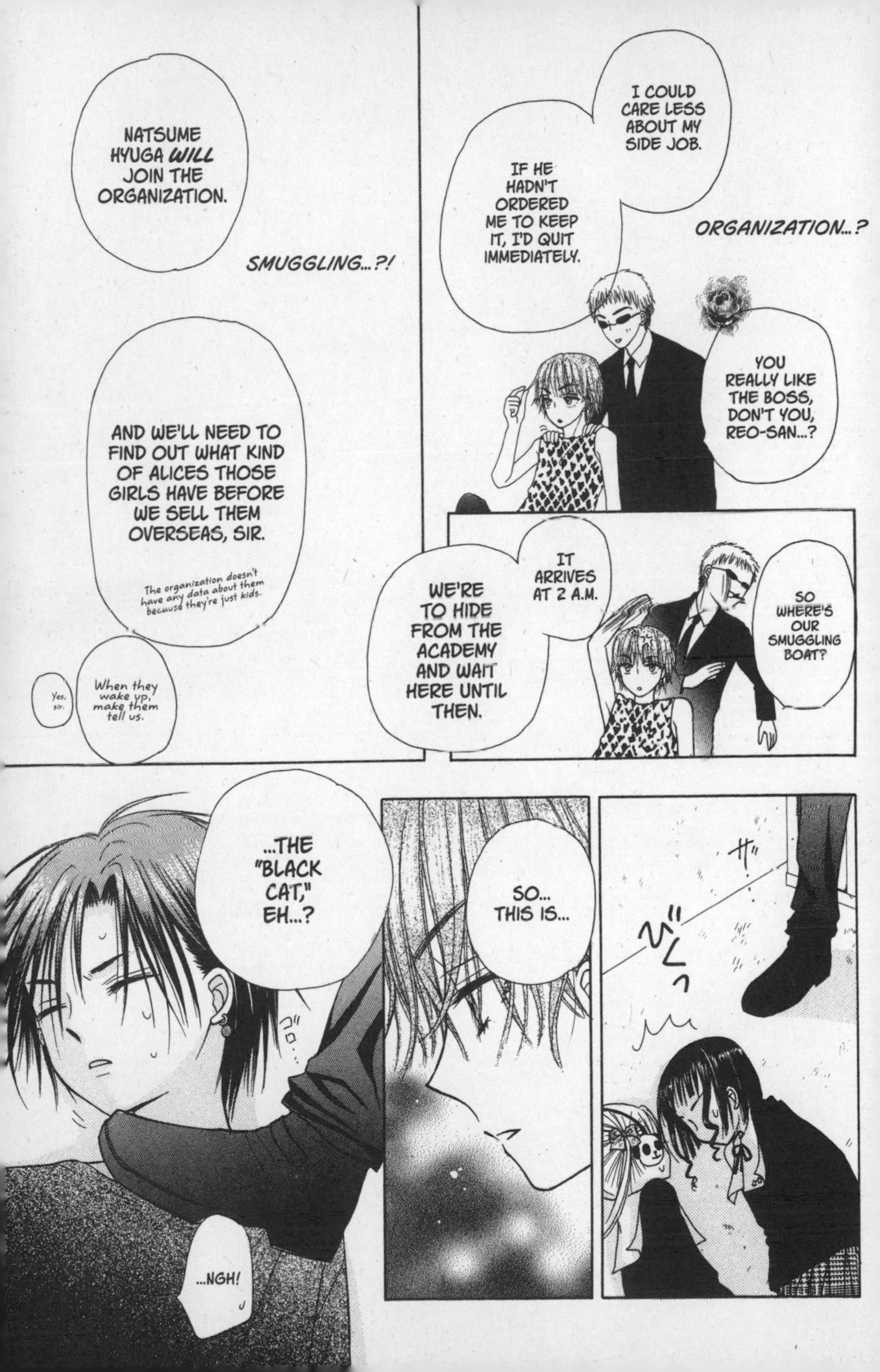

I COULD CARE LESS ABOUT MY SIDE JOB.
IF HE HADN'T ORDERED ME TO KEEP IT, I'D QUIT IMMEDIATELY.
ORGANIZATION...?
YOU REALLY LIKE THE BOSS, DON'T YOU, REO-SAN...?
SO WHERE'S OUR SMUGGLING BOAT?
IT ARRIVES AT 2 A.M.
WE'RE TO HIDE FROM THE ACADEMY AND WAIT HERE UNTIL THEN.
NATSUME HYUGA WILL JOIN THE ORGANIZATION.
SMUGGLING...?!
AND WE'LL NEED TO FIND OUT WHAT KIND OF ALICES THOSE GIRLS HAVE BEFORE WE SELL THEM OVERSEAS, SIR.
The organization doesn't have any data about them because they're just kids.
When they wake up, make them tell us.
Yes, sir.
SO... THIS IS...
...THE "BLACK CAT," EH...?
...NGH!

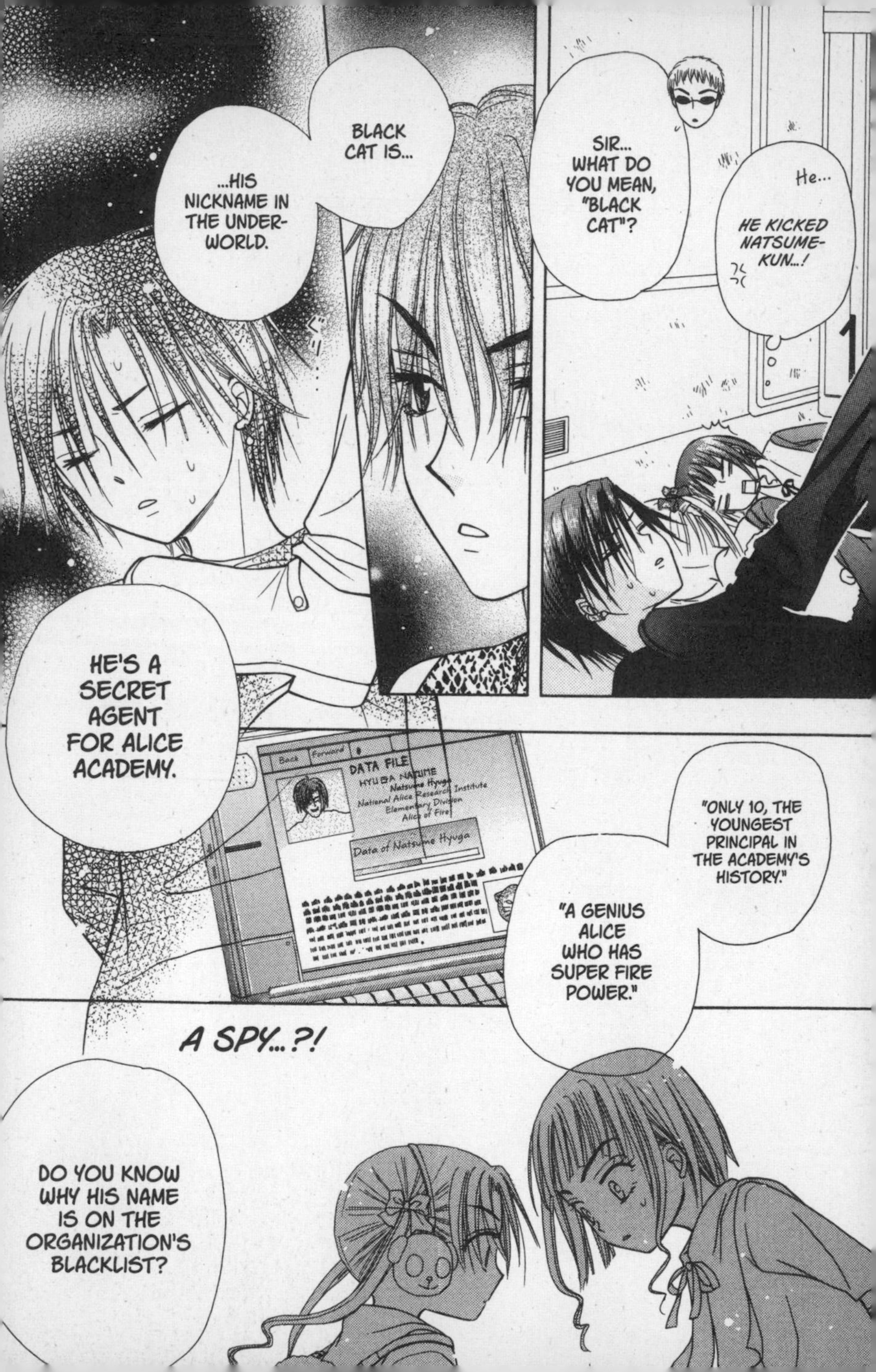
He...
HE KICKED NATSUME-KUN...!
SIR... WHAT DO YOU MEAN, "BLACK CAT"?
BLACK CAT IS...
...HIS NICKNAME IN THE UNDER-WORLD.
HE'S A SECRET AGENT FOR ALICE ACADEMY.
Back
Forward
DATA FILE
HYUGA NATSUME
Natsume Hyuga
National Alice Research Institute
Elementary Division
Alice of Fire
Data of Natsume Hyuga
"ONLY 10, THE YOUNGEST PRINCIPAL IN THE ACADEMY'S HISTORY."
"A GENIUS ALICE WHO HAS SUPER FIRE POWER."
A SPY...?!
DO YOU KNOW WHY HIS NAME IS ON THE ORGANIZATION'S BLACKLIST?

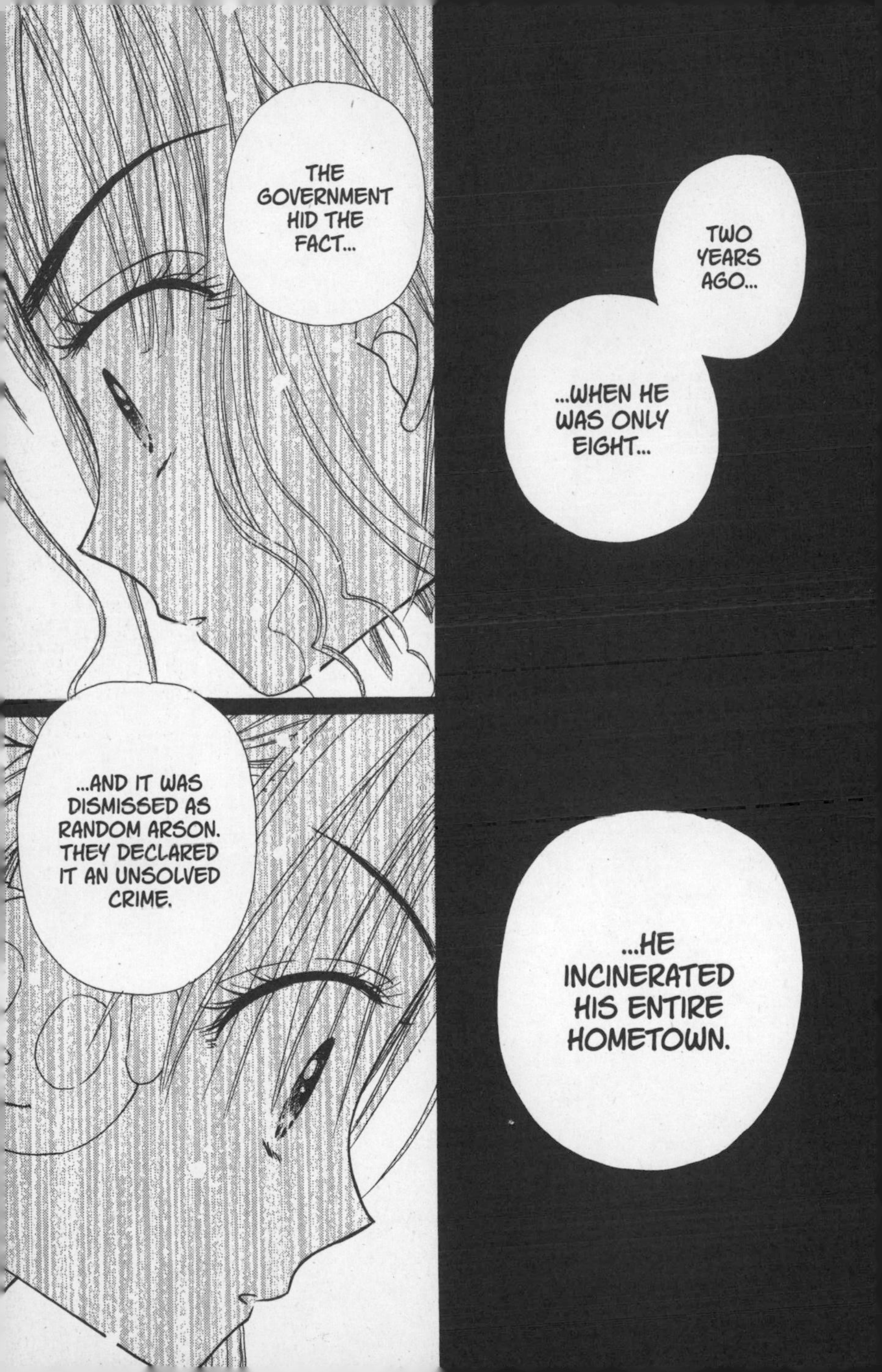
TWO YEARS AGO...
...WHEN HE WAS ONLY EIGHT...
...HE INCINERATED HIS ENTIRE HOMETOWN.
THE GOVERNMENT HID THE FACT...
...AND IT WAS DISMISSED AS RANDOM ARSON. THEY DECLARED IT AN UNSOLVED CRIME.

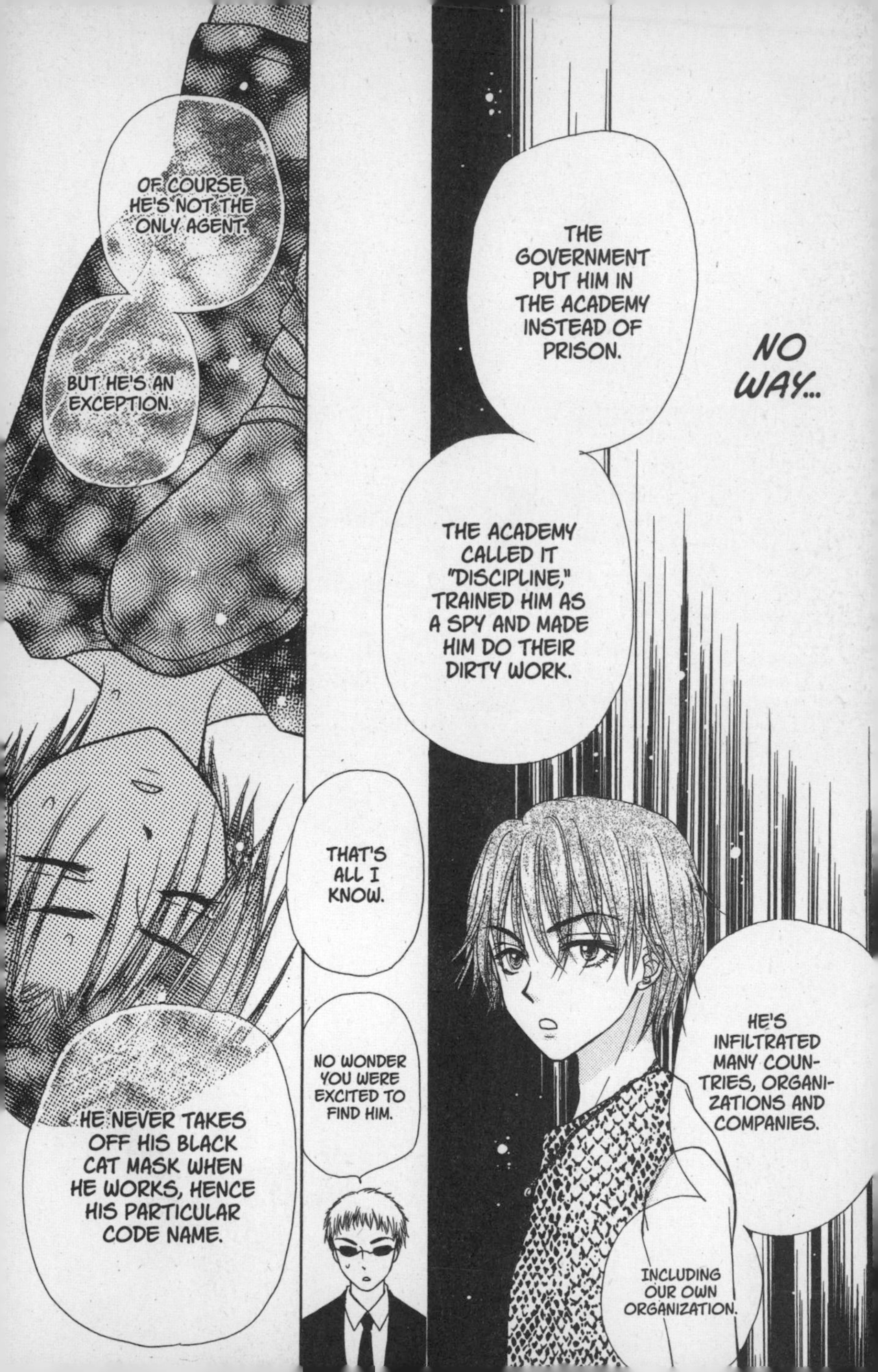
THE GOVERNMENT PUT HIM IN THE ACADEMY INSTEAD OF PRISON.
NO WAY...
THE ACADEMY CALLED IT "DISCIPLINE," TRAINED HIM AS A SPY AND MADE HIM DO THEIR DIRTY WORK.
HE'S INFILTRATED MANY COUNTRIES, ORGANIZATIONS AND COMPANIES.
INCLUDING OUR OWN ORGANIZATION.
THAT'S ALL I KNOW.
NO WONDER YOU WERE EXCITED TO FIND HIM.
OF COURSE, HE'S NOT THE ONLY AGENT.
BUT HE'S AN EXCEPTION.
HE NEVER TAKES OFF HIS BLACK CAT MASK WHEN HE WORKS, HENCE HIS PARTICULAR CODE NAME.

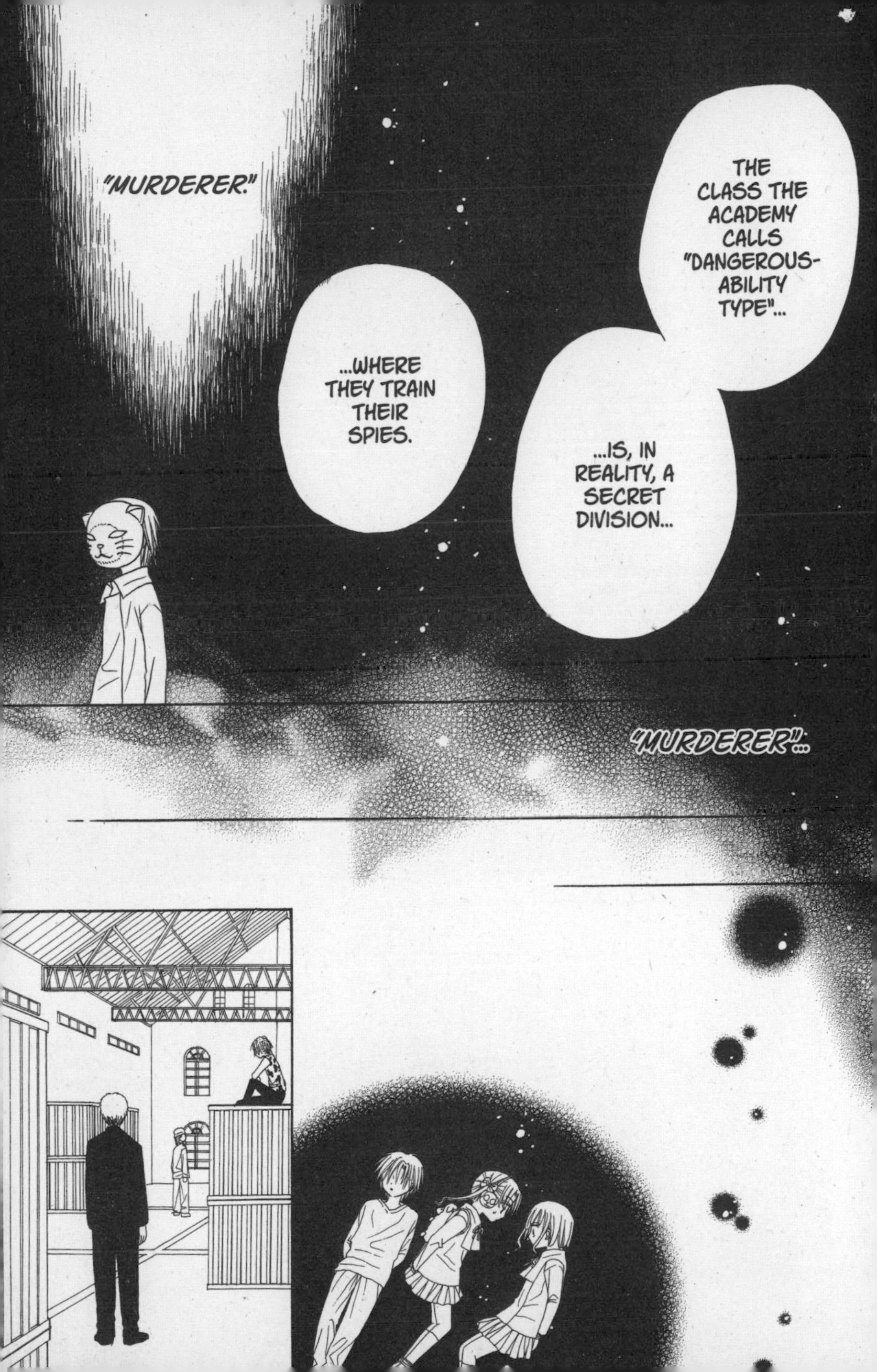
THE CLASS THE ACADEMY CALLS "DANGEROUS-ABILITY TYPE"...
...IS, IN REALITY, A SECRET DIVISION...
...WHERE THEY TRAIN THEIR SPIES.
"MURDERER."
"MURDERER"...

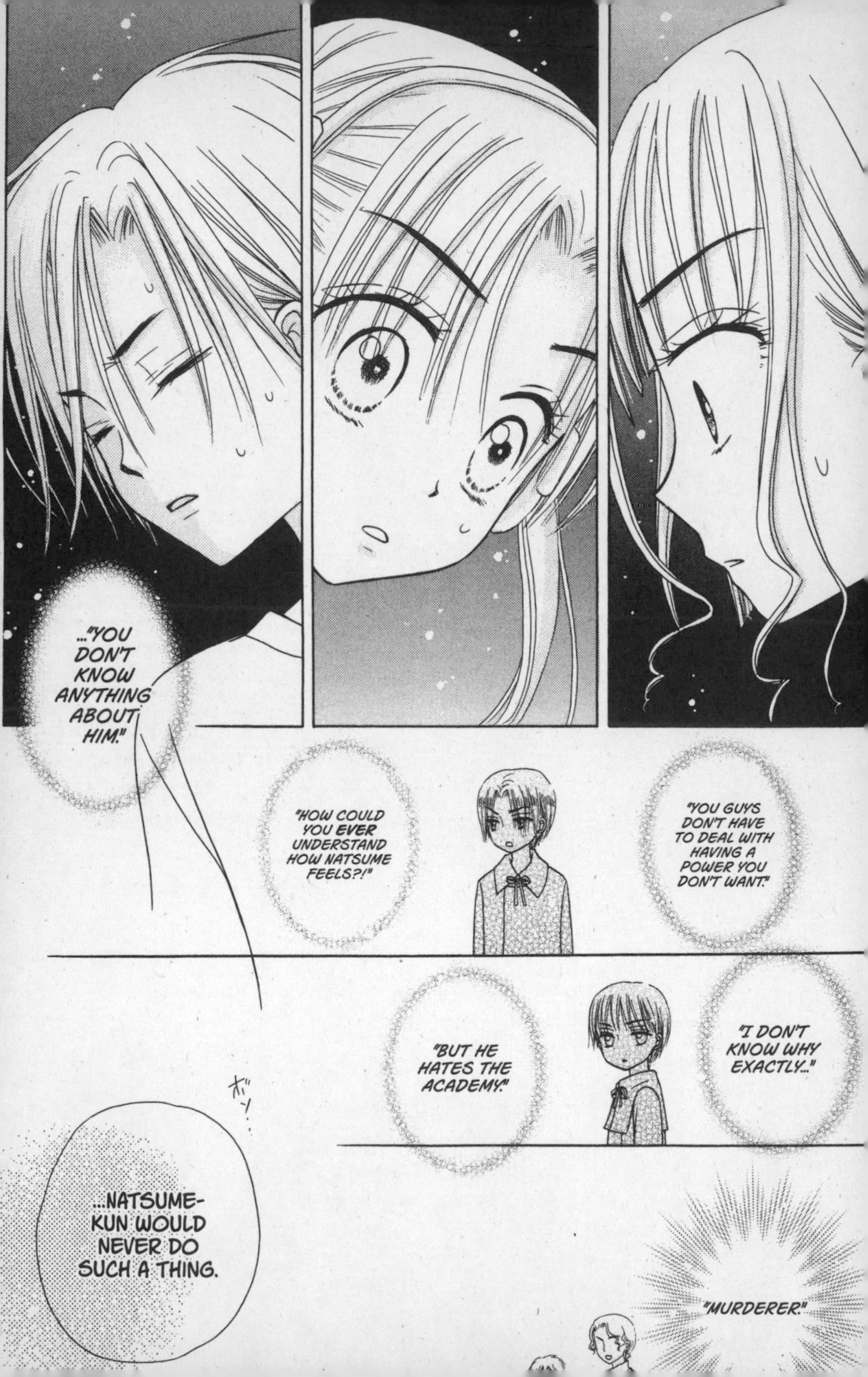
..."YOU DON'T KNOW ANYTHING ABOUT HIM."
"YOU GUYS DON'T HAVE TO DEAL WITH HAVING A POWER YOU DON'T WANT."
"HOW COULD YOU EVER UNDERSTAND HOW NATSUME FEELS?!"
"I DON'T KNOW WHY EXACTLY..."
"BUT HE HATES THE ACADEMY."
"MURDERER."
...NATSUME-KUN WOULD NEVER DO SUCH A THING.

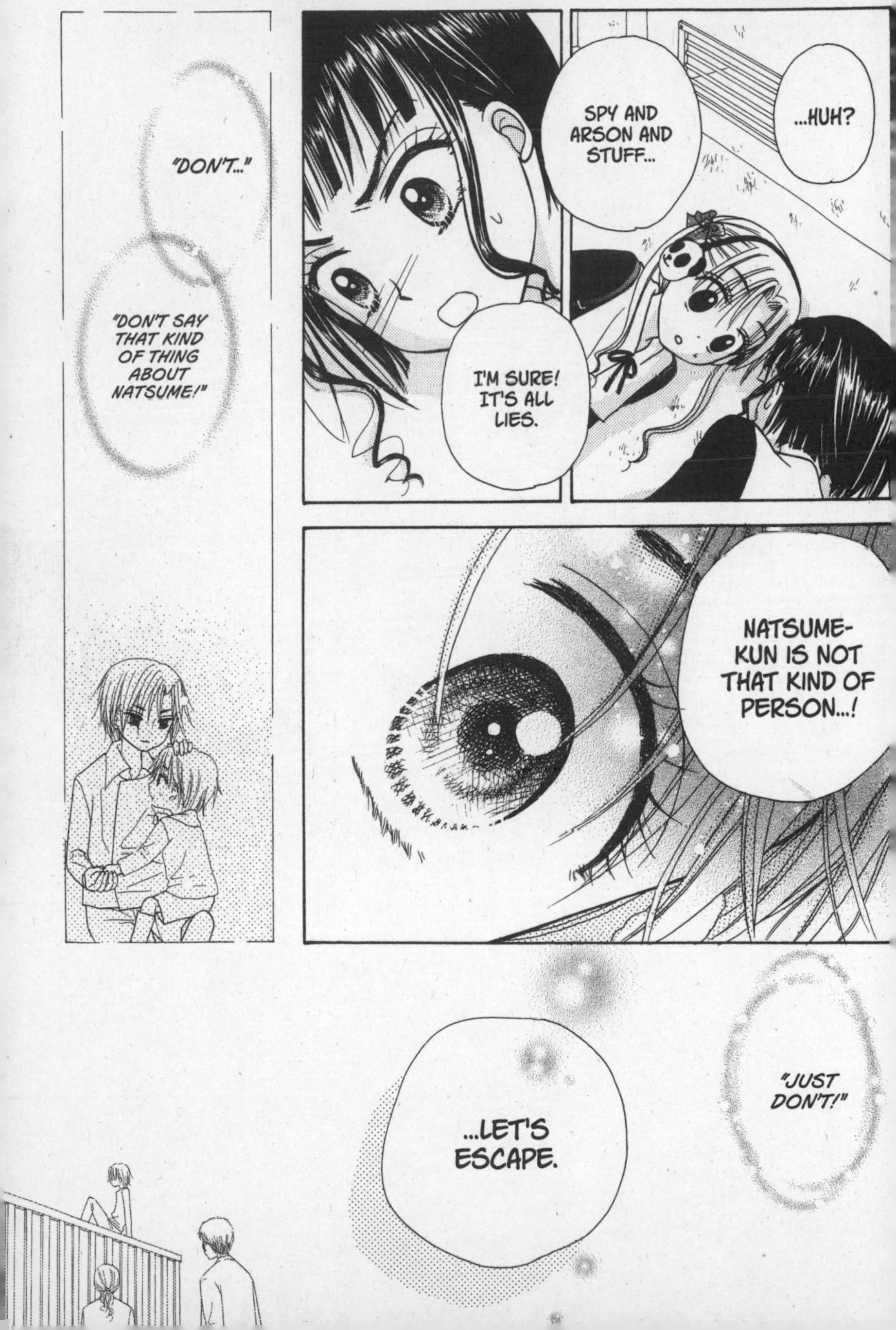
...HUH?
SPY AND ARSON AND STUFF...
I'M SURE! IT'S ALL LIES.
NATSUME-KUN IS NOT THAT KIND OF PERSON...!
"DON'T..."
"DON'T SAY THAT KIND OF THING ABOUT NATSUME!"
"JUST DON'T!"
...LET'S ESCAPE.

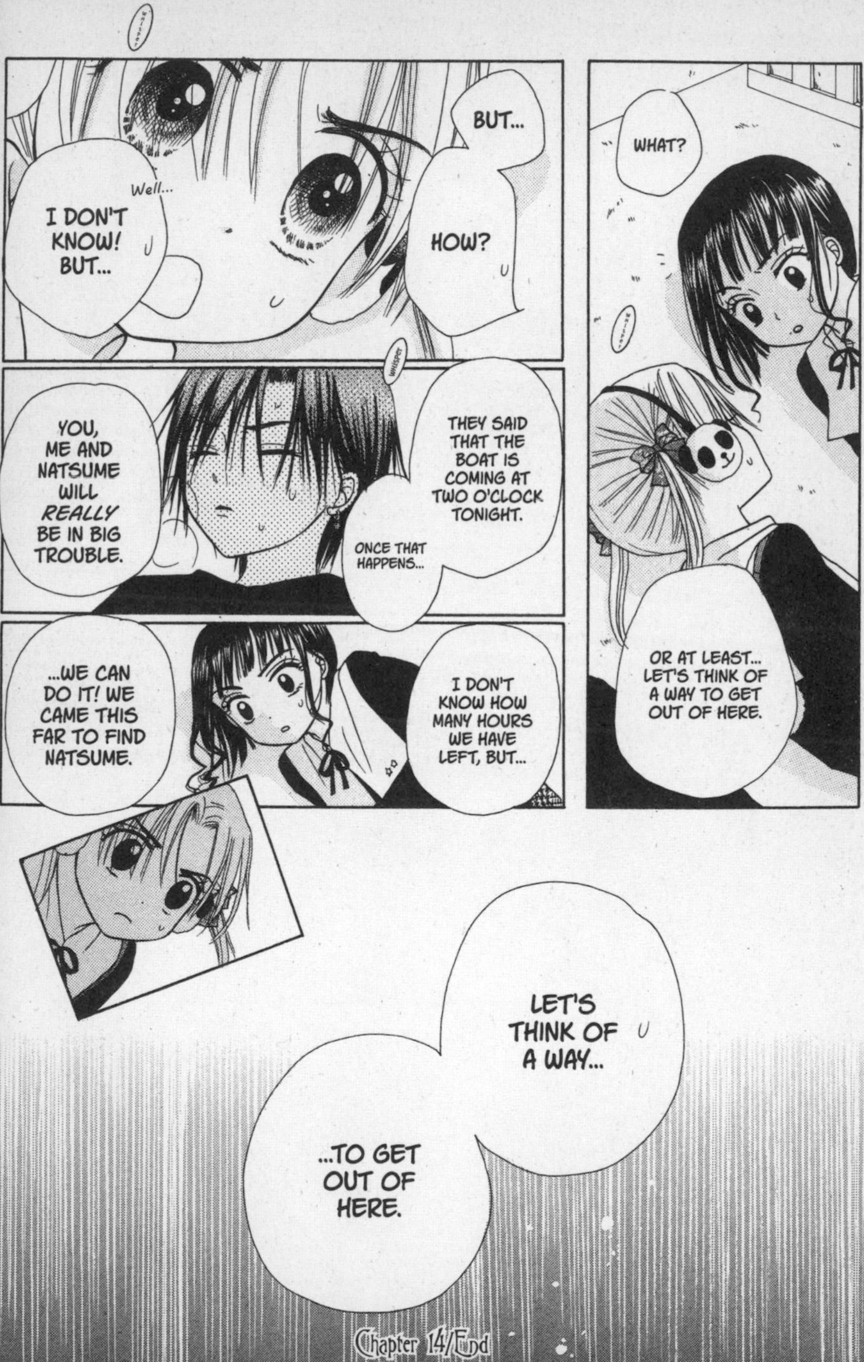
WHAT?
Whisper
OR AT LEAST... LET'S THINK OF A WAY TO GET OUT OF HERE.
Whisper
BUT... HOW?
I DON'T KNOW! BUT...
Well...
Whisper
THEY SAID THAT THE BOAT IS COMING AT TWO O'CLOCK TONIGHT.
ONCE THAT HAPPENS...
YOU, ME AND NATSUME WILL *REALLY* BE IN BIG TROUBLE.
I DON'T KNOW HOW MANY HOURS WE HAVE LEFT, BUT...
...WE CAN DO IT! WE CAME THIS FAR TO FIND NATSUME.
LET'S THINK OF A WAY...
...TO GET OUT OF HERE.
Chapter 14/End

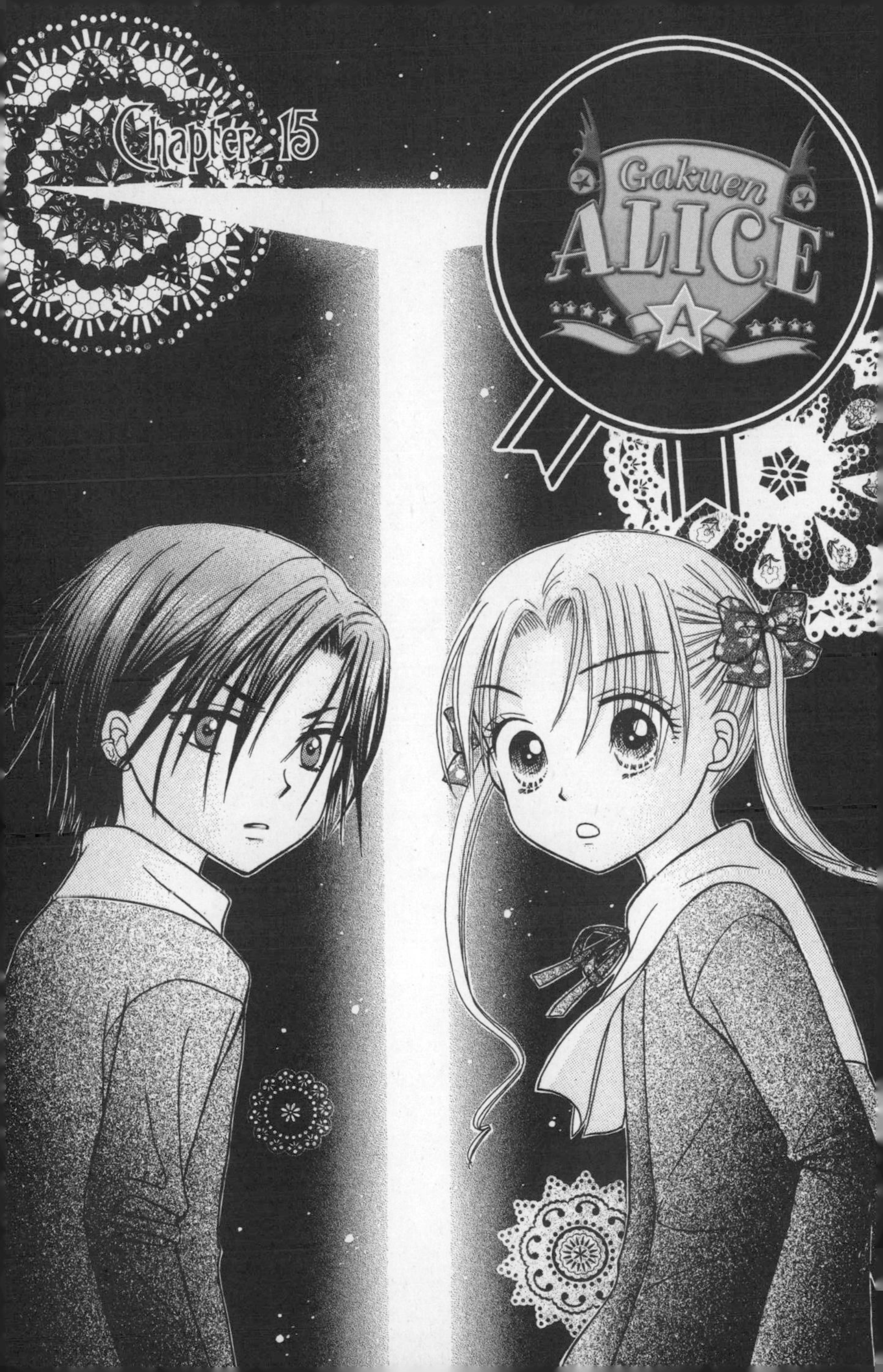
Chapter 15
Gakuen
ALICE
A

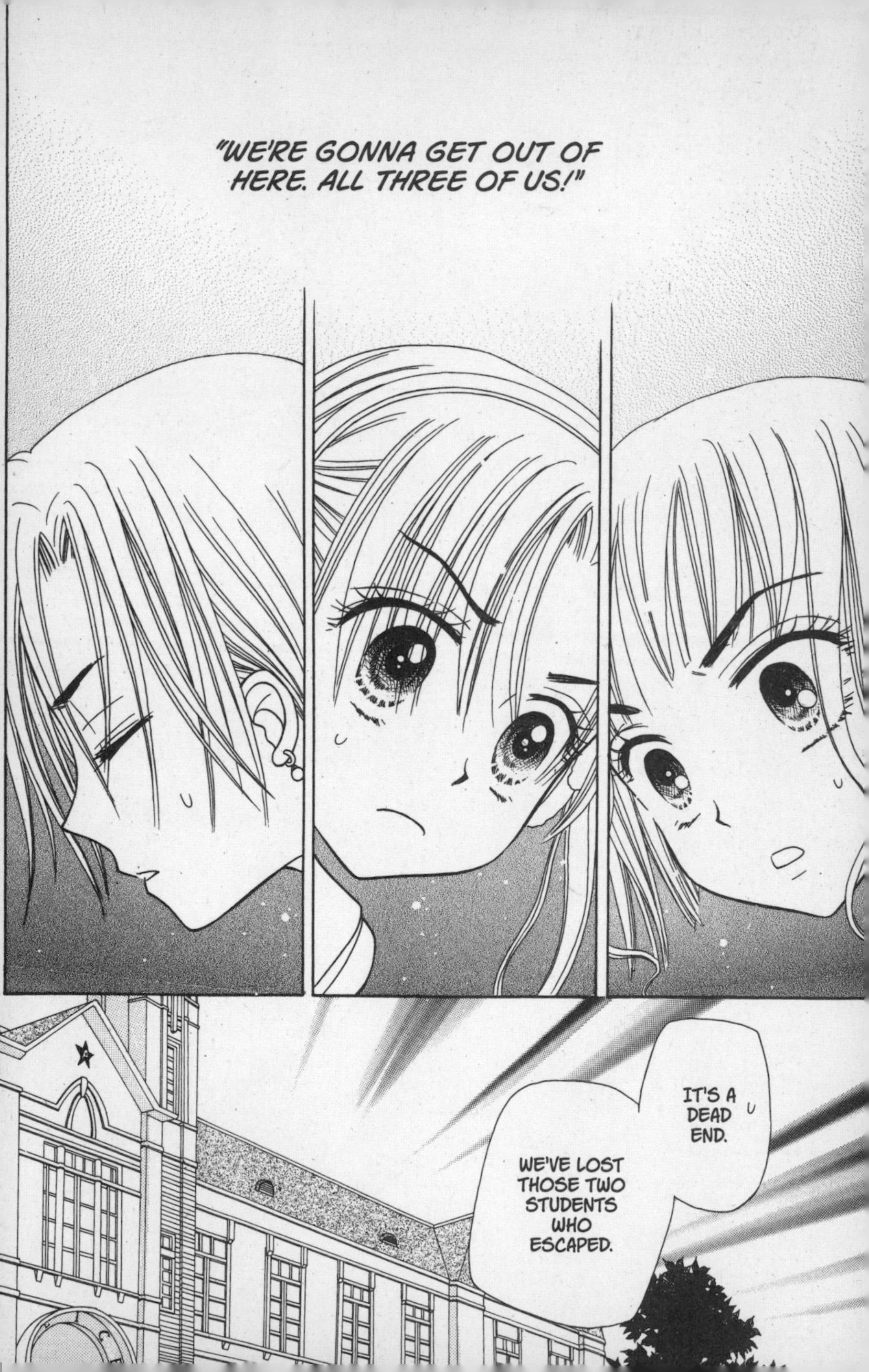
"WE'RE GONNA GET OUT OF HERE. ALL THREE OF US!"
IT'S A DEAD END.
WE'VE LOST THOSE TWO STUDENTS WHO ESCAPED.

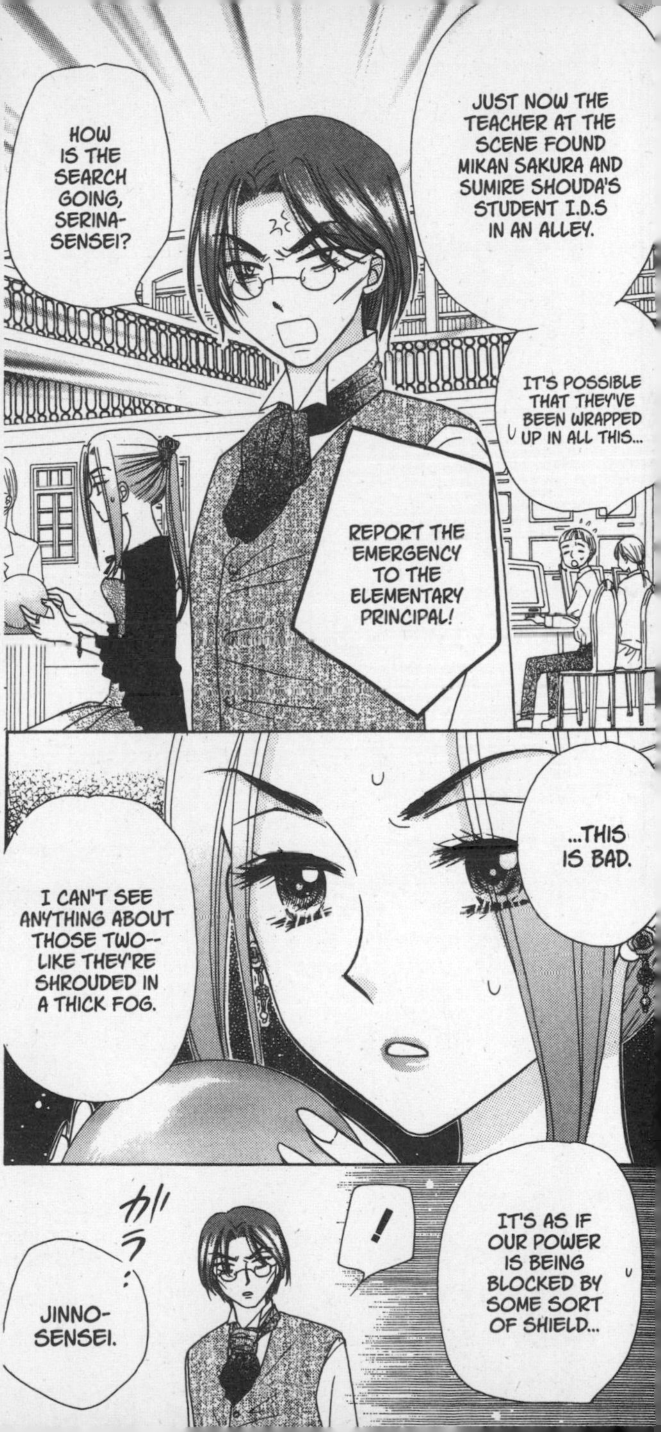
JUST NOW THE TEACHER AT THE SCENE FOUND MIKAN SAKURA AND SUMIRE SHOUDA'S STUDENT I.D.S IN AN ALLEY.
HOW IS THE SEARCH GOING, SERINA-SENSEI?
IT'S POSSIBLE THAT THEY'VE BEEN WRAPPED UP IN ALL THIS...
REPORT THE EMERGENCY TO THE ELEMENTARY PRINCIPAL!
...THIS IS BAD.
I CAN'T SEE ANYTHING ABOUT THOSE TWO-- LIKE THEY'RE SHROUDED IN A THICK FOG.
IT'S AS IF OUR POWER IS BEING BLOCKED BY SOME SORT OF SHIELD...
!
ガラ
JINNO-SENSEI.

Higuchi's Room 5

PROFILE 8

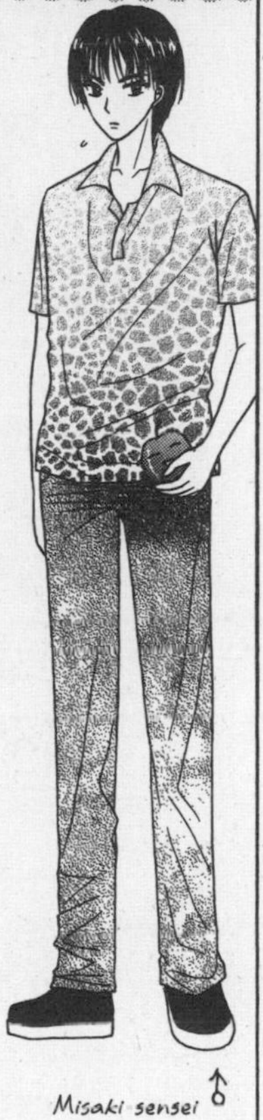

Misaki sensei

Born on Sept. 3,
27 years old
Virgo, blood type A

Even though he doesn't appear in the story much, he's unexpectedly popular. Come to think of it, what're his and Naru's first names? It's fun to draw the fruit he always has in his hands every time he appears. You'll see some more teachers in the story later. They're all Alice Academy graduates, so they still have the upper-underclassman thing going. He and Naru are friends but Naru did something to him in the past and Misaki-sensei hasn't forgiven him for it.

Go to 6.

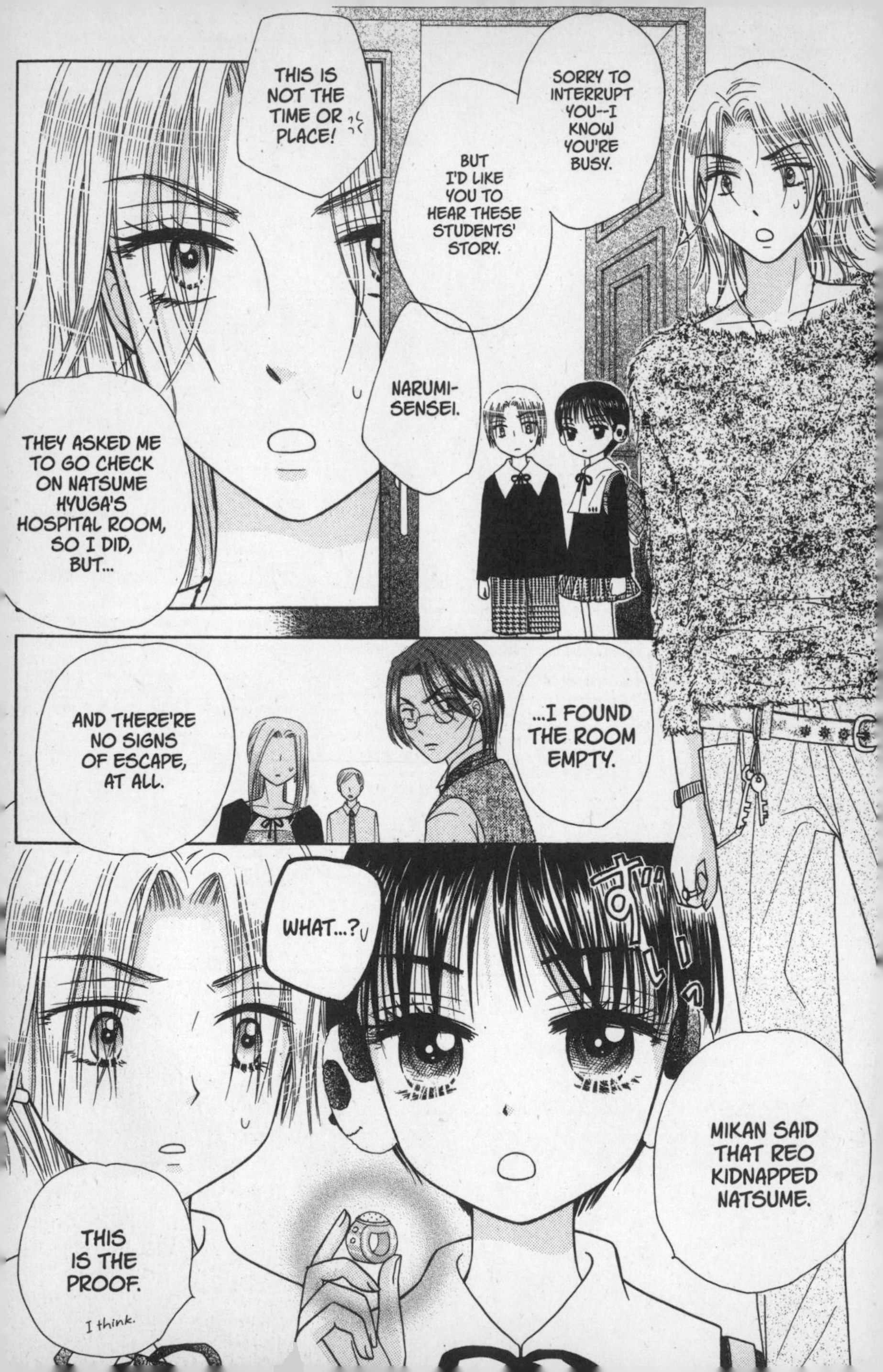
SORRY TO INTERRUPT YOU--I KNOW YOU'RE BUSY.
BUT I'D LIKE YOU TO HEAR THESE STUDENTS' STORY.
NARUMI-SENSEI.
THIS IS NOT THE TIME OR PLACE!
THEY ASKED ME TO GO CHECK ON NATSUME HYUGA'S HOSPITAL ROOM, SO I DID, BUT...
...I FOUND THE ROOM EMPTY.
AND THERE'RE NO SIGNS OF ESCAPE, AT ALL.
MIKAN SAID THAT REO KIDNAPPED NATSUME.
WHAT...?
THIS IS THE PROOF.
I think.

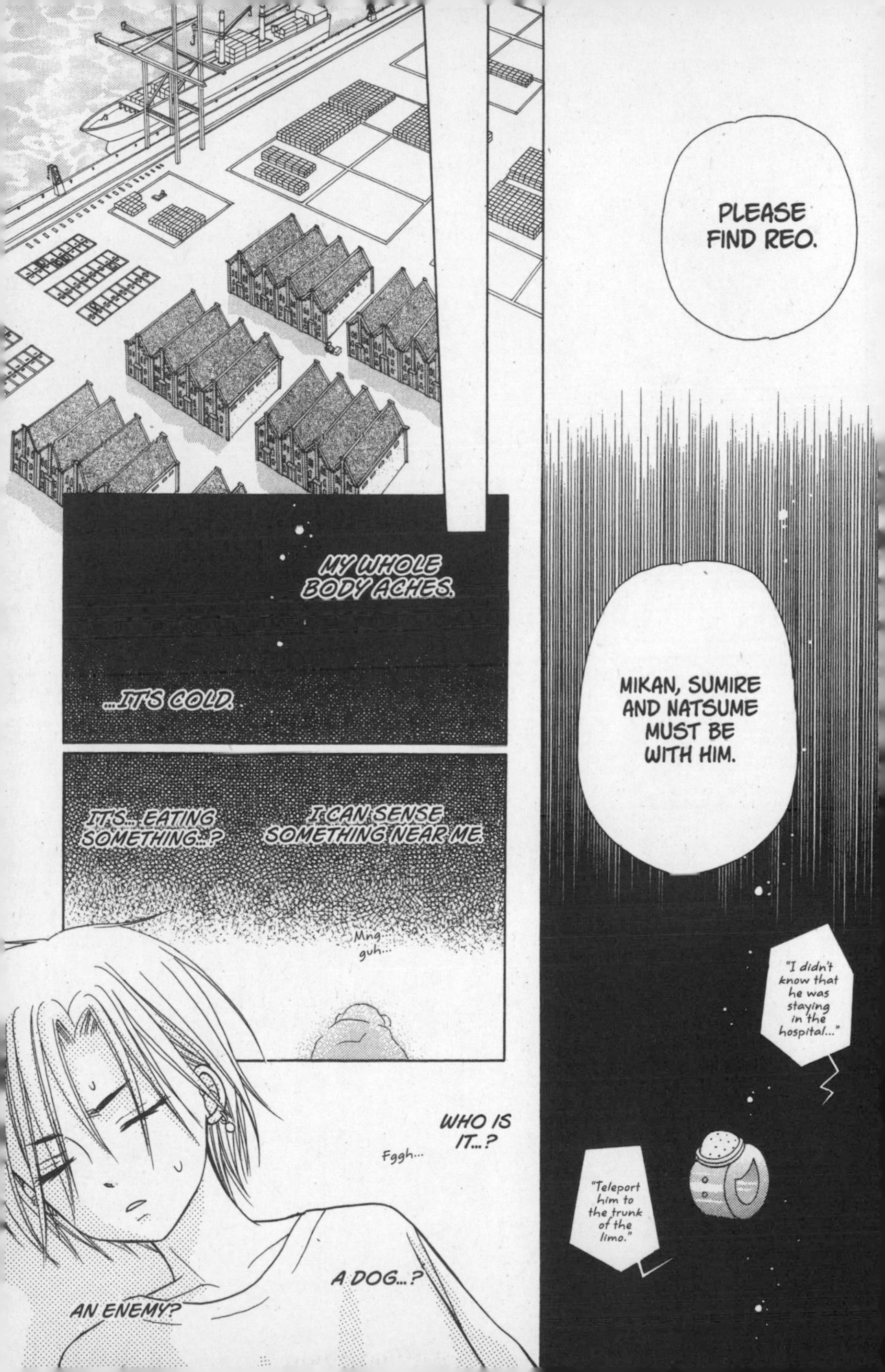
PLEASE FIND REO.
MIKAN, SUMIRE AND NATSUME MUST BE WITH HIM.
"I didn't know that he was staying in the hospital..."
"Teleport him to the trunk of the limo."
MY WHOLE BODY ACHES.
...IT'S COLD.
I CAN SENSE SOMETHING NEAR ME.
IT'S... EATING SOMETHING...?
Mng guh...
WHO IS IT...?
Fggh...
A DOG...?
AN ENEMY?

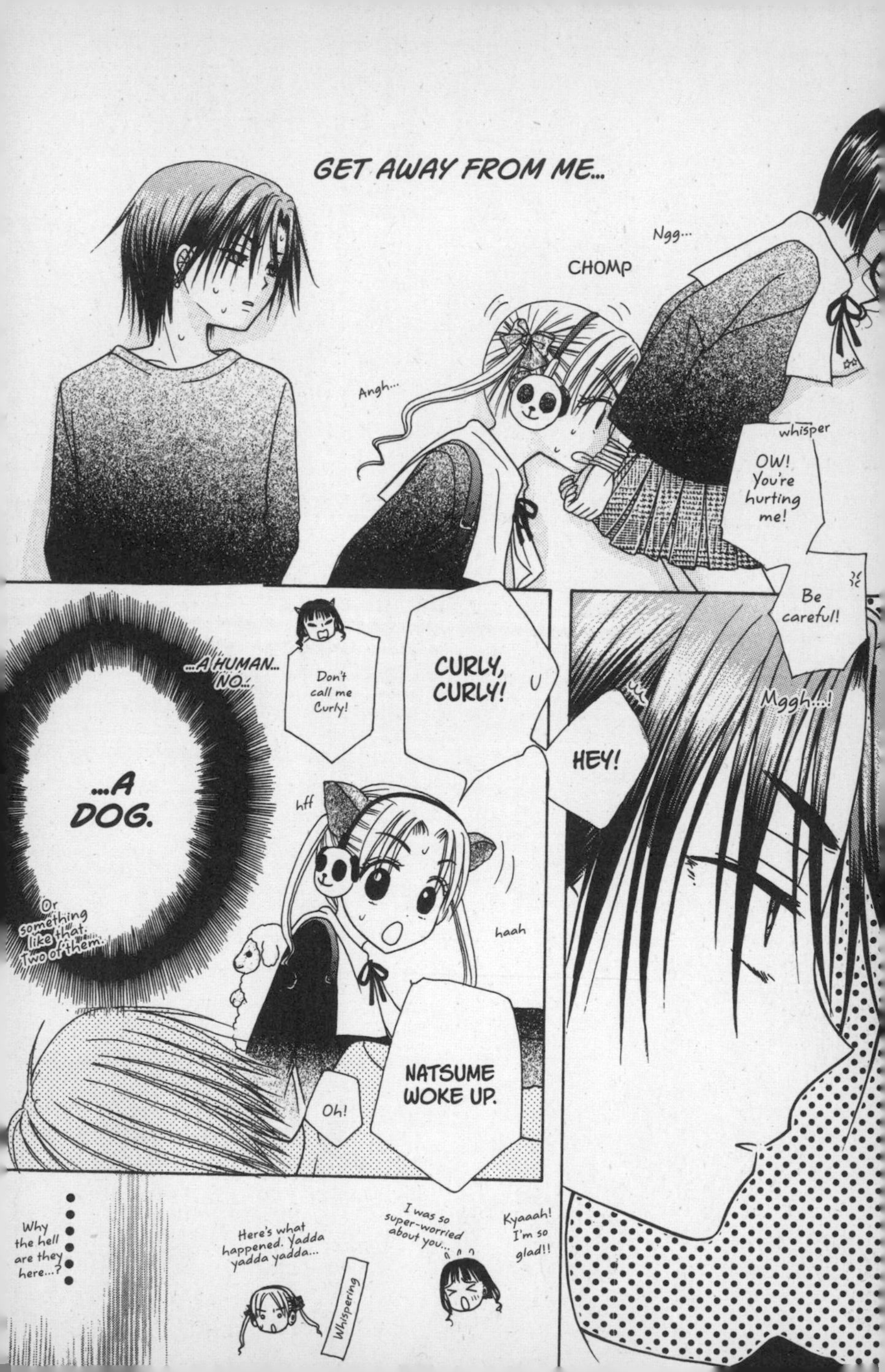
Ngg...
whisper
OW! You're hurting me!
Be careful!
GET AWAY FROM ME...
CHOMP
Angh...
Mggh...!
HEY!
CURLY, CURLY!
Don't call me Curly!
hff
haah
NATSUME WOKE UP.
Oh!
...A HUMAN... NO...
...A DOG.
Or something like that. Two of them.
Kyaaah! I'm so glad!!
I was so super-worried about you...
Here's what happened. Yadda yadda yadda...
Whispering
Why the hell are they here...?

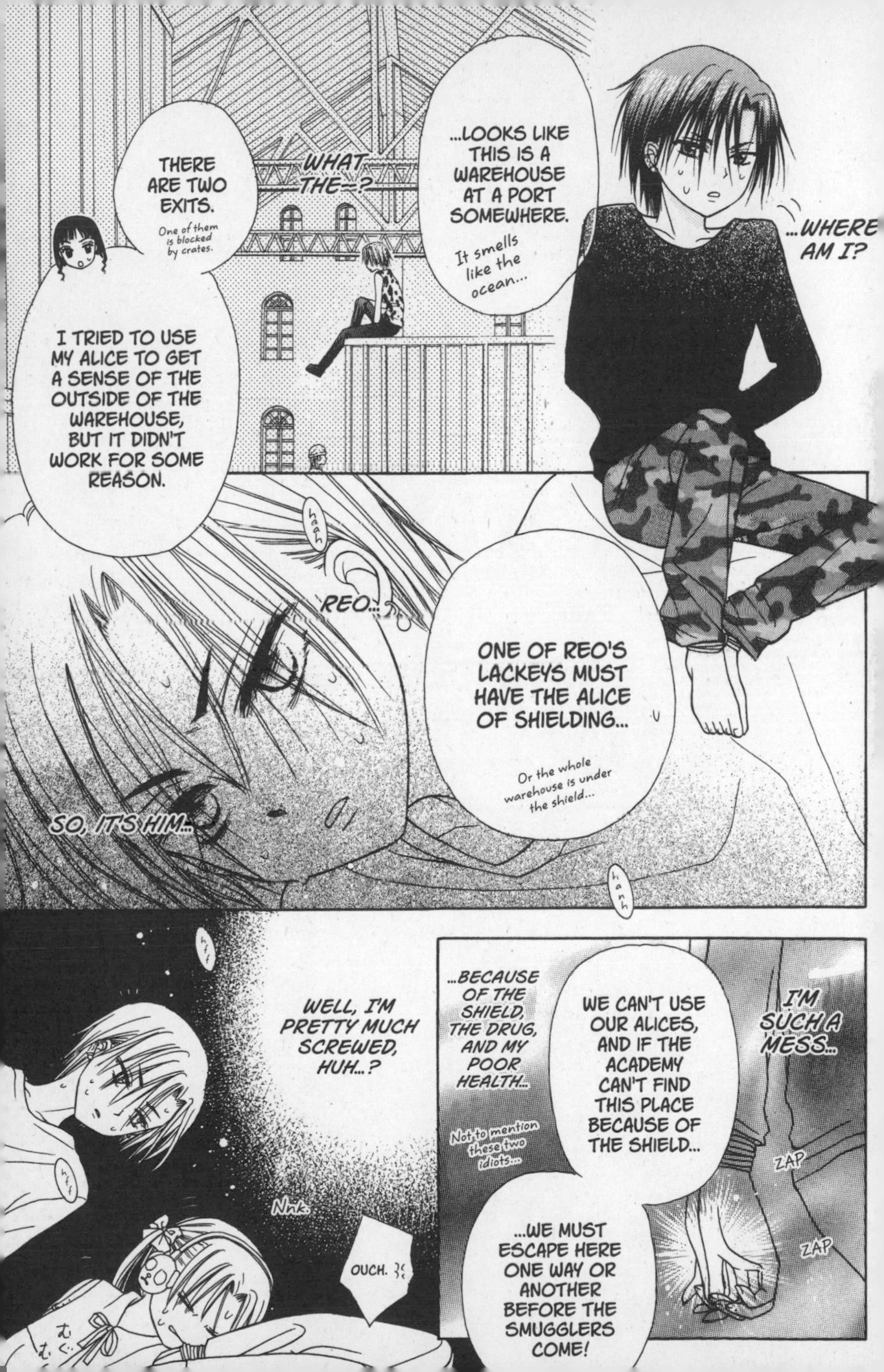
...WHERE AM I?
...LOOKS LIKE THIS IS A WAREHOUSE AT A PORT SOMEWHERE.
It smells like the ocean...
WHAT THE--?
THERE ARE TWO EXITS.
One of them is blocked by crates.
I TRIED TO USE MY ALICE TO GET A SENSE OF THE OUTSIDE OF THE WAREHOUSE, BUT IT DIDN'T WORK FOR SOME REASON.
ONE OF REO'S LACKEYS MUST HAVE THE ALICE OF SHIELDING...
Or the whole warehouse is under the shield...
haah
REO...
SO, IT'S HIM...
haah
I'M SUCH A MESS...
ZAP
ZAP
WE CAN'T USE OUR ALICES, AND IF THE ACADEMY CAN'T FIND THIS PLACE BECAUSE OF THE SHIELD...
...WE MUST ESCAPE HERE ONE WAY OR ANOTHER BEFORE THE SMUGGLERS COME!
...BECAUSE OF THE SHIELD, THE DRUG, AND MY POOR HEALTH...
Not to mention these two idiots...
WELL, I'M PRETTY MUCH SCREWED, HUH...?
hff
hff
Nnk.
OUCH.

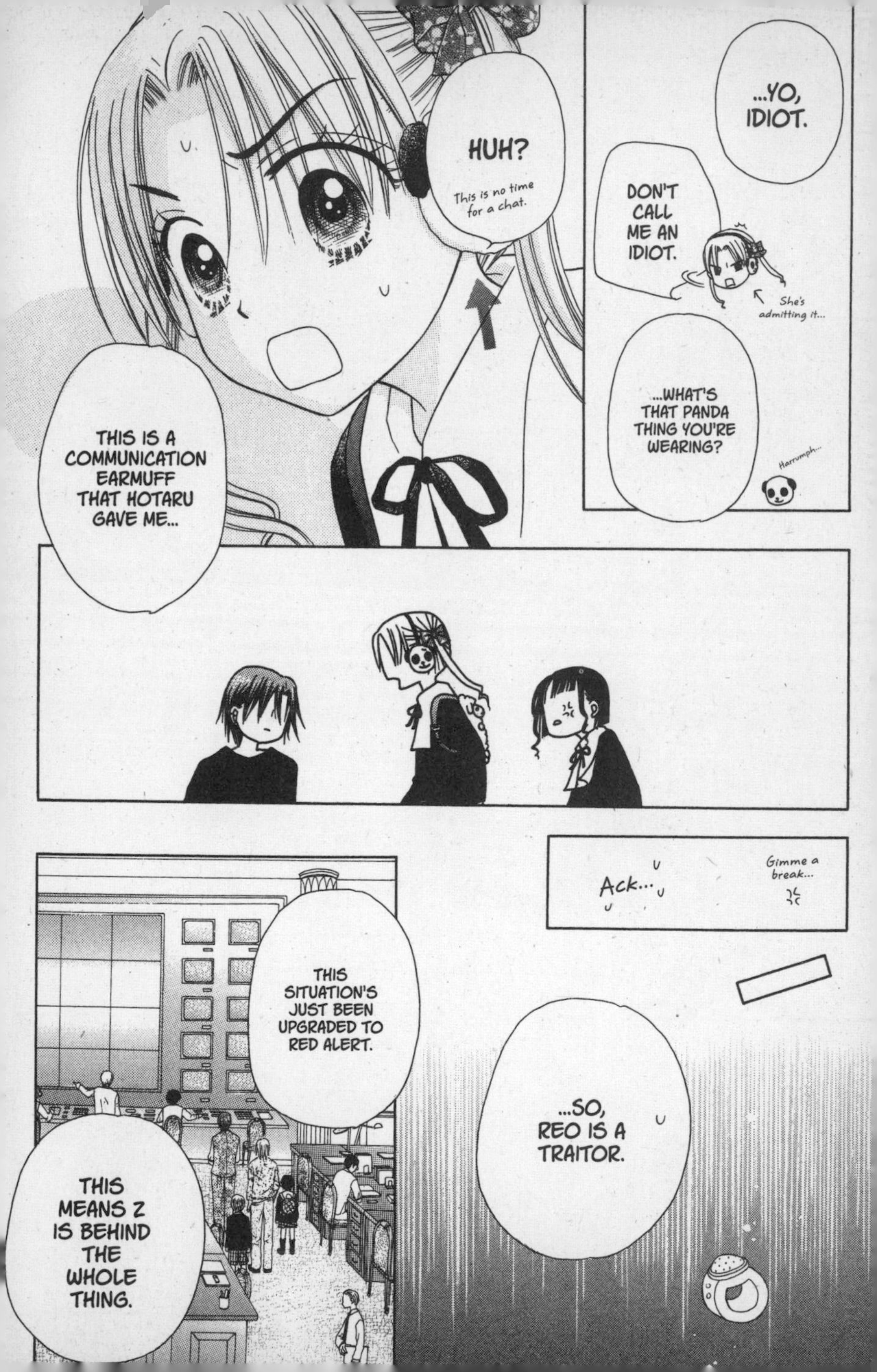
...YO, IDIOT.
DON'T CALL ME AN IDIOT.
She's admitting it...
...WHAT'S THAT PANDA THING YOU'RE WEARING?
Harrumph...
HUH?
This is no time for a chat.
THIS IS A COMMUNICATION EARMUFF THAT HOTARU GAVE ME...
Gimme a break...
Ack...
...SO, REO IS A TRAITOR.
THIS SITUATION'S JUST BEEN UPGRADED TO RED ALERT.
THIS MEANS Z IS BEHIND THE WHOLE THING.

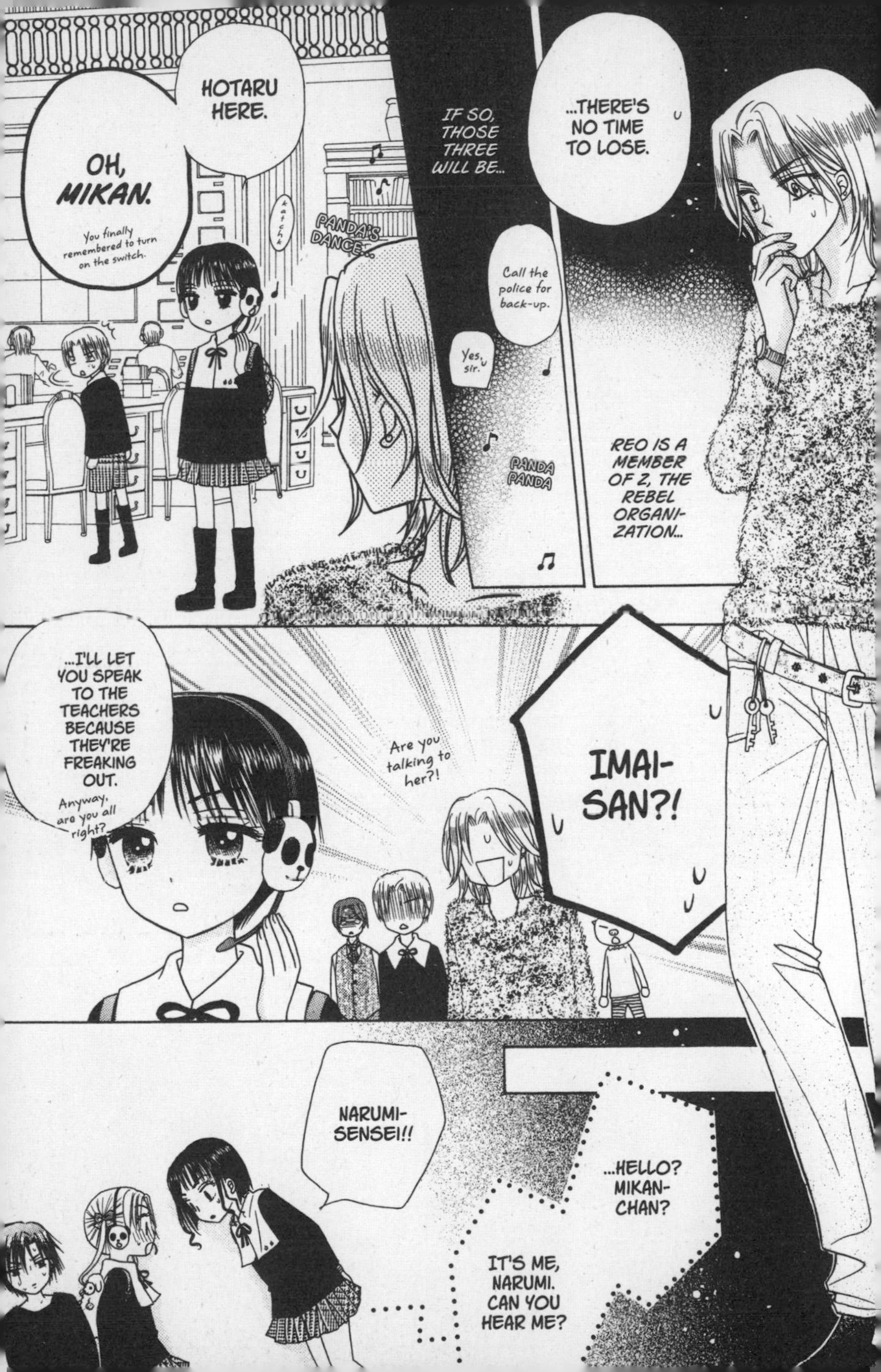
...THERE'S NO TIME TO LOSE.
IF SO, THOSE THREE WILL BE...
Call the police for back-up.
Yes, sir.
PANDA PANDA
REO IS A MEMBER OF Z, THE REBEL ORGANIZATION...
HOTARU HERE.
OH, MIKAN.
You finally remembered to turn on the switch.
katchk
PANDA'S DANCE...
IMAI-SAN?!
Are you talking to her?!
...I'LL LET YOU SPEAK TO THE TEACHERS BECAUSE THEY'RE FREAKING OUT.
Anyway, are you all right?
...HELLO? MIKAN-CHAN?
IT'S ME, NARUMI. CAN YOU HEAR ME?
NARUMI-SENSEI!!

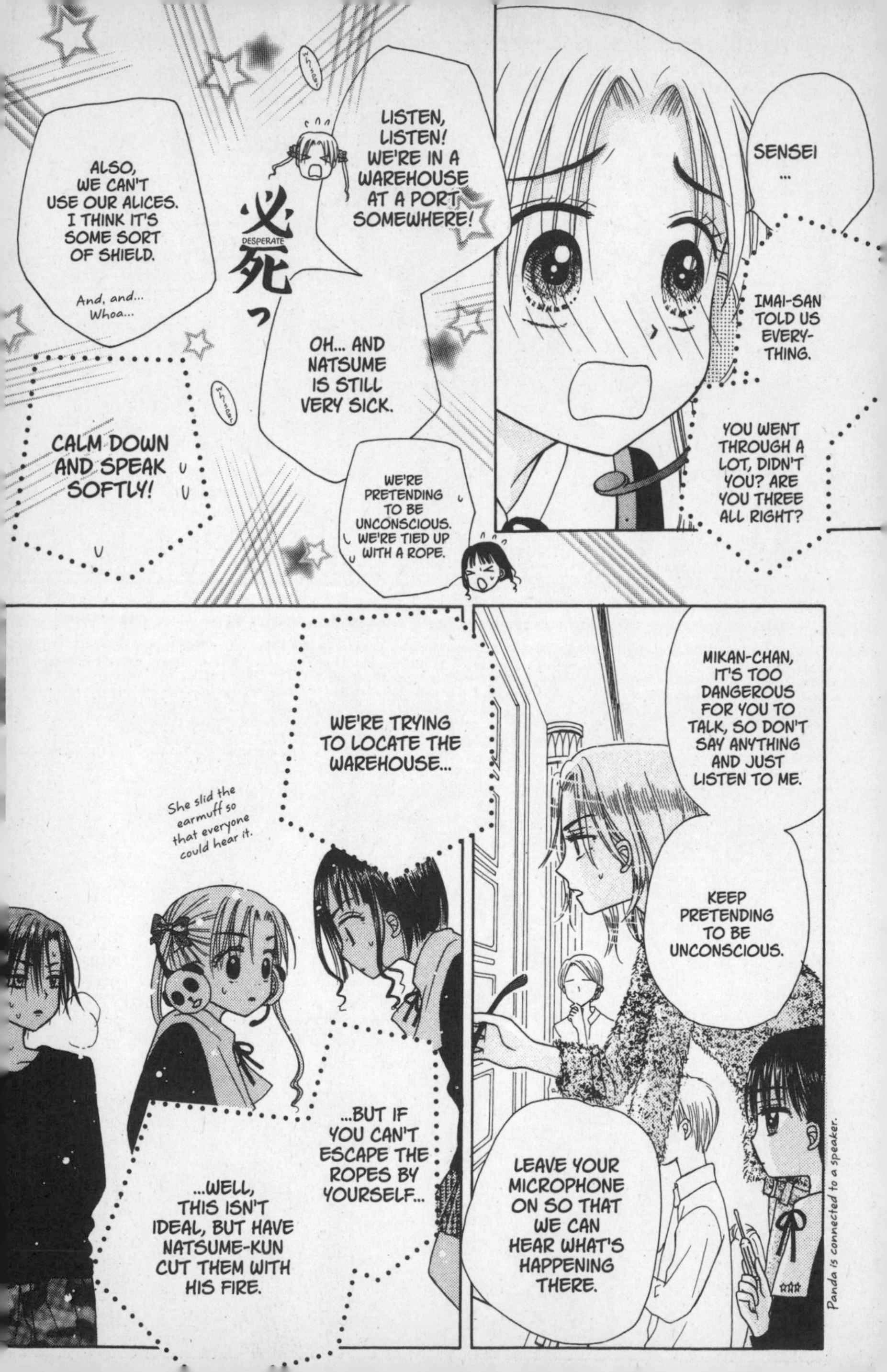
SENSEI ...
IMAI-SAN TOLD US EVERY-THING.
YOU WENT THROUGH A LOT, DIDN'T YOU? ARE YOU THREE ALL RIGHT?
LISTEN, LISTEN! WE'RE IN A WAREHOUSE AT A PORT SOMEWHERE!
必死っ
DESPERATE
ALSO, WE CAN'T USE OUR ALICES. I THINK IT'S SOME SORT OF SHIELD.
And, and... Whoa...
OH... AND NATSUME IS STILL VERY SICK.
WE'RE PRETENDING TO BE UNCONSCIOUS. WE'RE TIED UP WITH A ROPE.
CALM DOWN AND SPEAK SOFTLY!
MIKAN-CHAN, IT'S TOO DANGEROUS FOR YOU TO TALK, SO DON'T SAY ANYTHING AND JUST LISTEN TO ME.
KEEP PRETENDING TO BE UNCONSCIOUS.
LEAVE YOUR MICROPHONE ON SO THAT WE CAN HEAR WHAT'S HAPPENING THERE.
Panda is connected to a speaker.
WE'RE TRYING TO LOCATE THE WAREHOUSE...
She slid the earmuff so that everyone could hear it.
...BUT IF YOU CAN'T ESCAPE THE ROPES BY YOURSELF...
...WELL, THIS ISN'T IDEAL, BUT HAVE NATSUME-KUN CUT THEM WITH HIS FIRE.

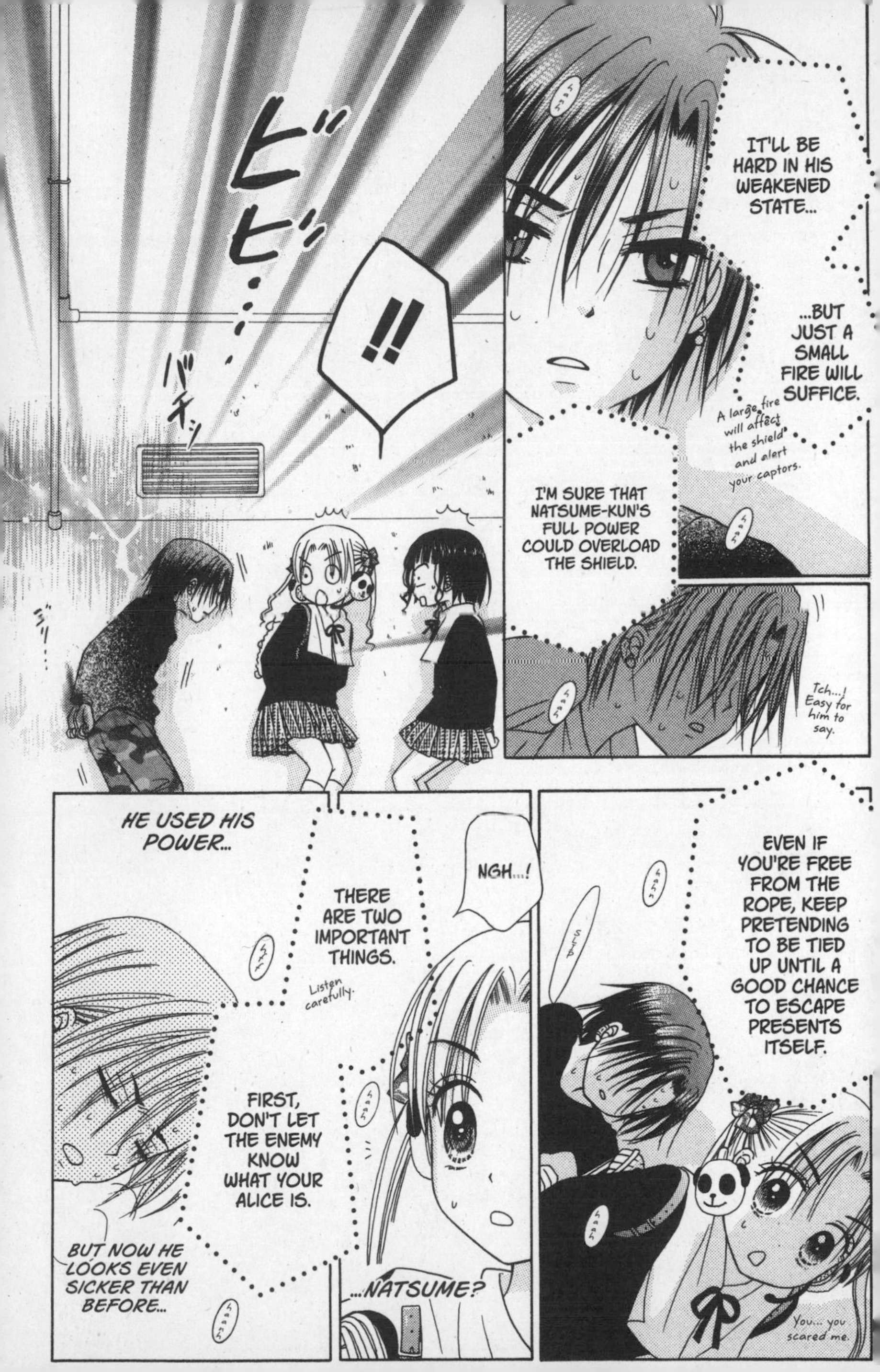
IT'LL BE HARD IN HIS WEAKENED STATE...
...BUT JUST A SMALL FIRE WILL SUFFICE.
A large fire will affect the shield and alert your captors.
I'M SURE THAT NATSUME-KUN'S FULL POWER COULD OVERLOAD THE SHIELD.
Tch...! Easy for him to say.
ビビ...
!!
バチッ
EVEN IF YOU'RE FREE FROM THE ROPE, KEEP PRETENDING TO BE TIED UP UNTIL A GOOD CHANCE TO ESCAPE PRESENTS ITSELF.
You... you scared me.
NGH...!
...NATSUME?
HE USED HIS POWER...
THERE ARE TWO IMPORTANT THINGS.
Listen carefully.
FIRST, DON'T LET THE ENEMY KNOW WHAT YOUR ALICE IS.
BUT NOW HE LOOKS EVEN SICKER THAN BEFORE...

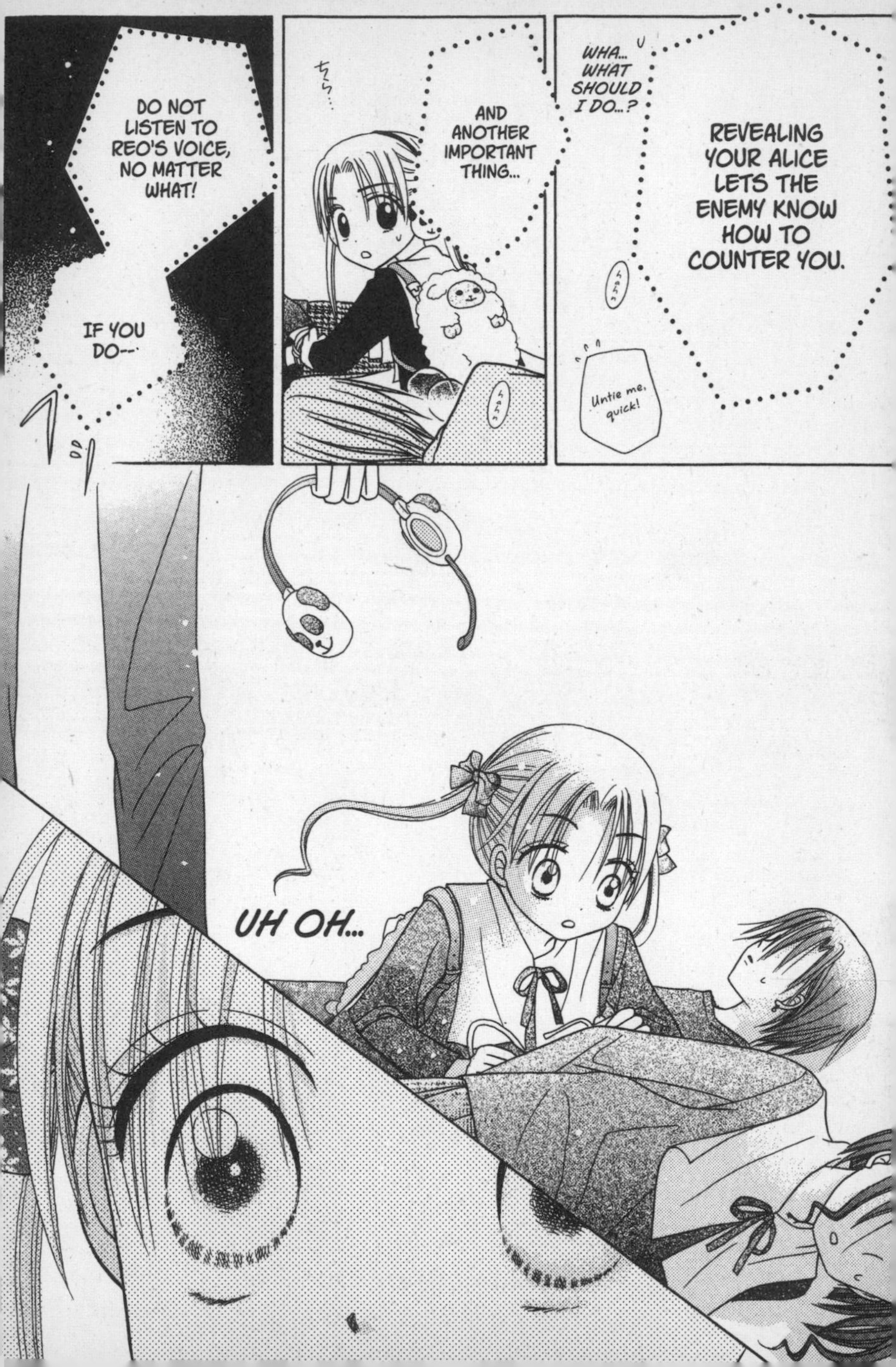
REVEALING YOUR ALICE LETS THE ENEMY KNOW HOW TO COUNTER YOU.
WHA... WHAT SHOULD I DO...?
Untie me, quick!
AND ANOTHER IMPORTANT THING...
DO NOT LISTEN TO REO'S VOICE, NO MATTER WHAT!
IF YOU DO--
UH OH...

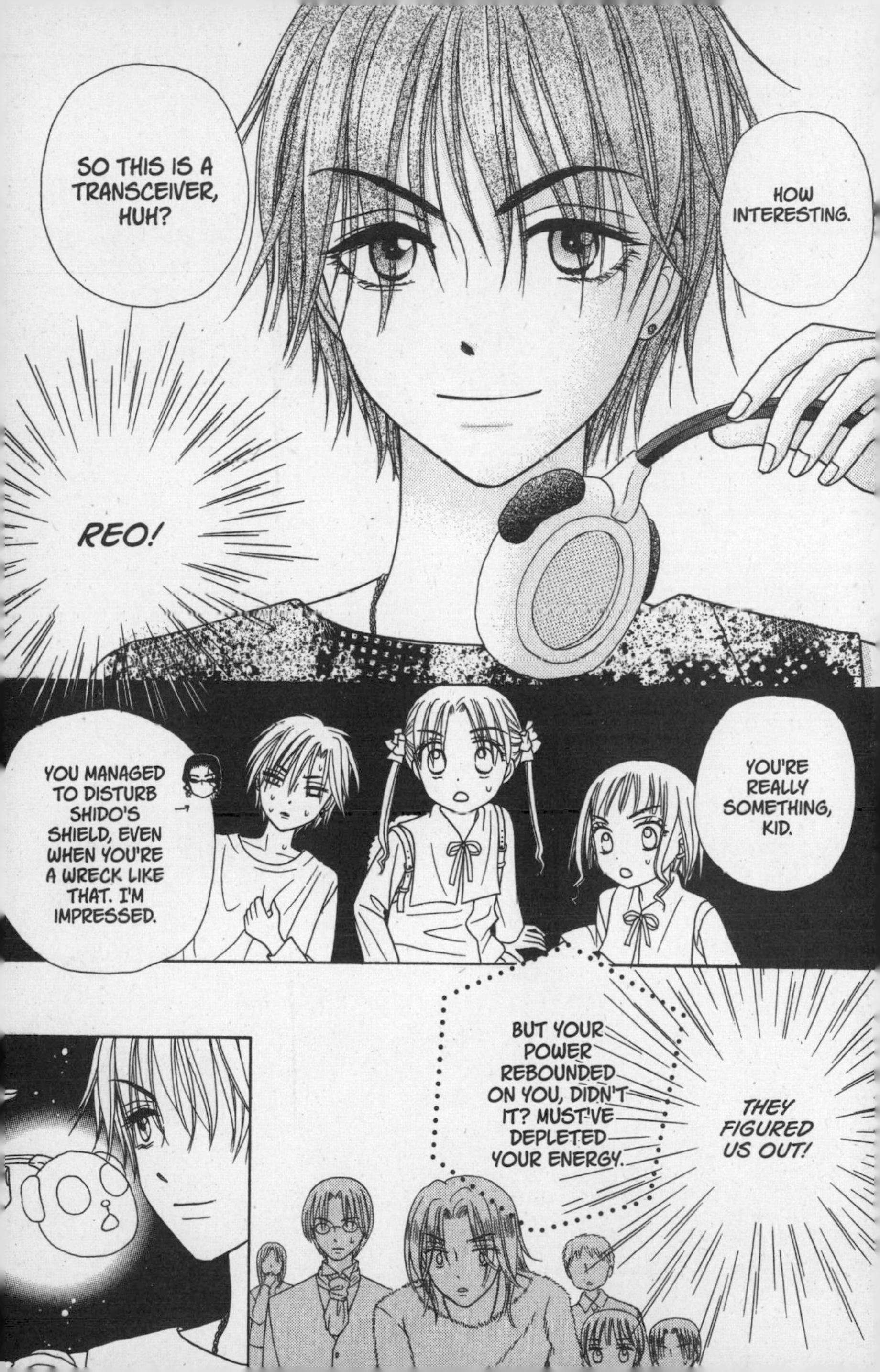
SO THIS IS A TRANSCEIVER, HUH?
HOW INTERESTING.
REO!
YOU MANAGED TO DISTURB SHIDO'S SHIELD, EVEN WHEN YOU'RE A WRECK LIKE THAT. I'M IMPRESSED.
YOU'RE REALLY SOMETHING, KID.
BUT YOUR POWER REBOUNDED ON YOU, DIDN'T IT? MUST'VE DEPLETED YOUR ENERGY.
THEY FIGURED US OUT!

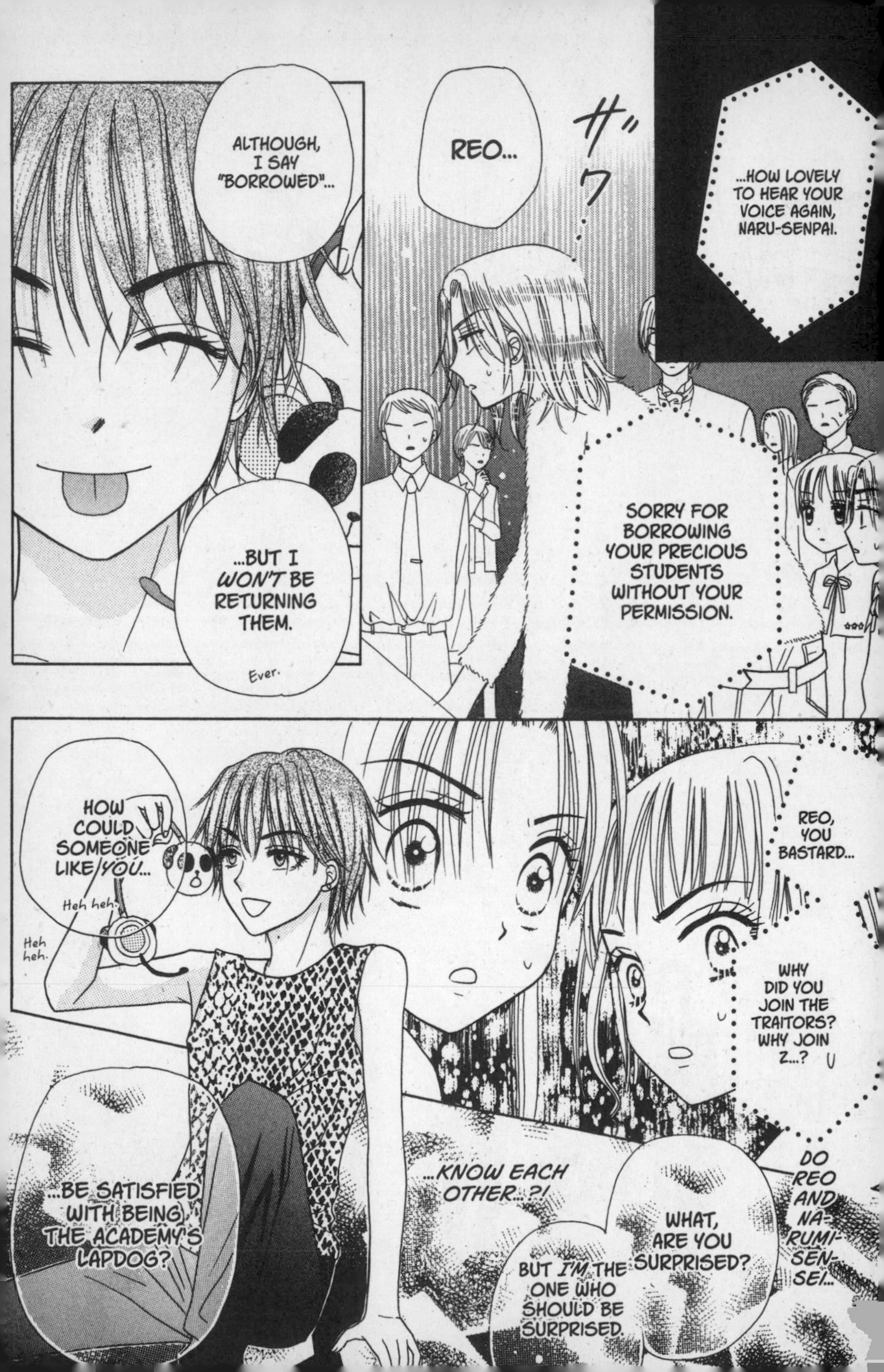
...HOW LOVELY TO HEAR YOUR VOICE AGAIN, NARU-SENPAI.
ザワ
REO...
SORRY FOR BORROWING YOUR PRECIOUS STUDENTS WITHOUT YOUR PERMISSION.
ALTHOUGH, I SAY "BORROWED"...
...BUT I *WON'T* BE RETURNING THEM.
Ever.
REO, YOU BASTARD...
WHY DID YOU JOIN THE TRAITORS? WHY JOIN Z...?
DO REO AND NARUMI-SENSEI...
...KNOW EACH OTHER...?!
WHAT, ARE YOU SURPRISED?
BUT *I'M* THE ONE WHO SHOULD BE SURPRISED.
HOW COULD SOMEONE LIKE YOU...
Heh heh.
Heh heh.
...BE SATISFIED WITH BEING THE ACADEMY'S LAPDOG?

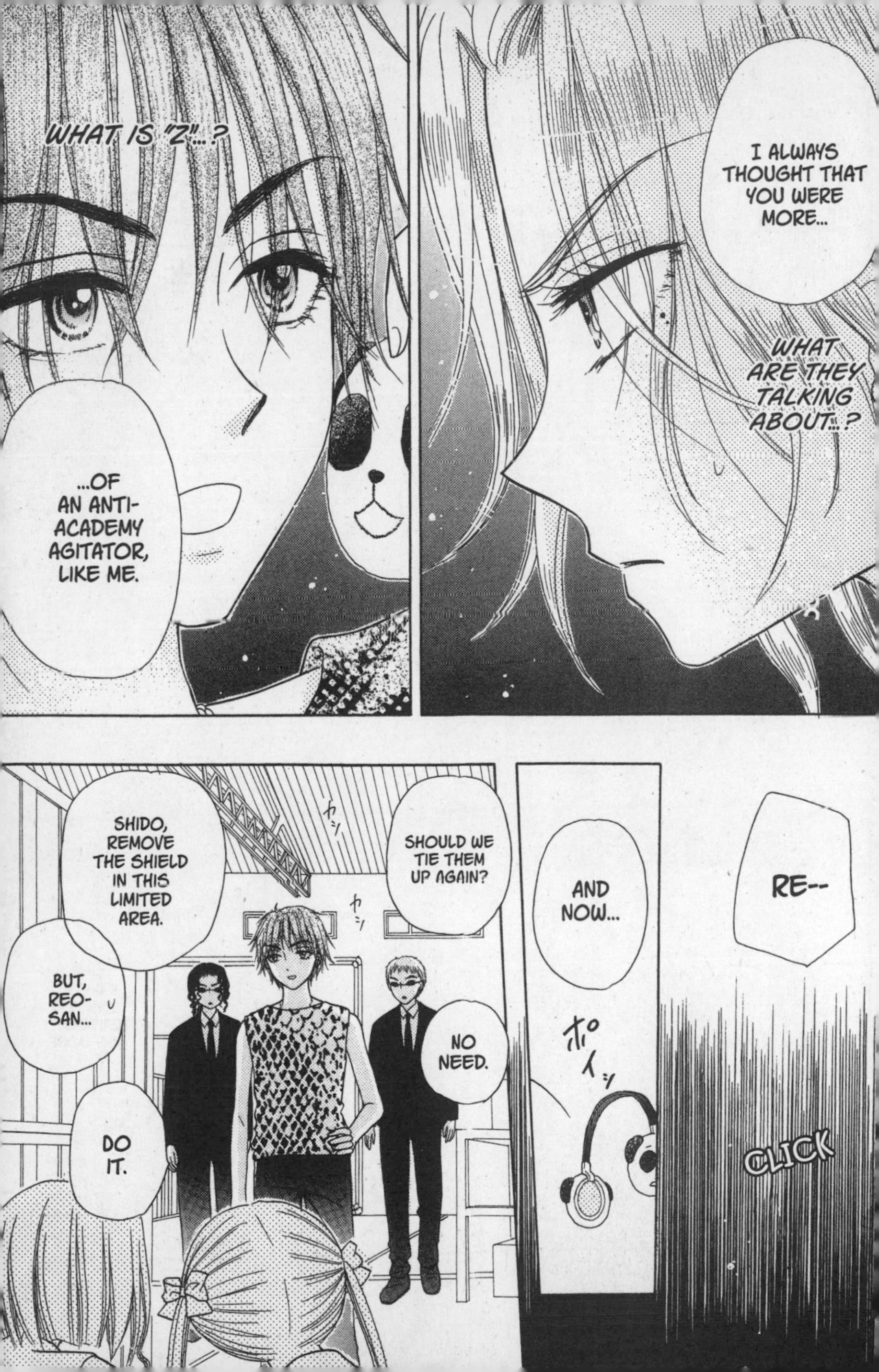
I ALWAYS THOUGHT THAT YOU WERE MORE...
WHAT ARE THEY TALKING ABOUT...?
WHAT IS "Z"...?
...OF AN ANTI-ACADEMY AGITATOR, LIKE ME.
RE--
AND NOW...
ポイッ
CLICK
SHOULD WE TIE THEM UP AGAIN?
NO NEED.
SHIDO, REMOVE THE SHIELD IN THIS LIMITED AREA.
BUT, REO-SAN...
DO IT.

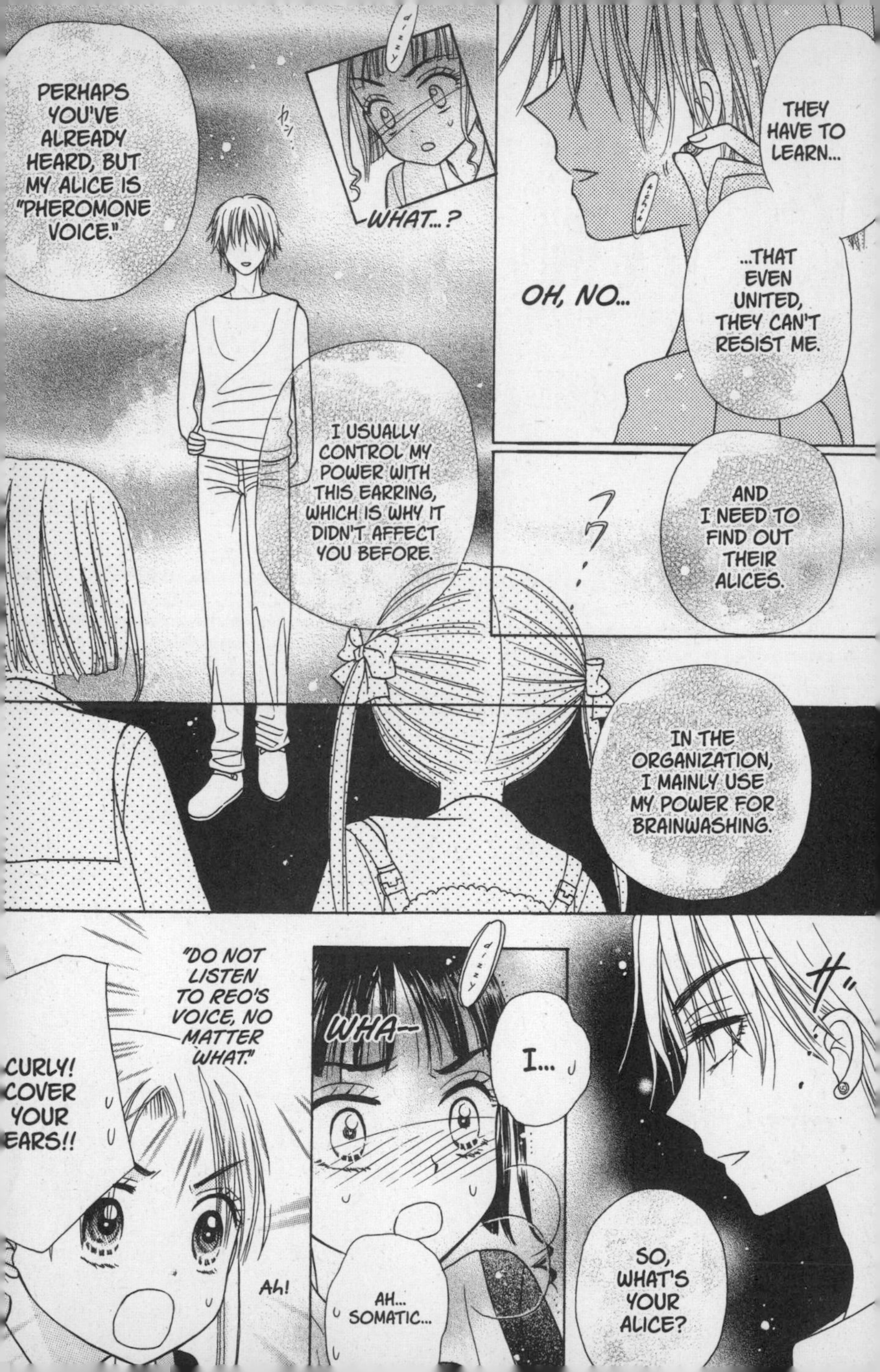

THEY HAVE TO LEARN...
...THAT EVEN UNITED, THEY CAN'T RESIST ME.
OH, NO...
dizzy
WHAT...?
PERHAPS YOU'VE ALREADY HEARD, BUT MY ALICE IS "PHEROMONE VOICE."
AND I NEED TO FIND OUT THEIR ALICES.
IN THE ORGANIZATION, I MAINLY USE MY POWER FOR BRAINWASHING.
I USUALLY CONTROL MY POWER WITH THIS EARRING, WHICH IS WHY IT DIDN'T AFFECT YOU BEFORE.
SO, WHAT'S YOUR ALICE?
dizzy
WHA--
I...
AH... SOMATIC...
"DO NOT LISTEN TO REO'S VOICE, NO MATTER WHAT."
CURLY! COVER YOUR EARS!!
Ah!

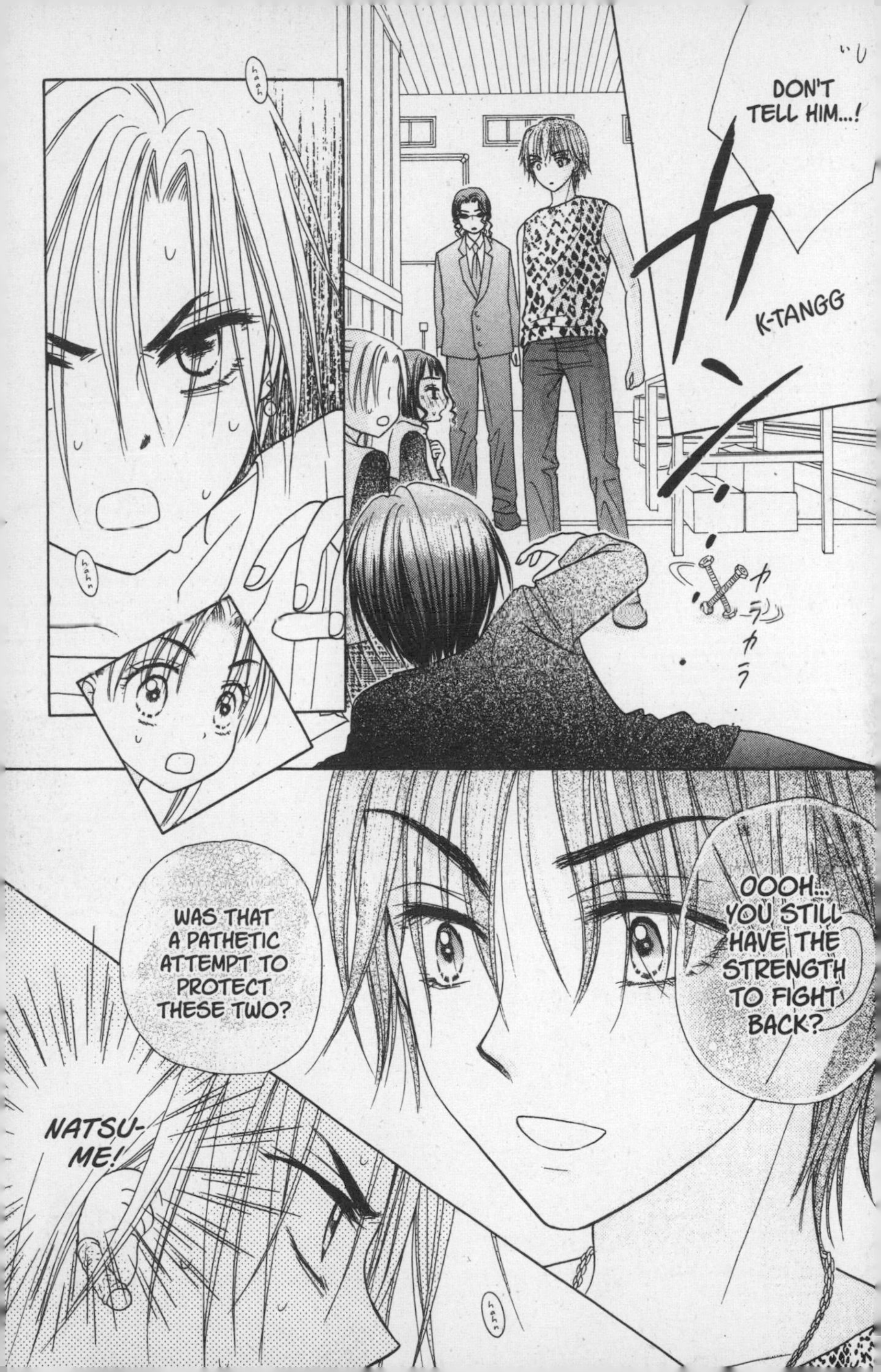
DON'T TELL HIM...!
K-TANGG
カラカラ
OOOH... YOU STILL HAVE THE STRENGTH TO FIGHT BACK?
WAS THAT A PATHETIC ATTEMPT TO PROTECT THESE TWO?
NATSU-ME!

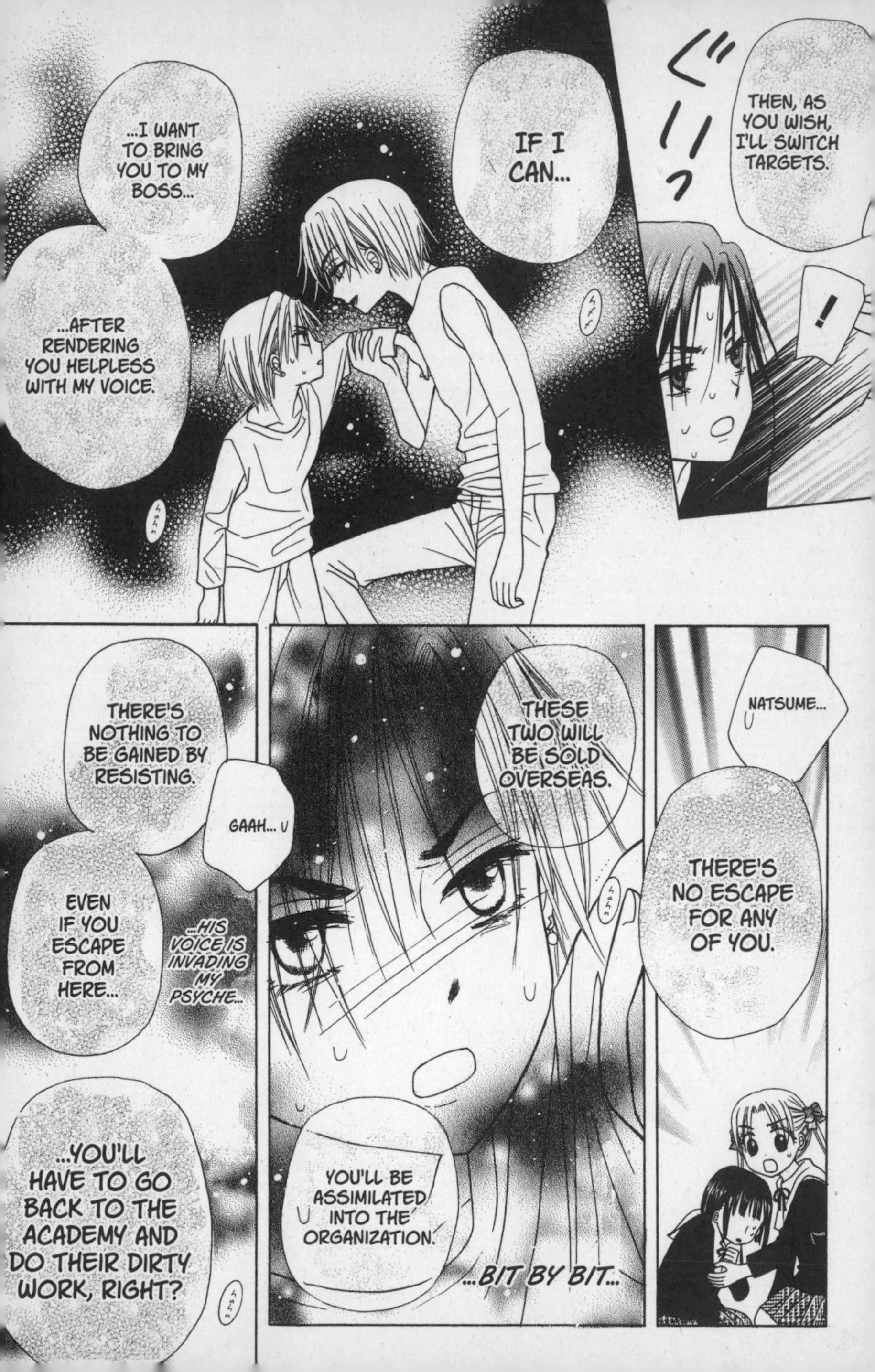
THEN, AS YOU WISH, I'LL SWITCH TARGETS.
!
IF I CAN...
...I WANT TO BRING YOU TO MY BOSS...
...AFTER RENDERING YOU HELPLESS WITH MY VOICE.
NATSUME...
THERE'S NO ESCAPE FOR ANY OF YOU.
THESE TWO WILL BE SOLD OVERSEAS.
YOU'LL BE ASSIMILATED INTO THE ORGANIZATION.
...BIT BY BIT...
THERE'S NOTHING TO BE GAINED BY RESISTING.
GAAH...
EVEN IF YOU ESCAPE FROM HERE...
...HIS VOICE IS INVADING MY PSYCHE...
...YOU'LL HAVE TO GO BACK TO THE ACADEMY AND DO THEIR DIRTY WORK, RIGHT?

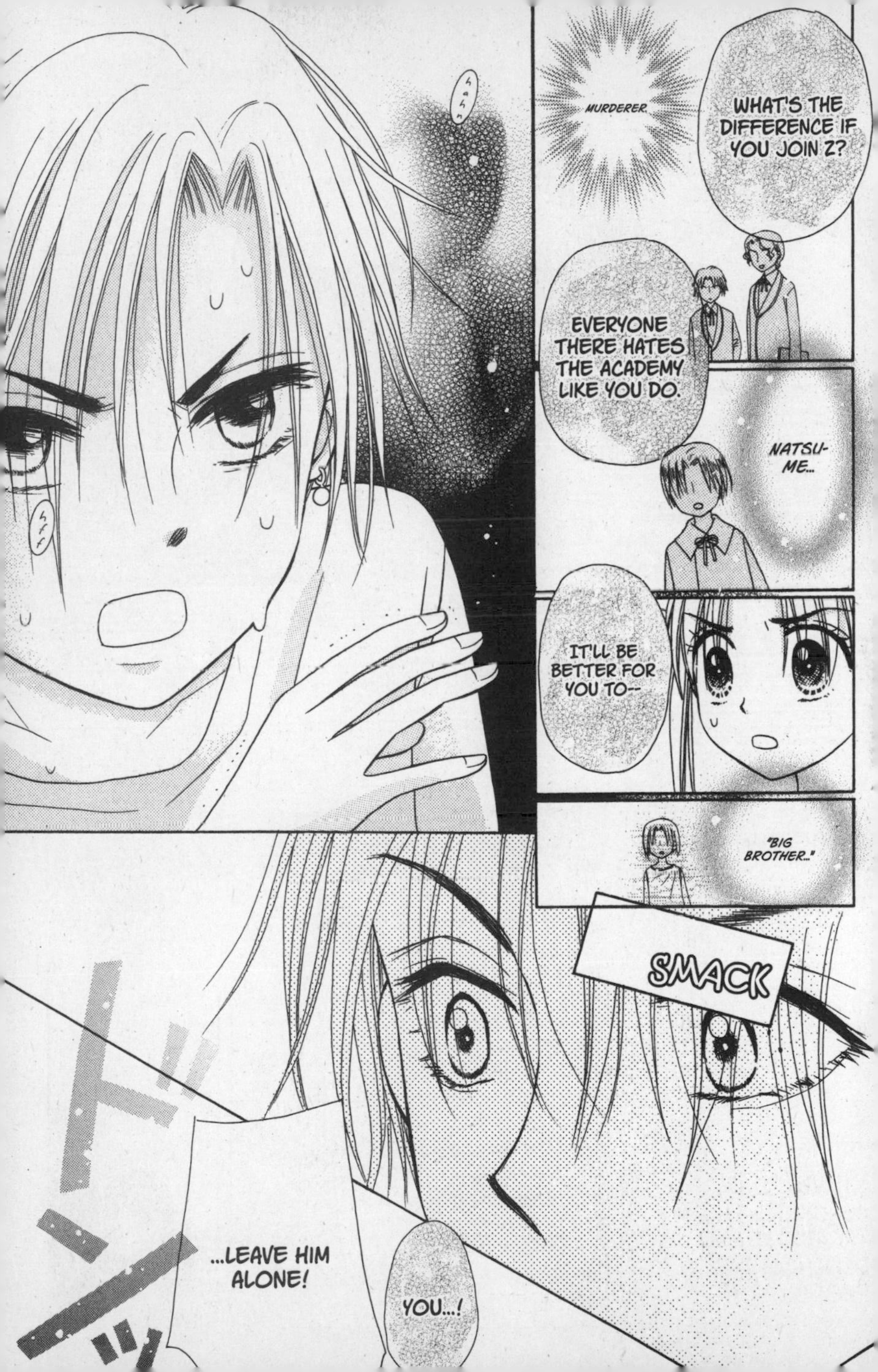
WHAT'S THE DIFFERENCE IF YOU JOIN Z?
MURDERER.
EVERYONE THERE HATES THE ACADEMY LIKE YOU DO.
NATSUME...
IT'LL BE BETTER FOR YOU TO--
"BIG BROTHER..."
SMACK
YOU...!
...LEAVE HIM ALONE!

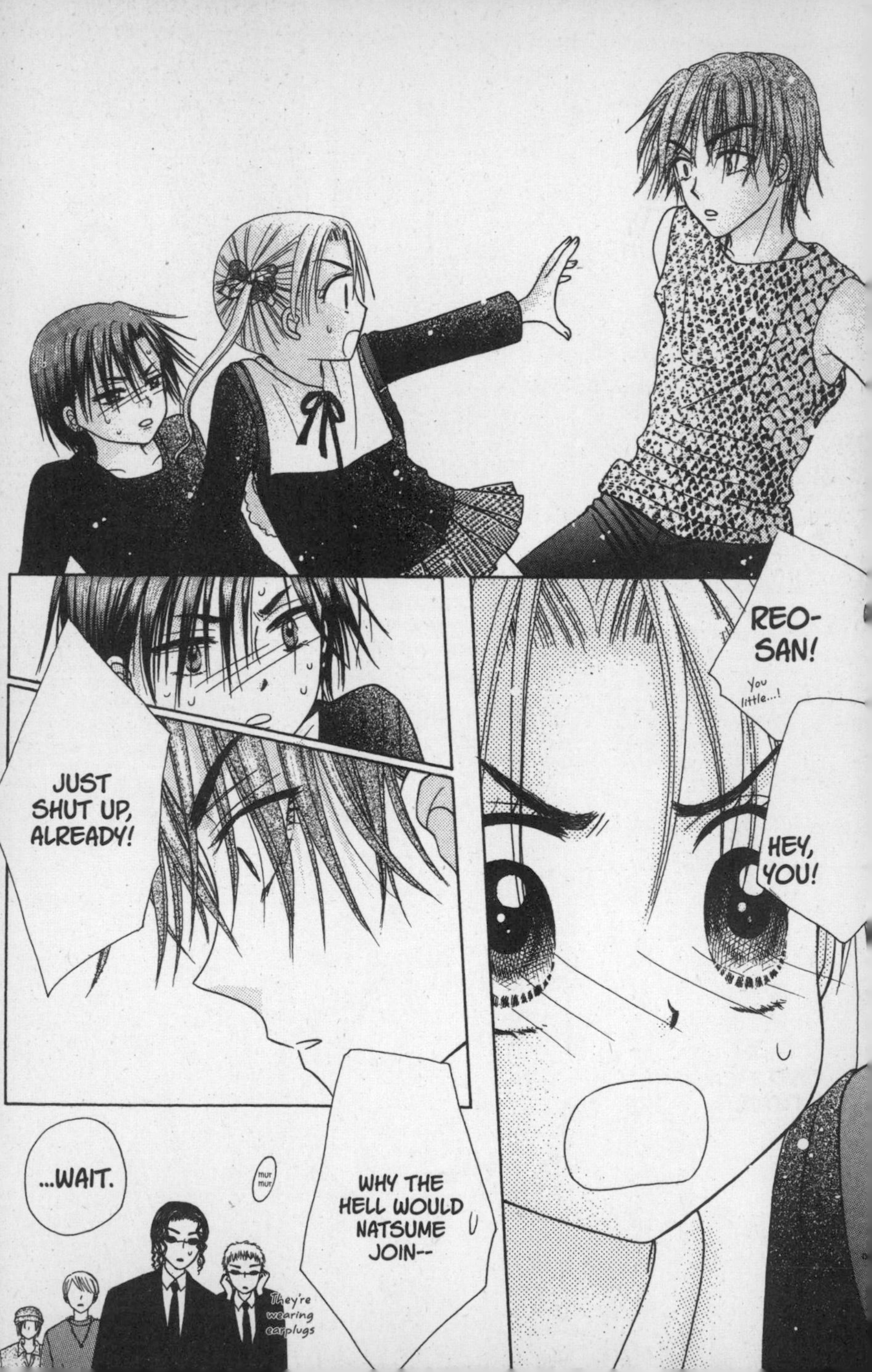
REO-SAN!
You little...!
HEY, YOU!
WHY THE HELL WOULD NATSUME JOIN--
JUST SHUT UP, ALREADY!
mut mut
...WAIT.
They're wearing earplugs

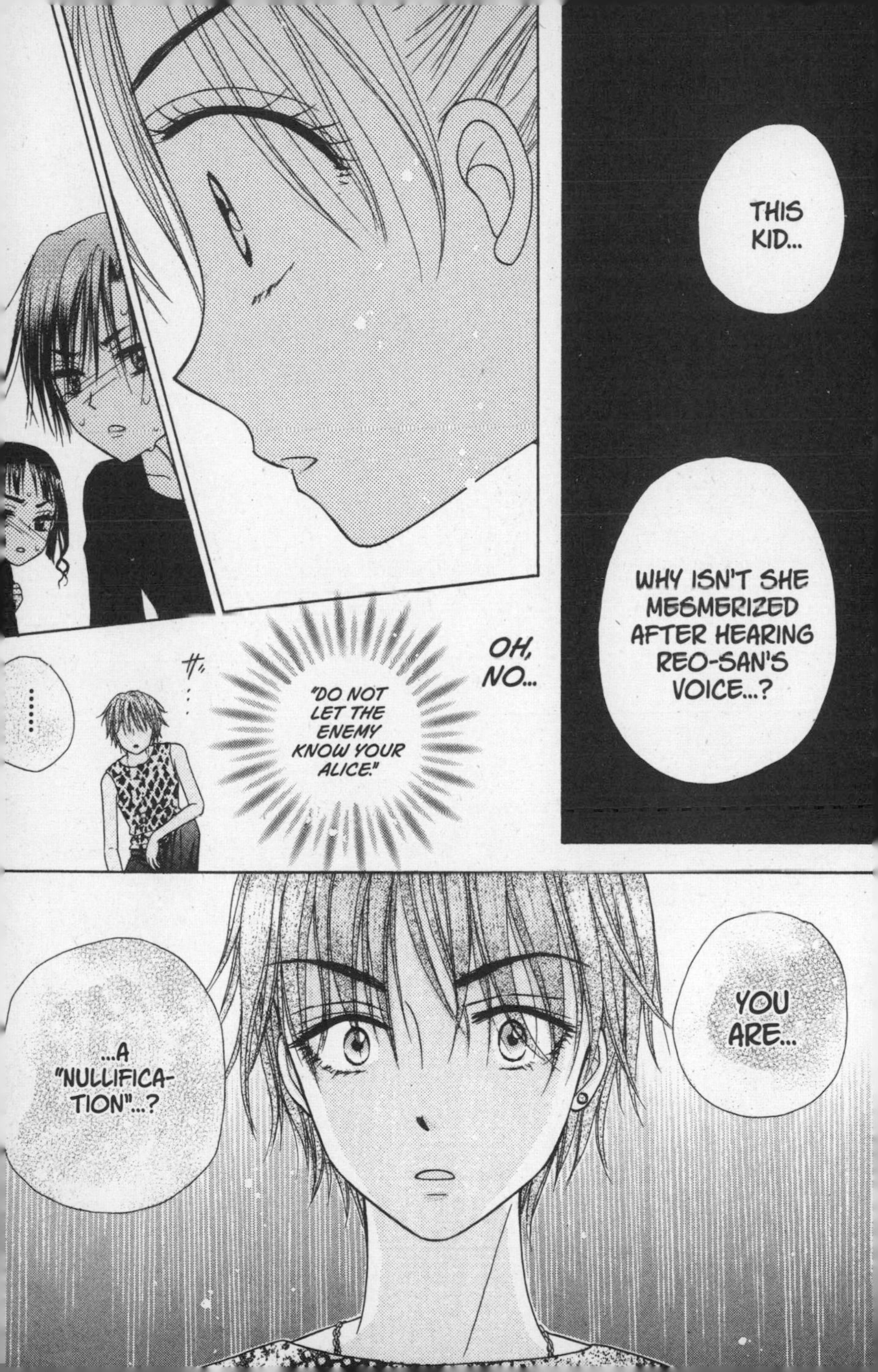
THIS KID...
WHY ISN'T SHE MESMERIZED AFTER HEARING REO-SAN'S VOICE...?
OH, NO...
"DO NOT LET THE ENEMY KNOW YOUR ALICE."
......
YOU ARE...
...A "NULLIFICA-TION"...?

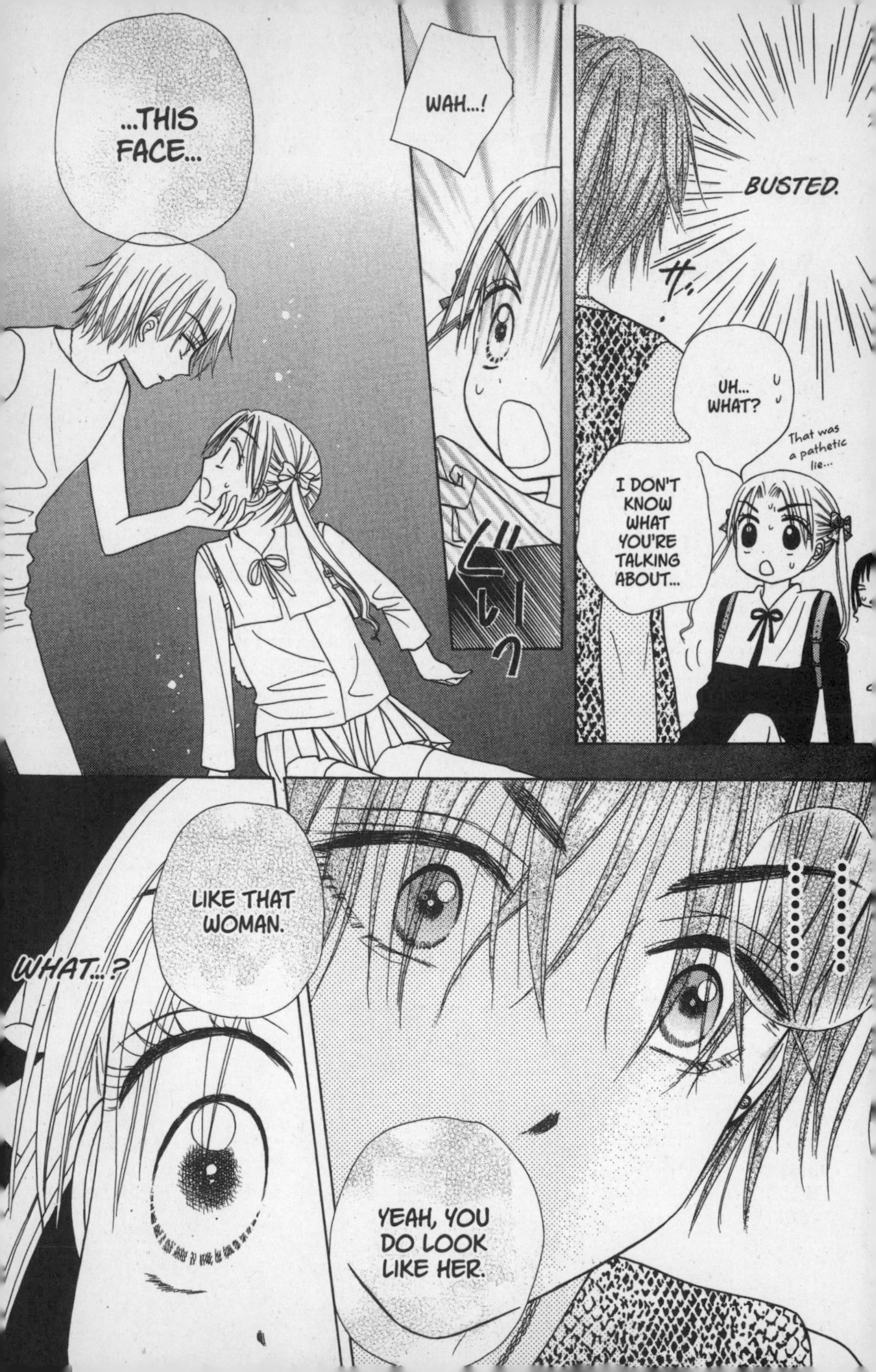
BUSTED.
UH... WHAT?
I DON'T KNOW WHAT YOU'RE TALKING ABOUT...
That was a pathetic lie...
WAH...!
ぐいっ
...THIS FACE...
!!
LIKE THAT WOMAN.
WHAT...?
YEAH, YOU DO LOOK LIKE HER.

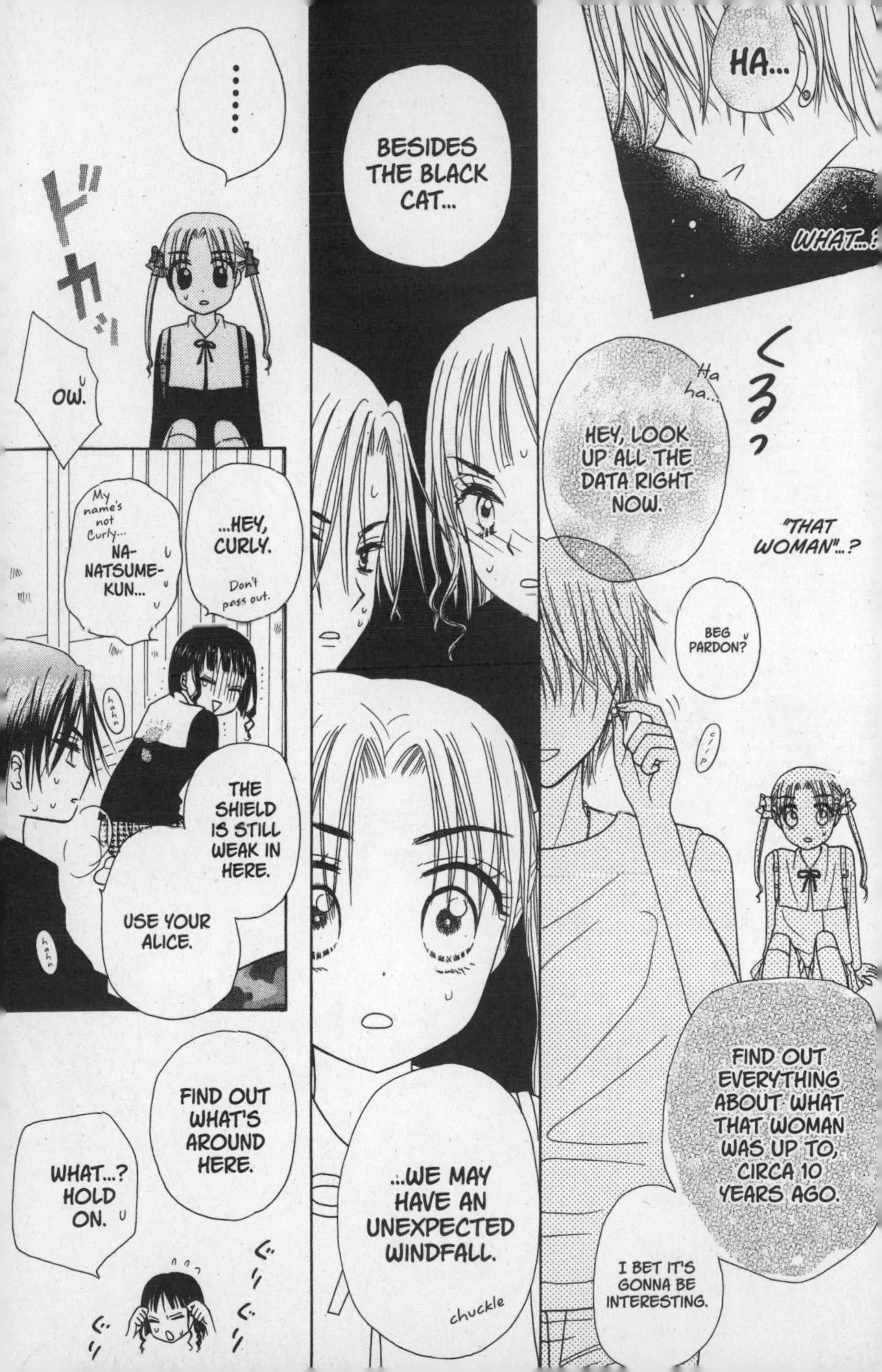
HA...
WHAT...!?
くるっ
Ha ha...
HEY, LOOK UP ALL THE DATA RIGHT NOW.
"THAT WOMAN"...?
BEG PARDON?
clip
FIND OUT EVERYTHING ABOUT WHAT THAT WOMAN WAS UP TO, CIRCA 10 YEARS AGO.
I BET IT'S GONNA BE INTERESTING.
BESIDES THE BLACK CAT...
...WE MAY HAVE AN UNEXPECTED WINDFALL.
chuckle
......
ドカッ
OW.
...HEY, CURLY.
Don't pass out.
My name's not Curly...
NA-NATSUME-KUN...
hahn
THE SHIELD IS STILL WEAK IN HERE.
USE YOUR ALICE.
hahn
FIND OUT WHAT'S AROUND HERE.
WHAT...? HOLD ON.

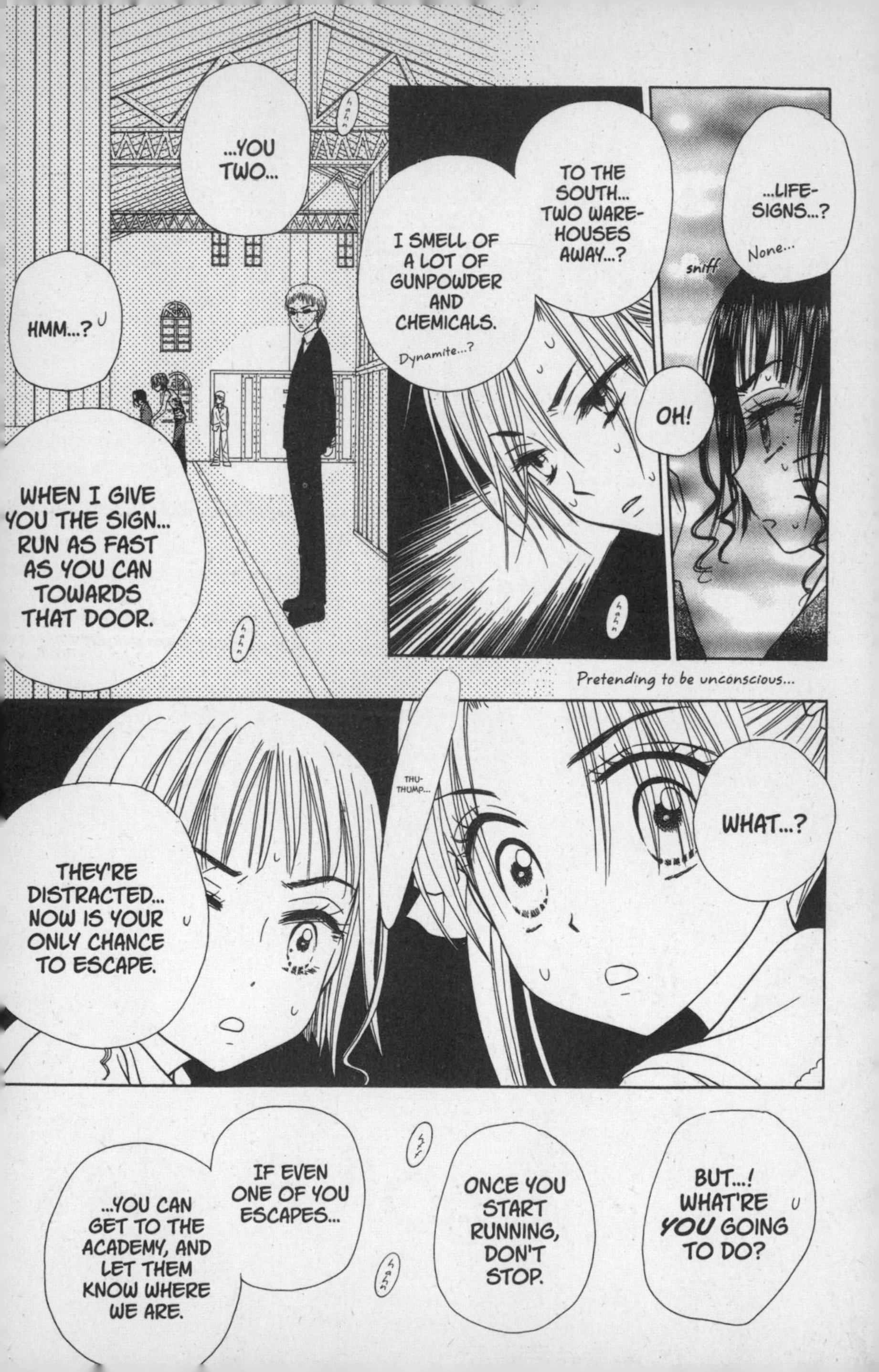
...LIFE-SIGNS...?
None...
sniff
OH!
Pretending to be unconscious...
TO THE SOUTH... TWO WARE-HOUSES AWAY...?
I SMELL OF A LOT OF GUNPOWDER AND CHEMICALS.
Dynamite...?
...YOU TWO...
HMM...?
WHEN I GIVE YOU THE SIGN... RUN AS FAST AS YOU CAN TOWARDS THAT DOOR.
WHAT...?
THU-THUMP...
THEY'RE DISTRACTED... NOW IS YOUR ONLY CHANCE TO ESCAPE.
BUT...! WHAT'RE YOU GOING TO DO?
ONCE YOU START RUNNING, DON'T STOP.
IF EVEN ONE OF YOU ESCAPES...
...YOU CAN GET TO THE ACADEMY, AND LET THEM KNOW WHERE WE ARE.

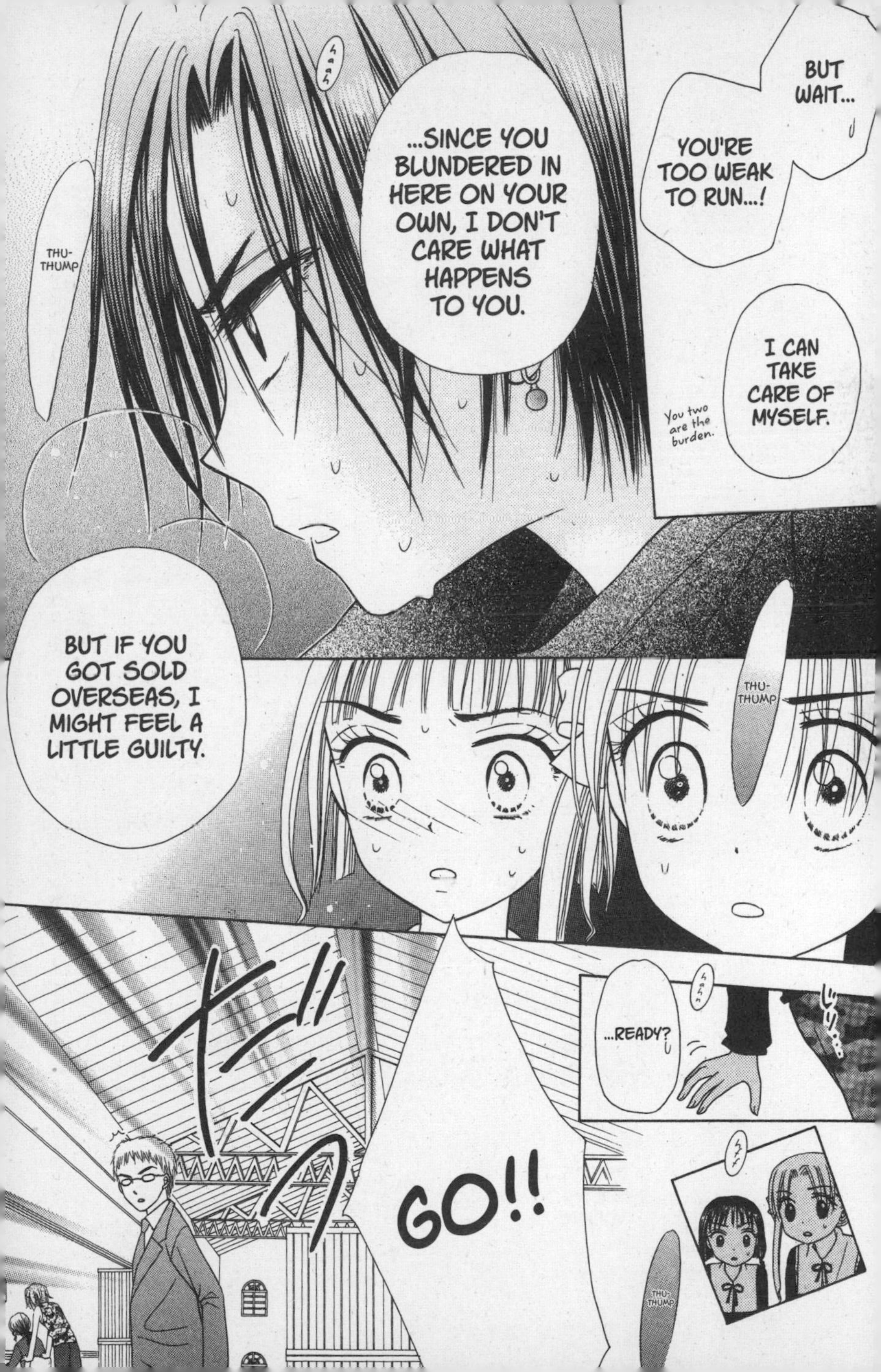
BUT WAIT...
YOU'RE TOO WEAK TO RUN...!
I CAN TAKE CARE OF MYSELF.
You two are the burden.
haah
...SINCE YOU BLUNDERED IN HERE ON YOUR OWN, I DON'T CARE WHAT HAPPENS TO YOU.
THU-THUMP
BUT IF YOU GOT SOLD OVERSEAS, I MIGHT FEEL A LITTLE GUILTY.
THU-THUMP
haah
...READY?
GO!!
THU-THUMP

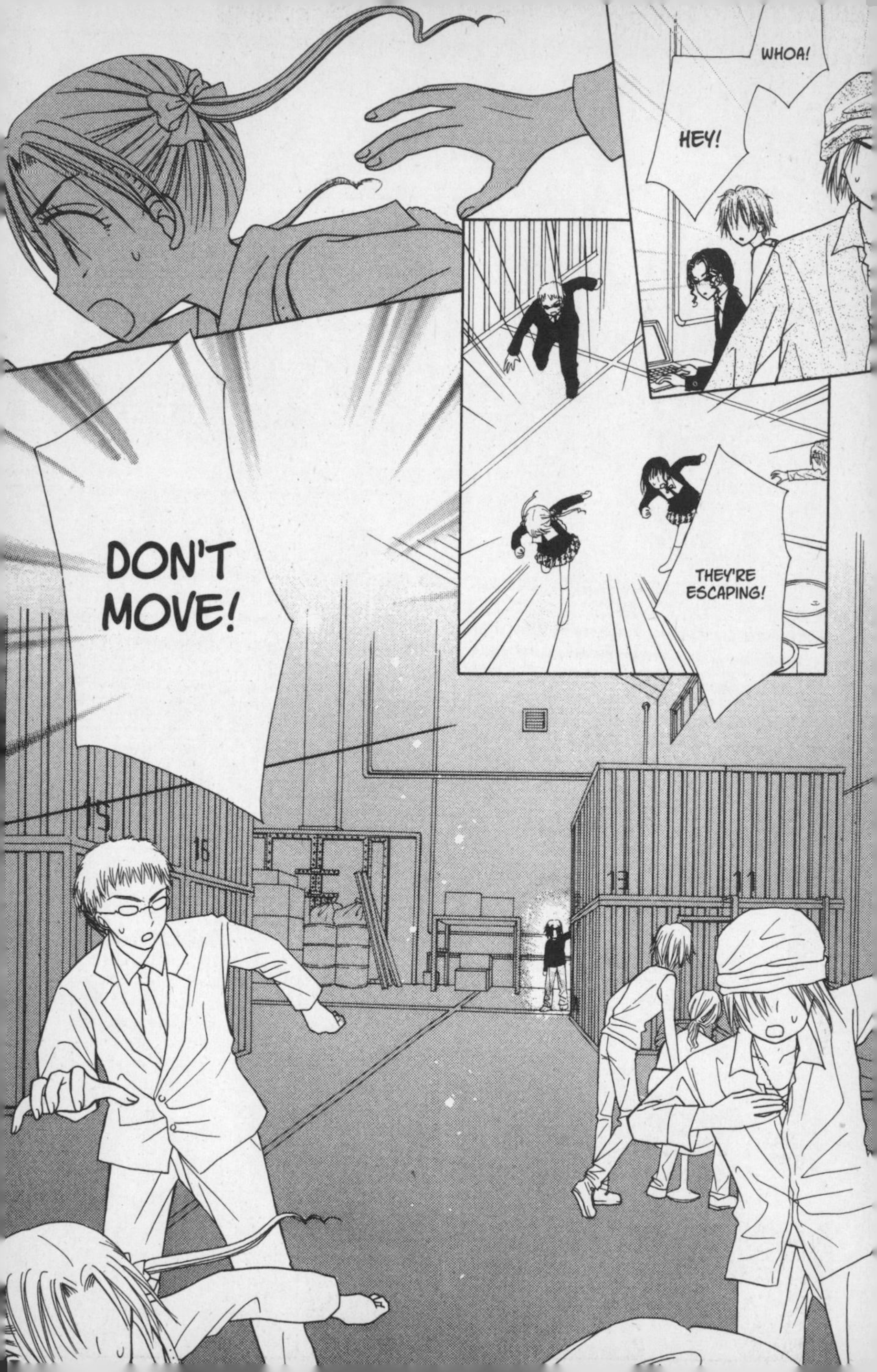
WHOA!
HEY!
DON'T MOVE!
THEY'RE ESCAPING!

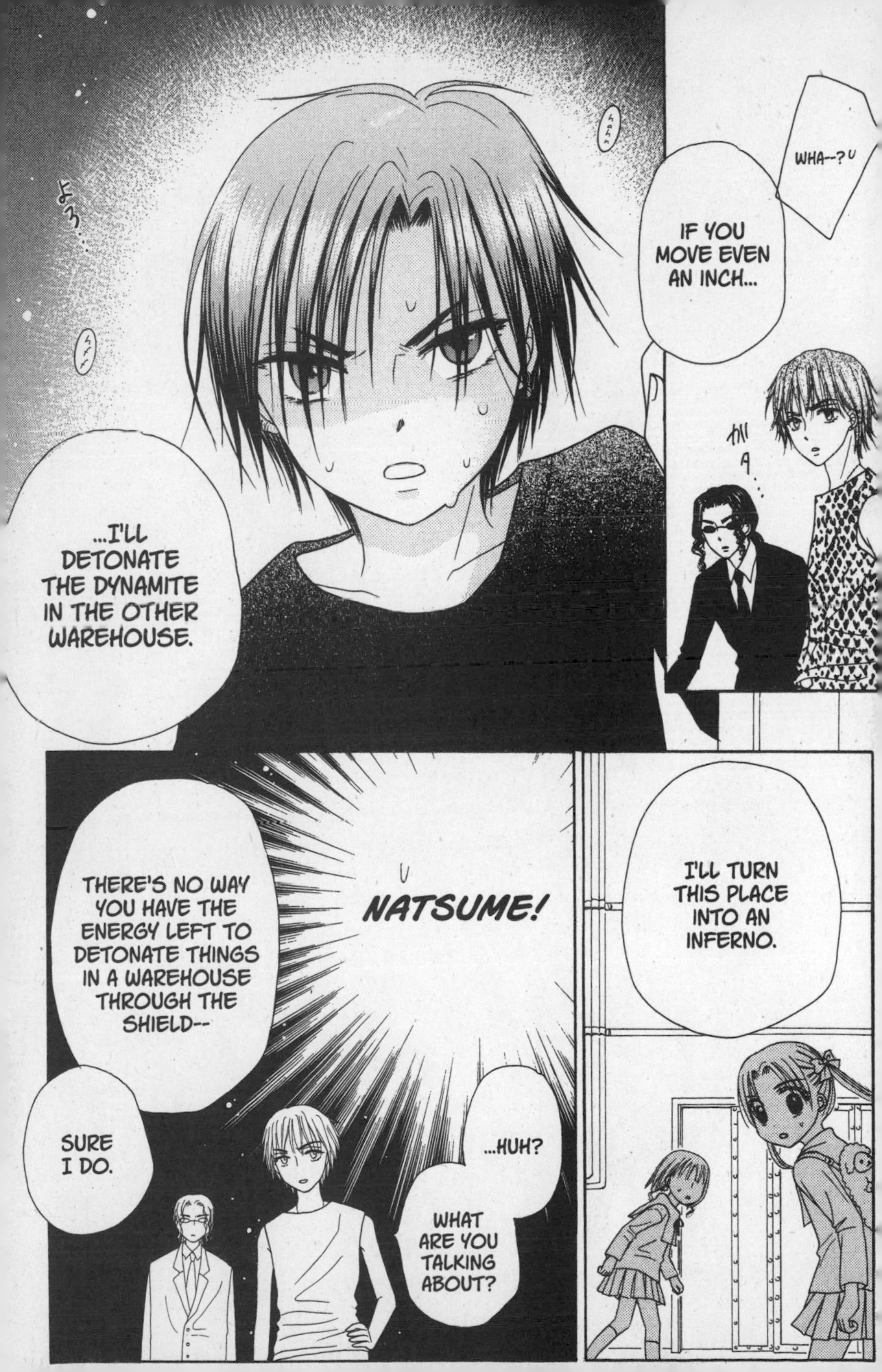
WHA--?
IF YOU MOVE EVEN AN INCH...
...I'LL DETONATE THE DYNAMITE IN THE OTHER WAREHOUSE.
I'LL TURN THIS PLACE INTO AN INFERNO.
NATSUME!
THERE'S NO WAY YOU HAVE THE ENERGY LEFT TO DETONATE THINGS IN A WAREHOUSE THROUGH THE SHIELD--
...HUH?
WHAT ARE YOU TALKING ABOUT?
SURE I DO.

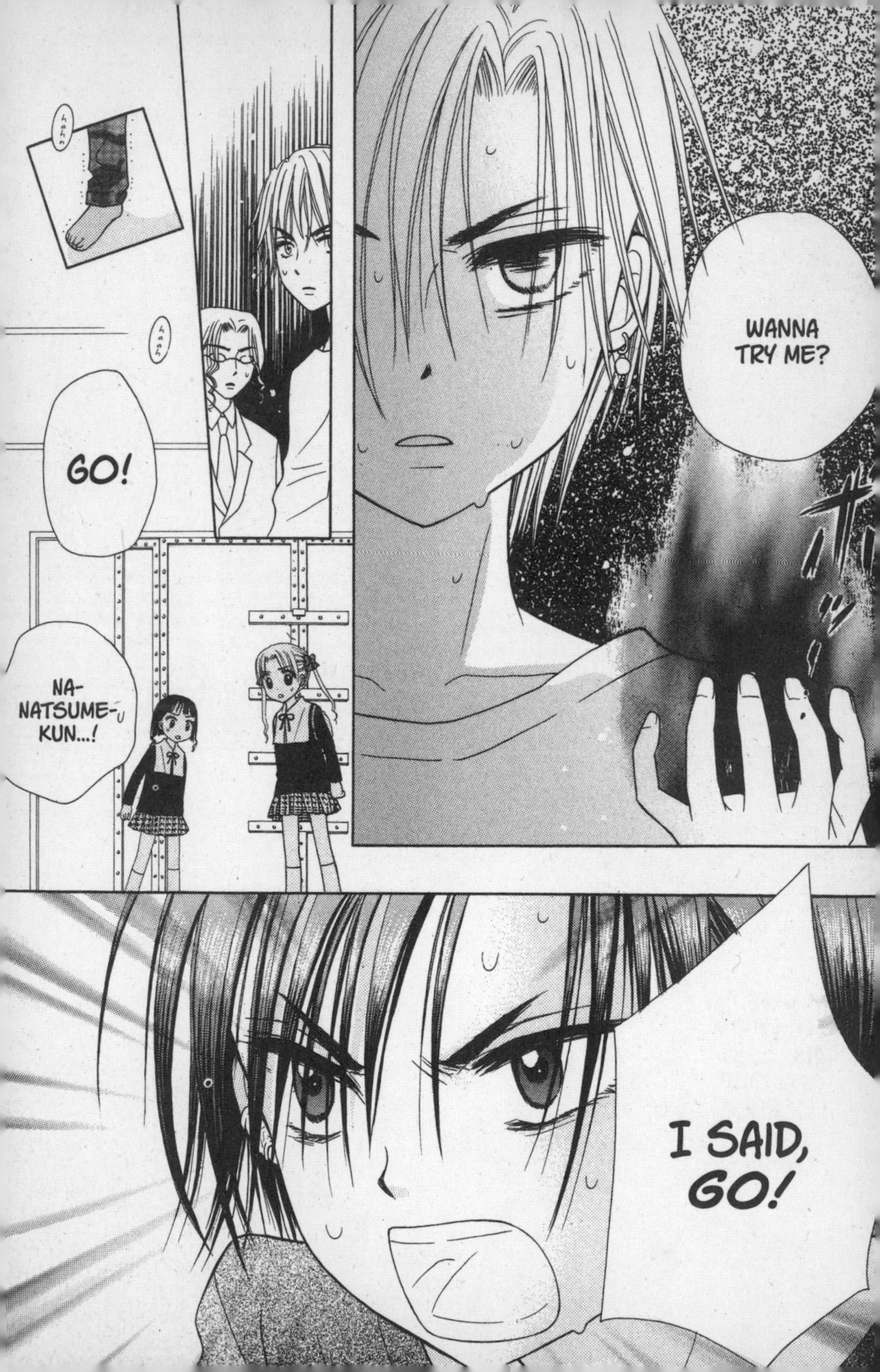
WANNA TRY ME?
hah
hah
GO!
NA-NATSUME-KUN...!
I SAID, GO!

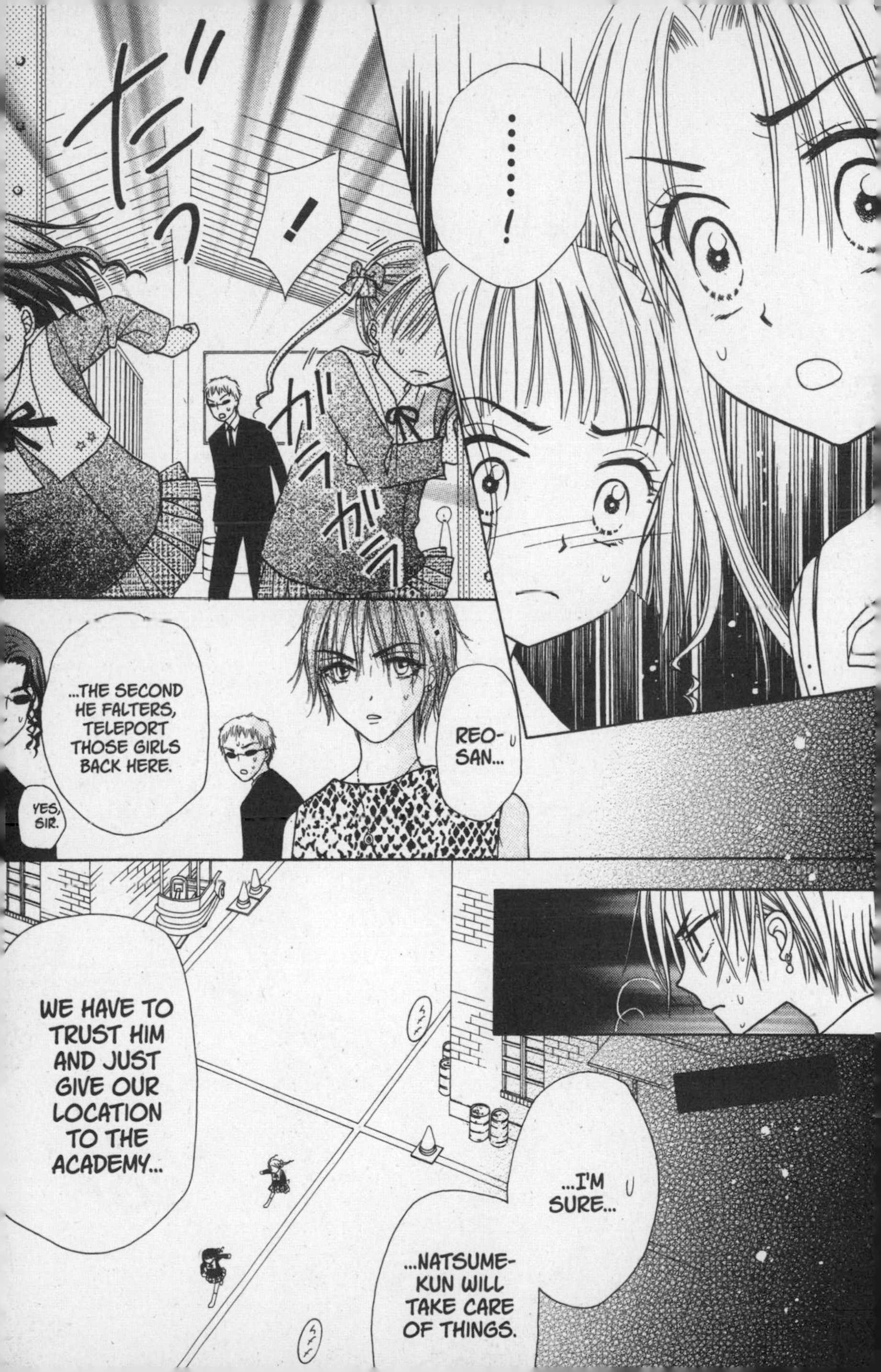

......!
!
REO-SAN...
...THE SECOND HE FALTERS, TELEPORT THOSE GIRLS BACK HERE.
YES, SIR.
...I'M SURE...
...NATSUME-KUN WILL TAKE CARE OF THINGS.
WE HAVE TO TRUST HIM AND JUST GIVE OUR LOCATION TO THE ACADEMY...

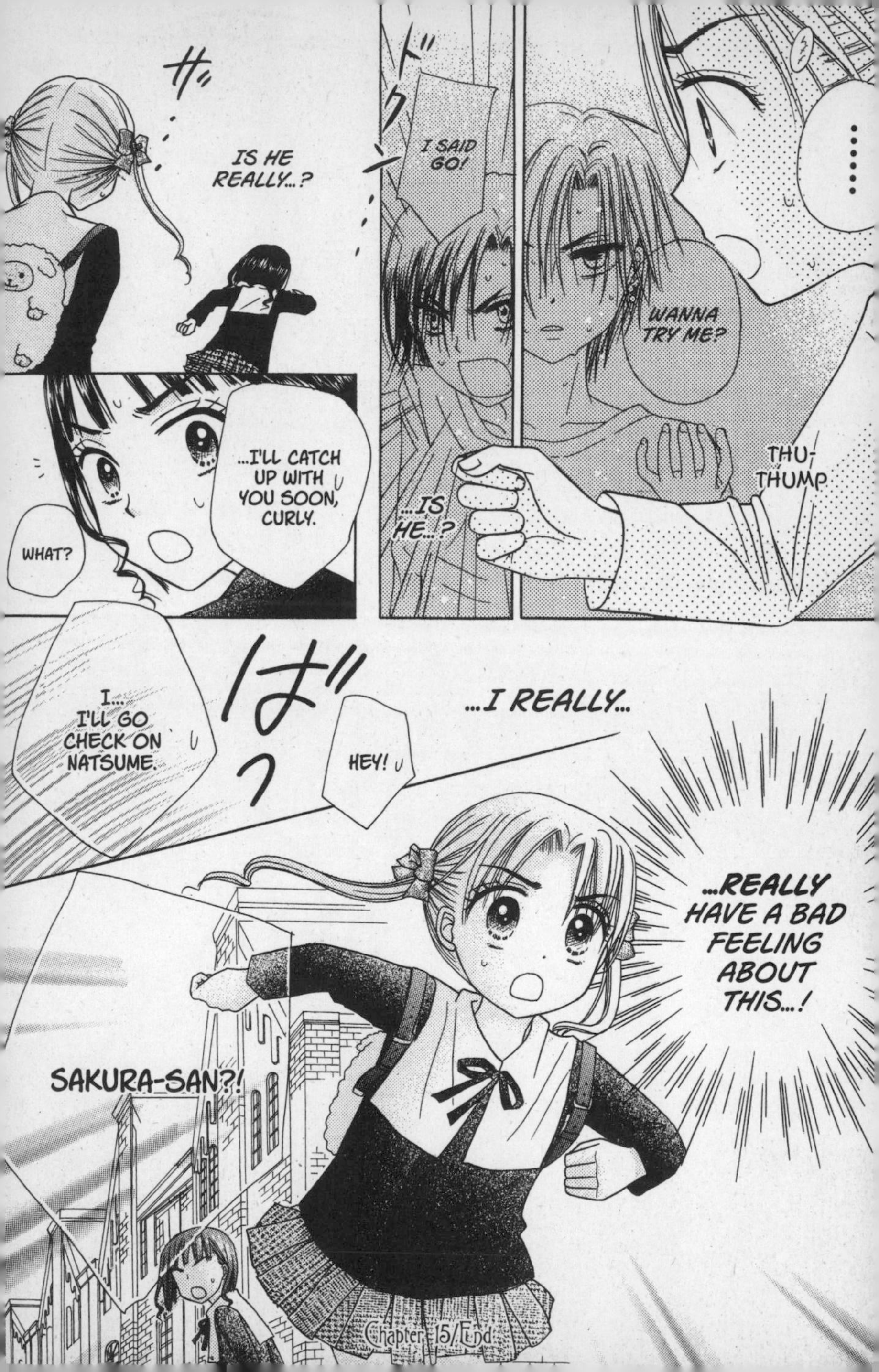

......
WANNA TRY ME?
THU-THUMP
ドク
I SAID GO!
...IS HE...?
ザッ
IS HE REALLY...?
...I'LL CATCH UP WITH YOU SOON, CURLY.
WHAT?
...I REALLY...
ばっ
HEY!
I... I'LL GO CHECK ON NATSUME.
...REALLY HAVE A BAD FEELING ABOUT THIS...!
SAKURA-SAN?!
Chapter 15/End

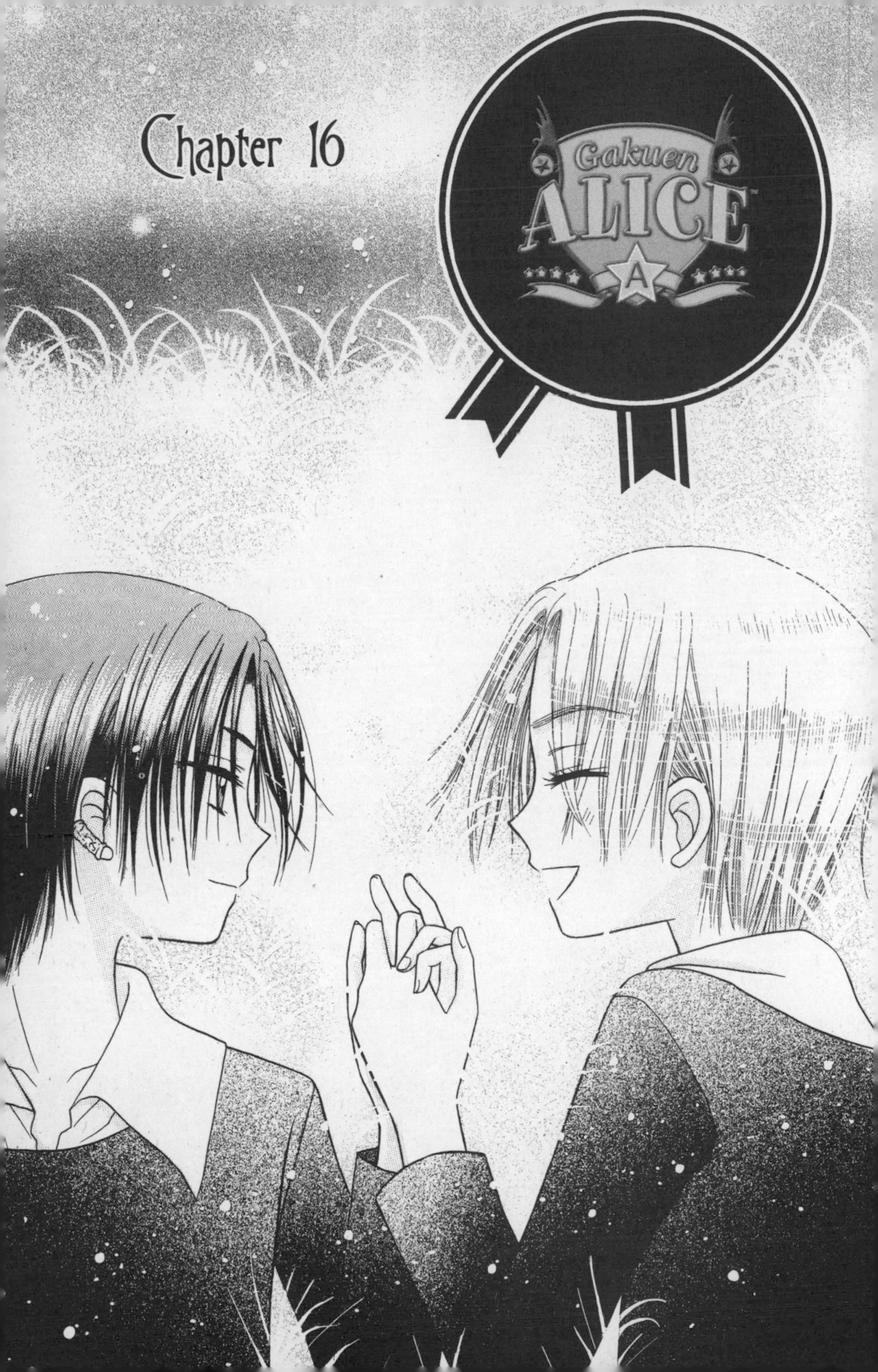
Chapter 16
Gakuen
ALICE

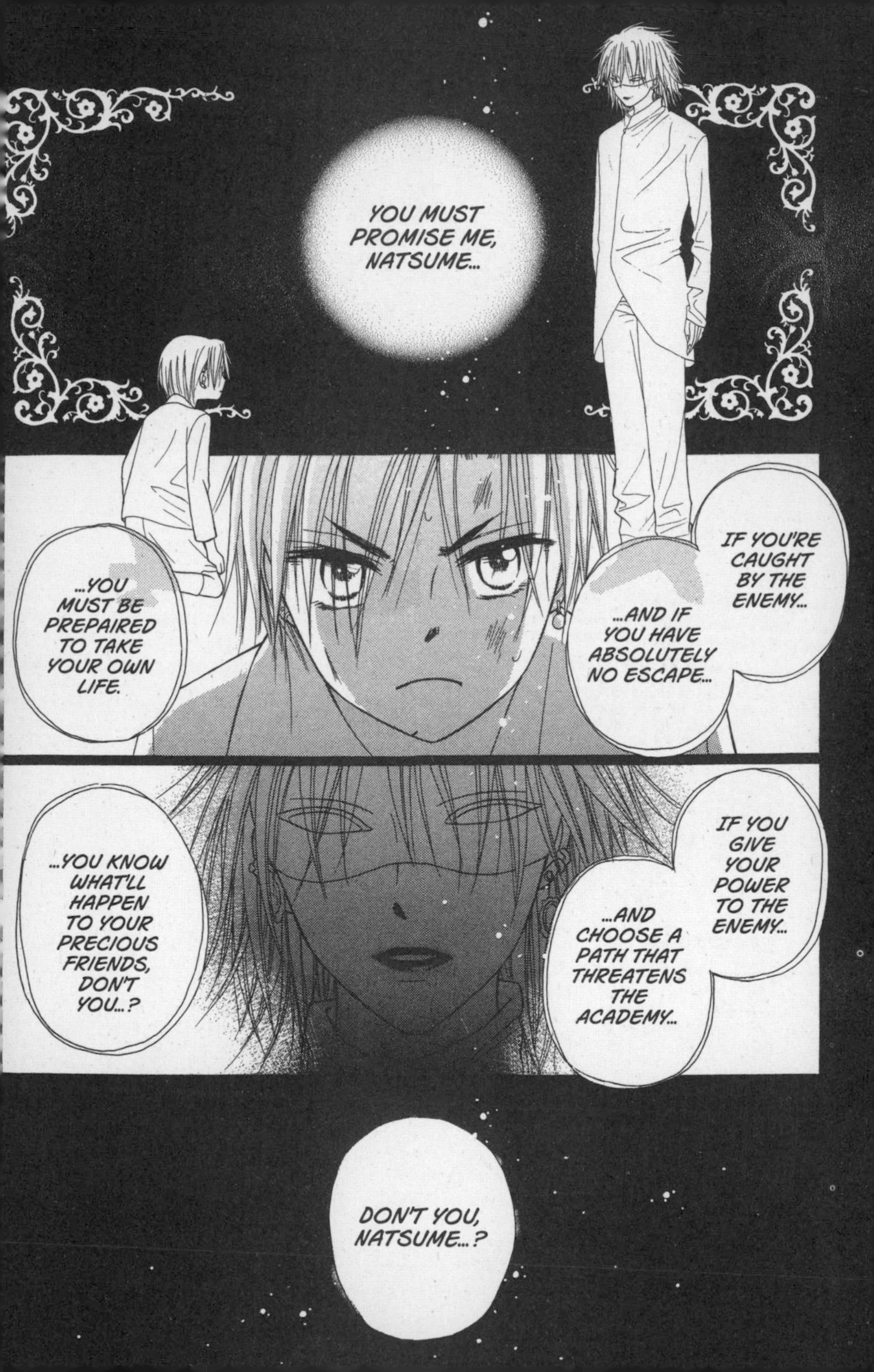
YOU MUST PROMISE ME, NATSUME...
IF YOU'RE CAUGHT BY THE ENEMY...
...AND IF YOU HAVE ABSOLUTELY NO ESCAPE...
...YOU MUST BE PREPAIRED TO TAKE YOUR OWN LIFE.
IF YOU GIVE YOUR POWER TO THE ENEMY...
...AND CHOOSE A PATH THAT THREATENS THE ACADEMY...
...YOU KNOW WHAT'LL HAPPEN TO YOUR PRECIOUS FRIENDS, DON'T YOU...?
DON'T YOU, NATSUME...?

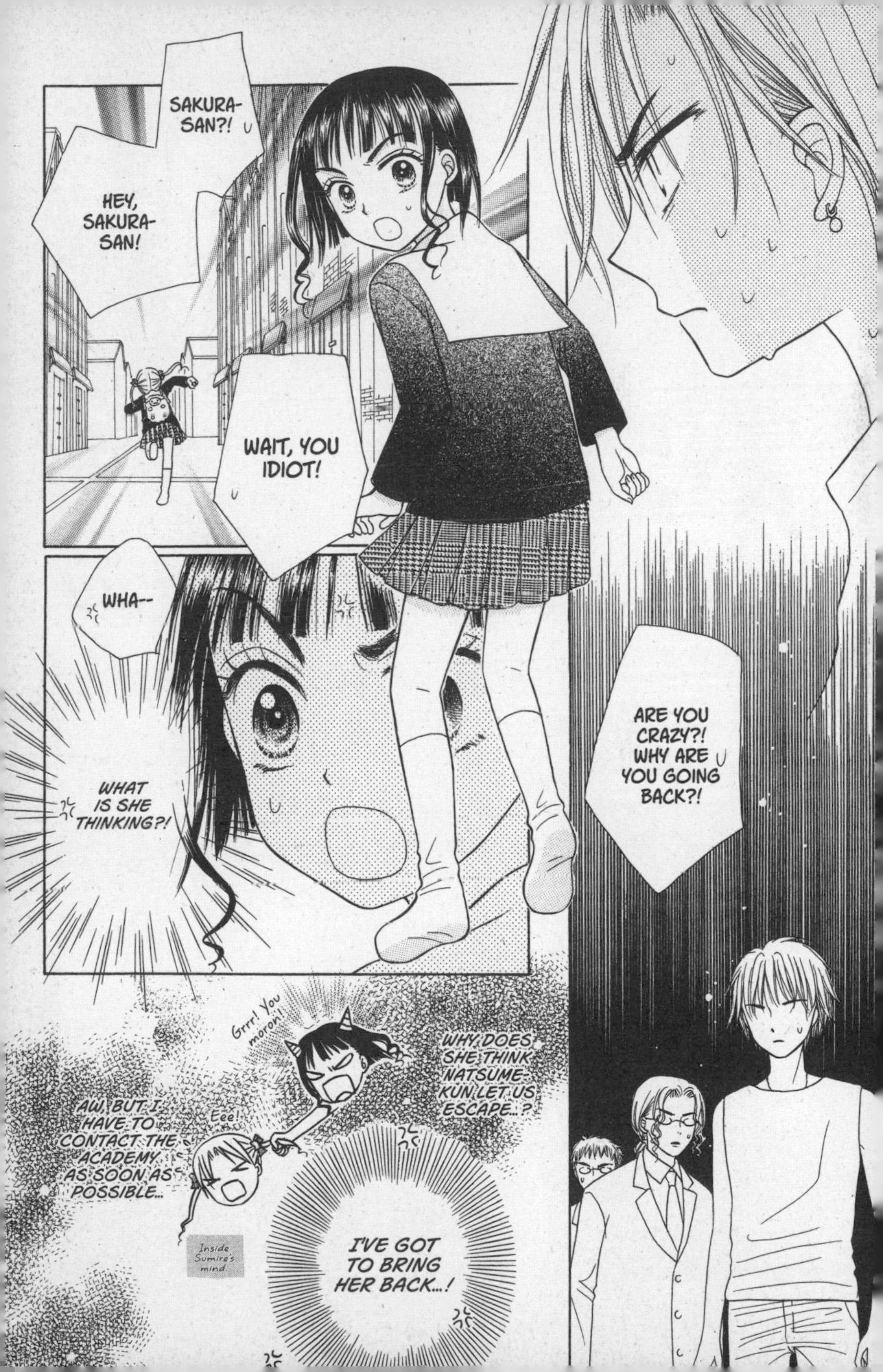
ARE YOU CRAZY?! WHY ARE YOU GOING BACK?!
SAKURA-SAN?!
HEY, SAKURA-SAN!
WAIT, YOU IDIOT!
WHA--
WHAT IS SHE THINKING?!
WHY DOES SHE THINK NATSUME-KUN LET US ESCAPE...?
Grrr! You moron!
I'VE GOT TO BRING HER BACK...!
AW, BUT I HAVE TO CONTACT THE ACADEMY AS SOON AS POSSIBLE...
Eee!
Inside Sumire's mind.

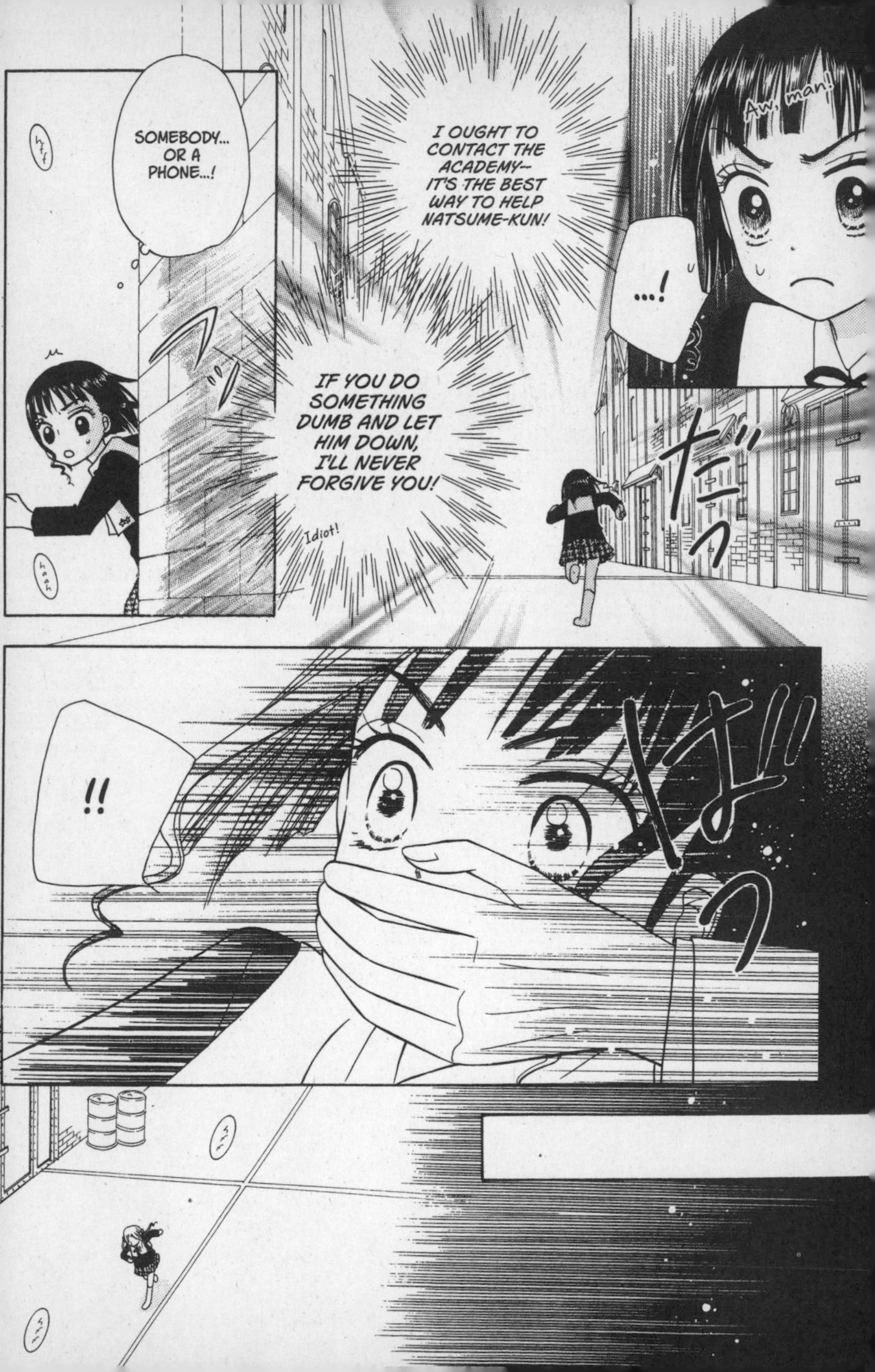
Aw, man!
...!
I OUGHT TO CONTACT THE ACADEMY-- IT'S THE BEST WAY TO HELP NATSUME-KUN!
IF YOU DO SOMETHING DUMB AND LET HIM DOWN, I'LL NEVER FORGIVE YOU!
Idiot!
SOMEBODY... OR A PHONE...!
!!

Read at your own discretion.

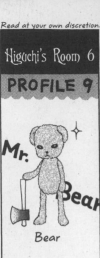

Higuchi's Room 6

PROFILE 9

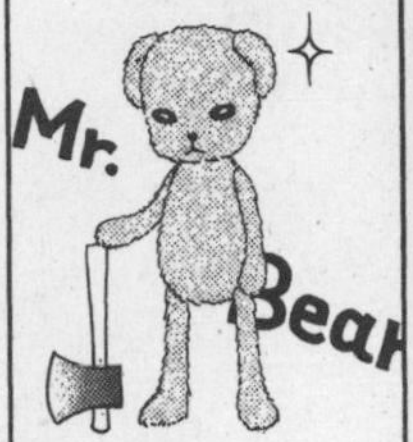
Mr. Bear

Bear

Born on Dec. 25,
7 years old
Capricorn (...),
blood type ? (...)

When I first thought about the story of *Gakuen Alice*, Mikan and Bear were the first characters that came into my mind. Bear's model is my favorite Teddy Bear (manufactured by Steiff). I love teddy bears!! So it's really fun to draw Bear. *ANIMATE* included a Bear stuffed toy in their *Gakuen Alice* merchandise. I was very happy. ♡ Someday I hope to show you a chapter about Bear's creator.

...Oops, I still have blank space.

The End!

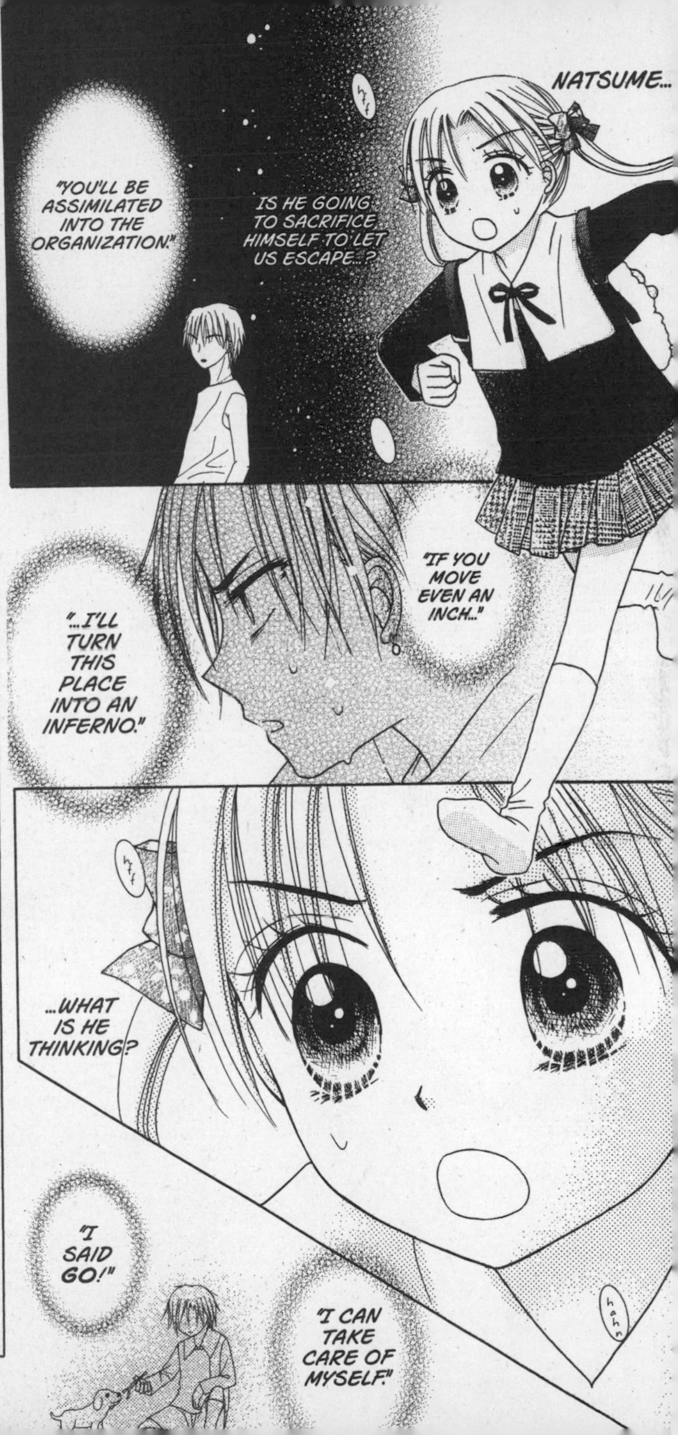
NATSUME...
IS HE GOING TO SACRIFICE HIMSELF TO LET US ESCAPE...?
"YOU'LL BE ASSIMILATED INTO THE ORGANIZATION."
"IF YOU MOVE EVEN AN INCH..."
"...I'LL TURN THIS PLACE INTO AN INFERNO."
...WHAT IS HE THINKING?
"I CAN TAKE CARE OF MYSELF."
"I SAID GO!"

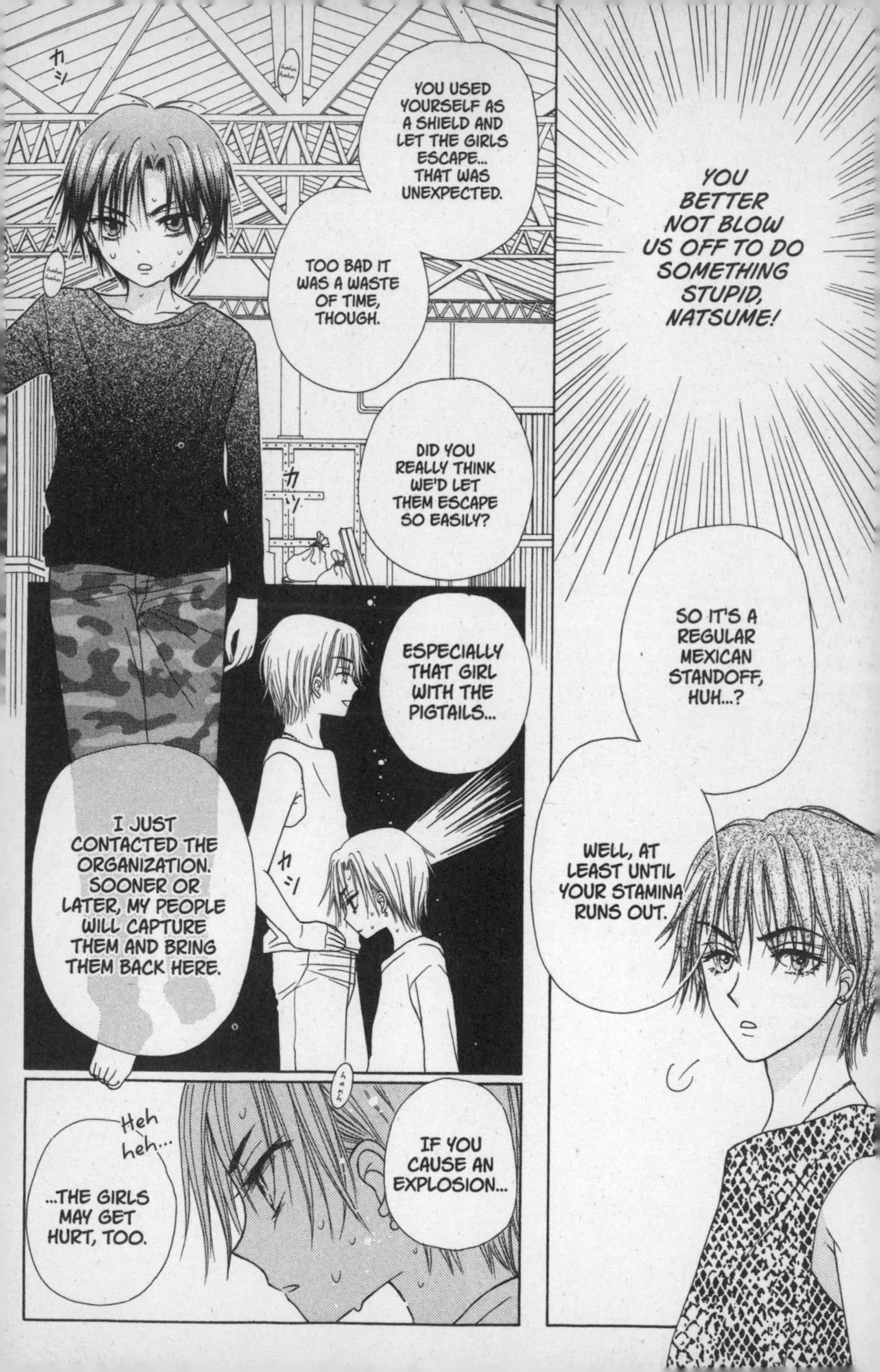
YOU BETTER NOT BLOW US OFF TO DO SOMETHING STUPID, NATSUME!
SO IT'S A REGULAR MEXICAN STANDOFF, HUH...?
WELL, AT LEAST UNTIL YOUR STAMINA RUNS OUT.
YOU USED YOURSELF AS A SHIELD AND LET THE GIRLS ESCAPE... THAT WAS UNEXPECTED.
TOO BAD IT WAS A WASTE OF TIME, THOUGH.
DID YOU REALLY THINK WE'D LET THEM ESCAPE SO EASILY?
ESPECIALLY THAT GIRL WITH THE PIGTAILS...
I JUST CONTACTED THE ORGANIZATION. SOONER OR LATER, MY PEOPLE WILL CAPTURE THEM AND BRING THEM BACK HERE.
IF YOU CAUSE AN EXPLOSION...
Heh heh...
...THE GIRLS MAY GET HURT, TOO.

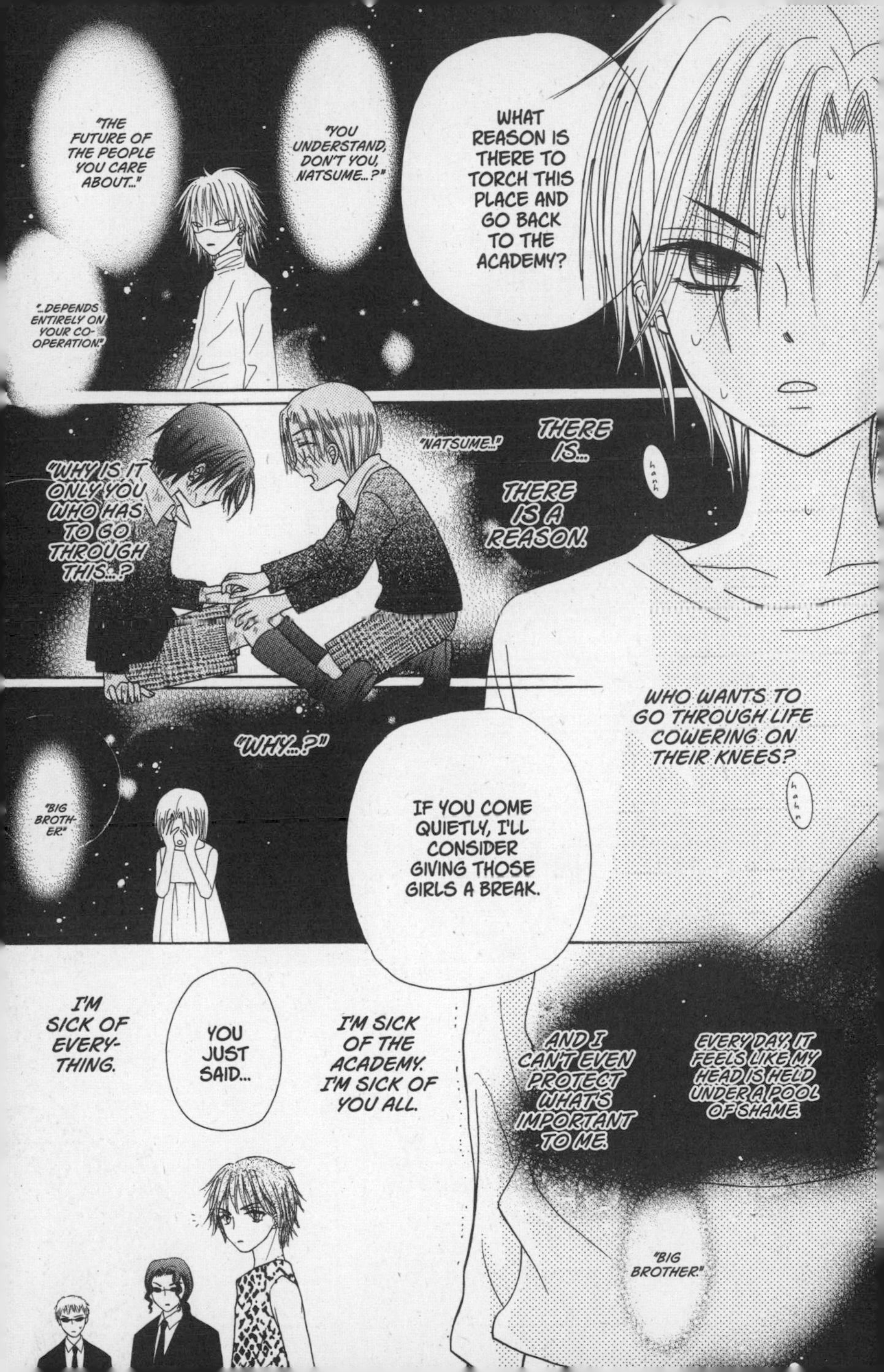

WHAT REASON IS THERE TO TORCH THIS PLACE AND GO BACK TO THE ACADEMY?
"YOU UNDERSTAND, DON'T YOU, NATSUME...?"
"THE FUTURE OF THE PEOPLE YOU CARE ABOUT..."
"...DEPENDS ENTIRELY ON YOUR CO-OPERATION."
THERE IS...
THERE IS A REASON.
hahh
"NATSUME..."
"WHY IS IT ONLY YOU WHO HAS TO GO THROUGH THIS...?"
"WHY...?"
"BIG BROTHER."
WHO WANTS TO GO THROUGH LIFE COWERING ON THEIR KNEES?
hahh
IF YOU COME QUIETLY, I'LL CONSIDER GIVING THOSE GIRLS A BREAK.
EVERY DAY, IT FEELS LIKE MY HEAD IS HELD UNDER A POOL OF SHAME.
AND I CAN'T EVEN PROTECT WHAT'S IMPORTANT TO ME.
"BIG BROTHER."
I'M SICK OF THE ACADEMY. I'M SICK OF YOU ALL.
YOU JUST SAID...
I'M SICK OF EVERYTHING.

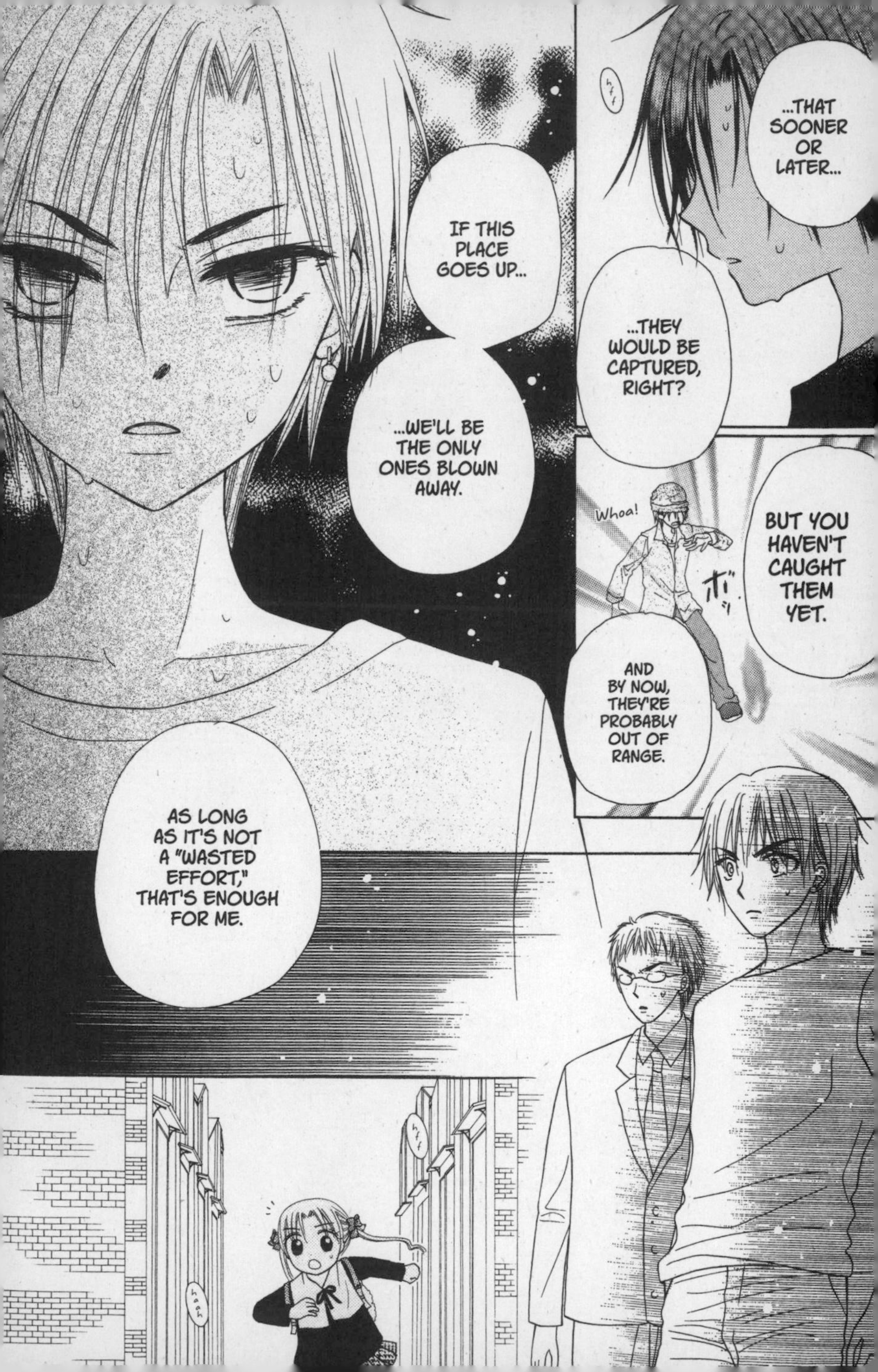
hff
...THAT SOONER OR LATER...
...THEY WOULD BE CAPTURED, RIGHT?
BUT YOU HAVEN'T CAUGHT THEM YET.
Whoa!
AND BY NOW, THEY'RE PROBABLY OUT OF RANGE.
IF THIS PLACE GOES UP...
...WE'LL BE THE ONLY ONES BLOWN AWAY.
AS LONG AS IT'S NOT A "WASTED EFFORT," THAT'S ENOUGH FOR ME.
hff
haah

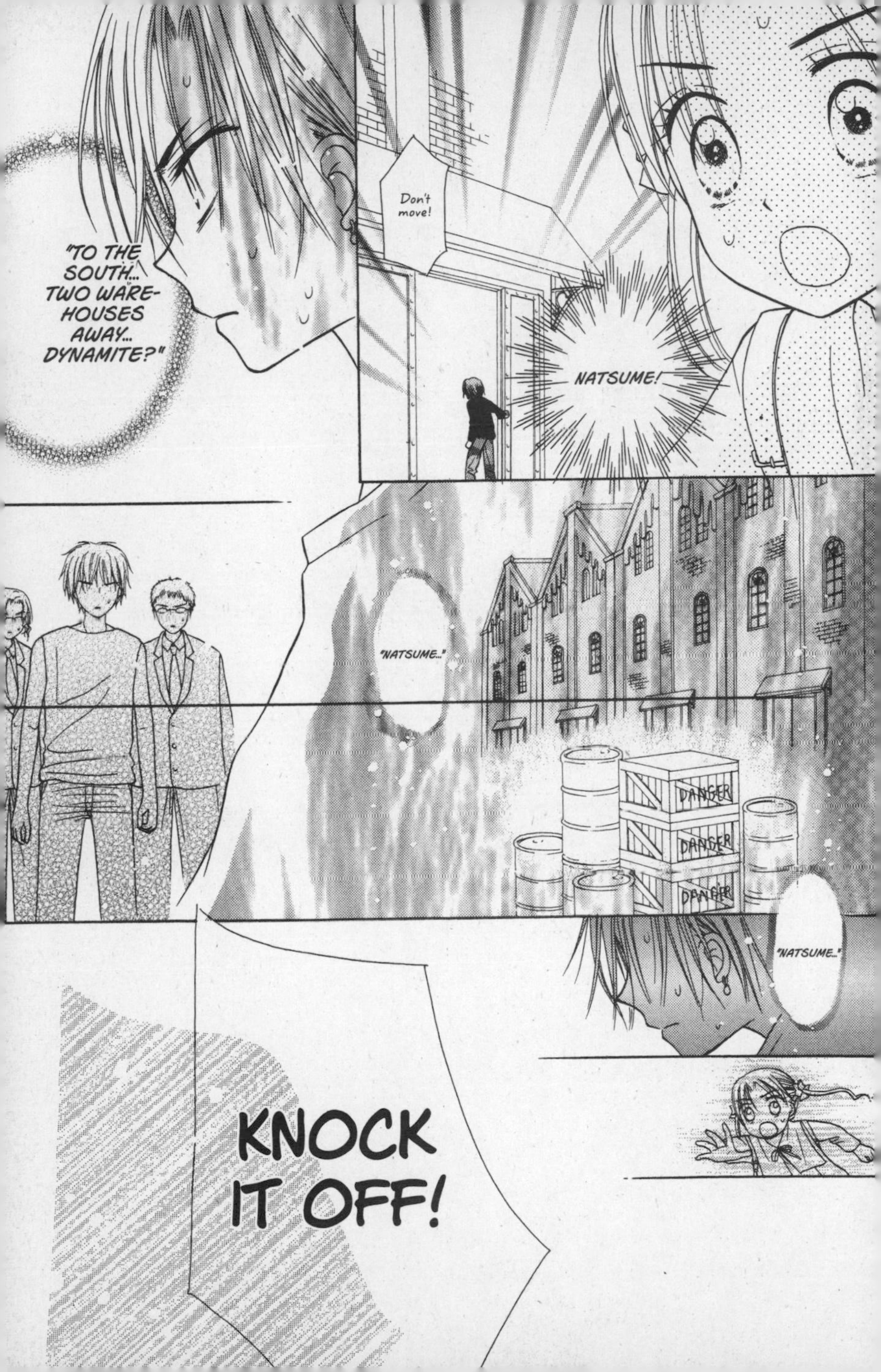
Don't move!
NATSUME!
"TO THE SOUTH... TWO WARE-HOUSES AWAY... DYNAMITE?"
"NATSUME..."
DANGER
DANGER
DANGER
"NATSUME..."
KNOCK IT OFF!

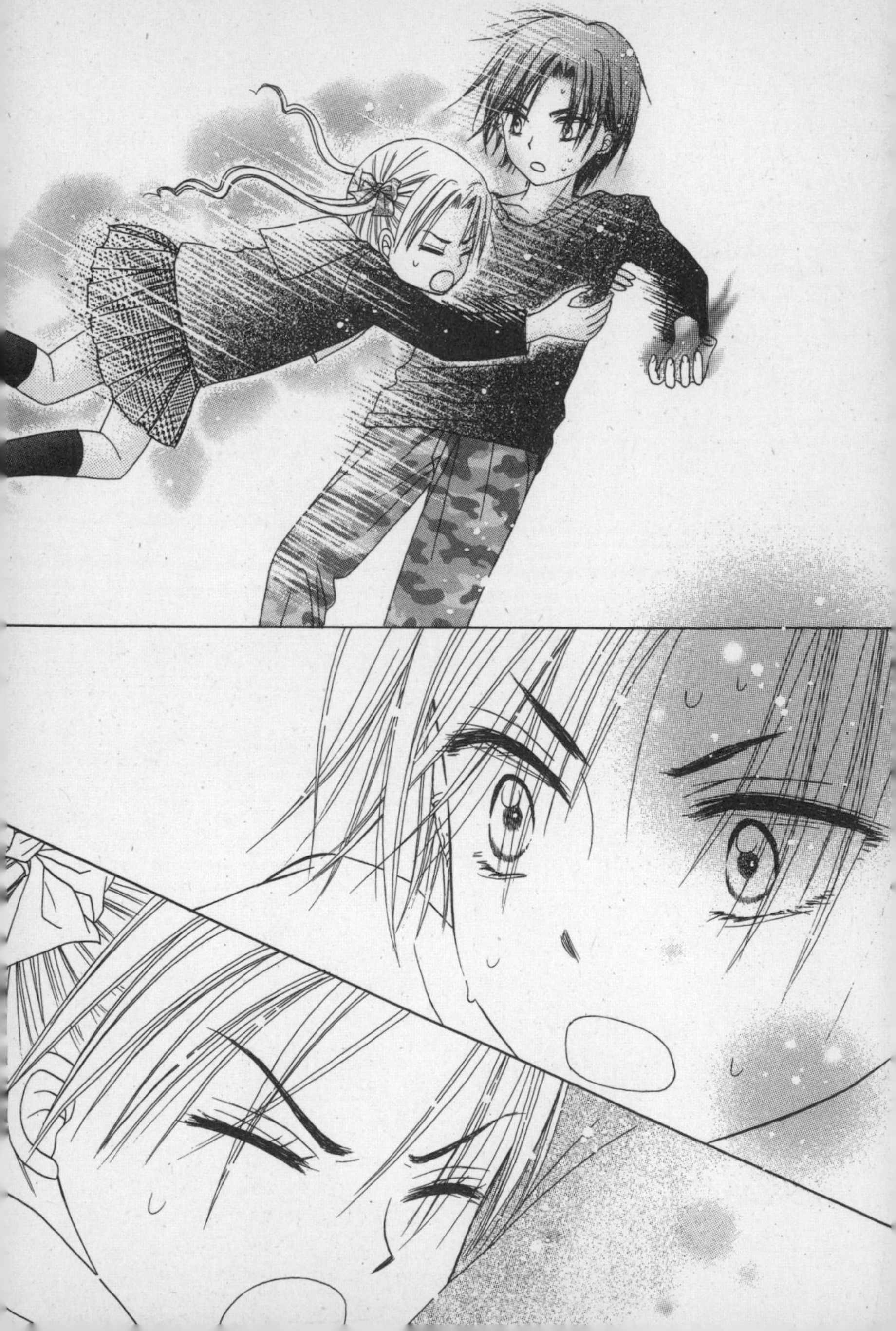

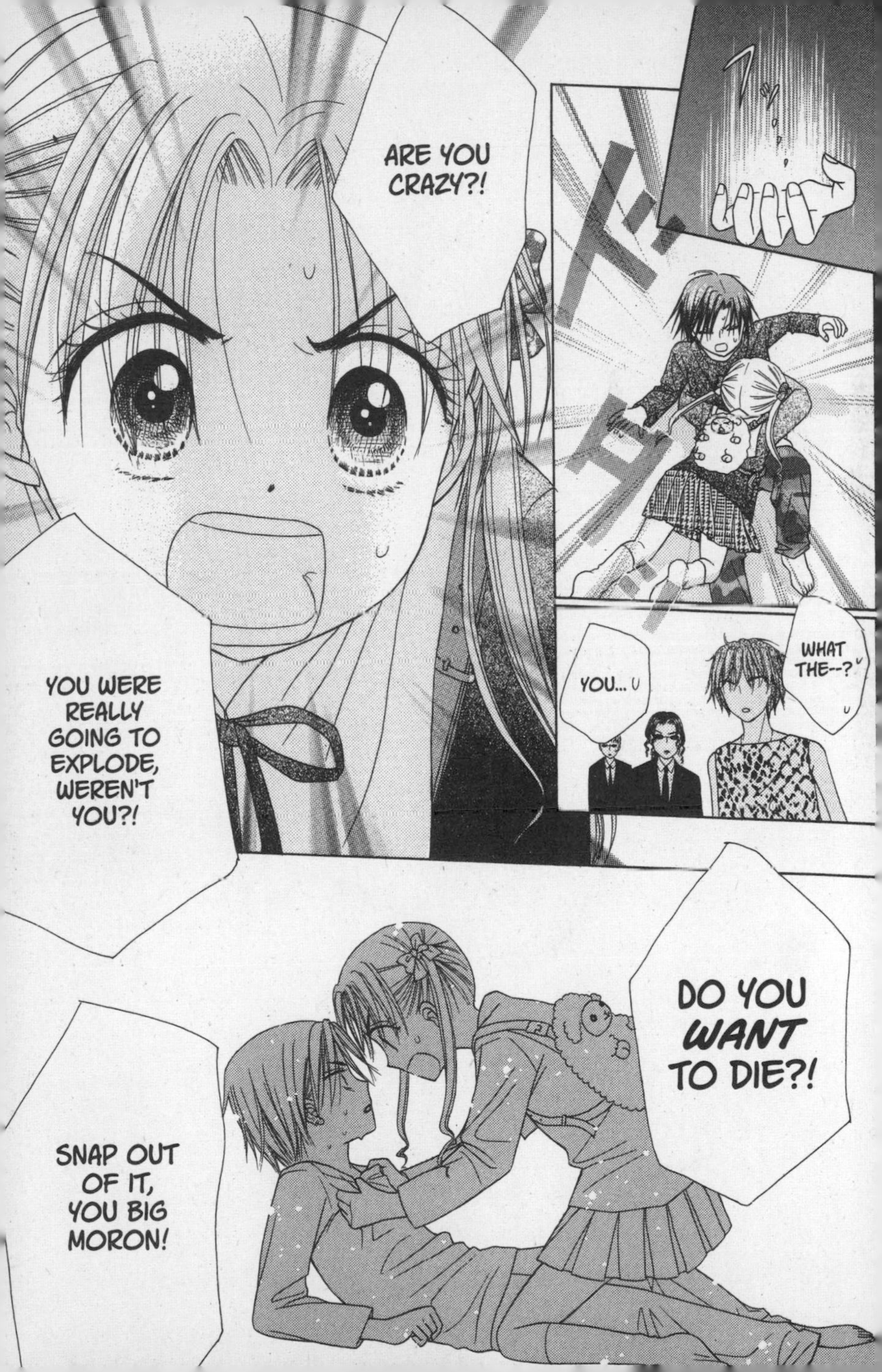
WHAT THE--?
YOU...
ARE YOU CRAZY?!
YOU WERE REALLY GOING TO EXPLODE, WEREN'T YOU?!
DO YOU *WANT* TO DIE?!
SNAP OUT OF IT, YOU BIG MORON!

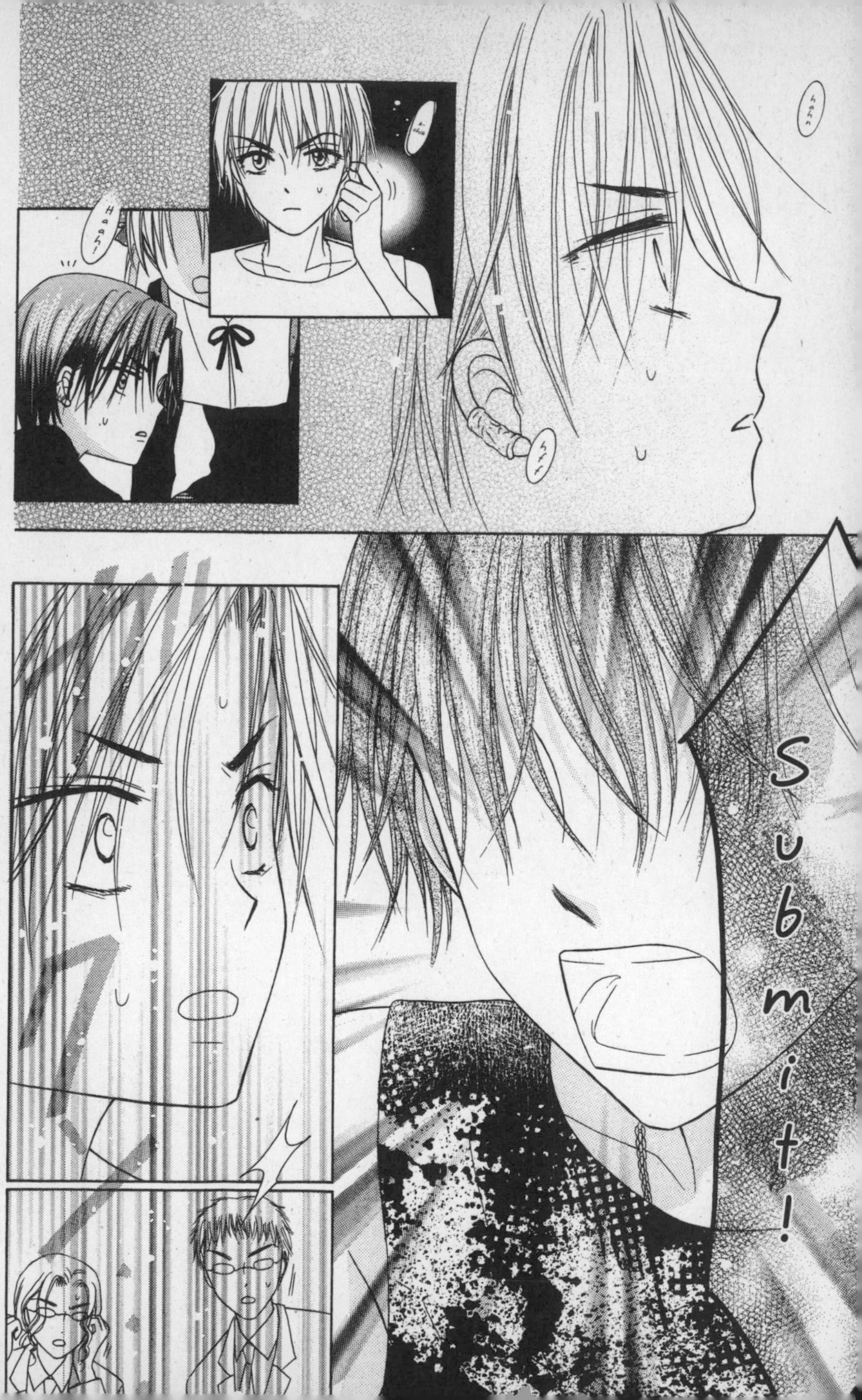
hahn
Haah!
Submit!

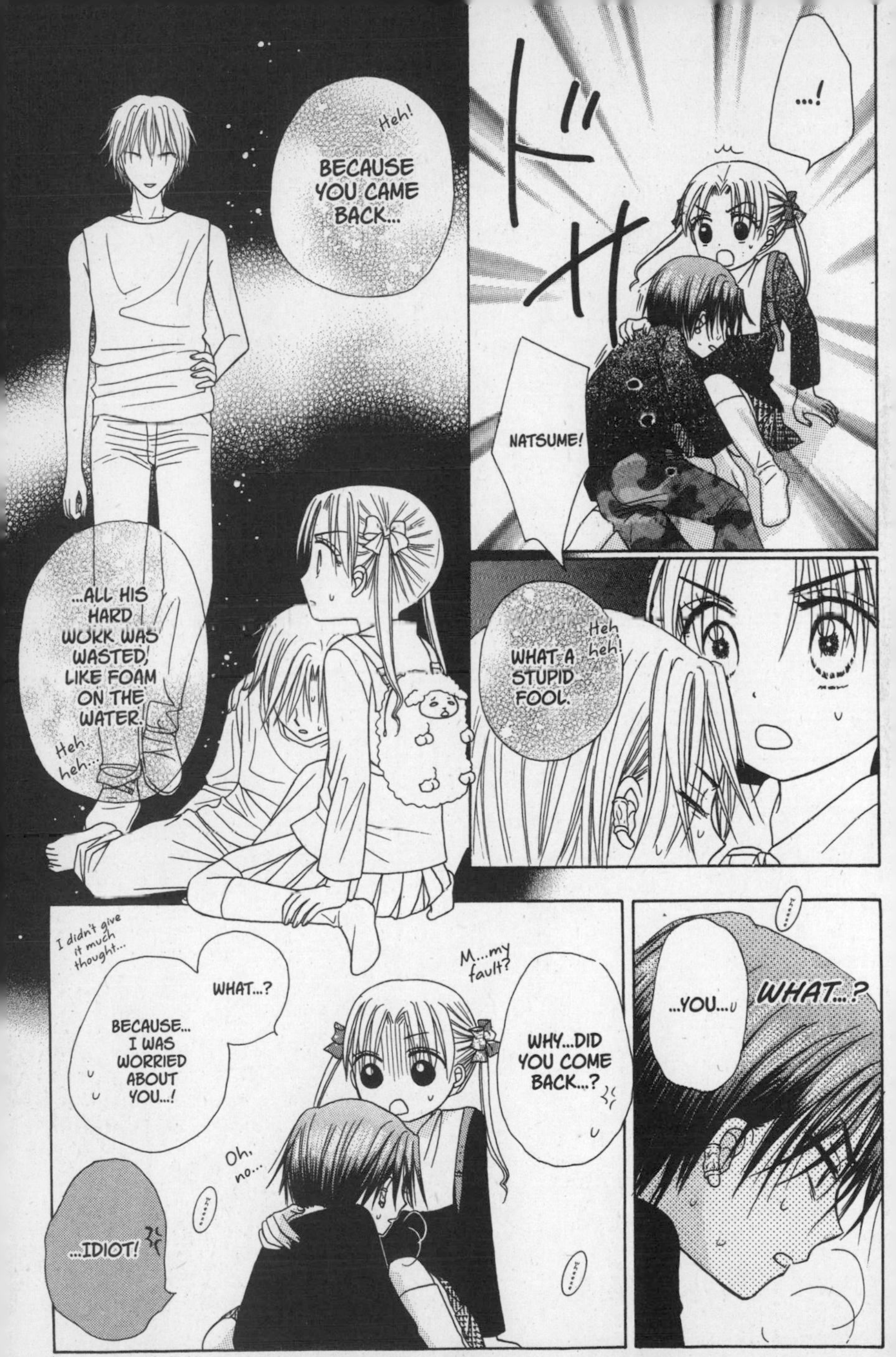
...!
ドサ
NATSUME!
Heh heh!
WHAT A STUPID FOOL.
Heh!
BECAUSE YOU CAME BACK...
...ALL HIS HARD WORK WAS WASTED, LIKE FOAM ON THE WATER.
Heh heh...
....!
WHAT...?
...YOU...
M...my fault?
WHY...DID YOU COME BACK...?
I didn't give it much thought...
WHAT...?
BECAUSE... I WAS WORRIED ABOUT YOU...!
Oh, no...
.....
...IDIOT!
.....

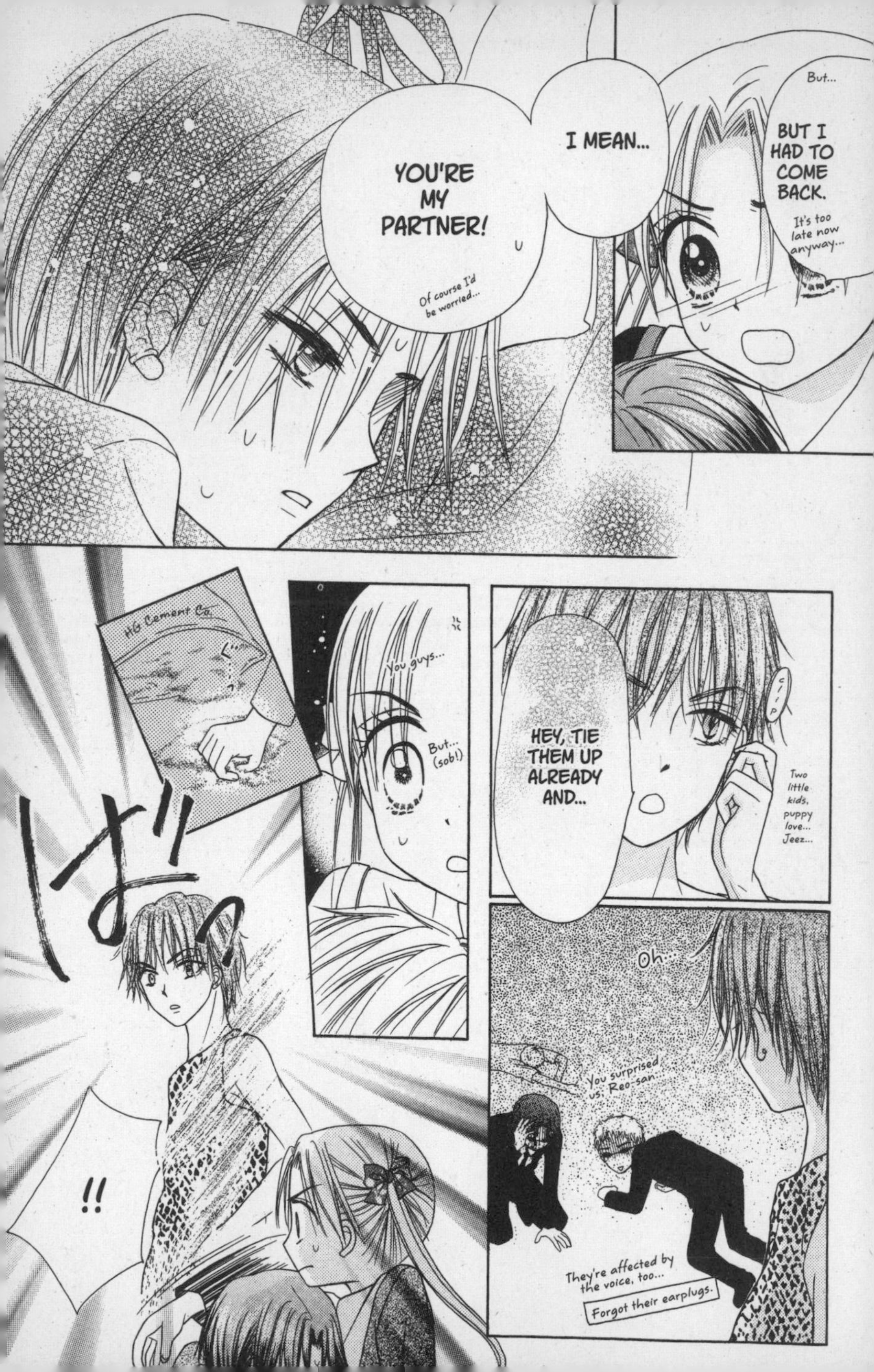
But...
BUT I HAD TO COME BACK.
It's too late now anyway...
I MEAN...
YOU'RE MY PARTNER!
Of course I'd be worried...
clip
HEY, TIE THEM UP ALREADY AND...
Two little kids, puppy love... Jeez...
Oh...
You surprised us, Reo-san...
They're affected by the voice, too...
Forgot their earplugs.
You guys...
But... (sob!)
HG Cement Co.
!!

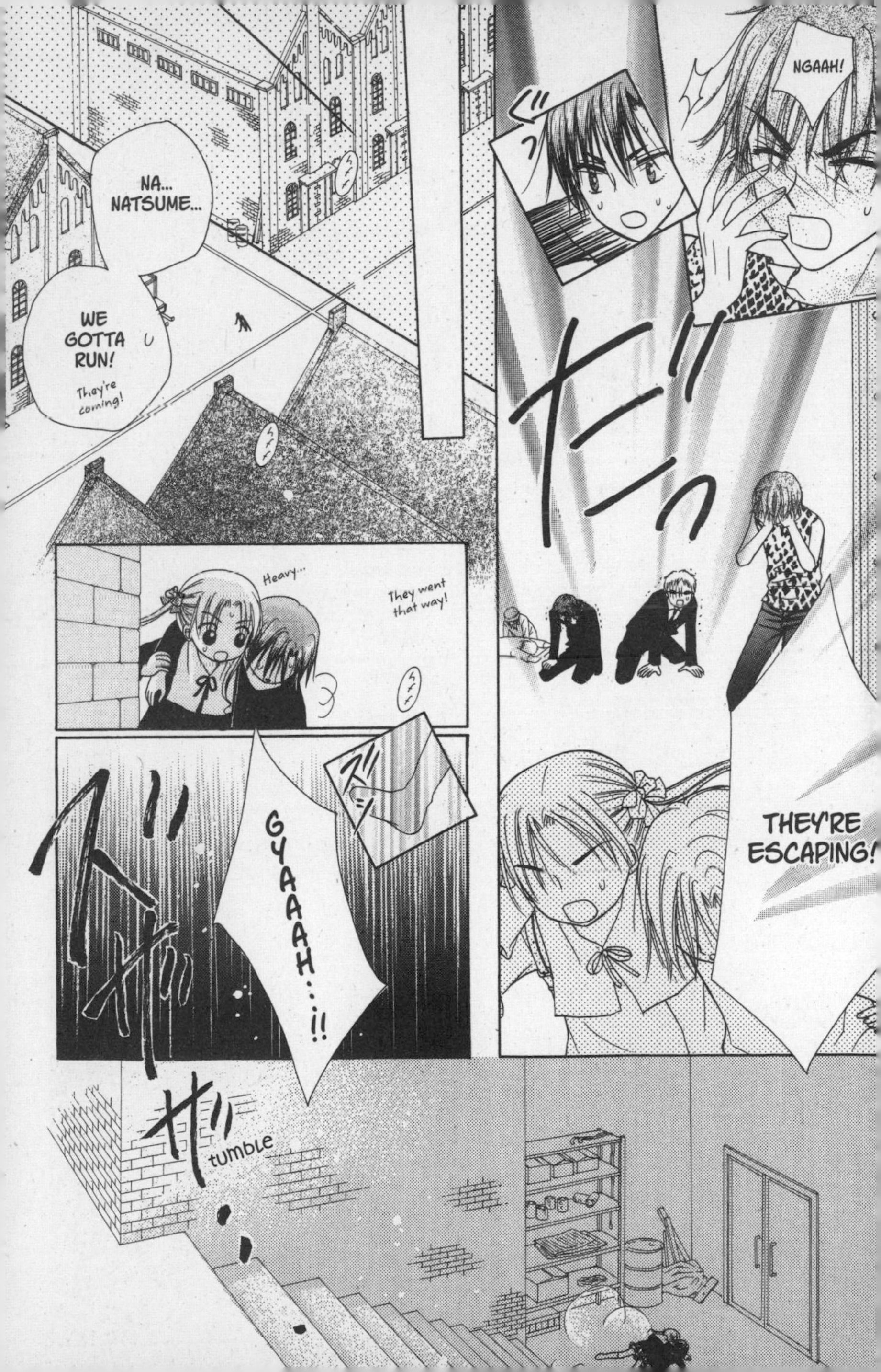
NGAAH!
THEY'RE ESCAPING!
NA... NATSUME...
WE GOTTA RUN!
They're coming!
Heavy...
They went that way!
GYAAAH...!!
tumble

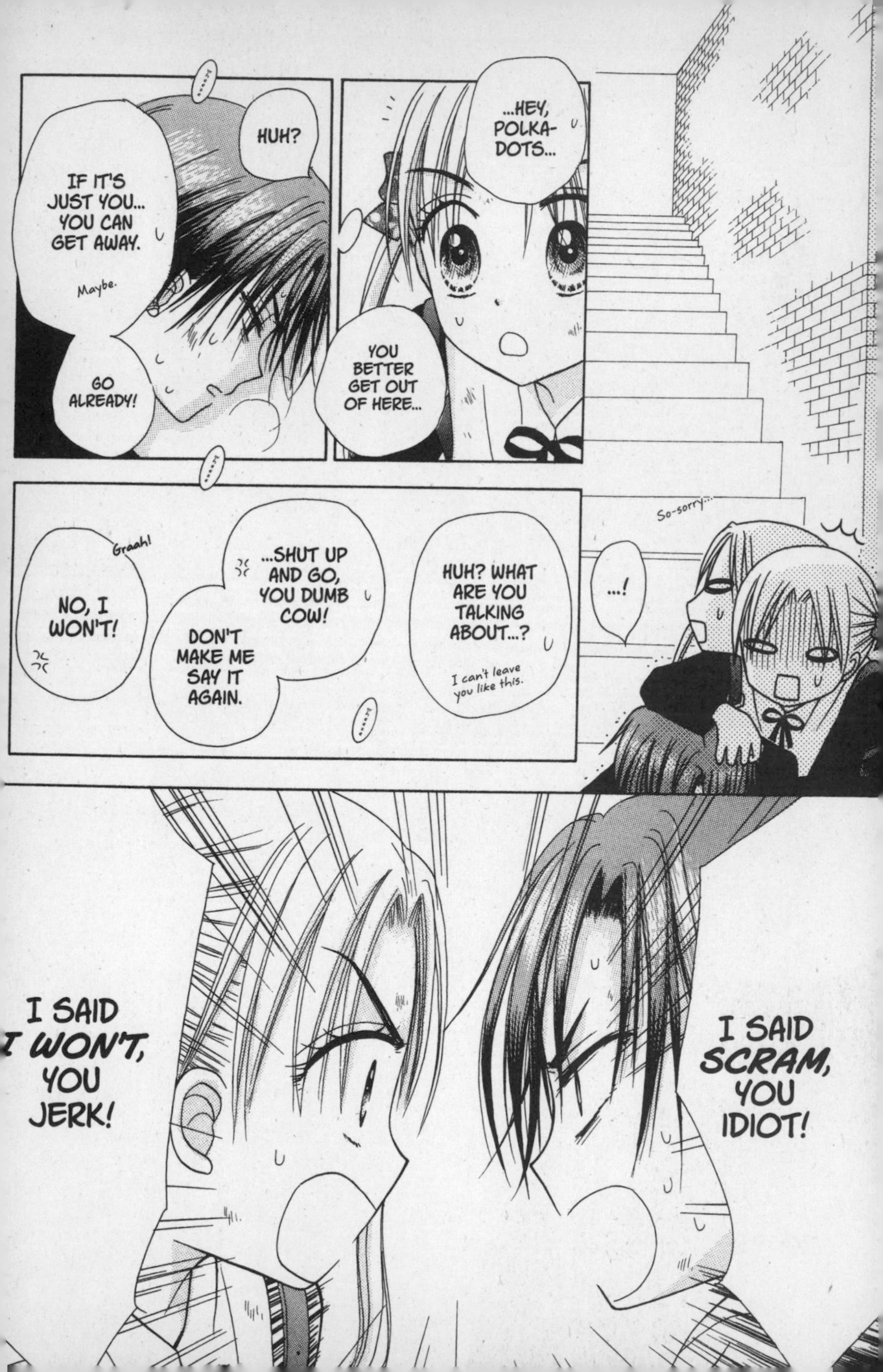
...HEY, POLKA-DOTS...
YOU BETTER GET OUT OF HERE...
HUH?
IF IT'S JUST YOU... YOU CAN GET AWAY.
Maybe.
GO ALREADY!
So-sorry...
...!
HUH? WHAT ARE YOU TALKING ABOUT...?
I can't leave you like this.
...SHUT UP AND GO, YOU DUMB COW!
DON'T MAKE ME SAY IT AGAIN.
NO, I WON'T!
Graah!
I SAID SCRAM, YOU IDIOT!
I SAID I WON'T, YOU JERK!

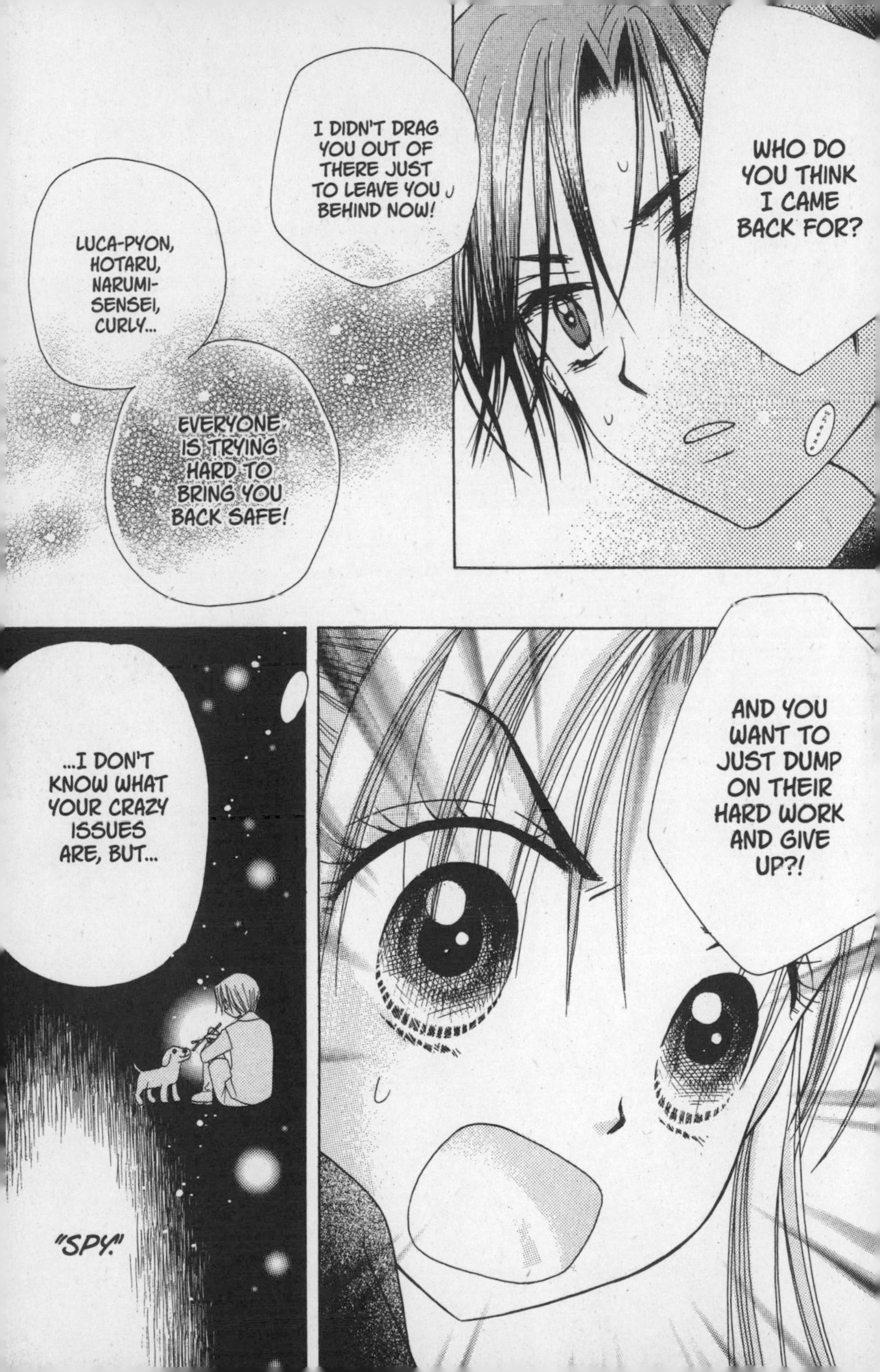
WHO DO YOU THINK I CAME BACK FOR?
I DIDN'T DRAG YOU OUT OF THERE JUST TO LEAVE YOU BEHIND NOW!
LUCA-PYON, HOTARU, NARUMI-SENSEI, CURLY...
EVERYONE IS TRYING HARD TO BRING YOU BACK SAFE!
AND YOU WANT TO JUST DUMP ON THEIR HARD WORK AND GIVE UP?!
...I DON'T KNOW WHAT YOUR CRAZY ISSUES ARE, BUT...
"SPY."

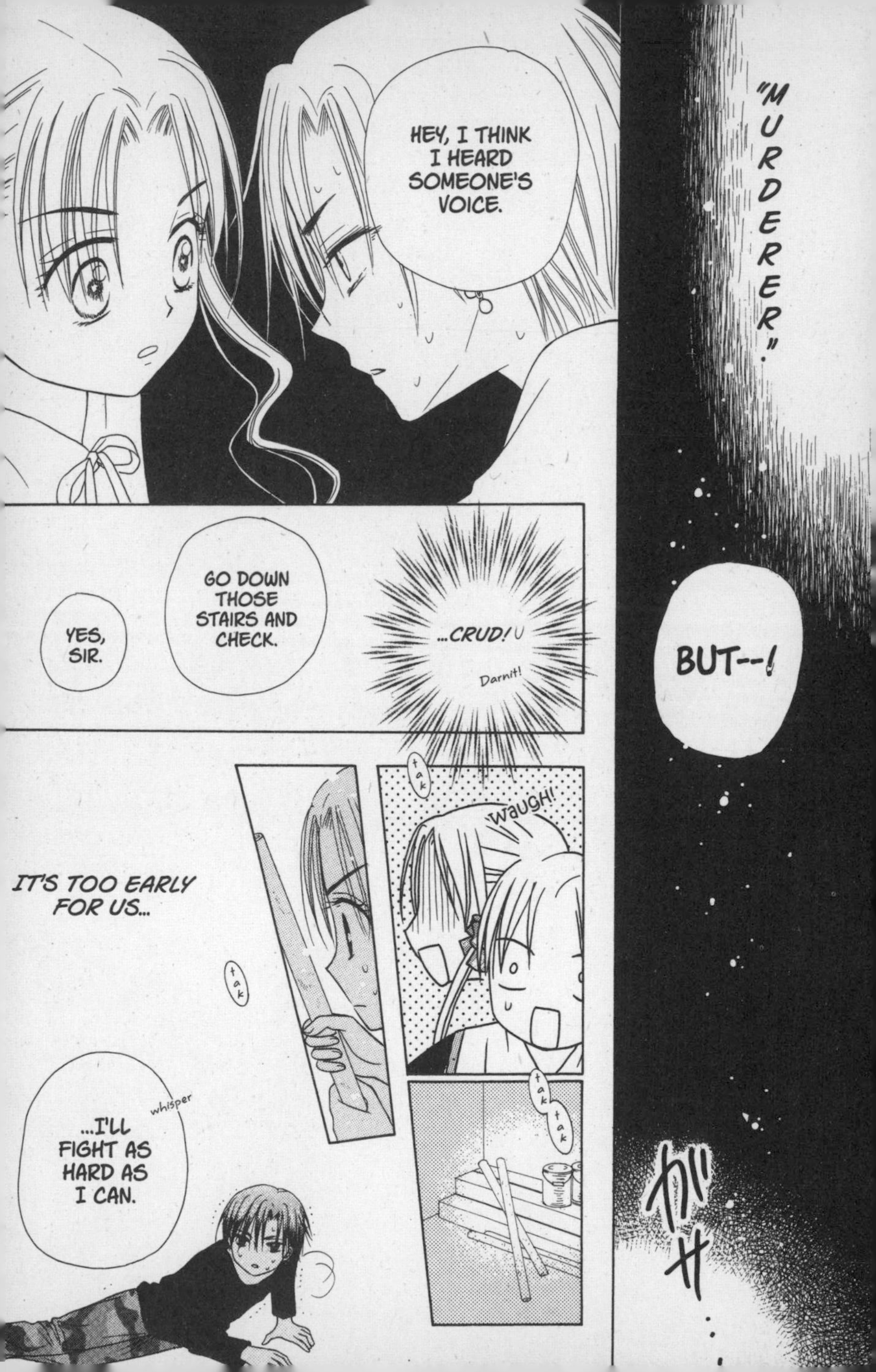
"MURDERER."
BUT--!
HEY, I THINK I HEARD SOMEONE'S VOICE.
...CRUD!
Darnit!
GO DOWN THOSE STAIRS AND CHECK.
YES, SIR.
tak
WAUGH!
tak tak
tak
IT'S TOO EARLY FOR US...
whisper
...I'LL FIGHT AS HARD AS I CAN.

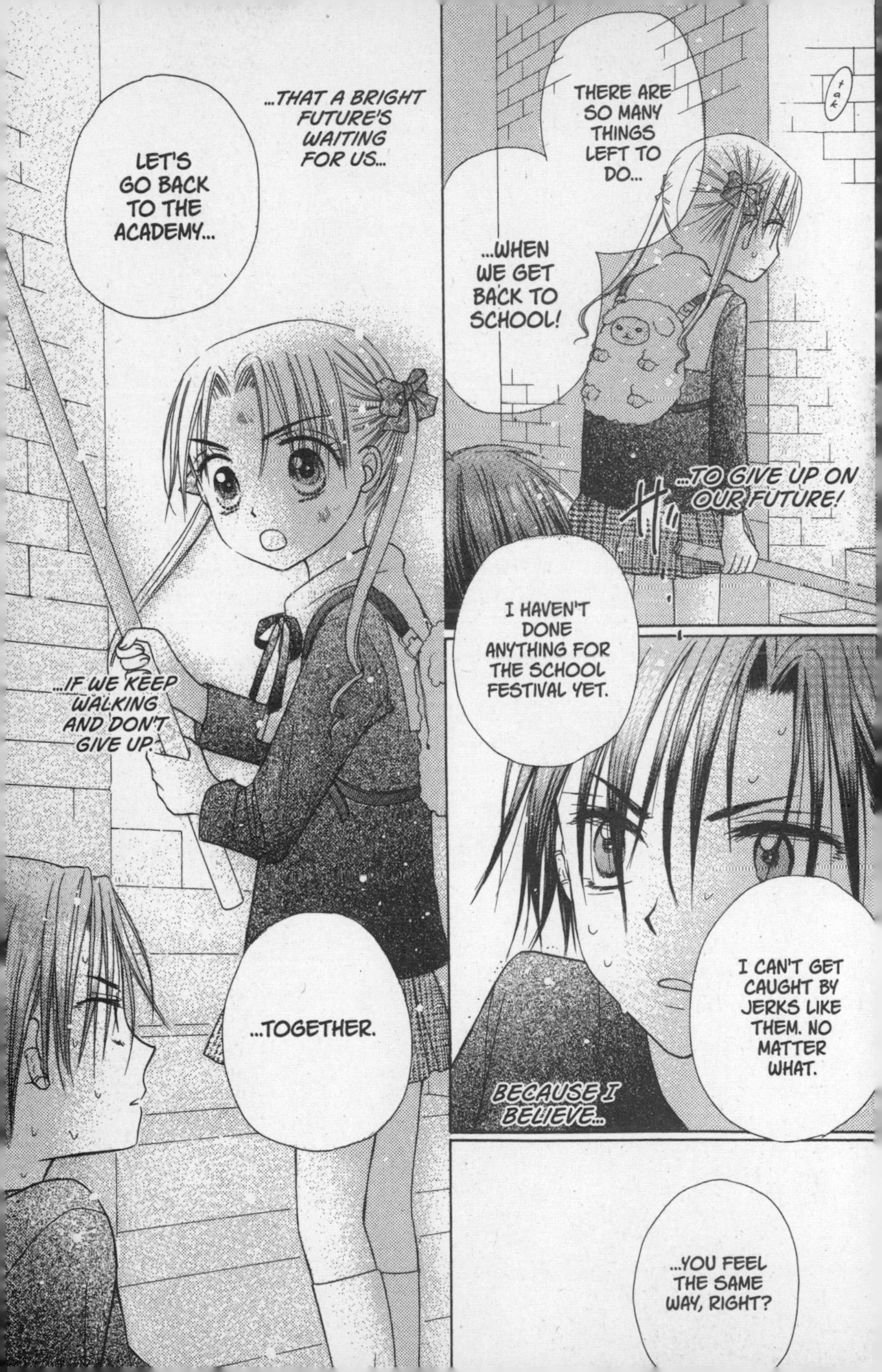
tak
THERE ARE SO MANY THINGS LEFT TO DO...
...WHEN WE GET BACK TO SCHOOL!
...TO GIVE UP ON OUR FUTURE!
I HAVEN'T DONE ANYTHING FOR THE SCHOOL FESTIVAL YET.
I CAN'T GET CAUGHT BY JERKS LIKE THEM. NO MATTER WHAT.
BECAUSE I BELIEVE...
...YOU FEEL THE SAME WAY, RIGHT?
...THAT A BRIGHT FUTURE'S WAITING FOR US...
LET'S GO BACK TO THE ACADEMY...
...IF WE KEEP WALKING AND DON'T GIVE UP.
...TOGETHER.

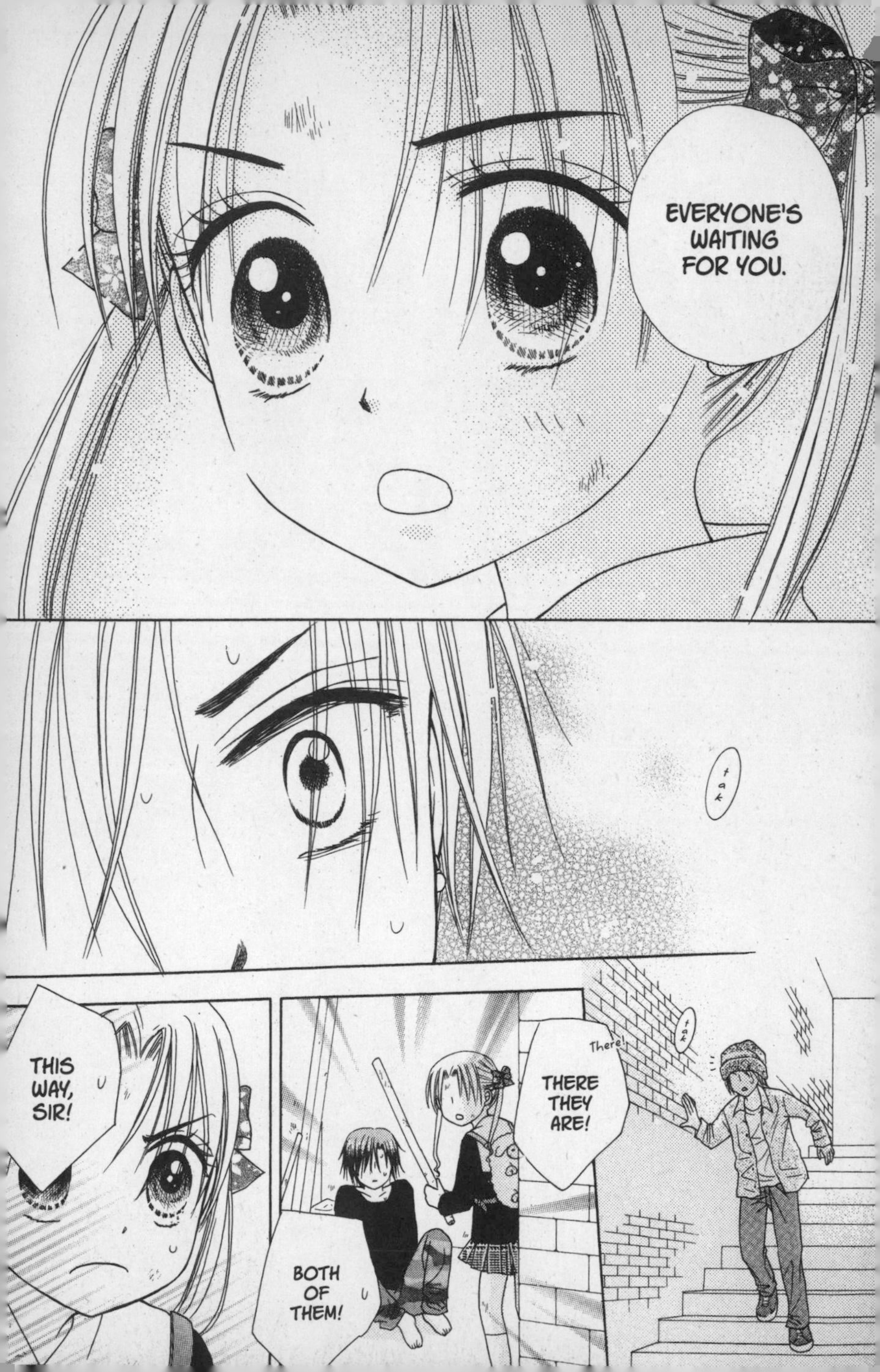
EVERYONE'S WAITING FOR YOU.
tak
tak
There!
THERE THEY ARE!
BOTH OF THEM!
THIS WAY, SIR!

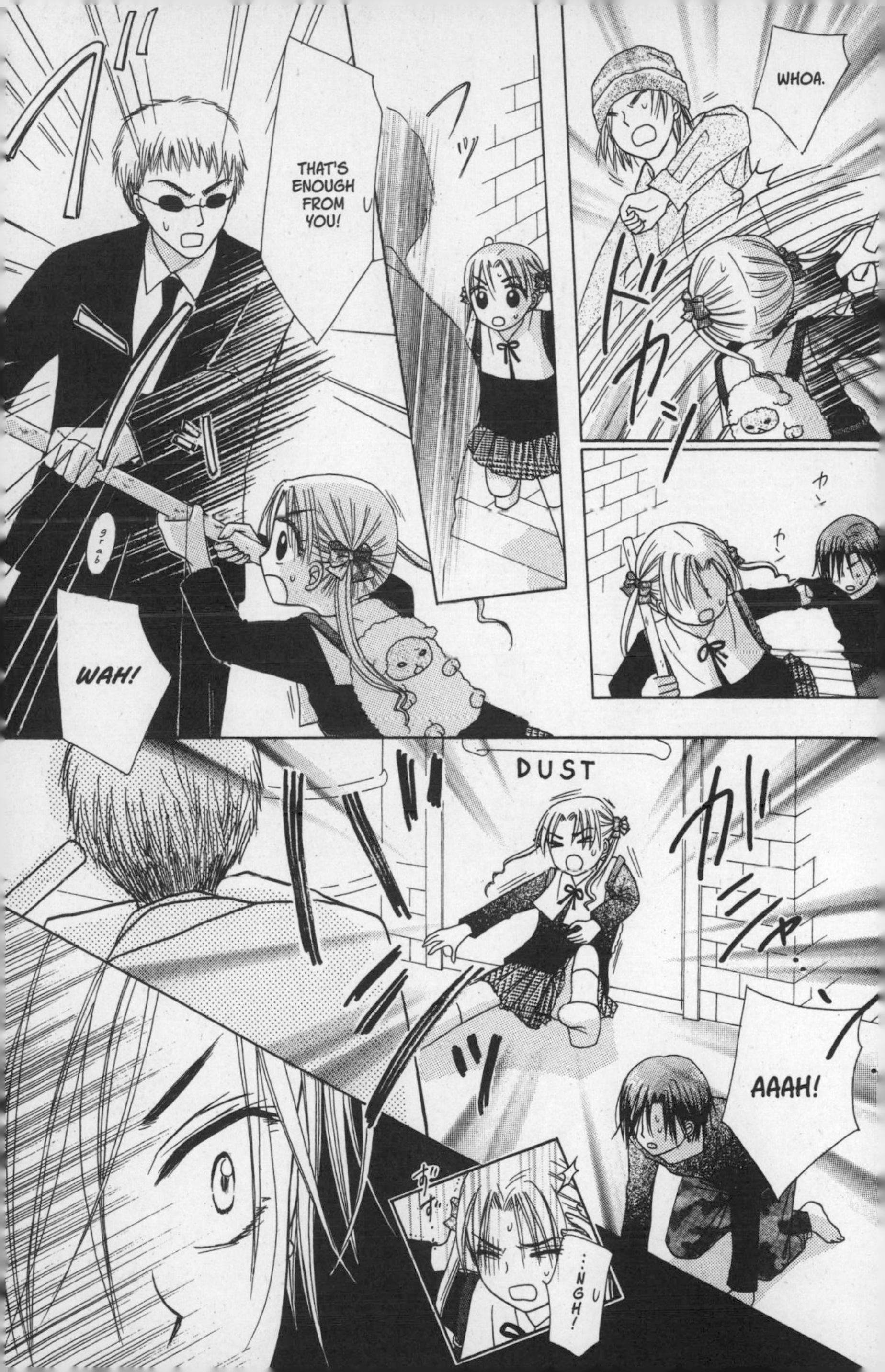
WHOA.
THAT'S ENOUGH FROM YOU!
grab
WAH!
DUST
AAAH!
...NGH!

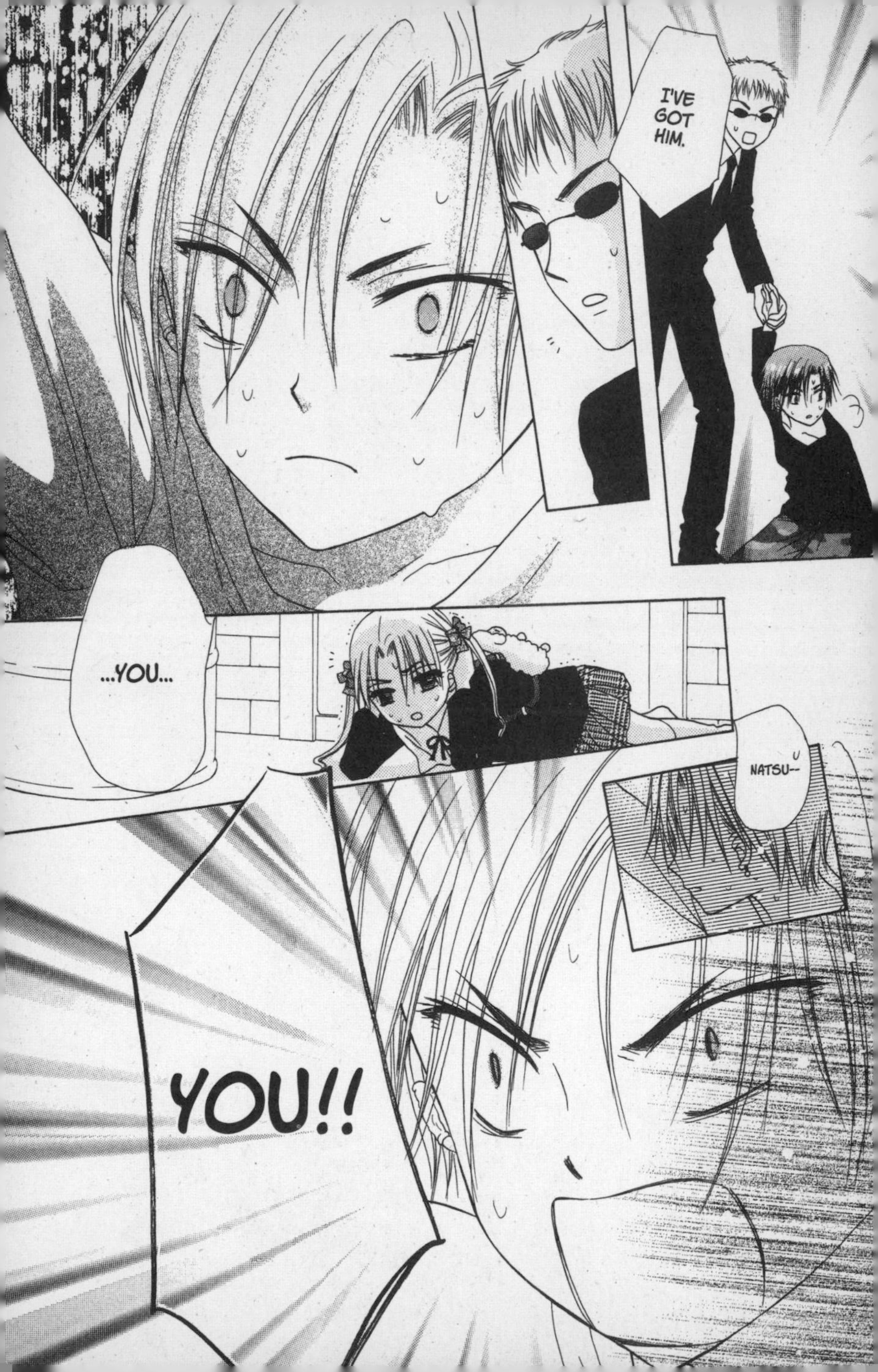
I'VE GOT HIM.
...YOU...
NATSU--
YOU!!

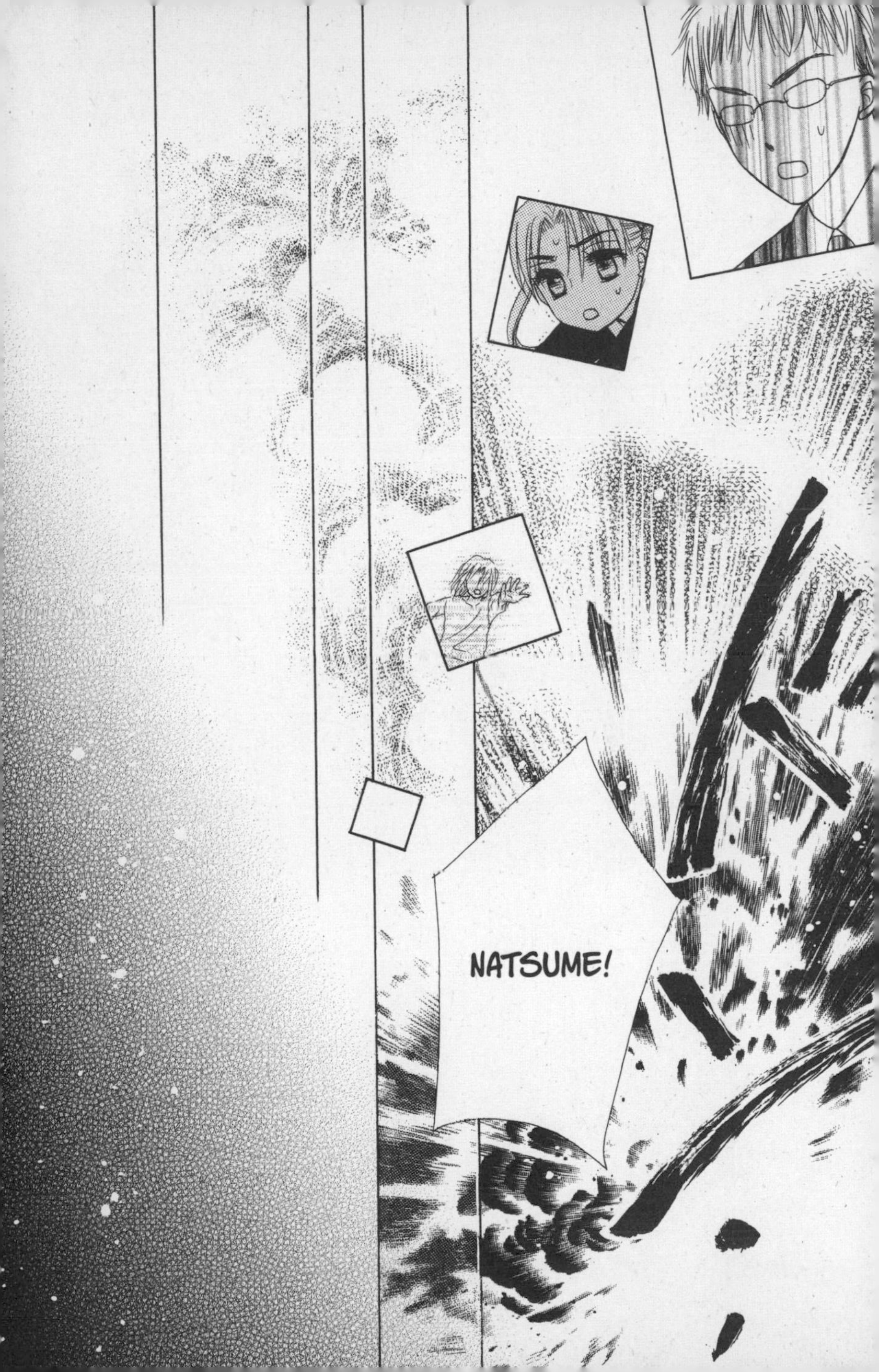
NATSUME!

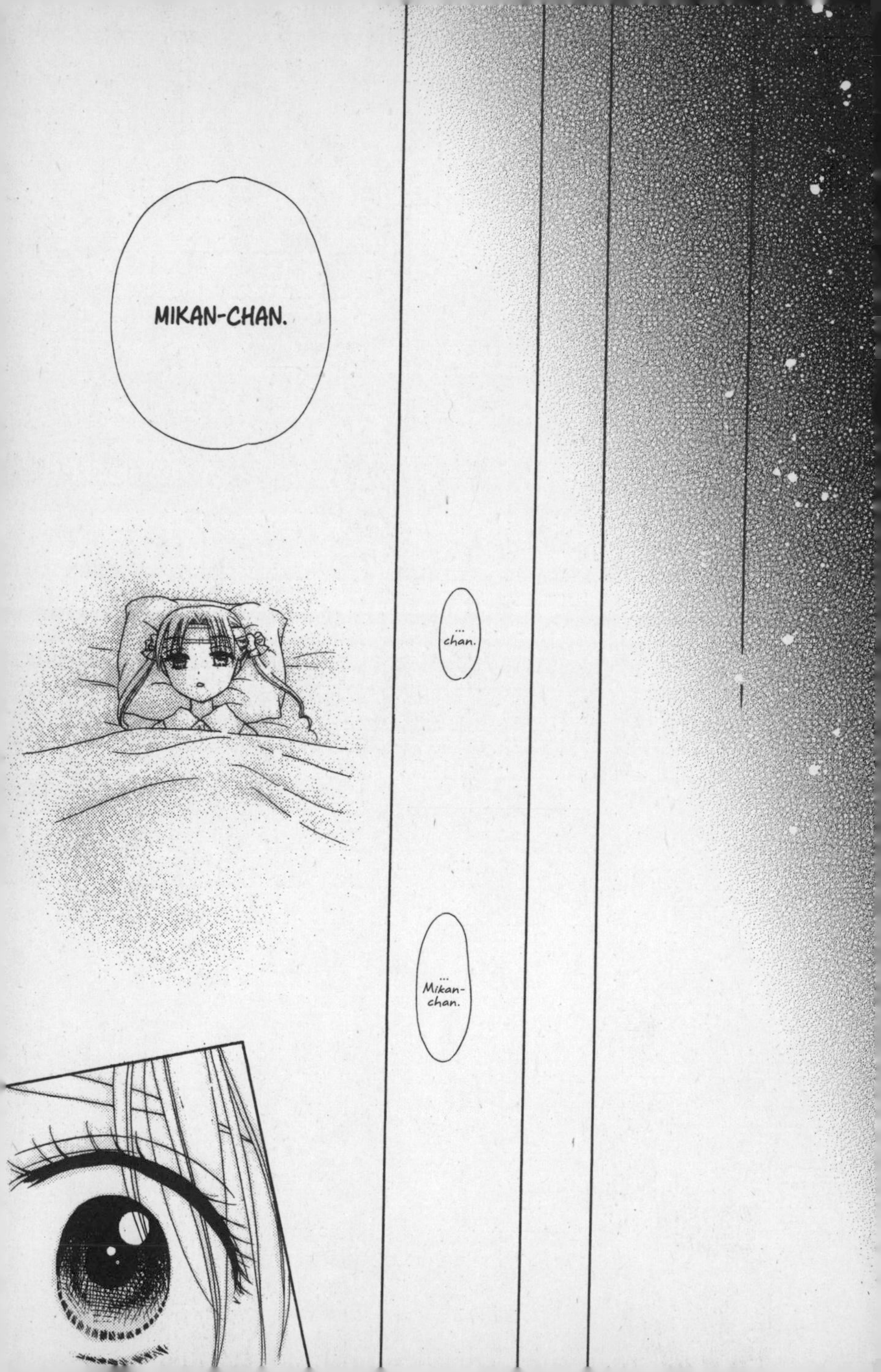

... chan.
... Mikan-chan.
MIKAN-CHAN.

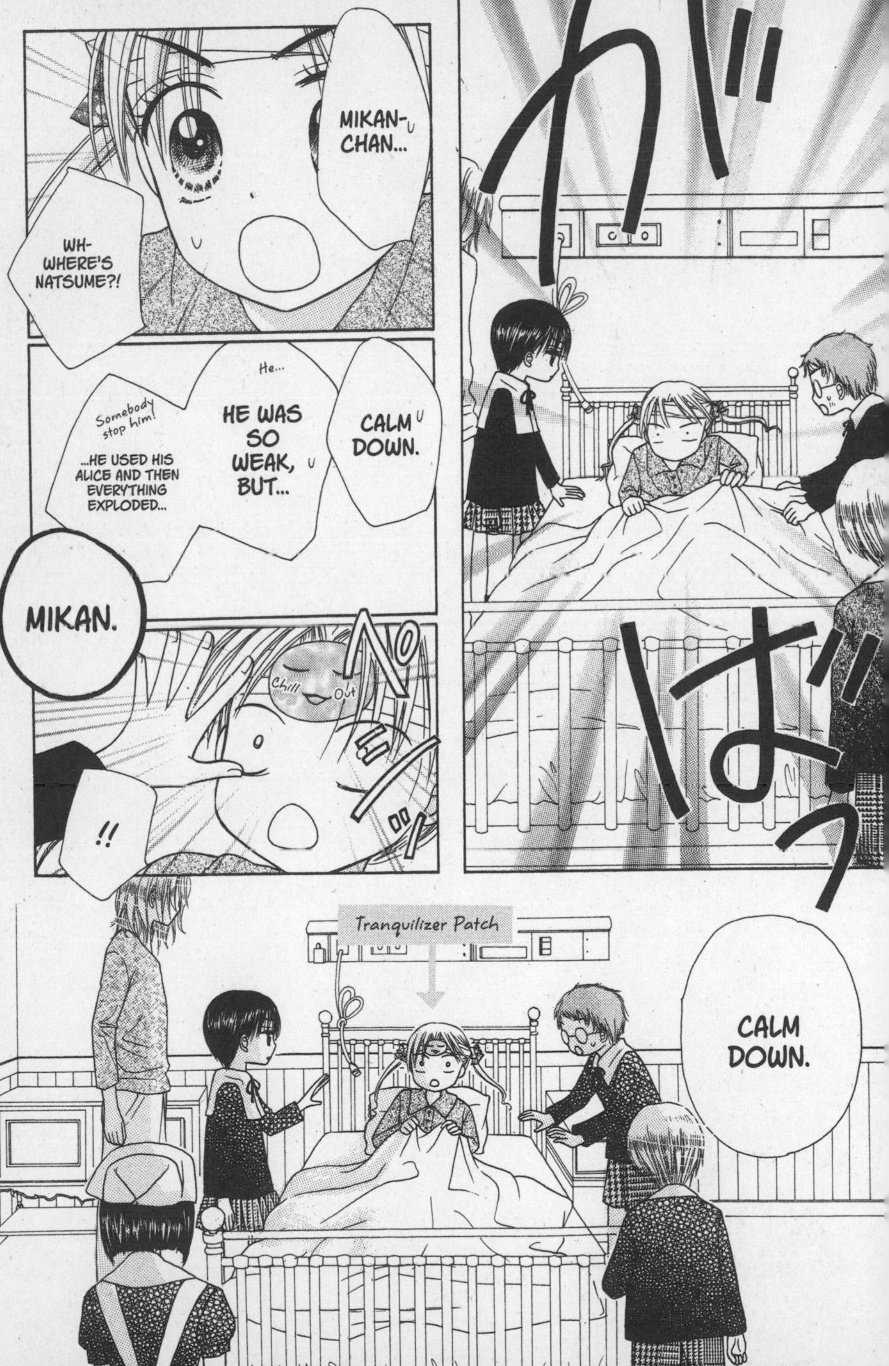
わド
ばっ
MIKAN-CHAN...
WH-WHERE'S NATSUME?!
CALM DOWN.
He...
HE WAS SO WEAK, BUT...
...HE USED HIS ALICE AND THEN EVERYTHING EXPLODED...
Somebody stop him!
MIKAN.
Chill Out
!!
CALM DOWN.
Tranquilizer Patch

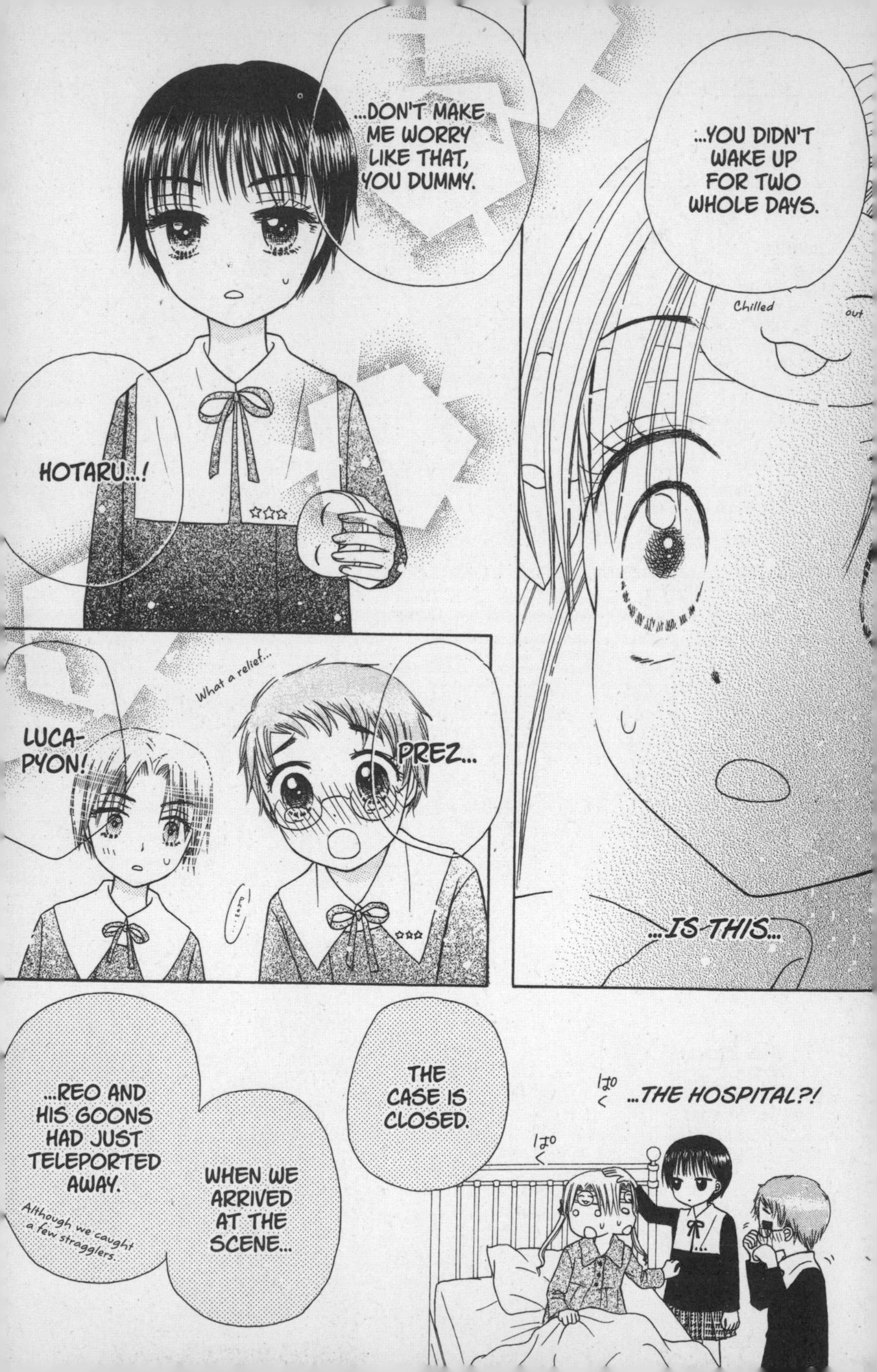
...YOU DIDN'T WAKE UP FOR TWO WHOLE DAYS.
Chilled out
...IS THIS...
...DON'T MAKE ME WORRY LIKE THAT, YOU DUMMY.
HOTARU...!
PREZ...
What a relief...
LUCA-PYON!
...THE HOSPITAL?!
THE CASE IS CLOSED.
WHEN WE ARRIVED AT THE SCENE...
...REO AND HIS GOONS HAD JUST TELEPORTED AWAY.
Although we caught a few stragglers.

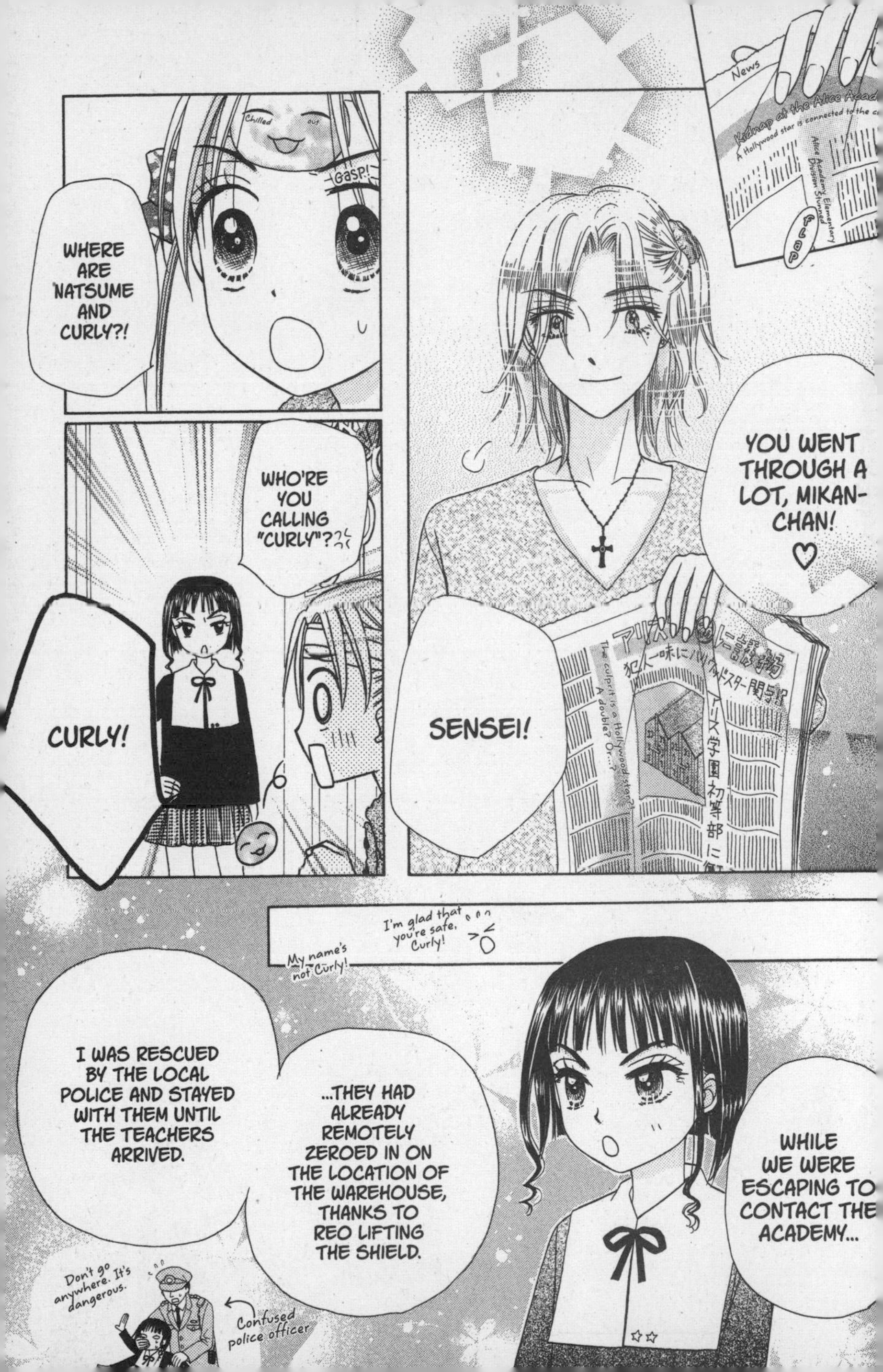
News
A Hollywood star is connected to the
Alice Academy Elementary Division Stunned
flap
The culprit is a Hollywood star? A double? Or...?
YOU WENT THROUGH A LOT, MIKAN-CHAN! ♡
SENSEI!
Chilled out
Gasp!
WHERE ARE NATSUME AND CURLY?!
WHO'RE YOU CALLING "CURLY"?
CURLY!
I'm glad that you're safe, Curly!
My name's not Curly!
WHILE WE WERE ESCAPING TO CONTACT THE ACADEMY...
...THEY HAD ALREADY REMOTELY ZEROED IN ON THE LOCATION OF THE WAREHOUSE, THANKS TO REO LIFTING THE SHIELD.
I WAS RESCUED BY THE LOCAL POLICE AND STAYED WITH THEM UNTIL THE TEACHERS ARRIVED.
Don't go anywhere. It's dangerous.
Confused police officer

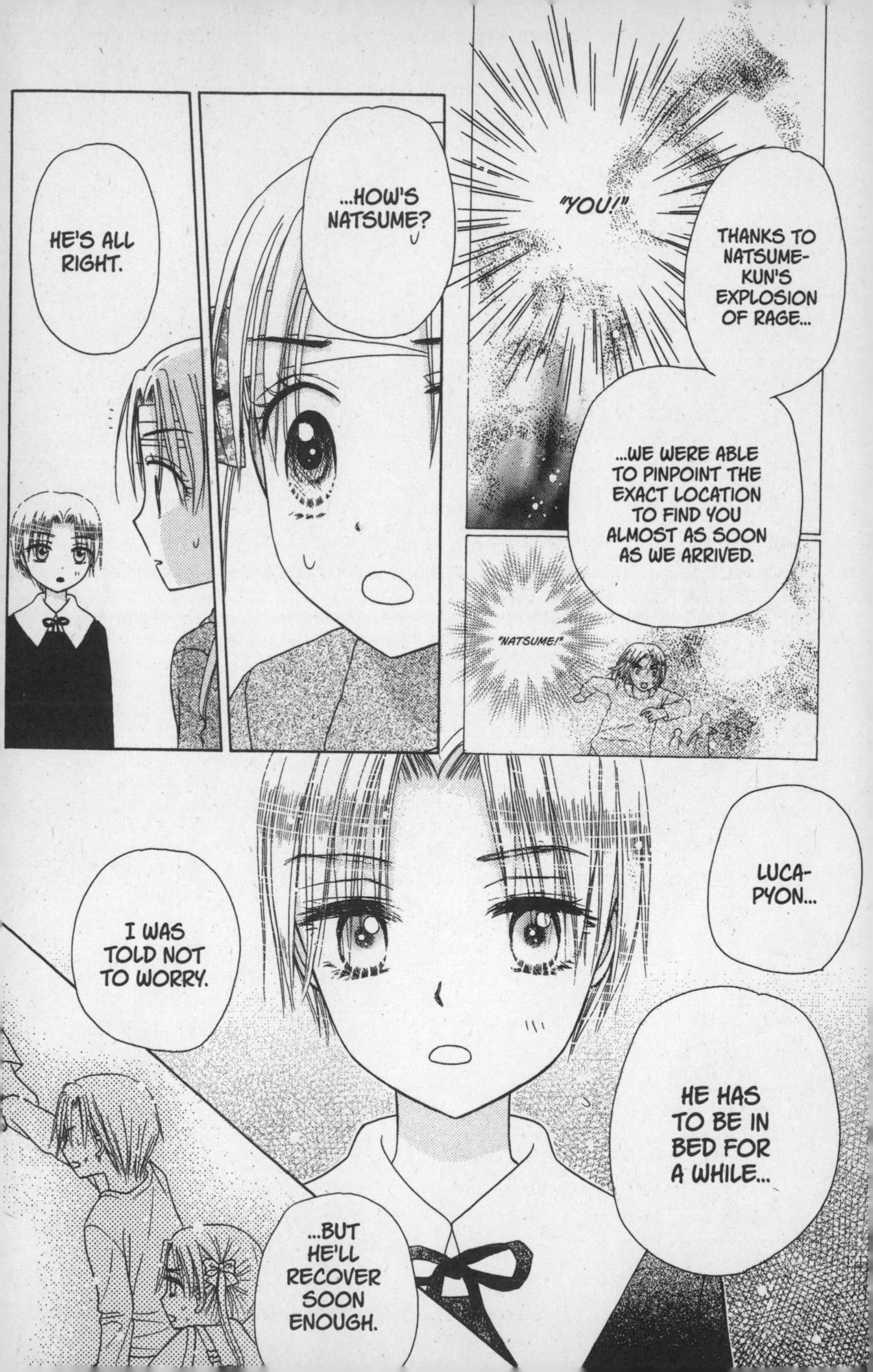
THANKS TO NATSUME-KUN'S EXPLOSION OF RAGE...
"YOU!"
...WE WERE ABLE TO PINPOINT THE EXACT LOCATION TO FIND YOU ALMOST AS SOON AS WE ARRIVED.
"NATSUME!"
...HOW'S NATSUME?
HE'S ALL RIGHT.
LUCA-PYON...
I WAS TOLD NOT TO WORRY.
HE HAS TO BE IN BED FOR A WHILE...
...BUT HE'LL RECOVER SOON ENOUGH.

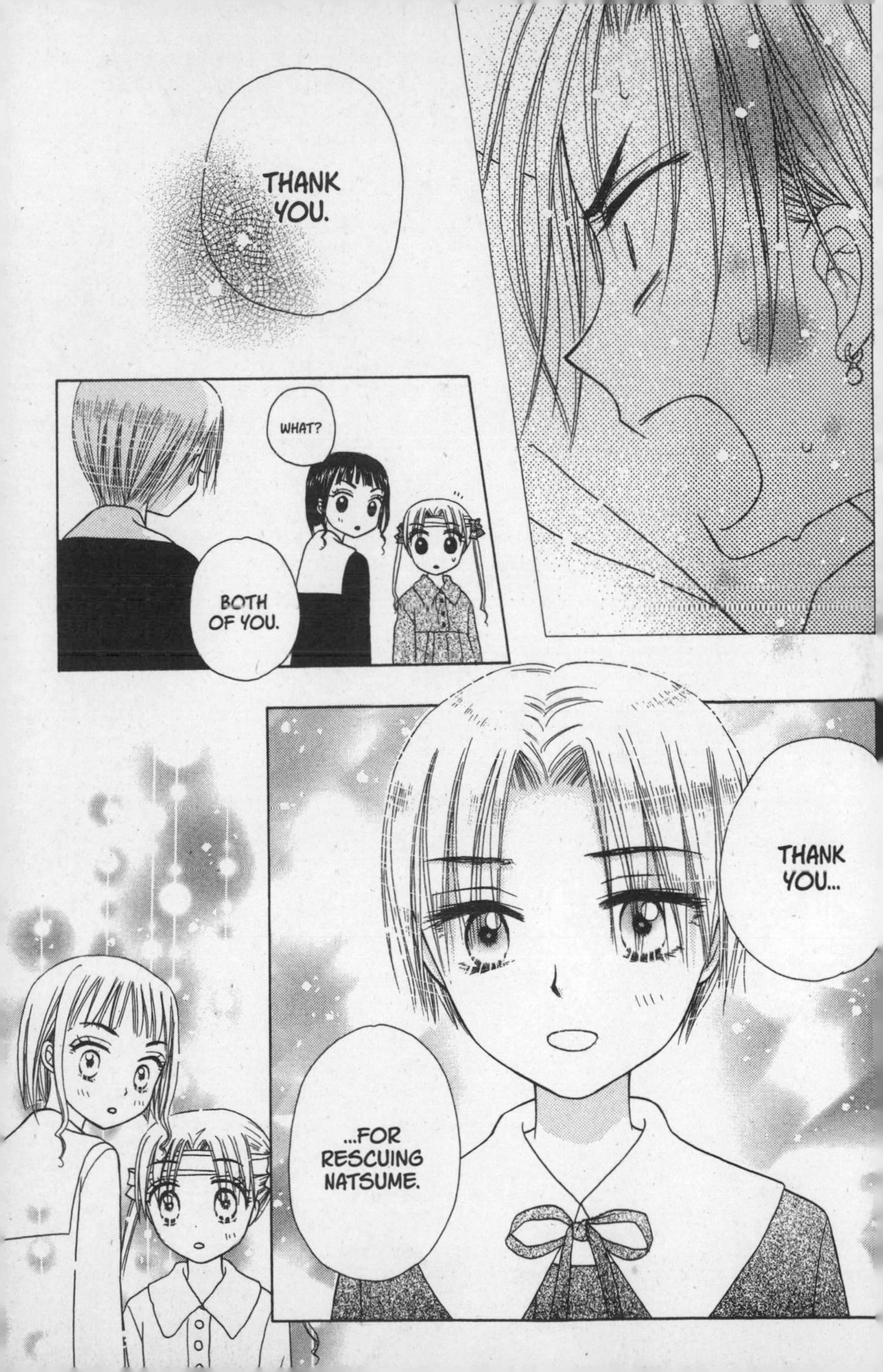
THANK YOU.
WHAT?
BOTH OF YOU.
THANK YOU...
...FOR RESCUING NATSUME.

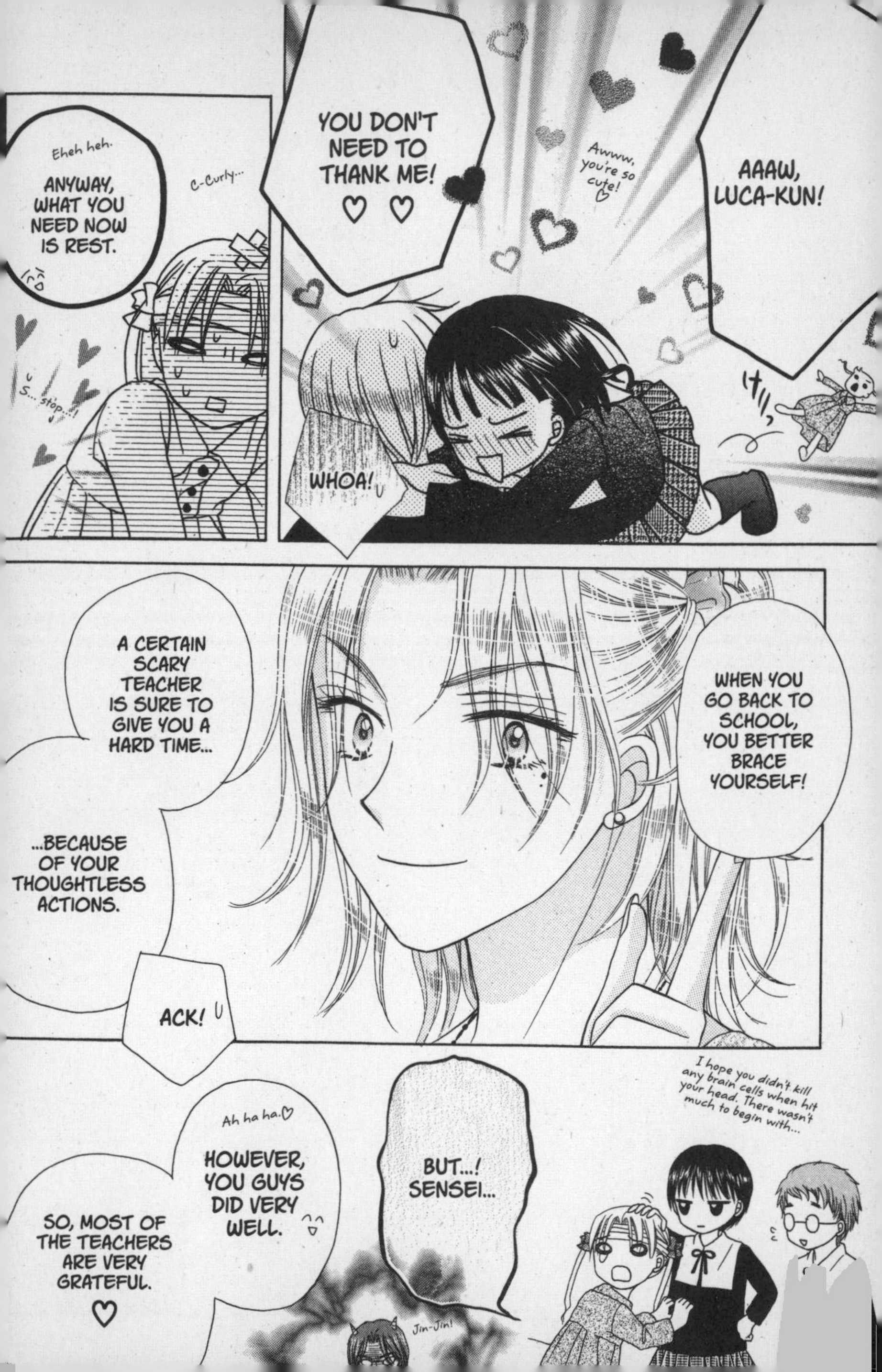
AAAW, LUCA-KUN!
Awww, you're so cute! ♡
YOU DON'T NEED TO THANK ME! ♡ ♡
WHOA!
Eheh heh.
ANYWAY, WHAT YOU NEED NOW IS REST.
C-Curly...
S... stop...!
WHEN YOU GO BACK TO SCHOOL, YOU BETTER BRACE YOURSELF!
A CERTAIN SCARY TEACHER IS SURE TO GIVE YOU A HARD TIME...
...BECAUSE OF YOUR THOUGHTLESS ACTIONS.
ACK!
I hope you didn't kill any brain cells when hit your head. There wasn't much to begin with...
BUT...! SENSEI...
Ah ha ha.♡
HOWEVER, YOU GUYS DID VERY WELL.
SO, MOST OF THE TEACHERS ARE VERY GRATEFUL. ♡
Jin-Jin!

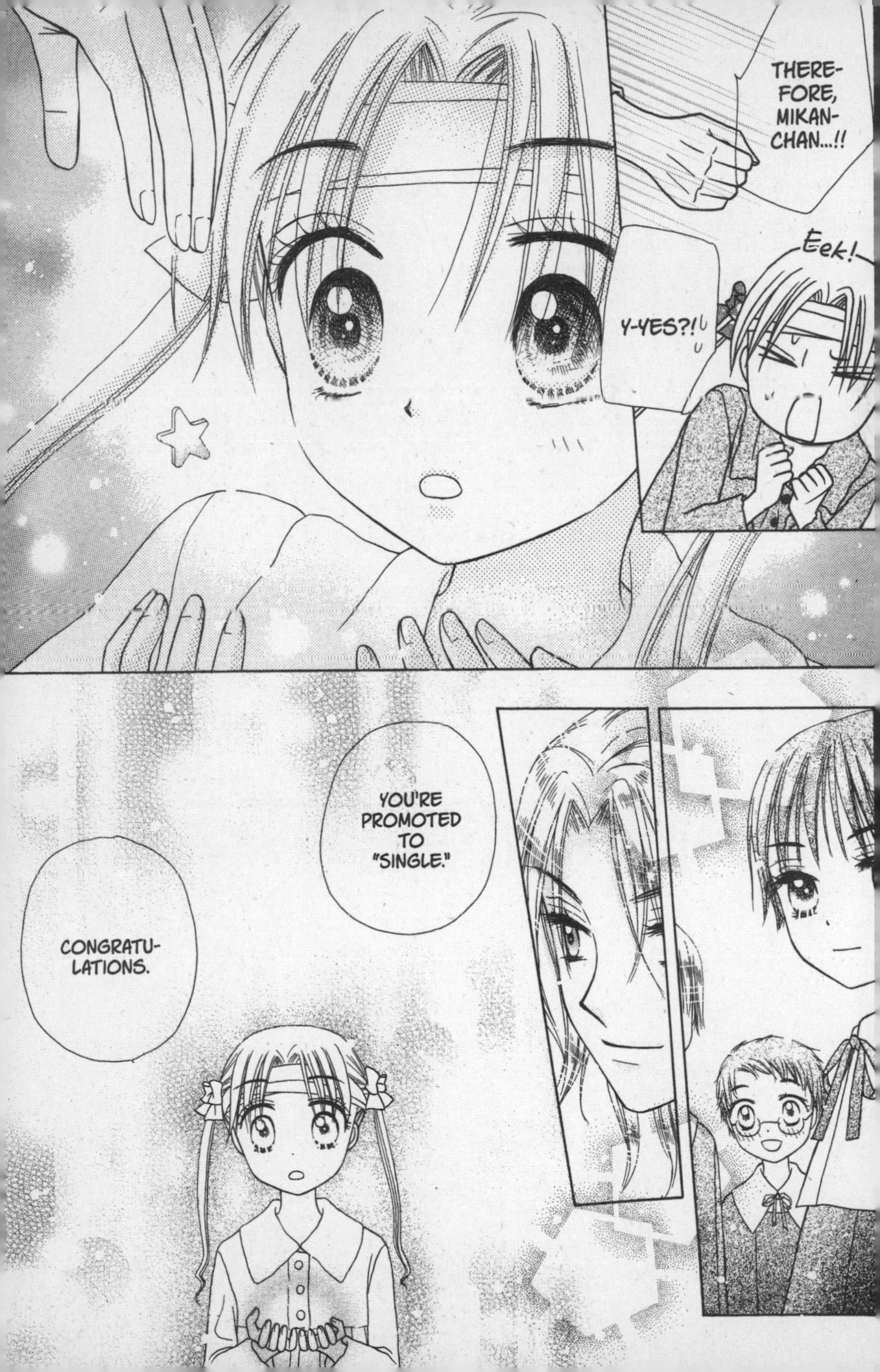
THEREFORE, MIKAN-CHAN...!!
Eek!
Y-YES?!
YOU'RE PROMOTED TO "SINGLE."
CONGRATULATIONS.

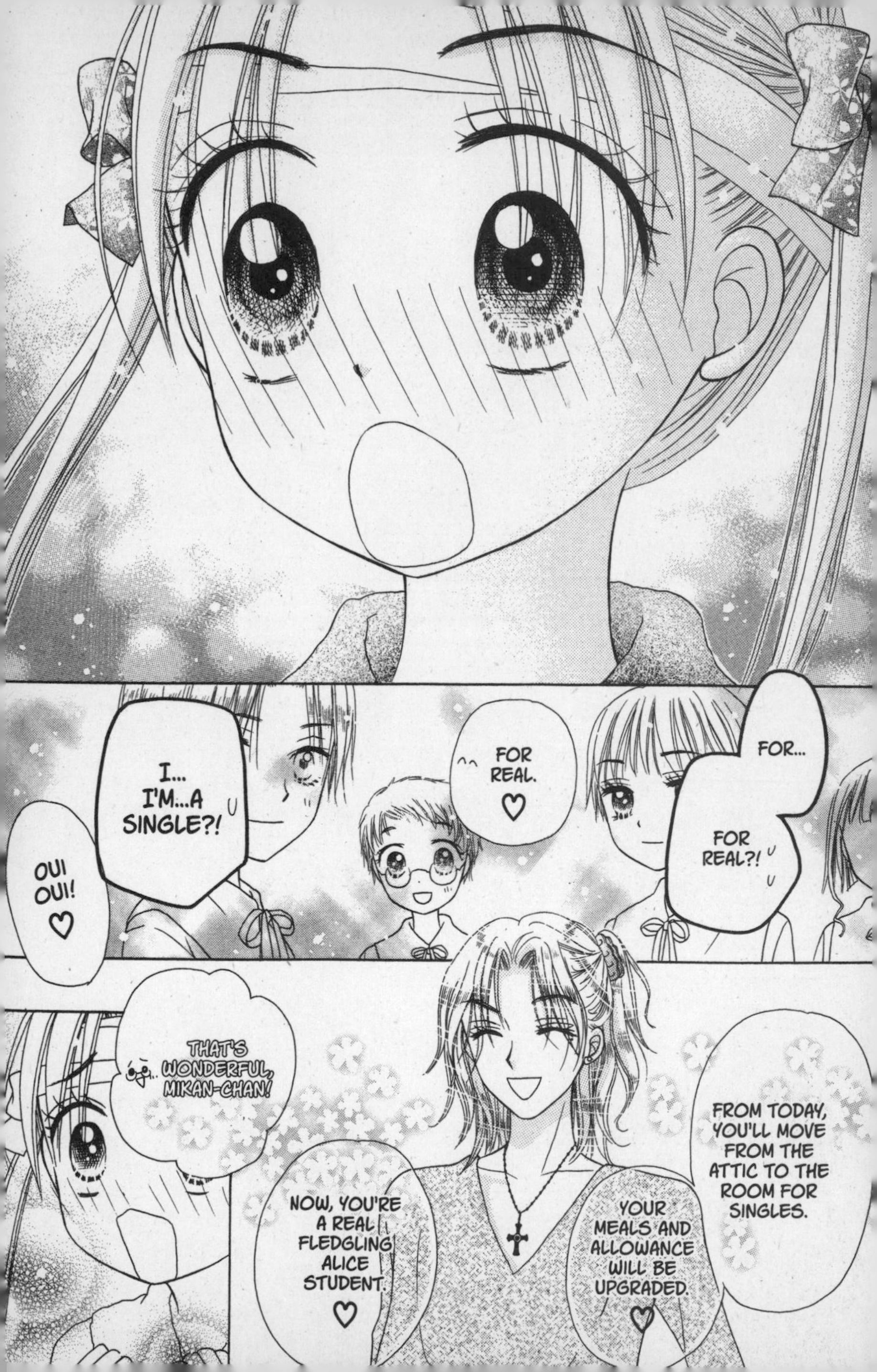
FOR... FOR REAL?!
FOR REAL. ♡
I... I'M...A SINGLE?!
OUI OUI! ♡
FROM TODAY, YOU'LL MOVE FROM THE ATTIC TO THE ROOM FOR SINGLES.
YOUR MEALS AND ALLOWANCE WILL BE UPGRADED. ♡
NOW, YOU'RE A REAL FLEDGLING ALICE STUDENT. ♡
THAT'S WONDERFUL, MIKAN-CHAN!

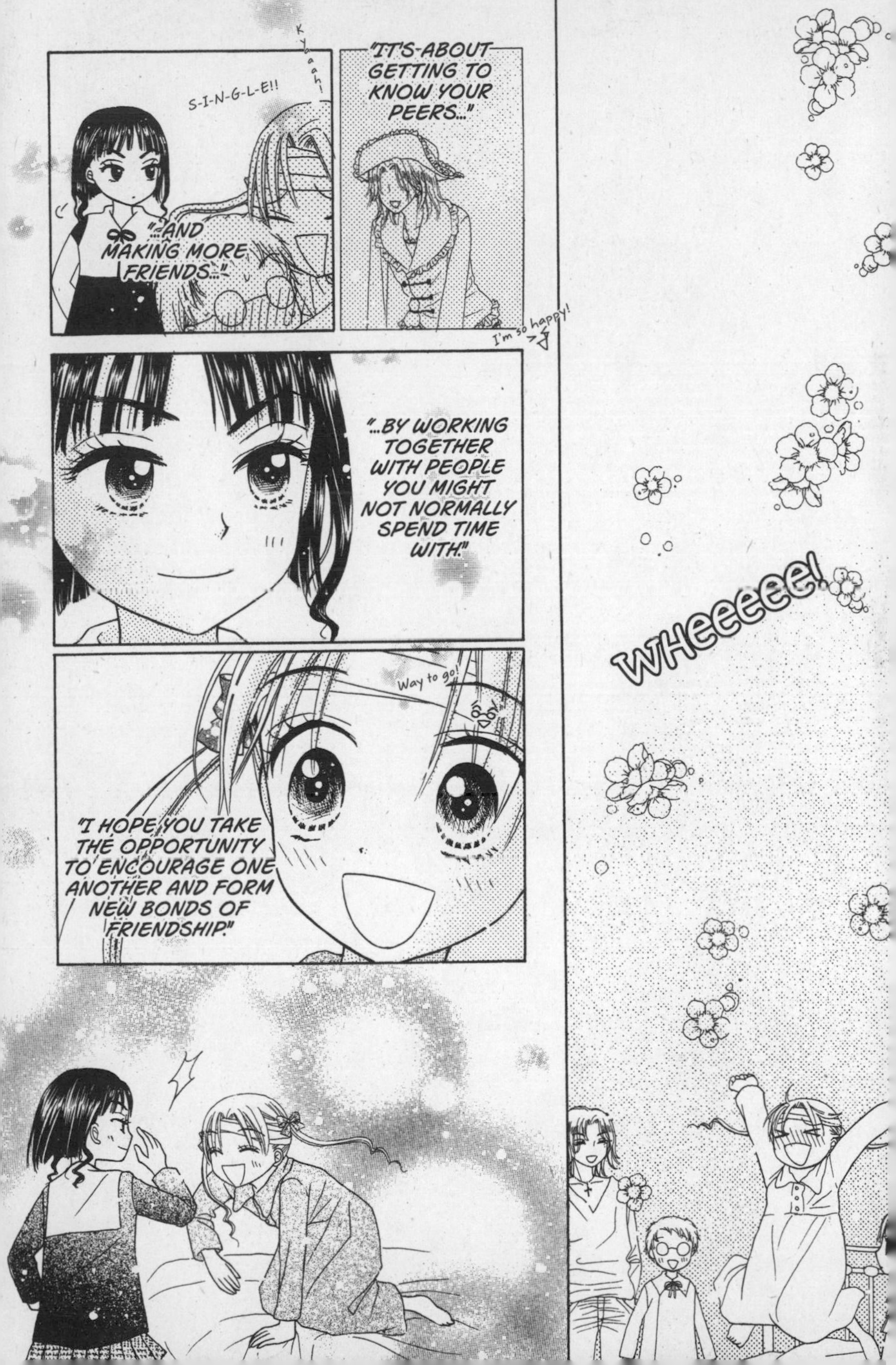
WHEEEEE!
"IT'S ABOUT GETTING TO KNOW YOUR PEERS..."
I'm so happy!
Kyaaah!
S-I-N-G-L-E!!
"...AND MAKING MORE FRIENDS..."
"...BY WORKING TOGETHER WITH PEOPLE YOU MIGHT NOT NORMALLY SPEND TIME WITH."
Way to go!
"I HOPE YOU TAKE THE OPPORTUNITY TO ENCOURAGE ONE ANOTHER AND FORM NEW BONDS OF FRIENDSHIP."

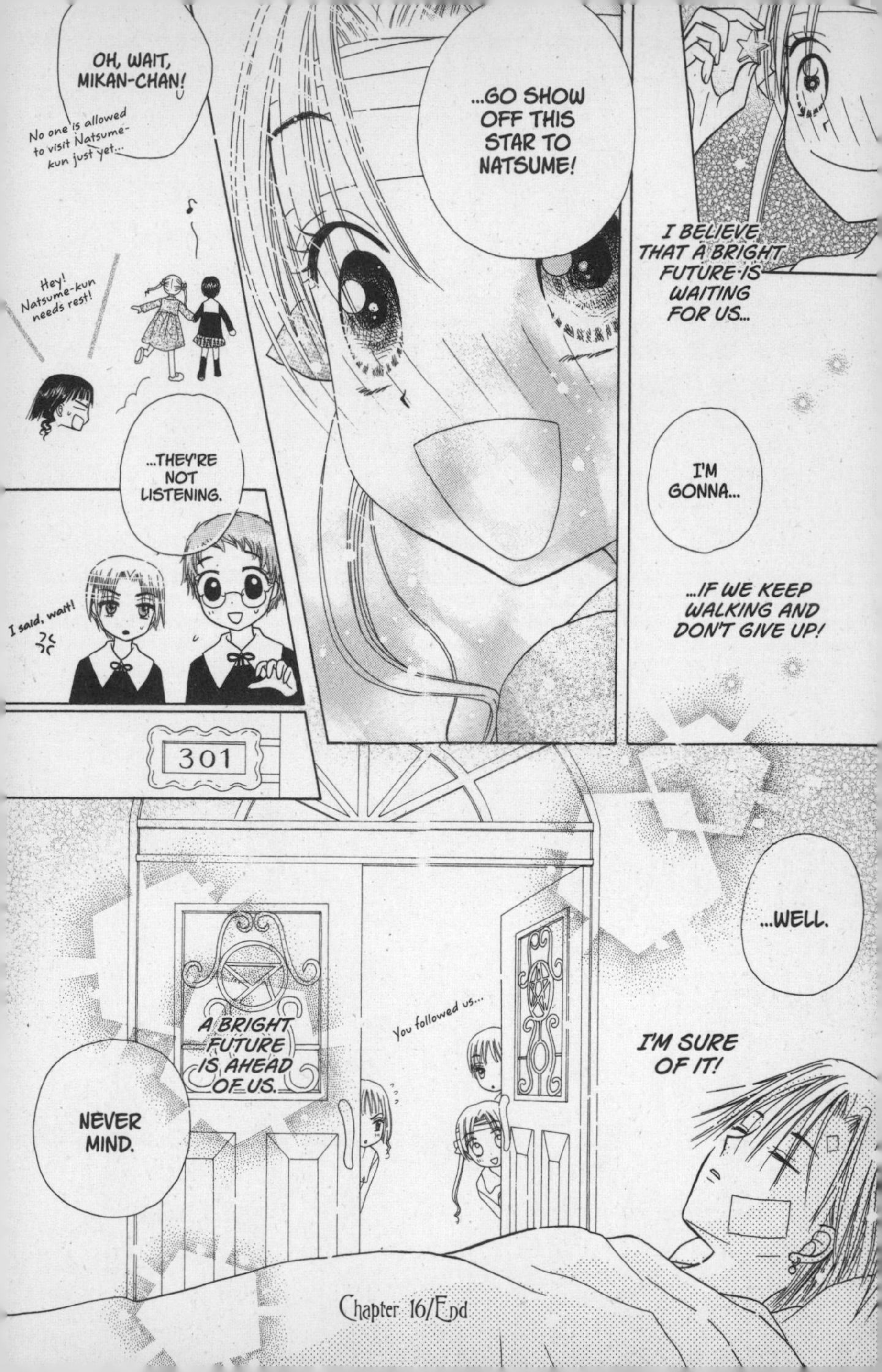
I BELIEVE THAT A BRIGHT FUTURE IS WAITING FOR US...
I'M GONNA...
...IF WE KEEP WALKING AND DON'T GIVE UP!
...GO SHOW OFF THIS STAR TO NATSUME!
OH, WAIT, MIKAN-CHAN!
No one is allowed to visit Natsume-kun just yet...
Hey! Natsume-kun needs rest!
...THEY'RE NOT LISTENING.
I said, wait!
301
...WELL.
I'M SURE OF IT!
You followed us...
A BRIGHT FUTURE IS AHEAD OF US.
NEVER MIND.
Chapter 16/End

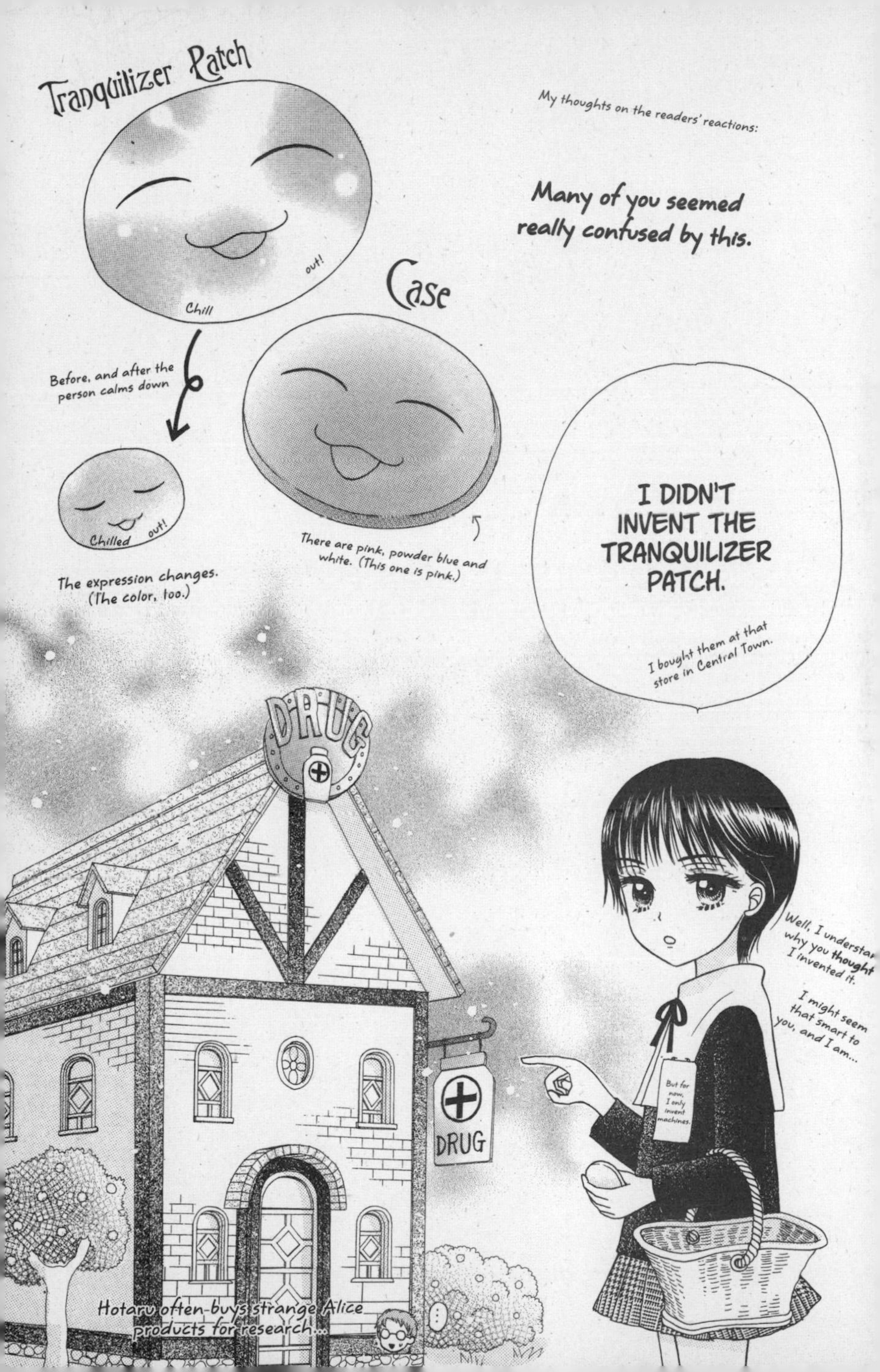

My thoughts on the readers' reactions:
Many of you seemed really confused by this.
I DIDN'T INVENT THE TRANQUILIZER PATCH.
I bought them at that store in Central Town.
Well, I understa why you thought I invented it.
I might seem that smart to you, and I am...
But for now, I only invent machines.
Tranquilizer Patch
Chill
out!
Case
Before, and after the person calms down
Chilled
out!
The expression changes. (The color, too.)
There are pink, powder blue and white. (This one is pink.)
DRUG
DRUG
Hotaru often buys strange Alice products for research...
...

BYE!

Next time in

Mikan's daring rescue of Natsume has earned her an upgrade to one-star rank, and just in time for the School Festival to start. Will she and the rest of the Special Ability class prove their worth to the rest of the school by knocking visitor's socks off with their great new attraction? And what is going on with the mysterious set of Principals?

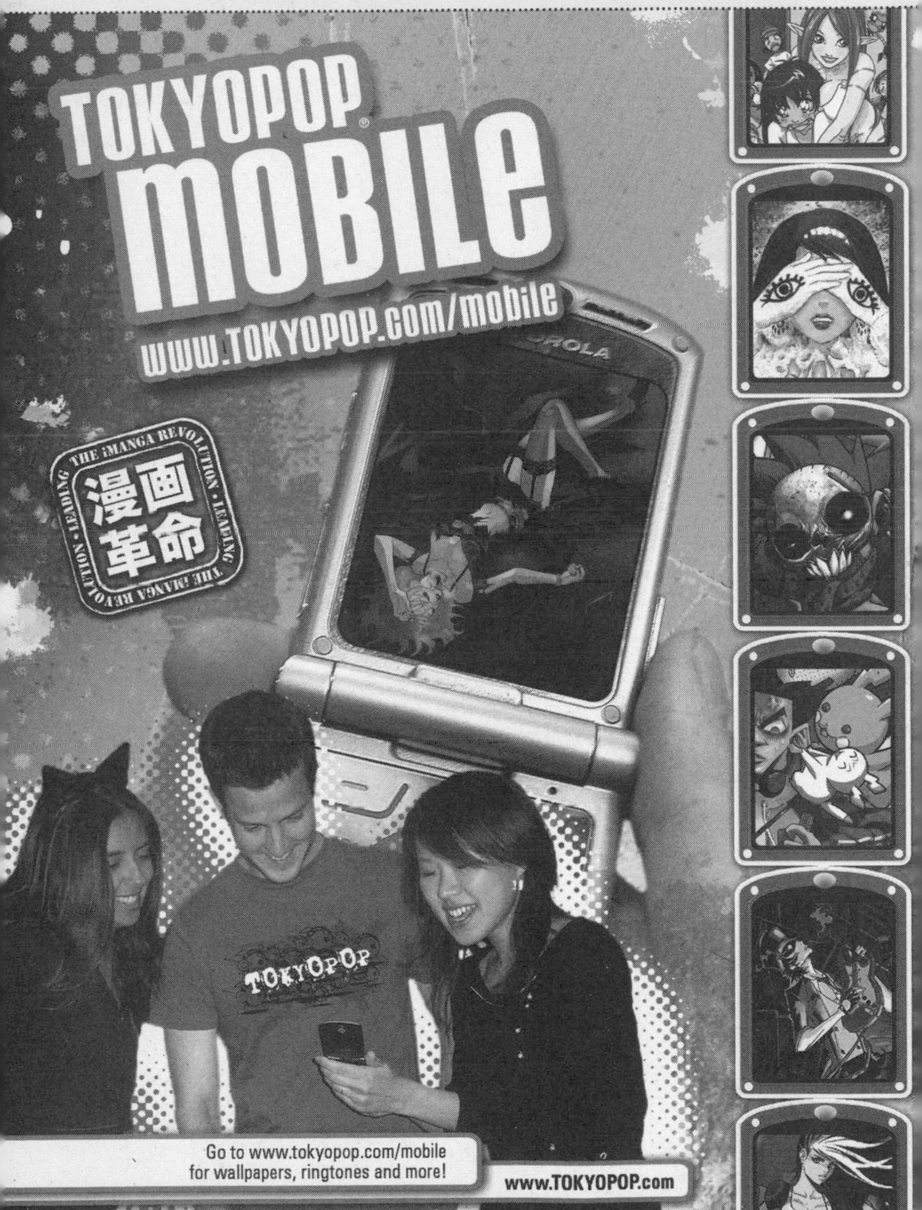
TOKYOPOP MOBILE
www.TOKYOPOP.com/mobile
THE iMANGA REVOLUTION · LEADING THE iMANGA REVOLUTION · LEADING
漫画革命
TOKYOPOP
Go to www.tokyopop.com/mobile
for wallpapers, ringtones and more!
www.TOKYOPOP.com

Bizenghast™

The Bizenghast Novel Debut!

When a young Dinah moves to the forgotten town of Bizenghast, she uncovers a terrifying collection of lost souls. As she is forced to help these wandering spirits, one thing becomes painfully clear: The residents of Bizenghast are just *dying* to come home. This is an unforgettable Gothic drama that will leave you haunted long after the last page is turned.

TOKYOPOP
Alice LeGrow's
Bizenghast:
THE NOVEL
ART NOT FINAL
One
Shawn Thorgersen

TOKYOPOP
Bizenghast

Check out the iManga at TOKYOPOP.com!
Bizenghast soundtrack available on iTunes

POP FICTION

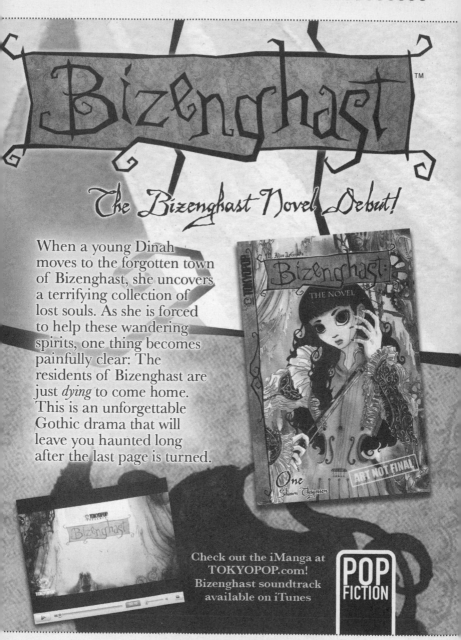

BIZENGHAST
BY M. ALICE LEGROW, NOVEL BY SHAWN THORGERSEN

Not every lost soul is a lost cause

Dinah must fight to keep her sanity
and life together, *and* keep all hell
from breaking loose in the
Mausoleum! The town of
Bizenghast holds many secrets, and
Dinah will have to grow up and
grow strong if she intends to seek
out the truth behind the mystery.

© M. Alice LeGrow and TOKYOPOP Inc.

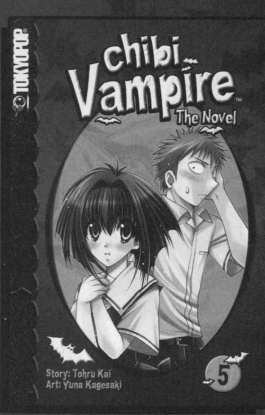

CHIBI VAMPIRE
MANGA BY YUNA KAGESAKI, NOVEL BY TOHRU KAI AND YUNA KAGESAKI

The HILARIOUS adventures of

chibi Vampire™

9

Created By:
Yuna Kagesaki

As Karin and Kenta's official first date continues, Anju shows up to keep an eye on the clumsy couple. When Kenta tells Karin how he really feels, will it destroy their relationship? Also, the new girl in town, Yuriya, begins snooping around in search of vampires. Why is she trying to uncover Karin's identity, and what secrets of her own is she hiding?

chibi Vampire™ Inspired the

FOR MORE INFORMATION VISIT:

STOP!

This is the back of the book.
You wouldn't want to spoil a great ending!

This book is printed "manga-style," in the authentic Japanese right-to-left format. Since none of the artwork has been flipped or altered, readers get to experience the story just as the creator intended. You've been asking for it, so TOKYOPOP® delivered: authentic, hot-off-the-press, and far more fun!

DIRECTIONS

If this is your first time reading manga-style, here's a quick guide to help you understand how it works.

It's easy... just start in the top right panel and follow the numbers. Have fun, and look for more 100% authentic manga from TOKYOPOP®!